THE POSTCOLONIAL AGE OF MIGRATION

This book critically examines the question of migration that appears at the intersection of global neo-liberal transformation, postcolonial politics, and economy. It analyses the specific ways in which colonial relations are produced and reproduced in global migratory flows and their consequences for labour, human rights, and social justice. The postcolonial age of migration not only indicates a geopolitical and geo-economic division of the globe between countries of the North and those of the South marked by massive and mixed population flows from the latter to the former, but also the production of these relations within and among the countries of the North. The book discusses issues such as transborder flows among countries of the South; migratory movements of the internally displaced; growing statelessness leading to forced migration; border violence; refugees of partitions; customary and local practices of care and protection; population policies and migration management (both emigration and immigration); the protracted nature of displacement; labour flows and immigrant labour; and the relationships between globalisation, nationalism, citizenship, and migration in postcolonial regions. It also traces colonial and postcolonial histories of migration and justice to bear on the present understanding of local experiences of migration as well as global social transformations while highlighting the limits of the fundamental tenets of humanitarianism (protection, assistance, security, responsibility), which impact the political and economic rights of vast sections of moving populations.

Topical and an important intervention in contemporary global migration and refugee studies, the book offers new sources, interpretations, and analyses in understanding postcolonial migration. It will be useful to scholars and researchers of migration studies, refugee studies, border studies, political studies, political sociology, international relations, human rights and law, human geography, international politics, and political economy. It will also interest policymakers, legal practitioners, nongovernmental organisations, and activists.

Ranabir Samaddar is Distinguished Chair in Migration and Forced Migration Studies, Calcutta Research Group, Kolkata, India. He belongs to the critical school of thinking and is considered as one of the foremost theorists in migration and forced migration studies. His writings on migration, forms of labour, urbanisation, and political struggles have signalled a new turn in postcolonial thinking. Among his influential works is *The Marginal Nation: Transborder Migration from Bangladesh to West Bengal* (1999). His recent works are *Karl Marx and the Postcolonial Age* (2018), *The Crisis of 1974: Railway Strike and the Rank and File* (2016), and *Beyond Kolkata: Rajarhat and the Dystopia of Urban Imagination* (2014, co-authored).

THE POSTCOLONIAL AGE OF MIGRATION

Ranabir Samaddar

Routledge
Taylor & Francis Group

LONDON AND NEW YORK

First published 2020
by Routledge
2 Park Square, Milton Park, Abingdon, Oxon OX14 4RN

and by Routledge
52 Vanderbilt Avenue, New York, NY 10017

Routledge is an imprint of the Taylor & Francis Group, an informa business

© 2020 Ranabir Samaddar

The right of Ranabir Samaddar to be identified as author of this work has been asserted by him in accordance with sections 77 and 78 of the Copyright, Designs and Patents Act 1988.

All rights reserved. No part of this book may be reprinted or reproduced or utilised in any form or by any electronic, mechanical, or other means, now known or hereafter invented, including photocopying and recording, or in any information storage or retrieval system, without permission in writing from the publishers.

Trademark notice: Product or corporate names may be trademarks or registered trademarks, and are used only for identification and explanation without intent to infringe.

British Library Cataloguing-in-Publication Data
A catalogue record for this book is available from the British Library

Library of Congress Cataloging-in-Publication Data
A catalog record for this book has been requested

ISBN: 978-0-367-34256-2 (hbk)
ISBN: 978-0-367-34257-9 (pbk)
ISBN: 978-0-429-32469-7 (ebk)

Typeset in Bembo
by Apex CoVantage, LLC

CONTENTS

Preface and acknowledgements   vi

1 Introduction: Revisiting *The Age of Migration*   1

2 Context, concepts, and method   23

3 Migrants in an earlier age of globalisation   43

4 The labouring subject of refugee economies   61

5 Postcolonial footprints of the ecological migrants   87

6 The spectral presence of the migrant   110

7 Insecure nation, insecure migrant   125

8 The postcolonial nature of Europe's migration crisis   142

9 Statelessness and the lost world of citizenship   167

10 Postcolonial marks on the principle of responsibility   191

11 The roadmap of global power and responsibility   213

Bibliography   *243*
Index   *272*

PREFACE AND ACKNOWLEDGEMENTS

For a long time, and to a large extent still today, refugees, migrants, internally displaced population groups, and illegally wandering bands of labour remained on the borders of several disciplines and were treated according to the norms of professional knowledge of care, protection, and above all population management and security. However, the massive population movements world over, in various forms overflowing their categorical boundaries (such as refugees, asylum seekers, jobseekers, migrants, seasonal and irregular immigrants, trafficked persons, etc.), have breached the structures of governance and rule, as well as our knowledge. After 1919 with the establishment of the League of Nations and certainly after 1951 when the Refugee Convention was born, forced population movements were perceived less in terms of "crisis". They did not indicate any crisis. Admittedly they were exceptional and had to be taken care of, while the regular and normal conduct of managing populations of nations could continue. Labour force was steady and would reproduce itself with reasonable certainty.

Then the crisis began with, on one hand technological change and change in the dynamics of accumulation, and on the other hand the number of legally and illegally moving people phenomenally increasing, throwing into the process the stability policies of governments in disarray. Various interventions and decisions to monitor and control the flows began in earnest. The first condition for the success of these new strategies was to isolate the phenomenon of massive and mixed migration, treat it as a serious "abnormal" phenomenon, and disconnect the power to protect and manage the migrants of the postcolonial world from the general effects of the neo-liberal transformation sweeping the globe. This is the postcolonial moment in the history of migration, which appears at the juncture where neo-liberal transformation and postcolonial politics and economy intersect. The current age of migration can be read historically only in this way. An understanding of this intersection is at the heart of this book.

When the great asylum structures were built after the formation of the League and then the United Nations, they were justified by a notion of a marvellous harmony between liberal democracy, welfare capitalism, the institution of citizenship, and the duty and responsibility to protect victims of forced migration. It was inevitable that the said harmony would not last long. Various asymmetries originating from the intersection of the two global structures of existence – the neo-liberal and the postcolonial – have put paid to the post-war history of welfare and protection. With this begins the postcolonial age of migration.

The moment is understood by many as "crisis"– a crisis in population and security policies of various countries, predominantly of Europe and the United States, as well as a crisis of perception. At the same time there is no doubt that the recent worldwide interest in migration and refugee flows has much to do with a series of events, known as the "European refugee crisis", the American "caravan crisis", the Rohingya crisis, and the two recent global compacts on refugees and migrants. This reawakened interest is only to be welcomed as this would now encourage and allow more investigation into global migration flows including massive internal displacements in various countries. Displacements of people due to persecution, developmental and environmental disasters, and above all neocolonial wars and fratricidal conflicts, are creating thousands of migrants as fodder for labour in the capitalist world. Living labour is turning virtually dead in the process. Yet we must not, however, use cataclysmic events as pretext to avoid investigations of longer trends. Any investigation into the ways in which the global economy uses the migrants as labour and the structure of global governance manages to keep the system running will open our eyes to the deep fault line in the landscape of migration. The origin, nature, and reproduction of the population flows makes our age irrefutably a postcolonial age of migration. With the transition to the neo-liberal mode of global accumulation of capital, the strategy of uprooting people has only exacerbated, and constitutes, to a significant extent the politics of our time. In the process it has thrown institutions like citizenship into disarray. Foundations of democratic order have been put into question. Modes of labour supply have to be continuously reorganised. For all these reasons this is a global age of migration. At the same time it is so because postcolonial realities of history, politics, and economy are profoundly shaping the global.

This is the reason why I wanted to engage with the way migration in recent academic scholarship was first conceptualised as a global issue and a global system. I had long desired to write a series of interventions around such a work, namely, Stephen Castles' (co-authored) *The Age of Migration*. The reason briefly was that the book at one level seemed rationally written, compact, rights sensitive, and aware of the global nature of the issue. Hence the term "age" seemed to justify the book. Yet, at another level, there seemed something fundamental missing. It was not just the postcolonial reality which was missing, and hence with all its qualities the book had clearly emanated from writers of the North (Australia is in the global North), positioned in the North, but also who viewed the age through Northern optics. But more troubling was the fact that it had not perhaps dawned on the authors that if this is an age of migration, it is because this age is postcolonial. It is a global age when globalisation and the postcolonial realities densely interact and at times become indistinguishable from each other. *The Age of Migration* seemed a perfect launching point for what I wanted to say. The book presented a massive scenario. It was an intriguing book. We had all grown up with it.

However a wise publisher cautioned me that it was not a good idea to write a book around a book, and that I should write something independently – on migration and forced migration, and not anchored to any specific book or discourse. But I was encouraged to lay out the various contours and dimensions of my main contention, namely, that this is a postcolonial age of migration. I have used the word "postcolonial" in a critical sense, which tells us of a global predicament symbolised by this word, and have not used it in the sense that informs postcolonial studies and cultural studies in Western academia.

Three successive annual short term visits (2017–19) to the IWM (Institut fur die Wissenschaften vom Menschen), Vienna, provided the opportunity to think of the plan in some detail, use the IWM library and its journal collection, re-read earlier versions of some of the chapters, write out some fresh ones, and give the material the shape of a coherent work. My thanks go to the Institute's rector, Shalini Randeria, who saw merit and possibility in my rough plan, extended me the invitations, and encouraged me to think ahead. To the librarian Katharina Gratz, who guided me patiently though its vast collections, and the Administrator of the Visiting Programmes Mary Kemle-Gussing, I remain similarly thankful. Indeed the IWM team and other visitors there provided encouragement to my ideas and this work.

Similarly, a three-month stay at the McGill University, Law School, under the O'Brien Residency Programme, gave me the scope to revise some of the chapters, but more importantly interact with well-known scholars in refugee studies and migration studies, whose value has been immeasurable for me. I must especially thank the Hans & Tamar Oppenheimer Chair in Public International Law, Francois Crepaeau, whose insights have helped me immensely. Nandini Ramanujam, Vrinda Narain, and Megan Bradley were likewise helpful. I must also mention the benefit I have drawn in the course of the last few years from discussions with colleagues at Carleton University, Ottawa – in particular William Walters, James Milner, and Martin Geiger.

Four other associations have helped shape the "global" perspective of the postcolonial age of migration. First, my involvement in the Refugee Research Network (RRN) based in the York University, Toronto, has been crucial for the development of my understanding. Participation in its meetings, exchanges with other members of the Network, arguments and reconciliation, writings and reviews – all these through the last ten years were helpful. My particular thanks go to Susan McGrath, Michele Millard, Wenona Giles, Jennifer Hyndman, Nergis Canefe, Susan Kneebone, Ranu Basu, Loren Landau, Chris Dolan, Susan Martin, Roberto Vidal-Lopez, James Simeon, Galya Ruffer, Mohammad Jalal Abbasi, and others of the Network – some based at the York University and others elsewhere. Second, participation in the work of the IASFM (International Association for the Study of

Forced Migration) in this and the preceding decade broadened my understanding of other regions and related issues. The IASFM panels were particularly helpful for putting in shape some of the chapters. Third, association with the IDP project directed by the Brookings Institution helped me understand better the global nature of internal displacement and the regional variations in patterns of internal displacement, and I remain singularly indebted to Roberta Cohen whose patience and sympathy guided me through some of the massive literature including reports, policy critiques, newspaper articles, and specific experiences of the UN process regarding the Guiding Principles on Internal Displacement. Finally – and this has been most important for the development of the postcolonial perspective in migration studies – I remain indebted to several critical scholars in migration studies who have not only raised the question of the "autonomy of migration" but also brought issues of labour, borders, supply chains, surveillance, regimes of control, refugee economy – the shadowy corners of the migrant world – into the literature on migration. They have urged me to extend my earlier work around "local" issues and experiences in South Asia and India, and encouraged me to project their relevance on the global scale. Of course, this has not been an easy task, but to the extent the postcolonial can be seen as global in the historical trajectory of migration, I remain indebted to Sandro Mezzadra, Brett Neilson, Ned Rossiter, Meghna Guha-thakurta, Hari Sharma, Alice Bloch, Paolo Novak, Giorgia Dona, Melissa Steyn, Lydia Potts, Itty Abraham, Liza Schuster, Federico Rahola, Catharine de Venden, Ayse Caglar, Bandana Purakayastha, Ravi Palat, Lawrence Juma, Manuela Bojadzijev, Imran Ayata, Subir Sinha, Chetan Bhatt, Sabine Hess, Alessandro Monsutti, Stephan Scheel, Nicolas de Genova, Julian Reid, Mark Frazier, Ashok Gurung, Rana Bose, Andrew Brandel, Andrew Baldwin, Giovanni Bettini, Shahram Khosravi, Sabine Hess, Kuntala Dutta Lahiri, and others.

Yet it was in India that my specific views on what makes this the postcolonial age of migration took present shape. My work on the so-called "local" issues of migration – Bangladesh-India trans-border migration, migratory movements of the internally displaced, growing statelessness in South Asia leading to forced population movements, border violence, partitioned refugees, borderland existences, local protection arrangements, bilateral agreements on protection, the juridical discourses of care and power, the protracted nature of displacement, labour flows, and the gamut of relationships between globalisation, nationalism, citizenship, and migration in South Asia – has had an intrinsic association with the Calcutta Research Group, a research collective working on, among others issues, migration and forced migration. It was there that my views, initially formulated in *The Marginal Nation* (1999), developed and the findings of my earlier works were taken further. I am only too happy to put on record my indebtedness to: Paula Banerjee, Sabyasachi Basu Ray Chaudhury, Samir K. Das, Nasreen Chowdhory, Subir Bhaumik, Madhuresh Kumar, Subhas Chakrabarty, Sanjay Barbora, Manish Jha, Monirul Hossain, Iman Mitra, Ritajyoti Bandopadhyay, Sibaji Pratim Basu, Samata Biswas, Samita Sen, Atig Ghosh, Prasanta Ray, Byasdeb Dasgupta, Moulehsri Vyas, Kalpana Kannabiran, Sucharita Sengupta, and the late Sharit Bhaumik. I also owe a debt to

B.S. Chimni, Tapan K. Bose, Walter Fernandes, and Ravi Nair whose writings on displacements, refugee law, and refugee protection have been pioneering in South Asia and have been helpful for me. They anticipated many of the postcolonial arguments of our time.

Finally, my acknowledgements are to those journals and books where some of the material had appeared in shorter and often different forms. My particular thanks go to *Conversation* (September 2018), *Current Sociology* (66:2, 2018), *Refugee Watch* (50, 2017), *IIC Quarterly* (winter 2016-spring 2017), *Refuge* (33:1, 2017), *Economic and Political Weekly* (50: 51, 2015), *International Journal of Migration and Border Studies* (2:2, 2016). Some parts of the material were published as book chapters in Alice Bloch and Giorgia Dona (eds.), *Forced Migration: Current Issues and Debates* (Routledge, 2018), Kuntala Lahiri-Dutta (ed.), *Between the Plough and the Pick: Informal, Artisanal and Small-Scale Mining in the Contemporary World* (ANU Press, Canberra, 2018), Andrew Baldwin and Giovanni Bettini (eds.), *Life Adrift: Climate Change, Migration, Critique* (Rowman and Littlefield, 2017), and my *A Postcolonial Enquiry into Europe's Debt and Migration Crisis* (Springer, 2016). I owe a debt of gratitude to the editors and publishers of these volumes. But of course, the encouragement from the editors of Routledge to the idea of the book was valuable. My sincere thanks go to their editors, Shoma Choudhury and Rimina Mohapatra.

Before I finish, let me explain briefly how the chapters address the main contention of the book.

The first chapter introduces a scrutiny of the classic, *The Age of Migration*, from a postcolonial angle. Through this scrutiny, the chapter anticipates the dimensions from which this book will try to visit the theme of the *age* again and again – only to argue that if it is the age of migration, it is because it is the postcolonial age of migration. The postcolonial gradient makes it the global age of migration.

This predictably brings in the issue of method of enquiry and its relation with context and concepts ruling this field. Chapter 2 introduces the problematic of the interrelation of context, concept, and method, and enquires what is postcolonial in forging a particular way of looking at issues, particular mode of analysis, or a particular mix of analyses. The chapter briefly traces the history of the development of forced migration studies in a postcolonial context – in this instance the context of India – and the implications of this context for the methodological question. Thus the issue of partition in migration studies, to give an instance, is discussed to show the implications of a postcolonial approach. Or, we can take the instance of internal displacement.

Chapter 3 argues for a return to the histories of immigration of the late nineteenth and early twentieth centuries to show the colonial origins of the current forms of migrant labour, forms and methods of migration control, and labour servitude. The chapter argues that a genealogical perspective is necessary for a deeper understanding of today's migration controls. It also argues that the received history of the past two centuries as one of the nation forms is to be complemented with a history of the labour forms in which migrant labour is a critical factor.

Chapter 4 deals with the issue of migrant and refugee labour in today's global capitalist economy. It discusses how the neo-liberal mode of inclusion of various sections in market economy reshapes the theme of humanitarianism and protection. In the process it engages in a critique of certain dominant writings on refugee labour.

Chapter 5 discusses the current ecological context of migration and brings out the overwhelming postcolonial nature of this context.

Chapter 6 continues the examination of migrant labour and engages in a detailed examination of the way in which mining and other extractive operations produce the precarious migrant. The more important purpose of this chapter is also to show why, notwithstanding its critical presence in neo-liberal economy, the migrant will have always a spectral presence. Its visibility/invisibility will be always a subject of play between economy and politics.

Chapter 7 presents a condensed history of conflicts within the Indian Northeast to show how the migrant invariably becomes the central figure in a generalised discourse of security/insecurity. The chapter argues that the particular nature of security discourse around the world today, built around the safety of chosen nations and population groups, draws substantially from the colonial past. The global discourse of security around issues of migration reflects colonial contentions about authentic blood, racialized differences, homeland and excluded territories, and enclave economies.

Chapters 4–7 are crucial to the purpose of the book, as they show how factors of economy, ecology, visibility, and security contribute to the development of a new type of power on a global scale, which we may call as the power to protect and secure. In a narrow sense the migrant (including the refugee) is the subject of this power; but its effect is general. It reorganises the entire society, or at least produces a model in which the footloose finds a "natural" place and will be governed by laws of care, protection, and security. At the same time the footloose subject will be a productive subject. It will be a part of the economy too.

The eighth chapter discusses the European scenario along with its present "migration crisis" in order to demonstrate the postcolonial impact on the global map of migration. In this context it discusses the idea of what is known as "autonomy of migration". It also refers to two "seaborne" migrations – the Mediterranean and the Bay of Bengal-Indian Sea.

Chapter 9 discusses the issue of statelessness. In this context it traces the evolution of the issue of the displaced Rohingyas into one of statelessness. It also discusses the issue of statelessness in the region, and particularly India, in the drive for registration of citizens' names. The chapter deliberates on the broad implications of growing statelessness for the political and legal reality of citizenship in the postcolonial world.

The tenth and eleventh chapters trace the disposition of power and responsibility in the global regime of protection and show the asymmetrical relation between the two. The tenth chapter discusses the postcolonial history of power and responsibility while the eleventh chapter places the issue on a global scale by formulating a critique of the new global compacts on refugee and migration flows.

These eleven chapters collectively reflect on the nature of the present age of migration. These chapters also argue that the project of elaborating a social transformation framework for the analysis of migration does not require starting from scratch. Rather the task is to bring together new approaches and insights in a detailed and systematic way so that they can serve as a coherent frame for migration theory and research methodology. A deeper understanding of the local experiences of migration can enhance our analysis of global social transformations.

This realisation also has influenced the way this study is framed. Instead of trying to make this book another massive factsheet along the lines of *The Age of Migration* (a stupendous achievement of *The Age of Migration* for which it needs to be studied again and again), I was guided by two possible ways of composing the book: one, selecting certain themes or areas for intervention, which will show that this age cannot be understood except in a postcolonial frame –historically, economically, or politically; and two, showing in the process how some of the fundamental tenets of humanitarianism such as protection, assistance, security, responsibility, and attending to degrees of vulnerability and victimisation, have been turned into problems in this age. Collectively these problems now make a simple understanding of rights equally problematic. Issues of historical justice, social justice, and political and economic rights now overwhelm the world of migration. At the same time population movements show one of the most intractable problems for modern capitalism. The ghost of Malthus has been resurrected. Refugees, migrants, shelter seekers, immigrant labour – nothing can be discussed today without reference to the issue of population. Migration management (both emigration and immigration) has become an issue integral to the population policies of countries and economies. But it could not have been otherwise in this time of neo-liberal capitalism.

1
INTRODUCTION
Revisiting *The Age of Migration*

Introduction

In some ways it makes sense to begin a book on the postcolonial imprint on current global migration question by discussing Stephen Castles' co-authored work, *The Age of Migration*. Stephen Castles has almost singlehandedly reshaped the field of migration studies through his stupendous writings in the last forty years or so. A combination of sociology, political economy, and global studies backed by immense scholarship marks his writings. They are mostly dry, factual, minimally theoretical, and strive to achieve balance in the sense of being careful, holistic, and by not excluding any factor or for that matter overstressing any such. The balance is there between a managerial approach, which marks much of the scholarship in migration studies, and a critical approach that is often post-national and autonomist. His co-authored (along with Hein de Haas and Mark J. Miller) *The Age of Migration* is a celebrated compulsory textbook in migration studies across the globe, particularly in countries of the north. *The Age of Migration,* appearing in the early years of the last decade of the last century, carries the imprint of Castles' approach and works. It is difficult to find any big loophole in the successive editions of *The Age of Migration* (the fifth edition came out in 2014).[1]

It does not mean however that *The Age of Migration* escapes the footprints of time. In attempting to be comprehensive, the book perhaps misses or underestimates certain factors or elements that require particular attention. Perhaps the *age* which the book discusses conceals from the latter's framework some fundamental features, which have become clearer after nearly thirty years of its first edition. I am referring to the postcolonial features of the age that the book aptly describes as one of migration. Hence, I shall begin this book by focusing in this chapter on the way Stephen Castles conceptualises the "age".

In his co-authored work with Godula Kosack, *Immigrant Workers and Class Structure in Western Europe,*[2] Castles had used as the main analytic framework to study migration trends a combination of race, class, and political economy. Race became in time a theme common to many writings on migration.[3] At the same time a sense of a "sociological culture" overwhelmed political economy, and a predominantly labour market mode of explanation gradually displaced in his writings political economy as a critical tool of analysis. This shift to labour market mode of analysis led to an emphasis on the study of policies, legislations, measures, and focus on the destination countries of the West where migrants were arriving to the neglect of other dimensions. Thus, for instance, ethnicity became increasingly a conceptual tool of greater importance. At the same time countries producing migrants were relatively neglected. As an overall consequence, while proposing this as the "age of migration" he refrained from any historical comparison with other ages, and from using historical tools in understanding migration in critical historical phases of capitalism. All these require reflecting on three great dimensions of migration, namely spatiality, temporality, and agency. We have to see how *The Age of Migration* fares in engaging with them. The interrogation of the "age" as conceptualised in *The Age of Migration* will proceed in this chapter through a discussion of three issues: (a) the limits of labour market approach, (b) treating migration as a product of globalisation, and (c) the dualities and paradoxes featuring the age, such as the near universal acceptance of the liberal norms of citizenship coupled with statelessness.

Beyond the labour market: the age of penalised labour

We may begin with the issue of labour market approach. Labour market approach evident in *The Age of Migration* makes it difficult for Stephen Castles to take into account one of the most fundamental causes of migration in the post–Second World War age, when developmental dispossession became widespread and acute[4] and considerably impacted states' policies of controlling migration.[5] The labour market approach conceals from us what Sylvia Federici calls the "reproduction crisis", when labour has no option but to become "outlaw" – illegally crossing the borders of economies and territories.[6] Though to be fair, Castles is aware of the factors shaping labour market dynamics, particularly in the neo-liberal age,[7] and shows awareness of how migration regulation policies have been shaped over time. He also inquires if the two events, the incident of 9/11 in 2001 and the financial crash of 2008, have impacted the migratory trends in our time. Yet the study of migration control practices reaches a dead end, for the book does not analyse themes relevant to the relation between forced migration and migration, which should have been the natural outcome of such an analysis. The book also refrains from analysing the widespread phenomenon of developmental displacement, migration in the wake of logistical frenzy[8] ("carriers", "body shopping", etc.), the dynamics of security, control, and migrant's autonomy, and the overarching concept of border. Yet today in the closing years of the second decade of the twenty-first century, the notion of migration is linked more than ever to *other* realities expressed by notions such as mobility, borderland, protracted displacement, penal colonies and settlements, statelessness, etc.

As I argue in next chapter, concepts move in groups or families. They are like signifiers working in tandem and suggest a reality that cannot be understood with the help of a single term or approach, in this case "labour market" or as Castles later advocated "social transformation". The empirical map of Castles and his co-authors is deceptive. In the process of emphasising the issue of labour market, it disguises, displaces, and reconfigures other realities of migration, which emanate from the relation between (a) forced migratory movements and what we consider to be "normal" migration flows; (b) between the dynamics of institutional practices of security and control and migrant's own autonomy; and finally (c) between border and migration. A predominantly labour market approach prevents the book from deploying the concept of border as a method to study migration and labour. Indeed it will be not an exaggeration to say that Stephen Castles' approach never engages with these three relations. Border is not treated as a critical analytic tool in rational analysis of migration,[9] of which *The Age of Migration* is an instructive example. Border is not linked to political economy either.[10]

Ronald Skeldon in his comments on *The Age of Migration* notes the complexity lurking behind the title of the book whose broad sweep we have come to admire over time through the preceding four (1993, 1998, 2003, and 2009) and the latest (the fifth, 2014) edition. In his brief note, Skeldon points out succinctly the problem of the concept of global migration that is behind the title and the book, even though as he says Castles and his collaborators gradually came to include in their book issues of internal displacement and internal migration, and admit – though indirectly – that the notion of mobility was gradually problematising the concept of migration. Skeldon also suggests that like our age perhaps some earlier age also could have been defined as an age of migration. *The Age of Migration* emphasises the specifically international character of migration today, while the specific characteristics of our particular age may be those of internal migrations and a dramatic rise in a series of forms of non-permanent population movements that can be better captured under the term "mobility".[11] Skeldon usefully points out that as percentage of global population the number of those involved in international migration is still insignificantly small, but people are becoming more and more mobile. Skeldon admits at the same time that "migration" as a term is better than "mobility", which as a term is opaque. "Mobility" does not attract the political and social controversy the term "migration" does – perhaps the reason as to why one should stick to the term "migration".

Others have noted that *The Age of Migration* focuses on how migration produces ethnicity, and in its "conscious choice to study the entire migratory process rather than focusing on either patterns and determinants of migration or the incorporation of migrants in receiving societies"[12] the aim of the book has been to avoid one-sided emphasis either on history or the explanatory value of the theme of "capital". Castles and his co-authors use an inter-disciplinary approach in order to address issues of the international politics of migration around irregular immigration, regional organisations such as the EU, and the linkages between migration and security. The book, evident in its approach, declares that the best way to prevent marginalisation and social conflicts is to grant permanent immigrants full rights in all social spheres, because if, as the book argues, the phenomenon of below-replacement-level fertility and increasing ageing populations in developed countries continues, it will increase the demand for labour from the developing world, and the immigrants would be there to stay for a long time to come. In this way, the book veers towards labour market analysis and assessment of labour market performance of migrants in receiving countries. As a result, the book moves increasingly towards statistical analysis and greater and greater presentation of facts and trends, calling for an altogether new website (www.age-of-migration.com) as access to further information used in the book.[13] So as one review shrewdly notes, the age of migration is the age of global markets. As global markets are formed by the terms of trade and commerce between nation states in their historical-colonial context and by the changes in the structures of firms and the spread of service-providing sectors today, the integration of economic regions and the new technologies of management and communication will lead to greater and greater incidence of migration. Clearly, the book suggests that these layers of complexity deny any single theory of migration as sufficient to tell the whole story. Yet *The Age of Migration*, perched between a labour market mode of analysis and a global template, oscillates between the two main branches of accounts of migration – functionalist accounts of push-pull factors, and historical-structural theories – with systemic explanation of the relationships of dominance and subordination between the developed and developing regions of the world intervening in both accounts.[14] There is no doubt that the book has evolved along with the evolution in migration studies in the last three decades, and it would be an interesting exercise to see how the changes and shifting of material from one section in the book to another signify evolving academic attention to various relevant issues.[15]

Castles and his co-authors are particularly sensitive to their hope that migration must not be seen as a phenomenon that can be judged by its own nature; as they emphasise, it has to be seen and judged only as facet of global change and development. This of course is an unexceptional point, given the particular sensitivity of the authors to various anti-immigrant discriminations and their own espousal of liberal norms of citizenship. Globalisation, acceleration, differentiation, and feminisation – all four marks of succeeding migration waves stand out as salient features of the discussion by Castles and his co-authors. Yet, something seems to be missing in the very fact of the breadth of coverage, intensity of data, and encyclopaedic discussion, namely the specific gradient that makes this an "age of migration".

Probably the answer is in the subtle shift of Castles' own trajectory. Castles, as I mentioned before, began in 1973 with a rigorous Marxist analysis of immigration and class structure in Western Europe. Then he (along with Booth and Wallace, 1984) moved towards sociological analyses by focusing on the shift from temporary labour migration to permanent settlement.[16] With *The Age of Migration*, the move away from Marxism is further. Labour market approach and liberal theory of citizenship now mark the writing. In trying to understand the "impact" of migration on societies, the authors attempt to cover too much,[17] and as a result miss the central question of our time, namely what does migration mean for capitalism, the bourgeois age, and the bourgeois society? How does history figure in this enquiry? What are the continuities and discontinuities in the migration narrative? What do borders signify? What are the meanings of the boundary-making exercises ordaining the lines of inclusion, differential inclusion, and exclusion? It is remarkable that *The Age of Migration* is without borders, border management, and border controls, jails, camps,[18] camp-like slums,[19] or detention centres,[20] all of which are shaping migration today.

Of these, camps and camp-like slums symbolise most the unreturnable nature of migration. One can only keep on moving on without firmly returning to the place of origin. As Edward Said had said, "Our age – with its modern warfare, imperialism, and the quasi-theological ambitions of totalitarian rulers – is indeed the age of the refugee, the displaced person, mass immigration."[21] How does this process continue unendingly? Precisely through forms of settlement (ironically called integration[22]) that paradoxically aim to end mobility by inventing a place which is neither inside nor outside, which contradicts the universal norms of membership of a political community called citizenship, and which is malleable to various forms, such as colonies, detention centres, protected areas, excluded zones, and relief settlements. The idea of the camp form thus underlies attempts to materialise a place which will be a substitute for, in Hannah Arendt's words, a "non-existent homeland".[23] Yet what is more important in this contradictory terrain of a place of stay but not a homeland is the colonial origins of such a terrain and such an apparatus of control. It was in the colonial time that the modern camp could be brought into existence and perfected. Federico Rahola reminds us,

> The trajectories of the camp-form delineate a movement that, from the colonies, is destined to move towards the centre, 'provincializing' Europe in the process, prior to its culmination in a problematic postcolonial scenario. Camps would be imported into the West during the First World War, as detention and labour facilities for war prisoners, as well as places to intern civilians of 'foreign' nationality and colonial subjects. They would then spread in the 1930s in a Europe saturated with borders and in a geopolitical situation that continued to be colonial but which was on the verge of catastrophe. . . . The tally of administrative dispositives and spectral 'substitutes for a homeland' would be reaffirmed at the end of the 1980s and scattered across the apparently smooth surface of the present. These represent the principal junctures in the specific history of camps.[24]

After studying the colonial origins of the camp form, Rahola concluded,

> The space of colonies had always exceeded and challenged forms of binary logic (such as inside-outside and friend-enemy) and conventional representations of borders. At most, it was a space characterized by a 'permanent war' and 'low intensity conflict' and therefore by security policies intent on compartmentalizing a territory and population.[25]

As consequence of the neglect of sites, terrains, and modes of migration, *The Age of Migration* appears to become what it wanted to avoid. It almost becomes a description of migration as a sui generis process without political specificity and apparatuses. The migrant as the stark figure of the outsider caught in various pulls and embodying contentions of various kinds does not appear there. The migrant is submerged beneath the generalities and multifarious descriptions. *The Age of Migration* thus, alas the fifth edition also, fails to answer, what is this figure of the migrant in this age of *mixed and massive flows*? What does settlement mean in such conditions as the one Europe perceived as "crisis" from 2015 onwards? Is there any migration system as the authors seem to suggest?[26] With "crises" appearing one after another will settlement mean anything? The emphasis on settlement actually derails the ambitious aim of the book to focus on migration as an act. In fact migration as an act is lost in the book. Migration as a process reigns, perhaps because the book rules out, as the philosopher would say, intention from action.[27] The migrant in *The Age of Migration* does not intend.

The result is that the political nature of migration as an act is missed, though Castles and others speak of how migration creates ethnic minorities,[28] whose formation is influenced by policies of host governments, and more importantly, because, "Never before has international migration seemed so pertinent to national security and so connected to conflict and disorder on a global scale" (*The Age of Migration*, first edition, p. 261). No wonder hundreds of doctoral theses and policy papers of strategic studies and conflict studies centres are written today on the theme of migration and national security. Keith Sword draws the conclusion, "This is surely a measure of how thinking on potential challenges to regional stability has changed since the Cold War period."[29] The age of migration is an age of globalisation also. But if it is globalisation of security concerns, it consequently globalises flexibility in norms of citizenship. This is the point where the question of postcolonial age enters with footloose illegal and quasi-legal immigrants playing havoc with settled norms of citizenship. These migrants straddle two worlds – the world of citizenship they leave and the world of alien-hood they move into. These two worlds do not present themselves to the migrants as mutually exclusive options. Instead a new world appears marked by coming, moving further, going back, coming again, going elsewhere – always returning.

If the book therefore leaves us with a sense of confusion and seems to miss something central to the details, we have to ask: Is the book then a displaced site of another reality, namely, that something more fundamental to our age is happening, which can tell us as to why this age is one of migration? Let us for instance take ethnicity. *The Age of Migration* pays much attention to ethnicity. Yet, while from a governmental angle migrants as ethnic groups may appear as important for policy making, administering, and controlling population mobility, for the migrant ethnicity may not be a life and death issue. Perhaps the governmental emphasis on ethnicity is only a way to control large sections of immigrant workers.[30] This is why it is important to focus on the figure of the migrant while we are studying migration as process.

Methodologically then it becomes a question of being selective as distinct from the all-encompassing method of Castles and his colleagues. In this book therefore I choose to focus on only those phenomena that throw light on the specifics of the "age" – on the postcolonial time as the principal gradient of this age.

Borders and other apparatuses of migration in an age of globalisation

In short, we have to be aware of the imperative to study migration with historical awareness. A genealogical sense will tell us that there are continuities and discontinuities in the forms and flows of migration; that the forms of forced migration too have varied, institutional forms of governing migration that may have originated decades back; and that migrant labour forms may carry strong historical traces. Some nations may behave consciously as a self-protected bounded entity *vis-à-vis* population flows, while others with imperial antecedents may show a more expansive attitude towards population flows. Frontier politics may influence immigration policies of states and empire-like unities, such as the EU. *The Age of Migration* neglects nation's histories *vis-à-vis* empire's lineages. It is caught in a binary of colony/nation. Thus, issues of colonial mobility, imperial region making, accumulation processes, universalism, concrete, etc. are left out. Nation appears in *The Age of Migration* as the natural site of migration.

The alternative I suggest is to think of a kind of revisionist history which weaves the idea of the nation form in terms of something like empires, states, and migration, and aims to qualify the given history of the nation form by way of looking at this history through the migration glass. In this task, the history of modern social governance (which combines coercion and management of conditions of accumulation) will be crucial. The nation will be problematised in that history, while the nation will still remain the locale. The history of social governance (from late nineteenth century) as a global phenomenon will give us new dimensions to what we know as globalisation, as well as to what we know as the nation. Indeed, history will also tell us the emergence of a distinct type of population politics in the wake of mass migrations – perhaps beginning with Irish and then Chinese migration, the Balkans and the "unmixing" of peoples after the territorial collapse of the Ottoman empire, the collapse of the Tsarist empire, Jewish refugees, Armenian refugees, and many more through to the first quarter of the twentieth century. Thousands of Germans, Austrians, Hungarians, Italians, and labour migration in even more thousands from Asia unsettled any idea of stable nations that theorists may have had imagined.[31] And remember, this was on the heels of great trans-Atlantic migration from Africa.

Population politics led to theories of birth control, notions of specific birth rates among immigration population groups, racism, and ideas of pure, protected nations. Delinking the history of the nation from that of the empire has cost us dearly, not only in terms understanding why nations behave in the way they do, at least certain nations, but also in terms of understanding the critical role migration played in shaping modern social governance and population politics.[32]

It seems that much of the literature on migration – again a perfect example will be *The Age of Migration* – engages with a subject called "global migration", which is built on a telos of globalisation: situating a past in which nation states reigned supreme alongside a present characterised by flows; fuzzy, permeable, and shifting borders; and footloose capitalism. In this scenario, empire as a concept is mostly treated in passing or in a way that fails to register as a historico-theoretical concept. On the other hand, the inquiry as I suggest here will give us a fresh angle to investigate the paradox of the juridico-political forms of citizenship (built in the age of colonialism) and the subject called labour. The paradox implies a transition to a bourgeois order of universalism but a universalism that must be marked by differences, subjugation, and absorption. With his writings framed in the liberal idea of citizenship, Castles (along with his co-authors) fails to see the paradox of liberal universalism and particularities of labour flows.

Yet, what can be the best form of such paradox if not the nation form? Inquiry of paradox can link the emergence of the *nation form* with the emergence of a specific form of labour (that is wage labour) as a *global commodity*. Yet, interestingly, the relation between the nation form and the labour form cannot actualise without the "global", "universal", "imperial", etc., within which migration happened as a phenomenon in the modern era. We may ask: Why does the concept of labour power as a mobile commodity appear only on the margins of the two other concepts (also realities) – empire and the nation with the colony as the mediator of two concepts? We can locate here footloose labour – invisible in social, political, and economic life of capitalism as well as in the received history of the nation form and the form of labour – as perhaps the most critical element in the making of the global.[33]

The world was never organised neatly along nation-state lines with tidy borders. It is a myth produced out of the received history of the national state and its supposed contrast with globalisation and a globalised order. Yet national institutions like boundaries of states serve the purpose of defining markets – markets of goods, labour, finance, etc. However, the resulting tension marking today's world is hard to find in *The Age of Migration*. At the same time this history gives an indication of the concrete nature of migration of our time, namely the *mixed and massive* nature of the population flows.[34] *The Age of Migration* does little to enlighten us on the specific nature of current migration flows. In the context of decades (or almost one century) of attempts to govern migration by classifying population flows under categories and inventing policies and administrative measures appropriate for these categories – such as asylum seekers, refugees, illegal immigrants, economic refugees, trafficked labour, trafficked women, seasonal or irregular migrants, etc.[35] – the failure is striking.

Any inquiry of the present age of migration has to therefore study the governance structures of global migration which have moulded power, humanitarianism, and human rights together into a governmental complex, and created an order where power and responsibility share an asymmetric relationship. This is the contention of the last two chapters of this book. While international law such as the Convention of 1951 and the 1967 Protocol have received global attention and discussion on their adequacy/inadequacy, migration governance framework has enjoyed the advantage of less scrutiny and thus relatively less controversy.

For instance, the IOM (International Organisation for Migration) declares that humane and orderly migration requires compliance with international law. As another principle, it states that since migration policy is often the subject of intense political debate and can be based on populist sentiments, migration policy must be based on facts and a well-founded analysis of the "benefits and risks the movement of people poses to the State". It says that in order to govern migration well, a State would collect, analyse, and use "credible data and information on, among other things, demographics, cross-border movements, internal displacement, Diasporas, labour markets, seasonal trends, education and health". It also advises the ways in which "a State can ensure that migration and mobility policy advances its broader interests". Further, governing migration requires partnerships to broaden the understanding of migration; and to develop comprehensive and effective approaches, business units are more and more brought in as partners and the road to privatisation of care begins. Also, as the IOM says "Addressing the root causes of crises and associated population movements need to be part of longer-term approaches towards recovery, transition and sustainable development". Thus, crisis becomes part of an understanding as to how migration is an inevitable consequence (of a crisis), and that recovery and transition efforts require consideration of the needs of migrants and their communities. All these mean that migration should take place in a safe, orderly, and dignified manner. What do all these mean if not more policing? The IOM recognises this as much as it says,

> Maintaining the integrity of migration and mobility schemes requires an ability to detect irregular migration and to prohibit illegal cross-border activity. Migration and border agencies would work with national and international justice and security agencies to collect and analyse and use information intelligence, to address among others terrorism, as well as trafficking in persons, smuggling in migrants and other trans-border criminal activity.[36]

The criminalisation of migration is based on this governmental approach that aims to permit migration according to the prescribed codes of regulation and forbid migration as an autonomous human act.

The importance of studying the migration governing structures also stems from the fact that the two interrelated processes of migration and forced migration are perched on, besides the global, various regional and national protection systems and migration control accords. These systems and accords tell us of the nature of the regimes such as the European Union along with its Schengen Zone and Frontex Force tasked with Europe's border protection and surveillance duties, or the Bali Process, or the national military deployment strategy of a country to intervene in the affairs of a neighbouring country to ostensibly control and stop migration from the latter. Governing structures cannot be understood without taking them into account in their totality and the range of impact. The UNHCR, ICRC, IOM,

EU, and various free trade compacts function as managerial modes and agencies of regulating population mobility. Their impact on the postcolonial world is collective and we shall fail to recognise the impact to a substantial extent if we conduct a country-by-country study or adopt a labour market–centric framework.

Modes of governing, in other words apparatuses of migration, also tell us how migrants move and the politics of their movement: the very act of moving, the politics of the road the migrants travel, and the politics of how the migrants move. William Walters calls it "viapolitics" (referring to the Roman word "via" for road). The vehicular is a contested field and indicates a form of mobile governmentality whose task is to police transport routes. Borders are thus sites of dynamic interactions and suggest the politics around the vehicles of transportation itself. Viapolitics tells us of how migrants today (or in the past) get smuggled onto ships, cross the seas or treacherous passes and snowy heights, enter tunnels and walk, board trains and try to remain anonymous, use specific modes of contact and communication, register or de-register and flee, which is say that boats, trains, wagons, vans and pick-up trucks, planes, roads, hills, and tunnels hitherto – ignored in studies of migration – become the deserved themes of study. They merit theoretical and empirical investigation in their own right.[37] The terrain, with which a mode of movement is connected, becomes a significant object of theorisation. Clearly once again only with a postcolonial approach and sensitivity the mode of moving will become a central point in a study of migrant's movement.[38]

Sea is now one of the most used terrains for mobility and forced migration.[39] Reports tell us of the voyages by smuggled people on sea amidst conditions of unimaginable distress and infamy. Uncounted deaths of refugees, employment seekers, trafficked girls and children, and shelter seekers tell us of the entangled world of mixed and massive forms of migration, employment agencies, state indifference, and the nature of global labour market which is only a scientific expression of what we call a supply chain of labour-as-commodity whose origin is often in countries like the Philippines, Myanmar, Bangladesh, and countries of sub-Saharan Africa.[40] Slave labour on the high seas, lawlessness including mayhem, crime, piracy, pollution, and finally using the on-sea platforms as prisons and detention centres – all mark the sea as the terrain of mobility. And in all these, race as the governing mode is the unsettling theme. Labour market norms and fixed labour market realities are eternally unsettled by race. Thus, countries like UK which welcomed labour from East Europe back in 2002 now treat the latter as burden. A decade and half later East European whiteness is not enough, and the plumber from, say Poland, after all belongs not to Europe, but outside.[41] It is thus not enough to say that migration is perched on racial divisions, because migration in turn produces new races. The globalization-migration framework of studying human mobility misses the reality of an over-determined presence of race in migration.

At stake in this discussion is obviously the approach to what is known as globalisation. *The Age of Migration* synchronises with the received narrative of the age of globalisation, and the book leaves the reader in no doubt that this is the age of globalisation whose main mark or one of the main marks is global migration. Yet the question looms large, is globalisation and by inference migration a "totalising process involving a kind of 'economic' rationality, which is devoid of agency" and various deep fault lines?[42] Referring to the writings of William Walters, one analyst wrote of the process of reproducing borders and extending them (conversely the borders shrink for others),

> For over a decade now, the 'border-work' of EU Member States has stretched far beyond the physical borders of the Union. The UK was one of the first to formally propose a 'new off-shore line of defense' for policing migration flows in 2008, but the mantra that 'successful borders' stop unwanted flows (of people, or other 'un-wanted') long before they reach the actual territorial borders of the state has by now become commonplace. Border officials now routinely speak of 'remote control borders' (or 'bordering at a distance'), of 'layered inspection strategies', or of the 'thickening of borders' through 'buffer-zones'.
>
> The EU's neighbours to the East and South have played a crucial role in these policies – whether through EU-financed hardening of controls at their own borders with states further afield . . . or by participating in joint policing operations designed to prevent migrants from reaching the EU's external borders. . . . It is useful to recall that Libya under Gaddafi had become a key partner for Europe in policing Mediterranean migrant flows.
>
> [. . .]
>
> Thanks to a series of agreements signed with Italy between 2007 and 2010, Libyan authorities carried out joint maritime patrols and surveillance operations at sea and on land and, from 2009 on, were engaged in 'push-back' operations that authorized the capture of all vessels carrying migrants in international waters and the removal of those on board back to Libyan shores.[. . .]
>
> But the de-bordering of the Union's borders has not only relied on such direct collaboration. . . . The control of the EU's borders has progressively been transformed into a highly complex and geographically-dispersed system of 'border management', relying on a much wider array of institutional and private actors, far beyond the territory of the Union. It now involves consular officials that assess visa applications and rights to asylum in migrants' countries of origin on the other side of the globe, as well as a growing cadre of immigration liaison officers (ILOs) deployed by Member States and whose task it is to carry out 'risk analyses' of potential flows of irregular migrants.[43]

In short, the picture of global migration drawn by Castles and his colleagues carries the logic of things imposed on human beings known as migrants, unmediated by the latter's autonomy and actions.[44] Yet aspects of migration governing technology, such as finance, markets, regulations, police deployment, admission, settlement, and labour absorption policies, find their true counterparts in the collective subject called the migrant.[45] The real world of globalisation is both, which is to say composed of both – the official aspects to which *The Age of Migration* draws our attention and the subaltern life of mobility which *The Age of Migration* leaves by the wayside.

Here then is a crucial problem of method for writing a book like the *Age of Migration*. As indicated in this chapter, the method of the book is structural. It is geared towards finding a system. As a goal, this is unobjectionable, provided one maintains a dialectical balance between structure and system on one hand and the element of human subjectivity, autonomy, and the uncertain flight paths on the other. The truth of "'autonomy of migration" cannot be grasped without an experiential method of study that takes into account historical experiences. History and experiences are the two crucial components we must add to the structural method of Castles. Today, we cannot produce a coherent account of global migration flows and their specificities without an experiential method, or at least one that draws heavily from existential accounts, such as the one we find in, say *Upheaval: The Refugee Trek through Europe*, which more than many scholarly analyses captures what has happened in the recent European migration crisis.[46]

The emphasis on the modes of governing migration and the modes of migration reflects on the entire theme of the autonomy of migration itself on which there has been a surge of interest among migration researchers in the wake of the European migration "crisis" since 2014.[47] Sadly *The Age of Migration* even in its last edition misses the meta-political question – indeed a double question – of how migration is governed and how migration remains an autonomous act with all its political and economic implications, and the interrelations of this dual problematic. As a result, themes such as how border as an institution functions, borderlands work as sites of migration and untold violence and at the same time of interaction, circulation, and exchange, how border management becomes one of the principal modes of rule, and how borders of migration become the consequence of continuous boundary drawing and reproduction of boundaries – all these are mentioned – if at all – in passing, and do not occupy the central place in reflection. The focus on settlement and resettlement results in over-emphasis on aspects like ethnicisation. The apparatuses of migration such as camps, borders, frontier forces, legislative design, new technological modes, forms of movement and mobility, capital-labour dispositions that redistribute populations, deployment of force, etc. do not receive in the book the attention they deserve in any exhaustive migration study of our time.

Dualities and paradoxes in the age of migration

Ironically, precisely at a time when Stephen Castles was putting hope of ensuring justice for the migrants through grant of citizenship to immigrants, more and more people in this period were becoming stateless. They were being stripped of their citizenship, and/or driven out of the lands where they were living and working, consigned to an endlessly protracted state of displacement. For instance, as I show later (in Chapter 9), people such as the Rohingyas in Myanmar were becoming stateless even before migrating or being compelled to migrate, while at the same time a protracted state of displacement was leading in many cases to de facto stateless situations, as with many South Bhutanese refugees in Nepal or perhaps many Tibetans or Chakma refugees in India. In order to avoid international censure and disciplinary steps, a state that may prevent a population group from leaving the country at the same time will deprive the latter of full citizenship rights. Race, religion, and resource (the three Rs) become factors in production of statelessness. Similar to "refugee and refugee-like situation" we have now situations of "statelessness and de facto statelessness". In the latter case international law is of little help, precisely because what we may call Geneva-based wisdom (with international law overwhelmed by that wisdom) fails to take into account the actual processes of statelessness, and how laws, policies, and administrative measures contribute to statelessness and forced migration. Most of Castles' and his colleagues' analyses miss the de facto processes. In the course of emphasising the liberal norms of citizenship they forget that citizenship is overwhelmingly a "birth right", and the transition almost everywhere from *jus soli* to *jus sanguinis* shows that citizenship and migration do not happily sit together. It is doubtful if the institution of citizenship can be an effective remedy to statelessness.[48]

There may be several reasons. As hinted previously, international legal wisdom emphasises definitions and the enumerations of the said definitions. We may ask and get an answer to: *Who is a refugee*? But if we were to ask, *what is a refugee-like condition?*, probably we shall not make much headway. The jungle in Calais, the overcrowded camps in Idomeni in Greece, the huddled shanties in the borderlands in Turkey or the detention camps in Assam in India for the illegal immigrants – these places tell us of *situation*, a *condition*. A condition or a situation cannot be always legally defined,[49] because such a situation as statelessness is defined by some *lack*: lack of facilities, lack of means of life and livelihood, lack of citizenship rights, and a lack of social entitlements, in short a lack of all that nationality would imply.[50] In the context of the worldwide shift from *jus soli* to *jus sanguinis*, the task of giving a positive definition of statelessness (that is legally providing a positive definition of statelessness) is becoming difficult. Central Asia, West Asia, some countries in Africa, South Asia – in all these regions and places citizenship and nationality rights are increasingly under different restrictions and qualification. Everywhere there is now a sub-population – a sub-national population consisting of disenfranchised minorities, immigrant groups, trafficked groups in labour and sex, and population groups in protracted situation of camp internment – which works as subaltern labour but without the free juridical status of citizenship. This is a fleet-footed population or a mobile labouring army, situated at one end of population distribution range, exemplifying the uneven and hierarchical situation of national populations throughout the world. As a global population group its characterisation as "stateless" tells only a formal story and that too only half of the story of sub-existence. It is a predatory situation causing maximum dispossession, evident in lives of urban refugees, and comparable to the penal existence of groups in islands and colonies in the nineteenth century. Refracted from citizenship rights, the condition of statelessness is therefore a grey zone. Today conditions have arisen where internal displacement too may lead to a situation of statelessness. Statelessness is the glass in which the sanitised picture of migration is laid bare.

The madness and the brutality in massive waves of migration strike one on its face. These massive waves of migration contain people who are moving due to all kinds of reasons – political persecution, statelessness, labour, environmental degradation, ecological disasters, and sexual oppression, as well as trafficking. The refugee and displacement problem becomes in this way one of the most complex humanitarian and political issues facing the world today, where existing legal avenues prove woefully inadequate. Migration is a "crisis" today – crisis for those countries that regularly accept and absorb refugees and for those from where people migrate. It is a crisis because, as said earlier, today's population movements are mixed and massive, throwing in disarray the tools and policies of classification, targeted relief, settlement, and return. Mixed and massive population flows ending up in cities and towns bring to the fore the critical relations between the migrants and the city. Cities look like camps while camps increasingly take on the character of small cities – the dual process signifying dispersal of population groups into resettlements of urban refugees as the city becomes a sanctuary, the boundaries within a city are redrawn, and migrants and asylum seekers move to the inner city. The sense of crisis as a consequence is overwhelming. The crisis, we are told, originates from the postcolonial world where anarchy, madness, uncertainty, regime instability, and developmental disorders prevail. The colonial past catches up, printing on the mobility map the course that human formations will take, for example, in journeys from the South and the East across sea and land to press on the borders of Europe.

In the context of this overwhelming idea of crisis affecting our senses, sensibilities, and discourses, migration and forced migration studies has to tie itself firmly with the three poles I mentioned at the beginning of the chapter, namely temporality, spatiality, and agency. In simpler words, these may be put as historical sense; significance of the question of place in refugee and migration studies (the place from where the migrants originate, where they reach, where they settle, and or move on, etc.); and finally the migrant's autonomy. I have tried to explain why Stephen Castles, notwithstanding his sincere advocacy of basing migration studies in social transformation framework,[51] fails to grasp the specificity of this age in historical perspective. It is a specificity that cannot be grasped by a systemic explanation of "global migration". Such systemic explanation misses the postcolonial temporality characteristic of the global migration of our time, because it neglects the three poles of migration studies: temporality, spatiality, and agency. Social transformation bereft of considerations of spatiality, temporality, and agency becomes less effective as an explanatory framework. The agency of the migrant becomes crucial for an agenda of hospitality and cosmopolitanism.[52]

This book is written from that disappointment with *The Age of Migration*, an instructive analytical treatise on migration, but missing some of the critical questions of our time, one of which is the autonomy of migration. Hence is the need for a postcolonial intervention in our understanding of migration. The figure of the migrant is produced out of what we can call a division of labour (migration and objectification of migration in a system). It is the schema of a duality that is producing the unwanted migrant today. On one hand, as Thomas Faist says, the liberal world is building a moral polity[53] in which many refugee-receiving countries in Europe have signed human rights conventions. Yet at the same time there is externalisation of migration control, more brutal border controls, and widespread rejection of forced migrants. This dualism of human rights on the one hand and an unwillingness to accept forced migrants on the other reflects the duality that the migrant represents and traverses.[54] *The Age of Migration* is perched on this paradox. Its schema aims to explain a system of global migration; contingency is ruled out from this schema. Hence the paradox is left unexplained. Events when mentioned have been offered as parts of that schema. Autonomy of the migrant as the subject's determination and capacity to escape is reduced to the context of policies, rules, and requirements of labour market. It is perhaps more relevant then to see *The Age of Migration* and the general corpus of Castles' writings as oscillating between a structural synthesis of pre-existing demographic trends and an intriguing admission that controls, policies, and systems fail in the wake of what is known as migration. The unruly subject of contemporary capitalism called the migrant and the refugee is the unsettling, quintessential postcolonial figure who has to be bound by market norms, laws of immigration, policies of stay or settlement and humanitarianism, and administrative-police measures, but who escapes all these measures aimed at stabilising the situation. We may have institutions like the World Bank, IMF, the G7 states, and the World Economic Forum promoting rights, and yet precisely the institutional framework of global governance violates claims of the migrants to justice. The limits of rights discourse manifest themselves at the moment when these two meet.[55]

To bring out the various contradictions in the migration world, also in the migration discourses, as suggested earlier in this chapter, we must move on to the question of method of inquiry. How do we unravel the principal gradient, namely the postcolonial nature, of the age of migration? How do we dissect the significance of the word "population" in the subtitle of the book, *The Age of Migration*? For after all, to the developed segment of the world, the vast segment known as the "underdeveloped" symbolises the population question: overpopulation, ecological crisis, abundant unskilled labour, wear, violence, poverty, and retarded transition. Migration from this underdeveloped world to the developed world is part of the population debate. The question will be: How does the population debate lodge itself in the issue of global migration?[56] Castles and his colleagues were silent about this, while this book will attempt to understand the problem. This is what we shall address from the next chapter onwards.

Notes

1 Stephen Castles, Hein de Haas, and Mark J. Miller, *The Age of Migration: International Population Movements in the Modern World*, 5th ed. (New York: Palgrave MacMillan, 2014).
2 Published by the Oxford University Press for Institute of Race Relations, London, 1973
3 See Martin Bulmer and John Solomos, "Migration and Race in Europe", *Ethnic and Racial Studies*, Volume 41 (5), 2018, pp. 779–784; Saskia Bonjour and Jan Willem Duyvendak, "The 'Migrant with Poor Prospects': Racialised Intersections of Class and Culture in Dutch Civic Integration Debates", *Ethnic and Racial Studies*, Volume 41 (5), 2018, pp. 882–900.
4 See on this, Thomas Faist, "Migrants as Transnational Development Agents: An Inquiry into the Newest Round of the Migration – Development Nexus", *Population, Space*

and Place, Volume 14 (1), 2008, pp. 21–42. It is important to point out that the issue of resources in shaping the relation between development and displacement is crucial, yet it was ignored by and large in the original literature on internal displacement, for instance in the UN Guiding Principles on Internal Displacement. Developmental measures altering land use, forest use, and water use have led to displacement. Castles' focus being on migration and displacement, one of the most important factors – development – shaping the migratory flows of our time has been thereby ignored. On the other hand postcolonial studies of migration have thrown light on the relation between resources, conflict, displacement, and migration, which include themes such as study of the forest policy of a modern developmental state like establishment of conserved areas for wildlife. See, Sanjay Barbora, "Riding the Rhino: Conservation, Conflicts, and Militarisation of Kaziranga National Park in Assam", *Antipode*, Volume 49 (5), November 2017, pp. 1145–1163. Barbora discusses in detail the relation between settlement pattern, mobility pattern, resource use pattern, and population conflict in forest areas of Assam in India. He notes that such resource use policies create conflict among population groups, lines of exclusion, and racialized class borders.
5 See for instance, Amit Bhaduri, "A Study in Development by Dispossession", *Cambridge Journal of Economics*, 2017, doi:10.1093/cje/bex026.
6 An interview with Sylvia Federici, "The Reproduction Crisis and the Birth of a New 'Out of Law' Proletariat", *Left East*, 10 July 2017, www.criticatac.ro/lefteast/the-reproduction-crisis-and-the-birth-of-a-new-out-of-law-proletariat-an-interview-with-silvia-federici/ (accessed on 15 December 2017); see also, Sandro Mezzadra, "What's at Stake in the Mobility of Labour? Borders, Migration, Contemporary Capitalism", *Migration, Mobility, and Displacement*, Volume 2 (1), 2016, pp. 31–43.
7 In an essay titled, "Migration, Crisis, and the Global Labour Market", *Globalizations*, Volume 8 (3), 2011, pp. 311–324, Stephen Castles reflected on two contrasting realities of the global labour situation and discussed the neo-liberal ideology of economic efficiency and shared prosperity that masked the exploitation of labour on a global scale. He also argued that the international mobilisation of workers and their differentiation on criteria of gender, race, ethnicity, origins, and legal status were a crucial part of the global economic order. Labour markets were being restructured, and there were hierarchies in citizenship. Thus the migration pattern in the phase of expansion of manufacturing in core economies from 1945 to the 1970s underwent changes in the early twenty-first century as what can be called the new economy emerged on a global scale with new migration from the Caribbean, Asia, and Africa and production jobs being outsourced to countries like Mexico and China, new jobs being created in retailing, personal services, etc., marked by sub-contracting, casual work, informalisation, and fragmentation of ethnic or community solidarity. Yet these insights are not pushed to their logical conclusion and thus are not integrated in the overall argument of *The Age of Migration*.
8 On this see for instance, Transnational Social Strike Platform, "Logistics, Power, Strike: Elements for the Political Infrastructure", *Logistics and the Transnational Social Strike*, Fall 2017, pp. 5–12, www.transnational-strike.info/wp-content/uploads/Logistics-the-Transnational-Social-Strike-%E2%80%94-TSS-Journal-Fall-2017-1.pdf (accessed on 20 January 2018).
9 On this, Paolo Novak, "Back to Borders", *Critical Sociology*, Volume 43 (6), September 2017, pp. 847–864. Novak analyses the responses of social theorists and writes that these theorists have failed to analyse the crisis in its complexity and have been primarily concerned with the realm of representation. Thus for some the crisis was provoked by the men, women, and children entering, but not yet integrated into, Europe and could be best characterized as one of demographic enlargement. For these theorists, the crisis should be overcome by offering these "virtual citizens" access to European citizenship. However, others were inclined to think that these migrant men, women, and children did not simply want to settle for a minimum of safety and well-being, but were rather pursuing a utopian dream that was out of reach for most Europeans. Europe, thus, should renew its commitment to provide for the dignified treatment of those fleeing "failed

states", but at the same time impose clear rules and regulations to control the stream of refugees.

However, William Walters prudently cautions us not to treat in migration studies the theme of control, governmentality, and in particular the institution of border as an all-weather, all-purpose serving analytic tool, but contingently. See, William Walters, "Reflections on Migration and Governmentality", 2015, http://movements-journal.org/issues/01.grenzregime/04.walters--migration.governmentality.html (accessed on 22 March 2018)

10 Sandro Mezzadra and Brett Neilson argue for linking the two in their *Border as Method: Or, the Multiplication of Labour* (Durham, NC: Duke University Press, 2013).
11 Ronald Skeldon, "What's in a Title? The Fifth Edition of *The Age of Migration*", *Ethnic and Racial Studies*, Volume 38 (13), 2015, pp. 2356–2361; the point about mobility indicating movements within a country is also noted by Michael Collyer in his review of the fifth edition of *The Age of Migration*, "Steel Wheels: The Age of Migration 5.0", *Ethnic and Racial Studies*, Volume 38 (13), 2015, pp. 2362–2365, 2365; same point noted by Russell King, "Migration Comes of Age", *Ethnic and Racial Studies*, Volume 38 (13), 2015, pp. 2366–2372.
12 Helena Ekelund, "Review of Stephen Castle and Mark Miller, *The Age of Migration: International Population Movements in the Modern World* (Fourth Edition)", *Journal of Contemporary European Research*, Volume 5 (2), Summer 2009, pp. 326–327, 326.
13 See for instance, Md. Kamrul Islam, "Review of Stephen Castle and Mark Miller, *The Age of Migration: International Population Movements in the Modern World* (2009)", *Canadian Studies in Population*, Volume 40 (1–2), Spring–Summer 2013, Special Issue on "Immigration and the Life Course", pp. 105–106. With regard to the use of resources it is important to note that Castles and his team deploy an astonishing range of data – but almost all originating from Western sources or UN corpus, but seldom use the data originating from the postcolonial world – governmental, research-based, and other such as NGO material.
14 Don's "Review of the Fifth Edition of *The Age of Migration*" appearing on Migrants' Rights Network (16 March 2014), www.migrantsrights.org.uk/blog. . . (accessed on 20 November 2017), now unavailable; originally appearing on www.goodreads.com/review/list/1478469-don?shelf=modern-society – here also now unavailable.
15 Michael Collyer notes this in "Steel Wheels: The Age of Migration 5.0", *Ethnic and Racial Studies*, Volume 38 (13), 2015, pp. 2362–2365.
16 Stephen Castles, Heather Booth, and Tina Wallace, *Here for Good: Western Europe's New Ethnic Minorities* (London: Pluto Press, 1984)
17 The sociological ambition of the book was noted as early as 1994 by Helene Lambert in a review of the first edition of the book in *Millennium: Journal of International Studies*, Volume 23 (2), 1994, pp. 436–437.
18 Studies of camps now occupy a central place in forced migration studies. See for instance, Frank Heidemann and Abhijit Dasgupta, "Learning to Live in the Colonies and Camps: Repatriates and Refugee in Tamil Nadu", *Economic and Political Weekly*, Volume 53 (8), 24 February, 2018, pp. 39–47; Michel Agier, *Maanging the Undesirables: Refugee Camps and Humanitarian Government* (Cambridge: Polity Press, 2010); also, Michel Agier, "Between 'War and City: Towards an Urban Anthropology of Refugee Camps", *Ethnography*, Volume 3 (3), 2002, pp. 317–366; also Michel Agier, "The Chaos and the Camps: Fragments of a Humanitarian Government", in Ursula Biemann and Brian Holmes (eds.), *The Maghreb Connection: Movements of Life Across North Africa* (Barcelona: Actar, 2006), pp. 260–282. Alessandro Petti in speaks of camp as a university in exile in discussing the "camp form", which he says is a new form of urbanism, also a site of political invention. – Alessandro Petti, "Campus in Camps: A University in Exile", in Sandi Hilal and Alessandro Petti (eds.), *Permanent Temporariness* (Stockholm: Royal Institute of Art and Art and Theory Publishing, 2018), pp. 209–214.
19 On the crucial role of migrant labour in the creation of slums, see for instance on the case of India a government report, *Slums in India: A Statistical Compendium, 2011*

(New Delhi: Government of India, Ministry of Housing and Urban Poverty Alleviation, National Buildings Organization, 2011); the report shows that slums are not given places of accommodation and work of migrants, but that to have migrant labour slums are needed. The report stated,

> While it is empirically evident that it is mainly the poor rural migrants who are forced into informal, even illegal land settlements; it is also true that tenure insecurity itself powers the vicious cycle of poverty. The insecurity of tenure along with urban poverty reinforces social exclusion and propagates squatter and slum settlements.
>
> *p. 39*

20 On the crucial role of camps in migration studies see, Tings Chak, "Undocumented: The Architecture of Migrant Detention", *Migration, Mobility, & Displacement*, Volume 2 (1), 2016, pp. 6–29. Chak showed in detail how since 2006, nearly 100,000 people had been jailed indefinitely in Canada, without charge or trial – with immigration detention being mostly invisible. Chak wrote that while migrants were incarcerated because they had no documents of nationality, there was little trace to be found of those sites of detention: drawings and photos were classified, and access was extremely limited. The detention centres, too, like the migrants were undocumented.

21 Edward Said, *Reflections on Exile and Other Essays* (Cambridge, MA: Harvard University Press, 2002), p. 174.

22 For instance, see the OECD Report, "The Economic and Social Aspects of Integration", by Anja Rudiger and Sarah Spencer, Brussels, 21–22 January 2003, www.oecd.org/migration/mig/15516956.pdf (accessed on 21 march 2018); see also, J Doomernik, *A Study of the Effectiveness of Integration* (Geneva: ILO Migration Programme Series, 1998).

23 Hannah Arendt, *The Origins of Totalitarianism* (New York: Meridian, 1958), p. 284.

24 Federico Rahola, "The Space of Camps: Towards a Genealogy of Places of Internment in the Present", in A. Dal Lago and S. Palidda (eds.), *Conflict, Security and the Reshaping of Society: The Civilisation of War* (Milton Park: Routledge, 2010), pp. 185–199, 193.

25 *Ibid.*, p. 198.

26 The assumption of a system was pointed out by Caroline R. Nagel in her review of the 1999 edition of *The Age of Migration* in *Political Geography*, 19, 2000, pp. 661–665, 662; on the assumption of a system, see also n 46.

27 Stuart Hampshire, *Thought and Action*, new ed. (London: Chatto and Windus, 1982), chapter 2, "Intention and Action", pp. 90–168

28 Volker Ronge noted very early the emphasis by Castles and his co-authors' on ethnicity, the production of "ethnic confusion" in the host country by a supposition of "some degree of ethnic homogeneity". See the review of the first edition, *Journal of European Social Policy*, Volume 4 (2), 1994, pp. 152–153, 152.

29 Review, *The Slavonic and East European Review*, Volume 74 (1), January 1996, pp. 186–188, p. 187.

30 It will be difficult to cite many instances of riots occasioned by migration. Everywhere riots become legitimate by becoming "ethnicised" supposedly against migrants or enacted by migrants. Even the Paris riots in 2005 or the killings in the Balkans were not acts against the "migrants" or for that matter enacted by "migrants", but by groups of "natives" trapped in the conflicting pulls of racism.

31 One of the insightful accounts of forced population movements in early twentieth century is Michael R. Marrus, *The Unwanted: European Refugees in the Twentieth Century* (New York: Oxford University Press, 1985). Marrus shows how the national world was being formed through the collapse of empires and the peace treaties which shaped population movements of that time. See chapters 1–2, particularly "Empires in Ruin" marking the Nansen era, pp. 52–74.

32 Typical of such close relation between immigration and population politics is the current controversy over the "windrush" generation in the UK – those who came to the UK for economic reconstruction of the country, and are now asked to go back after seventy years. On the "Empire Windrush" the vessel in which migrants arrived in England on 23 June 1948, the report in *The Guardian*, 30 June 2016, www.theguardian.

com/uk-news/2016/jun/23/immigration-windrush-west-indians-jamaica-britain 30 June 2016 (accessed on 20 April 2018).
33 For a detailed discussion see Chapter 6.
34 UNHCR noted the mixed nature of population flows that defy neat categorisation in2007. See, "Refugee Protection and Mixed Migration: A 10-Point Plan of Action", www.unhcr.org/protection/migration/4742a30b4/refugee-protection-mixed-migration-10-point-plan-action.html (accessed on 12 March 2018); yet not only was the document bereft of historical sense, it was extremely myopic in admitting that population flows are increasingly mixed, which means precisely that causes of migration are intermixed, modes of migration are mixed, and people are both migrants and potential refugees. The UNHCR noted,

> Migrant is a wide-ranging term that covers people who move to a foreign country for a certain length of time – not to be confused with short-term visitors such as tourists and traders. People migrate for a variety of reasons. Migrants are fundamentally different from refugees and, thus, are treated very differently under international law. Migrants, especially economic migrants, choose to move in order to improve their lives. Refugees are forced to flee to save their lives or preserve their freedom. Migrants and refugees increasingly make use of the same routes and means of transport to get to an overseas destination. If people composing these mixed flows are unable to enter a particular state legally, they often employ the services of human smugglers and embark on dangerous sea or land voyages, which many do not survive. To help states address mixed migration movements in a protection-sensitive way, UNHCR in 2006 launched a 10-Point Plan of Action on Refugee Protection and Mixed Migration. The plan sets out key areas where protection interventions are called for. Mixed migration movements are of concern mainly in the Mediterranean basin, the Gulf of Aden, Central America and the Caribbean, South-east Asia and the Balkans.

As can be seen, this was a view from Geneva, Eurocentric to say the least.
35 On this, Itty Abraham, "Refugees and Humanitarianism", *Refugee Watch*, Special Issue Nos. 24–26, October 2005, www.mcrg.ac.in/rw%20files/RW24.doc (accessed on 12 March 2018)
36 All quotations in this and the previous paragraph are from the IOM, "Migration Governance Framework", www.iom.int/sites/default/files/about-iom/migof_brochure_a4_en.pdf (accessed on 19 March 2018); See for a relevant discussion on IOM, Megan Bradley, "The International Organization for Migration (IOM): Gaining Power in the Forced Migration Regime", *Refuge*, Volume 33 (1), 2017, pp. 97–106, https://refuge.journals.yorku.ca/index.php/refuge/article/view/40452/36445(accessed on 20 March 2018); see also, on particular operations of the IOM in the postcolonial world, Asher Lazarus Hirsch and Cameron Doig, "Outsourcing Control: The International Organization for Migration in Indonesia", *The International Journal of Human Rights*, 17 January, 2018, doi:10.1080/13642987.2017.1417261.
37 William Walters, "Migration, Vehicles, and Politics: Three Theses on *Viapolitics*", *European Journal of Social Theory*, Volume 18 (4), 2014, pp. 469–488; see also, R. Andersson, "Hunter and Prey: Patrolling Clandestine Migration in the Euro-African Borderlands", *Anthropological Quarterly*, Volume 87 (1), 2014, pp. 119–149.
38 G. Garelli and M. Tazzioli, "Challenging the Discipline of Migration: Militant Research in Migration Studies", *Post Colonial Studies*, Volume 16 (3), 2013, pp. 245–249; see also, Bhaskar Mukhopadhyay who writes of the world around a crossing a bridge by the migrants to a city, "Crossing the Howrah Bridge: Calcutta, Filth and Dwelling – Forms, Fragments, Phantasms", *Theory, Culture, & Society*, Volume 23 (7–8), 2006, pp. 221–241. Mukhpadhyay writes,

> They come in hordes, mostly from Bihar, one of the poorest states of India, poor even by Indian standards. Clutching their tin suitcases, they arrive at the Howrah station and cross the bridge to Calcutta. The motif of moving to the city and becoming

a part of its underclass is so timeworn that even their folksongs have registered it. They come to Calcutta to work as rickshaws-pullers, *jamadars* [cleaners of sewers], day-labourers, porters, pavement-barbers, cobblers, potters, blacksmiths, and so on. In many cases, these are also their caste occupations and for generations now the Bihari countryside has been 'subsidizing' Calcutta, so to speak, by allowing the latter to draw from the former's pool of skilled labour. Menial work in the city being regulated by close-knit kin/caste networks, newcomers are mostly unwelcome. Yet, the lure of 'the city of cash', as Calcutta is known to these migrants, is great. One comes to the city not to become a citizen, not to become a city dweller, but to tide over lean seasons, to pay back a loan to the moneylender, to work as cash-earner for a big peasant family or to run away from the wrath of the upper-caste landlords or the *dadas*. A part of the (joint) family always stays back in the village and the bond with the village is never severed.

p. 221

39 From the Mediterranean to the Indian Ocean waters, sea is the preferred route. Indeed as reports suggest, in 2014, over 180,000 Libyan refugees are known to have attempted to cross the Mediterranean, with about 2,000 either having drowned or died because of dangerous sailing conditions. Although they are only approximate, these figures testify to at least two indisputable facts, i.e. the route has become much more attractive than ever before and unquestionably is more popular than two other popular routes – by sea from Morocco to Spain and over land from Turkey to Greece.

40 On this see the exceptional report on the Philippines, "Tricked and Indebted on Land, Abused or Abandoned at Sea" by Ian Urbina, *The New York Times*, 8 November 2015, www.nytimes.com/2015/11/09/world/asia/philippines-fishing-ships-illegal-manning-agencies.html (accessed on 15 March 2018). Urbina shows how illegal "manning agencies" trick villagers in the Philippines with promises of high wages and then send them to ships notorious for poor safety and labour records.

41 József Böröcz and Mahua Sarkar, "The Unbearable Whiteness of the Polish Plumber and the Hungarian Peacock Dance around 'Race'", *Slavic Review*, Volume 76 (2), Summer 2017, pp. 307–314; see also Joseph Pugliese, "Race as Category Crisis: Whiteness and the Topical Assignation of Race", *Social Semiotics*, Volume 12 (2), August 2002, pp. 149–168.

42 Bhaskar Mukhopadhyay writes on what he calls the "rumor of globalization",

More broadly, 'The Rumor of Globalization' seeks to capture the wider historic unease surrounding 'globalization' Critical studies of globalization phrase it as a totalizing process involving a kind of "economic" rationality which is devoid of agency – the inhuman, 'fantastic' logic of 'things' comes to impose itself on what is directly lived – human 'belonging' which is necessarily local, autochthonous, resistant and unmediated by representation. It is my contention that globalization is also an imaginary; it is imagined through metaphors, narratives, and rumors. Even its moments of violence are mediated by structures of meaning. These meanings are constitutive of 'globalization' and not simply its flip-sides or ideological chimeras that mask forms of oppression that are external to them. Finance, interest rates, markets, tariffs and regulations emerge from a discursive process because the 'economy' itself is a re-presentation, and not the 'real' world itself.

The Rumor of Globalization: Desecrating the Global Forms from the Vernacular Margins *(London: C. Hurst & Co., 2012), p. 37.*

43 Luiza Bialasiewicz, "Where Do We Want the EU's Borders to Lie?" *Transit Online*, 9 November 2015, www.iwm.at/transit/transit-online/want-eus-borders-lie/ (accessed on 20 March 2018).

44 Refugee activism in occupying the City Plaza in Athens for 39 months is one of several examples of migrant subjectivity – an aspect of the present time and ignored in *The Age of Migration*. On 22 April 2016, the Economic and Political Refugee Solidarity Initiative squatted the empty City Plaza building with a twofold goal: (a) to create a space of safety and dignity in which to house refugees in the centre of the city, and (b) to create a centre

of struggle against racism, borders, and social exclusion, for the freedom of movement, and for the right to stay. On 10 July 2019, the keys of occupied City Plaza were handed back to the former employees of the hotel. All refugees living at City Plaza were moved to safe housing within the city – Report by Economic and Political Refugee Solidarity Initiative, 15 July 2019, https://socialistproject.ca/2019/07/greece-39-months-city-plaza/ (accessed on 8 September 2019).

45 Stephen Castles drew our attention to the poorly crafted policies with respect to migration. See the discussion – Bridget Anderson, "Towards a New Politics of Migration?" *Ethnic and Racial Studies*, Volume 40 (9), 2017, pp. 1527–1537; Stephen Castles, "A Response to Bridget Anderson: Migration Policies Are Problematic – Because They Are About Migration", *Ethnic and Racial Studies*, Volume 40 (9), 2017, pp. 1538–1543; Stephen Castle wrote there of the complexity of migration processes and the poor responses in form of policies, which fail to understand the complexity. See Stephen Castles, "Why Migration Policies Fail", *Ethnic and Racial Studies*, Volume 27 (2), 2004, pp. 205–227; Castles observed in this article that even though immigration and asylum were key political issues in Britain and the European Union, their state and collective policies fail. He cited three types of reasons for policy failure: factors arising from the social dynamics of the migratory process, those linked to globalisation and the North-South divide; and those arising within political systems. He concluded by saying that migration policies might be more successful if they were explicitly linked to long-term political agendas concerned with trade, development, and conflict prevention, and reducing North-South inequality. Yet Castles does not link this to either the dynamics of apparatus building or migrant's relative autonomy.

46 Navid Kermani, *Upheaval: The Refugee Trek through Europe*, trans. Tony Crawford (London: Polity Press, 2017).

47 Stephen Castles in 2004 had noted the issue of migrant's agency with these words, "migrants are not just isolated individuals who react to market stimuli and bureaucratic rules, but social beings who seek to achieve better outcomes for themselves, their families and their communities through actively shaping the migratory process" ("Why Migration Policies Fail", *Ethnic and Racial Studies*, Volume 27, 2004, pp. 205–227, 209–210); yet the theme of autonomy of migration never featured centrally in his analysis. See on the question of autonomy of migration, Nicholas De Genova (ed.), *The Borders of "Europe": Autonomy of Migration, Tactics of Bordering* (Durham, NC: Duke University Press, 2017); also, Stephan Scheel, "Autonomy of Migration despite Its Securitisation? Facing the Terms and Conditions of Biometric Rebordering", *Millennium – Journal of International Studies*, Volume 41, 2013, pp. 575–600.

48 On this see the Calcutta Research Group study of statelessness in South Asia, Paula Banerjee, Atig Ghosh, and Anasua Basu Ray Chaudhury, *The State of Being Stateless: An Account of South Asia* (Hyderabad: Orient Blackswan, 2015); Engin Isin, "Citizens Without Nations", *Environment and Planning D: Society and Space*, Volume 30 (2), June 2012, pp. 450–467; also, Sabyasachi Basu Ray Chaudhury and R. Samaddar, *Rohingya in South Asia: People Without a State* (London: Routledge, 2018).

49 There are cases which for instance the Refugee Convention of 1951 will try to define as a situation of fear.

50 For instance, immigrants in India are declared illegal, Indian government says that they are from Bangladesh, and Bangladesh refuses to take them back saying they are not citizens of Bangladesh. What happens to the rights of the migrants in such case? They lose nationality rights and other human rights. In the context of the preparation of the Draft National Register of Citizens in Assam in India one analyst commented,

> The option adopted by the government, under such circumstances, has been the detention of detected illegal migrants. Assam has six detention camps so far and the state has also planned to develop a full-fledged detention centre for foreigners in Goalpara district. However, the pressing question is whether detention ought to be the solution. Can a person declared a foreigner, be detained in a camp forever? Will this not be a violation of human rights by the state, in the eyes of the international

community? . . . If by amending the Citizenship Act, Hindus and other religious minorities are granted citizenship, will only illegal Muslims be forced to live in detention camps? Urgent measures need to be undertaken to avoid such eventualities.

Akhil Ranjan Dutta, "Political Destiny of Immigrants in Assam: National Register of Citizens", *Economic and Political Weekly,* Volume 53 (9), 3 March 2018, pp. 18–21.

51 Stephen Castles, "Understanding Global Migration: A Social Transformation Perspective", *Journal of Ethnic and Migration Studies,* Volume 36 (10), 2010, pp. 1565–1586; Castles stresses the need of a systemic study grounded in social transformation perspective. See also his, "Migration and Social Transformation", Lecture at the London School of Economics, London, 15 November 2007, www.lse.ac.uk/website-archive/. . ./20071115Migra tionStudies (accessed on 25 February 2018). Castles wrote there,

> Thus the project of elaborating a social transformation framework for the analysis of migration does not require starting from scratch. Rather the task is to bring together new approaches and insights in a detailed and systematic way so that they can serve as a coherent frame for migration theory and research methodology. This task cannot be attempted here. Rather one example will be presented to show briefly how the understanding of local experiences of migration can be enhanced through analysis of global social transformations.

52 Alessandro Monsutti, "Mobility as a Political Act", *Ethnic and Racial Studies,* Volume 41 (3), 2018, pp. 448–455. Monsutti suggests that it is time to re-examine our conceptual framework on human mobility, cross-dress forced migration and find a way to reveal the human cost of existing dichotomous categories. "The massive arrival to Europe of Syrians, Afghans, Iraqis, Eritreans, and sub-Saharan Africans does not only result from a series of regional conflicts or an individual quest for labour. The people knocking at the door of Europe tell something that needs to be listened to; they also tell their moral fatigue in front of the increasingly fast gap between the wealthiest and poorest segments of humanity. They are active participants in the global moral polity in showing how immoral it might be. Their mobility represents a protest against the global repartition of wealth and security, as well as a subversion of classical forms of political territoriality. As such, it can be conceived as a political act".

53 Thomas Faist, "The Moral Polity of Forced Migration", *Ethnic and Racial Studies,* Volume 41 (3), 2018, pp. 412–423.

54 See on this duality, Radha D'Souza, *What Is Wrong with Rights: Social Movements, Law, and Liberal Imaginations* (London: Pluto Press, 2018); see for another explanation of the duality, Gregor Noll, "Why Human Rights Fail to Protect Undocumented Migrants", *European Journal of Migration and Law,* Volume 12 (2), 2010, pp. 241–272.

55 A classic instance of trying to make these two meet in a governance framework with ethical legitimacy is Alexander Betts and Paul Collier, *Refuge: Transforming a Broken Refugee System* (London: Allen Lane, 2017); Betts and Collier's antipathy to mass refugee migration is clear in the book. Yet they want the refugee rights to be acknowledged and a broken system repaired.

56 As a background to this query, see Yves Charbit, *Economic, Social, and Demographic Thought: The Population Debate from Marx to Malthus* (Singapore: Springer, 2009).

2
CONTEXT, CONCEPTS, AND METHOD[1]

Introduction

Studying forced migrations in the postcolonial context is a question of method also. Context and method overlap in this case, as context makes a method necessary, while through a distinct method the context emerges. Now, in the refugee studies literature, and in the general literature on forced migration, the refugee condition or the condition of forced migration is considered exceptional, following Hannah Arendt and Giorgio Agamben.[2] In this idea of exception there is a tremendous force of generalisation. It is based on the binary of exceptionality and banality. The power of the binary compels the scholars of refugee and forced migration studies to think of the subject in the framework of exception.[3]

Yet one can ask in colonial and postcolonial context, does not the theory of exception ignore concrete postcolonial conditions, which are both exceptional as well as part of the general history of democracy and human rights? Or to pose the question differently, does not this theory of exceptionality take the liberal-democratic condition as universal to which refugeehood would be the supposed exception? More importantly, what does this theory of exception look like if we consider the role of historical intelligibility as crucial in the making of a concept? I want to address in this chapter the role of historical intelligibility in our choice of how we study a phenomenon – in this case migration, and forced migration in particular. I seek to do this by reviewing and examining (a) the context in which ideas and concepts of refugeehood and forced migration have emerged in a postcolonial country like India; (b) the ways in which these concepts have been problematised, (c) similarly the way post colonial political sense has combined rights, ethics, and law in generating specific ideas related to forced migration, and finally (d) the problem of locating the idea of exception in a critical postcolonial milieu.

India: the postcolonial context of crossing boundaries of times and themes

Research on forced migration in India and broadly South Asia has advanced greatly in the last thirty years. Especially, the fiftieth year of partition and independence of India and Pakistan in 1947 occasioned a spurt in refugee and partition studies. A critical feminist perspective produced two of the finest studies on partition and forced population movements.[4] These were pioneering works. By 2001, though not the first, the most extensive volume on refugees in West Bengal, the institutional practices of their protection, and the production of the refugee identity came out in a postcolonial context of partitioned states.[5] Within two years or so of that publication the first comprehensive account of refugees in post-Independent India along with the history of her asylum practices was published (2003).[6] Researching on the edges of ethics, law, and history, the study of refugees in India for the first time produced a framework that was distinctly postcolonial and critical, but at the same time engaging and challenging the dominant paradigms of refugee studies, refugee law, and refugee protection policies. These studies brought out public events and cases (particularly connected with the population flows after partition) that had no answer from international refugee law.[7] The last named study in particular produced a framework that since its publication has attracted wide readership, reviews, appreciation, comments, and encouraged many others to study forced migration in the frame of postcolonial history. Insights gained from these two researches helped researchers to undertake systematic studies of internal displacement in South Asia, the relevance of UN Guiding Principles, and the relevance of the IDP issue to studies on forced migration, the first of this genre of studies coming out in 2005.[8] The studies of the IDPs, attending governmental practices, legal definitions and their limit, and finally the massive nature of the internal population flows in the context of recurrent communal riots and developmental displacement also helped forced migration researchers to see refugee movements in a new and broader light, beyond the existing international legal framework or a dominantly cultural framework that had hitherto limited the understanding of refugee condition to mainly symbols and identities. We have to also mention the writings of Indian jurists like B.S. Chimni on the particularity of sovereign nation states of the South in the background of the Cold War origins of the refugee protection framework symbolised by the Convention of 1951.[9]

These three phases or milestones – first, the Partition of 1947 as the birthmark of refugees in the South Asian sub-continent constituting the understanding of what a refugee flow is; second, historical understanding of refugee care in India by a postcolonial state; and third, the study of the IDPs in the broad framework of forced migration flows – have produced and defined a critical, postcolonial mode of investigation that is now part of the valued methods in forced migration studies. Strong empirical base, historical understanding of issues in question, critical legal theory, gender-sensitive approach, deploying the concept of border and frontier as method of study, understanding of the epochal significance of issues of colonialism, partitions, borders and boundaries, the play of migrant and refugee subjectivity in coping with the birth of divided postcolonial states, and a critique of neo-liberal developmentalism – these are some of the aspects of this critical postcolonial approach.[10] Studying borders in particular has occupied a critical place in the evolution of a postcolonial mode of studying migration as historians and ethnographers soon found out that borders are both visible and invisible, they keep on reproducing themselves, and invisible borders in particular keep immigrants strangers for generations. At the same time they make the migrant ever deportable. These researches show how to study subjectivity materially grounded in historical experiences.

The development of the historical intelligibility of the phenomenon of forced migration has been possible due to a nuanced understanding of the relation between migration and forced migration, out of which came the concept of mixed and massive flows. Two works carried the evidence of this nuanced understanding. One was *The Marginal Nation*, written around the time of the fiftieth year of Indian independence. It linked in a detailed texture the institution of border, the event of Partition, peasant migration and historical continuities in migration patterns, network theory, and the production of forced migrants, to prove the particularities of the postcolonial milieu.[11] The second was the Reader on International Refugee Law, which in its selection of the material and commentary again pointed to the inter-linked nature of migration flows, the limits to a positivist legal understanding, and new approaches to refugee law.[12]

An important stage in the evolution of this critical mode came in the last decade when empirical studies on camps of refugees and IDPs in South Asia with emphasis on mapping the voices of IDPs in camps became available.[13] Around the same time there were other reports on the displaced due to communal disturbances and developmental disorders, and collectively these reports and studies broke many myths and wrong ideas on acceptance and legitimacy of laws, their efficacy and relevance, the comparative roles of development projects and violence in producing IDPs,[14] etc. These studies also helped the researchers in the postcolonial world conceptualise the notion of massive and mixed flows of populations.[15] These writings also anchored refugee studies firmly in forced migration studies and border and borderland studies. Indeed postcolonial studies have shown how frontiers and borders as governmental technologies have been used to regulate immigration and in turn have produced population flows. Population flows have produced new border-centric and frontier-centric thinking among states and governments. States have resorted to frontier-centric thinking where borders are found relatively less effective. Classic is the case of India's relations with neighbours to the Northeast. The results can be seen in writings on two crucial themes: (a) spatial dimensions of population flows and protracted displacement, and (b) the governmental technologies of border-making that produce the identity of the migrant. All in all, postcolonial historical sensibility has helped deepen our understanding of the relations between space, migration, and borders and boundaries.[16]

These studies have been followed appropriately or were carried out around the same time by researches on refugee situations in Sri Lanka, Nepal, Pakistan, Bangladesh, Afghanistan, and Burma – producing in relatively short time a wide understanding of the interlinked nature of recurrent refugee crises in the region, nature of camps, great power interventions, etc.[17]

In the context of decolonisation, research on an extensive scale began also on statelessness.[18] In the engagement with the theme of statelessness readers can sense the same unique method: careful selection of case studies that tell us of the minor, subjugated histories of various population groups, genealogical orientation, and a critical, postcolonial mode of investigation. Statelessness is seen in these studies less as a positive definition that sets down complete conditions towards a legal definition of statelessness. Statelessness is seen in these studies more as refraction of a reality known as citizenship. These studies show citizenship as an institution that, to use the word of a philosopher, always "incompletes" itself.[19] Statelessness can be defined only on the basis of a kind of displacement of a reality – the reality of state, nationality, citizenship. Therefore the postcolonial commentaries on statelessness are studies of permanent incompleteness – a reality that always seems to fall short of a hyper-reality, and therefore the ideal reality of citizenship, entitlements, legal protection, full proof identity, solemn recognitions by courts of law, and the avowals by the State. Statelessness is thus more a situation, a condition, or a set of conditions that make what can be called a limit situation – limit of a situation or condition called citizenship. Such an understanding must at some point in time brush against the positivism of law. It is up to law (in this case international law) to live up to these refracted, displaced realities, whose function is to tell the society the limits of the assured knowledge of institutions like border, state, citizenship, rights, humanitarianism, constitution, etc. If the subject of the State is the citizen, the stateless is the alien.[20]

There is no doubt that the study of stateless population groups will become increasingly significant in forced migration studies. As states once again go to war; come up and go down in history; countries fight newer forms of colonialism; newer forms of decolonisation occur; and borders and boundaries play havoc with settled configurations, the number of the stateless people will increase. We may see a reduction of de jure statelessness, but at the same time a rise in de facto stateless population around the world. It may also become increasingly difficult to distinguish between a refugee group and a stateless group. Newer identity practices imposed by States may produce stateless conditions. If the preceding century was a century of partitions, this century may become known as the century of stateless people. In Chapter 9 we shall deal with the problem of statelessness in greater details.

Suffice it to say now that the postcolonial perspective is important to appreciate the particular way in which forced migration studies have developed in wider parts of the world. The reason is that this perspective has combined the exceptionality of the events of forced migration with the structure and the daily experiences of colonialism, decolonisation, and the postcolonial realities of society and politics.

Concept as an epistemological category and the function of problematising

In this way concepts in forced migration studies have emerged as steps in the development of a postcolonial historical understanding of the phenomenon.

These concepts have given birth to certain definite methods in pursuing studies in this field.

To repeat, concepts and methods are interlinked in this history, because these concepts have emerged through a process of critique of the realities of partition, colonialism, decolonisation, riots, boundary setting and border drawing exercises of the departing colonial power, developmental policies of the postcolonial State, migration of labour in servitude and semi-servitude, and capitalist conquest of land and other resources such as forest belonging to indigenous communities. Critique means in this context not so much re-framing a philosophical idea through reworking on some of the aspects of the latter, but criticism from "presentist" concerns of existing practices, policies, and discourses of a theme. In this way critique has turned a given knowledge (or phenomenon) into a problem. This is distinct from the usual problem-setting exercise, a favourite pastime in policy exercises in migration management. Critique has become in this way a step towards formulation of new themes. As a result, there are clashes of concepts, such as over the definition of a refugee in India. Questions are asked: Who is a *refugee*?[21] What does *security* mean in forced migration studies in the postcolonial context?[22] What does the concept of *care* signify in studies on forced migration?[23] Ethics brought in the question of the postcolonial self, traditions of hospitality, etc., and questioned the nationalist common sense, reminding us of the way philosopher Derrida raised the question, "Is not hospitality an interruption of the self?"[24] In this way, the legal community, policy circles, the human rights community, political forums, and scholarly academia began referring to the cosmopolitan ideas in the pre-colonial and colonial time, the duty to protect the shelterseekers, ethics of kith and kin ties, and if and how far these ethical principles sit with security and economic imperatives.[25]

Yet, even though battles are fought over concepts, and concepts may work against each other, generally concepts work in groups. We can speak of a family of concepts, and a particular concept may be known by its family identity. Studying concepts is thus inherently genealogical. Not only we need to discuss the historical evolution of a concept in a "presentist" framework, the purpose is to lay bare the "hidden" structure of the concept, its anatomy, laws of its formation, function, and affinity with other concepts. Given our postcolonial existence, the mode is always to turn the received theme into a problematic through a critical procedure.

For instance: refuge, asylum, non-*refoulement*, protracted displacement, environmental refuge, statelessness, situations in limbo, regime of protection, protection agencies, refugee laws and conventions, borders, illegal immigration, irregular migration, voluntary and forced migration – and we can go on – belong to a family of concepts.[26] We can bring in also associated concepts, such as acculturation, assimilation, borders, brain drain, chain and circular migration, deportation, diaspora, ethnicity, ethnic conclaves, gendered migration, guest workers, integration, migration networks, social capital, undocumented migration, etc. These are like signs of a phenomenon moving together, making sense only in association with each other. Indeed, after a point they are empty signs almost exhausted of any further reference. Possibly they cannot be called strictly empty, because collectively they point to a particular structure of ideas, and thus of power. Postcolonial experience suggests that problematising these concepts and categories is a political task aimed at critiquing existing knowledge and power structures. In some cases problematising means showing the impossibility of certain claims, let us say in this case, the ethical claims of protection by the state or a community.[27]

Problematising signifies also an attempt to make sense of the migrant as the *abnormal* figure of our time because the migrant represents insecurity in various forms.[28] The insecurity the migrant poses for an urban regime, and the insecurity that the migrant in a city is eternally subject to, has been brought out in studies of labour migration, in particular migration of the rural poor to the city. The theme of "expulsion", to quote from the title of Saskia Sassen's famous book, has been followed up and interrogated in detail in many postcolonial analyses of labour migration – particularly within a country.[29]

In order to get a sense of the relation between migration and security we can think of five dimensions (there may be more) of a genealogical method of enquiry:

(a) The postcolonial nature of the current phenomenon of population flows;
(b) The protracted nature of displacement;
(c) The mixed and massive nature of forced population movements;
(d) Borders, security, and borderland existence; and
(e) Migrant as the subject of a neo-liberal global economy.

Contemporary law, administrative practices, and mainstream economy consider the borderland existence of population groups and their flux as threats to security, which is built around the idea of stable population groups. A genealogical investigation of these issues will enrich our understanding of the unresolved problematic in the science of ruling – settled governments and the unsettled populations of our time.

However, we must keep in mind that problematising a given knowledge is possible only in the context of the historical intelligibility of some of the contemporary studies. As we discuss in the following chapter, the nation is not at the centre of political understanding in these writings; instead, significant in such studies is the inadequately explored history of governing a mobile, unruly world of population flows. These works have given us a sense of the hidden histories of conflicts, of desperate survivals, itinerant movements, transportations of coolies, spread of famines, shipping of children and adult girls, and pieces of welfare legislation to cope with this great infamy. These writings suggest the extra-nationalist universe of mobile labour. In fact, it was largely on the condition of making labour mobile that globalisation had proceeded earlier.[30] It was in the colonial age that care emerged as a function of power. It became crucial for refugee protection. Production of the refugee or the illegal immigrant took place in what we can call the social factory.

This context was by and large ignored in the research agenda of forced migration studies, while this is the context that has given birth to frontier concepts in forced migration studies. Hitherto researchers of the global South were expected to work on case studies that would support the meta-narratives produced in the

North.[31] However, with the emergence in the last two decades of critical scholars from the global South that picture has changed to some extent. These new scholars have pointed out that categorisation of forced migrants into rigid groups of refugees, IDPs, forced migrants, environmental migrants, and economic migrants is unhelpful to say the least. They have also pointed out that forced migrants are always vulnerable people irrespective of whether the particular vulnerability comes from poverty or political situation within a society, or environmental degradation, and that it always results in discrimination and persecution. There is little to choose between death by genocide or hunger, and in fact, most conflicts at the end are conflicts over resources.[32]

As a result of research done by these new age scholars, *avant-garde* centres have grown up in hitherto unknown quarters in the postcolonial world. New issues such as mixed and massive flows, labour migration in semi-servitude, statelessness, etc., are now debated. The post-1989 political situation also contributed to these developments. Focus on terror bought to the forefront the critique of the role of global North in producing forced migrants in the South in the name of anti-terror operations. Pakistan, Afghanistan, Syria, and Iraq are burning instances of this. More and more research now focuses on vulnerable groups and their own narratives of living as forced migrants. Subjectivity of the victims in this way has become an important theme of research. There is also an accompanying shift from a focus purely on refugee laws. Critical juridical discourse is one of the outcomes of this shift. It is increasingly pointed out that in the end it should be remembered that research on forced migration is research on human beings who are severely discriminated and dispossessed of power. Demands have also emerged that knowledge networks should play the role of a bridge between research institutions of global North and global South towards joint research, and that there should be more emphasis on qualitative research and joint leadership of research projects. The challenge is how to escape the tentacles of policy driven research, because good research always produces policy critiques and policy implications.[33]

In other words, only through a rigorous mapping of critical work in forced migration studies, such as research, knowledge exchange, and dissemination, can we make sense of the historical intelligibility of certain ideas, say of partition, borderlands, or border violence, or smuggling, or divided people, or statelessness.

All in all, this forms the context in which we are now witnessing a strategic displacement in the epistemology of forced migration studies. When in the beginning of the nineties forced migration studies began for instance in India in different universities and centres of research, researchers were not unaware of bonded labour, indentured labour, or village-to-city migration of labour in forms of servitude – in short different forms in which the "forced" comes into play – but refugee studies until then had not looked into them as integral to the field of inquiry. But "forced migration" soon emerged as a holistic concept. The reason for this change was the realisation that only with a postcolonial sense of history can we move on from the old, restricted, "northern", governmental way of looking at things to the broader, more historical, political way of looking at the phenomenon of forced migration. It is in this sense, studies of partition as well as natural calamities – that is political as well as environmental events – have shaped the postcolonial intelligibility of refugee and other forms of forced migration flows. Whereas the influence of partition studies on our sensitivities regarding forced migration was only to be expected,[34] it is the critical sensibility about disasters and migration that brought in changes in approach, and made our sensibilities regarding forced migration more acute.[35] Disaster, politics, partition, long history, memory, critique of the state, verdict on colonialism, and an awareness of a postcolonial destiny – all have meshed into a complex sensibility about forced migration.

A critical postcolonial approach is therefore important. It enables the researcher to go beyond the binary of exceptionality and banality, and forge newer ways of chronicling and analysing various forms of forced migration. The writings of new scholars and reports framed by them are marked by collaborative research and a sense of the significance of the local in this globalising time. Through all these, the postcolonial researchers are now able to take a long view of citizenship and alienhood, histories of hatred, reconciliation, friendships and enmities, the significance of camp as a liminal space of subjectivity and submission, of control and escape, despair and inefficacy of international norms, laws, and arrangements, and victims' own voices about how and what could be done. In short one can say that forced migration studies has come out of the restrictive framework of refugee studies,[36] and has evolved to embrace many other aspects of migration. This is a case of strategic displacement of our classical ideas of refugee-hood and camp, which had treated these realities as exceptional. The related concepts were considered as sovereign. The historical-critical mode is now able to place migration in the grey zone of force/volition, subjectivity/conditions, human rights/humanitarianism, exception/normal, and all other binaries that at times lead us to a blind alley. To take an instance of what we mean by problematisation: The Indian partition of 1947 on the occasion of its fiftieth year – also the fiftieth year of Indian Independence – became a turning point in forced migration studies in India. The problem of refugee flows in the context of decolonization became historically intelligible. Partition led to forced migration – refugee flows and flows of other types. Partition also made the question of return crucial. Questions cropped up: Did partition refugees have right to return?[37] If they had the right to return, then what was the period they were to enjoy the right? Also, would there be certain conditions? How was one to differentiate between right of return and forced return? In this way, partition became the prism in which the stakes in the study of forced migration became sharper.

However, there was a danger also. Many partition scholars took post-partition migration to be a unique process and ignored the possibility that post-partition migration could be built on lines of historical continuity. However, it was important to find out the continuities and discontinuities in the migration process. Or, there is now a need to study for instance the nature of forced migration in Europe in Europe's century of religious wars, and compare that with what happened in India when the great religious war broke out in the second half of the forties of the last century. If the mobile subjectivity evoked in Brecht's *Mother Courage* speaks of the former, Manto's *Toba Tek Singh* speaks of the latter.[38] We are still to appreciate the stakes in studying partition as a major marker in forced migration studies. Partitions of India, Ottoman Empire, Germany, Palestine, Korea, Yugoslavia, and other de facto partitions in the last century and this one – these are only some of the major events to shape the story of forced migration.[39] Perhaps we shall have to master the art of writing event-centric history to bring out the global nature of the phenomenon of forced migration. There are so many unnoticed events, which are neither as major nor as infamous as the Indian Partition of 1947, but which have their own histories of migration. These small histories will enrich forced migration studies.

We may consider another instance. Few eminent scholars in refugee studies care to embark on research on the IDPs. Yet the inclusion of issues of the IDPs has widened forced migration studies. Consequently, researchers can now study the phenomenon of displacement more reliably. They are able to link issues of nation, sovereignty, economy, globalisation, social violence, environment, developmental displacement, and justice in a more meaningful way. Recognition of the rights of the IDPs has been a major development.

In the wake of globalisation population flows have become massive and mixed. These flows make us sit up and wonder how worthy the various norms are with which we categorise displaced population groups, and use these categories in terms of analysis and policy response. The UNHCR in one of its recent notes has taken cognisance of this.[40] Old protection strategies are failing. New strategies are needed to ensure the rights of victims of protracted state of displacement.[41] Old forms of refugee status determination do not make much sense in this new situation. Likewise, old guarantees of asylum do not make sense in the light of restrictive and preventing strategies of the states. How does one distinguish between a classic refugee, a person escaping hunger, or fleeing in search of work by any means, and say, trafficked labour in servitude?

To repeat then, problematisation will mean challenging settled concepts and received binaries. In the light of colonial and postcolonial accounts of forced migration, this chapter has sought to address a crucial question: namely, how much of the binary of routine/exception is relevant to these migratory movements? Indeed is not the received category of *exception* a problematic in forced migration scholarship?

Rights, ethics, and legal pluralism

Rights are indivisible. Yet the way forward may not be to do away with all the institutions governing different categories of rights and set up new ones, because that may result in more centralisation of bureaucratic mechanisms resulting in further controlling and regulating population movements. Probably a more dialogic relationship between victims of forced migration, law, and institutions is necessary. Also efforts at minimising – if not doing away altogether – the hold of security-related thinking, provisions, and practices in matters of recognising and protecting the rights of the victims of forced migration have to continue. Institutions have their vested interests; they zealously guard their domains. To try to reduce them is the need of the hour. To do so we have to begin with working out the implications of the theoretical recognition, to repeat, that population flows are massive and mixed. The reality of these mixed and massive flows questions old polarities. They need to be recognised in their variety, plurality, and amorphous nature – and this is possible only when we have a more federal way of looking at things, not from an institutional-pyramid point of view, that is to say from the top, but from the point of understanding how it works on the ground. We shall then be able to challenge the customary distinction between episodic violence and structural violence in terms of protection policies and institutions.

We shall be able to ask also if constructing a hierarchy of the victims is the appropriate way to frame protection policy. As indicated earlier, this way of analysing through interrogation of received binaries is already evident in the ongoing studies on statelessness. These binaries such as refugee/IDP, episodic violence/ structural violence, citizen/stateless, movement due to fear/movement due to economic imperative, international norms/national responsibility,[42] and human rights/ humanitarianism have been subjected to critical inquiry today. Such critical inquiry is possible only when we consider forced migration studies not as an isolated discipline or a subject, defined by some strange esoteric rules, but as a field marked by lines of power and flight paths of various subjectivities.

This brings us to the important issue of legal pluralism. The Convention on Refugees has completed nearly seventy years and the Guiding Principles on Internal Displacement have also been in existence for two decades. Yet the question is: Are they adequate in the contemporary context of massive displacement of population groups the world over? If they are not adequate, how can we replicate the instances of regional conventions and/or protocols? We all know that the 1951 Convention is dated for all kinds of reasons. The Cold War perspective is long over. The nature of forced migration has changed. New forms of servitude have appeared along with new vulnerabilities. The 1951 Convention also does not address the issue of burden sharing. It does not principally address the question of escapees of war. But no one wants to open that can of worms, because refugees, notwithstanding all protestations, are at the end of the day "burdens"; also because there is an apprehension that the next Convention to replace the existing one will be even more problematic.

Likewise, the Guiding Principles emphasise a particular context. It is too much rooted in a particular reading of the contexts of Africa, some parts of Latin America, and the Caucasus. It ignores to a large extent developmental displacement,[43] and places the issue in the framework of what is known as sovereignty as responsibility. While the Guiding Principles have done service to the cause of the displaced population groups, it has left open occasions for abuse. Great Powers can intervene on the pretext of saving endangered population groups (recall Syria) while the Great Powers may be substantially responsible for the unsettling scenario. Again while they may be responsible for economic catastrophes in many countries and regions, they can appear as saviours. Besides, while the origin of the Guiding Principles in the human rights principles is clear, its structure carries an old state of international law. In a sense the Guiding Principles has removed the focus from the issue of developmental displacement in today's world. However, the modality of *guiding principles* is significant and has dialogic potentiality. It offers new insights into the process of law making.

If we take the Refugee Convention of 1951 we can see the reason for its wide acceptance. It creates a legal person (of the refugee), a whole penumbra of institutions, an office, etc., without making any one – nation, government, big powers, individual – responsible for creating refugee-hood. It has been able to merge in a milieu of a fantasy the ethics of humanitarian protection and guarantee of rights of a rightless person, that is to say the refugee. Likewise, the Guiding Principles are not law, yet they have the appearance of some kind of moral injunction with at least the partial effectiveness of law. So countries may not have signed the Principles, for they are only a resolution. Yet they appear as giving birth to some kind of law. How do we retain this fantasy and proceed? Possibly, not only we need to move on to the regional level as the most crucial level in framing the international, but there too we shall have the need to innovate the art of successful law making by combining fantasy with injunction. The art of governmentality will never cease to be relevant.

The important point here is how to produce the consent that is necessary for enacting what is termed as soft law. On one hand we have sovereignty as an important factor in treaty making process, which is a crucial part of international law making, and we have great power concord and combined pressure to produce the law; on the other hand there is the effort to produce consent of the probable treaty parties. This is a process which is getting more and more intriguing. How to produce consent for a treaty is a serious problem for the international that we speak of today. It may be that the more we decentralise the process the more we shall produce the consent necessary for law. After all we may not need grand and universal laws anymore, or at least not to the extent to which we are led to believe. As if the world will break down if we do not have a single treaty, a single convention, a single office. In its place, what we need is more work on the process of producing the consensus at different levels and making that consensus work. For this purpose, the idea of "soft law" (because the soft may be more insidious, as we have seen this in the iniquitous application of the principle of intervention on humanitarian grounds) and legal pluralism may be a significant area of work.[44] In view of the need for decentralisation of the legal apparatus of protection, the postcolonial context becomes even more important.

The practices of South Asian countries including India give us a faint idea of the likely nature of legal pluralism. None of these countries is a signatory to the 1951 Convention for refugee protection; there is no national refugee law in India for instance; yet most of these countries have borne tremendous load of refugee protection. Indian courts have referred to international human rights laws also in matters of adjudicating issues of grant of asylum and non-refoulement.[45] One important reason behind such a pluralist approach to law is an underlying concept of ethics born out of anti-colonialism and postcolonial sense of the world. It is important therefore to historicise the concept of ethics of care and protection.

To the extent the ethical practices of care and protection are present in the legal mechanisms for protection they are like a double-edged sword. They strengthen the principles of humanitarianism, which we need in our individual and collective lives. Yet when applied they tend to reduce the persons they seek to protect and care for to being objects of sympathy and charity. Therefore, in the refugee protection literature there is this debate on charity or rights. Some argue that whatever protections people get are not due to the principles of care and hospitality, but through struggle for rights. How is basic rightlessness removed? A philosopher may say that while the principle of care and hospitality is unavoidable, we care only to the extent self-care allows. Thus, there is always a limit to the care that these international legal mechanisms offer. At times a great power will bomb a country, create refugees, displace millions, and then the so-called international community will invoke the principles of care to rush in aid for those bombed-out countries, and help the displaced within the limits set by the big power. That is why people in war-ravaged countries sometimes despise the humanitarian workers, many of whom are inspired with the noblest values; yet they appear to the war-ravaged people as those who come to supply artificial legs in the evening after their legs have been blown off in the morning by invading bombers. The process of infusing the legal and administrative mechanisms of protection of the displaced with the principles of care and protection is thus a contradictory one. Examination of the extent to which self-care is present in the operations of care becomes significant in this context.

In this respect, we need to interrogate the concept of humanitarianism itself. It may be an ideology that works like a machine. It may be based on sentiments, but we create institutions to give effect to those sentiments, and then we legitimise those institutions with an overarching ideology of care, which may gloss over the injustices of the entire process through which persons have been reduced to being objects of care and protection. And then there is the fact that a large number of the displaced millions, possibly the majority of the displaced persons, do not depend at all on these legal arrangements. Care operates in the lives of the millions in a different way. We can find this paradox then even in the legal and administrative mechanisms for the protection of the displaced. There is no one single arrangement of care, for instance in India. Care of the displaced due to violence is organised along one line, or set of lines, while care of the displaced due to developmental activities runs along another set, while again the care of the displaced due to natural disasters is organised in a different set of ways. There are similarities in these three cases, yet the principle of care operates in a differential way.

Humanitarianism in the nineteenth century was for the destitute, the abnormal, and the poor in the colonies. Yet we cannot do away with the principle of care. The task possibly will be to organise the principle in a different way, to see how this operates in popular life, to entrust the people with the task of protecting rather than making the mighty the protector of imperiled lives. Federalisation of care is important. Likewise important is the task of making dialogic the principles of care and protection. This requires the insertion of the principle of justice, which will bring back the issues of claims and rights. We thus cannot avoid the contradiction between care and rights. A balanced view is necessary. Can justice be compatible with the principle of care? Probably the main task in public ethics today is to make the principle of care compatible with the notion of justice. The evolution of the jurisprudence on disability rights is an instance.[46] It shows how a paramount sense of justice can lead to deliberation towards greater care.

There is a running thread through these three points, which to recapitulate are: (a) the historical context of forced migration studies in India; (b) the significance of problematisation in an analysis of the historical intelligibility of the concepts in forced migration studies; and (c) the historical obligation in crossing the boundaries of rights, law, and ethics. The running thread is the postcolonial idea that there is no pure field of concepts. Concepts in forced migration studies are linked to several modes such as problematising, thematising, conceptualising, critique, genealogy, observing, narrating, and several others including ones that are deployed to de-construct a concept. In fact, methods turn in time into concepts. The field of forced migration studies is a particular one with specific concepts and its own history. As a field of scientific research besides having policy implications, it deals with human beings in vulnerable situations. It is thus inescapably a study of power. It has quantitative dimensions. Also its concepts are embodiments of social relations.

For all these reasons, we always begin with concepts, never with pure descriptions. Even the purest description has an underlying concept. Therefore, concepts are like signs. They are also at times metaphors. Thus for instance, one of the questions presently marking forced migration studies is around the institution of border. We may say, *border is a concept, a sign, a concept that works as a metaphor, and therefore it is an analytical method.*

We may raise a point as a second level of analysis. The point is: while forced migration studies aim to understand the nature of "force" in migratory movements, it has to still ask why what we call "force" assumes particular forms. Hence the questions: why does the migrant appear as the abnormal subject, why is border ubiquitous, why has forced migration a pronounced gendered nature, or, why does the power of the government require an element of care? Indeed, "force" as the subject of analysis will call for the inquiry, namely, why does the concept of human rights need as its complement the ideology of humanitarianism, and why camps exist as abnormal sites? Yet this abnormality is only discrete. Camps function only as one end of a series of forms of confinement and protection. Such inquiry implies also asking as to why vulnerability has to be measured most of the time (for instance by duration, such as protracted or short) and by the magnitude of the protection involved. These research questions bear the unmistakeable imprint of an age when the process of displacement appears to have overwhelmed societies to an extent where the concepts and policies relating to displacement appear as nature-imposed necessity. Hence the given knowledge of forced migration studies appears to treat all non-official, non-legal knowledge, particularly pre-existing non-official and non-legal knowledge on migration, as belonging to nature, which is pre-scientific and pre-practical in this age. Therefore important is the historical intelligibility of a concept, also to see the history of migration in long-term continuities and discontinuities, which will require inter-epoch comparisons, handling of large series of data, making sense of what Charles Tilly had called more than two decades back history through big data.[47] Researches show remarkable historical continuities in patterns of migration and forced migration flows for instance in India.[48]

To conclude, discussion on the phenomenon of forced migration along the line of exceptionality faces several methodological problems, such as the problem posed by the ruling concepts in this field, that of multiple units of analysis, or the problem of linking forced migration studies to its context. In *Homo Sacer*, Agamben had likened the natural life to Hannah Arendt's description of the refugee's naked life.[49] The effect of *homo sacer* was a cleavage between one's biological and political lives. The state of the refugees *and others* persecuted in similar outlawed conditions, were the states of the *homo sacer*. Although human rights were conceived of as the ground for civil rights, the deprivation of those civil rights (as, for example, in the case of stateless people or refugees) made them comparable to "savages", many of whom periodically perished as in camps. This condition was opposed to the life considered "normal". It was a state of exception. One can of course say that the legal resolution of conflicts under democracy happens by putting rights of "man" and "citizens" together, which closes any chance of exclusion of some from political life altogether. Yet if as response to the power of the sovereign, bare life becomes the subject of politics, then we may ask, how does the fact of bare life evolving into a subject of politics become possible? In short, does bare life ever reconcile to the "bare" position in politics? In that fissure, epitomised in refugee-like conditions, we can see the emergence of the possibility of political subjectivity not exhausted by the rules of liberal politics.

Yet as we analyse the trajectory of care and protection begun in the wake of decolonisation and its legacy over the years – and this not only in India but in large tracts of the decolonised world – we can see at the same time that refugee care contributed to the power of the postcolonial state. It contributed to its much broader and ambitious agenda of a nationalist welfare and security, and the stabilisation of a national labour force by including refugee labour in it, and inaugurating various relief and resettlement programmes for the internally displaced though on a severely inadequate scale. The constitution of political power in this way came to rely on a sort of grand utopia of a harmonious social functioning. Mechanisms of protection ensured a reserve army of workers to be employed whenever needed and a ready-made labour force for all kinds of scattered, decentralised, informal productions on which the country's economy depended to a great extent. Protection was not limited to the confines of the camps of the refugees and the displaced. It came out to the larger social arena and contributed to the appearance of the postcolonial state as a singular power.

In other words, historical analysis of the postcolonial refugee and forced migration flows should not be subject to an a priori theory of knowledge that depends on received binaries, but to a theory of discursive practices that does not privilege any concept anterior to discourse. Then we shall be able to ask, can the refugee be reduced to "bare life", which is a life without politics? Can we afford to minimise the political significance of postcolonial condition supposedly symbolized by "bare life"?[50] Towards an answer to that question we shall have to repeatedly visit the question of historical intelligibility of the present age of migration. That indeed is the basis of our claim that ours is the postcolonial age of migration.

Notes

1 A shorter version of this essay was published earlier as R. Samaddar, "Forced Migration Situations as Exceptions in History?" *International Journal of Migration and Border Studies*, Volume 2 (2), 2016, pp. 99–118, doi:10.1504/IJMBS.2016.075579. Used with permission.
2 Hannah Arendt, "We Refugees", in Marc Robinson (ed.), *Altogether Elsewhere: Writers on Exile* (London: Faber and Faber, 1994), pp. 110–119; Giorgio Agamben, *State of Exception*, trans. Kevin Attell (Chicago: University of Chicago Press, 2005); however, to be truthful, while Arendt considered the refugee situation as one of basic rightlessness, she also in the closing paragraph of "We Refugees", wrote, "outlawing of the Jewish people in Europe has been followed closely by the outlawing of most European nations", p. 119.
3 For details on the question of exception, see R. Samaddar, "Forced Migration Situations as Exceptions in History?" *International Journal of Migration and Border Studies*, Volume 2 (2), 2016, pp. 99–118.
4 Urvashi Butalia, *The Other Side of Silence: Voices from the Partition of India* (new edition, Delhi: Penguin Random House, 2017) and Ritu Menon and Kamla Bhasin, *Borders and Boundaries: Women in India's Partition* (New Delhi: Kali for Women, 1998)
5 Pradip K. Bose (ed.), *Refugees in West Bengal: Institutional Practices and Contested Identities* (Kolkata: Calcutta Research Group, 2000); It took forward the discussion on the condition of partition refugees first initiated by Prafulla K. Chakrabarti, *The Marginal Men – The Refugees and the Left Political Syndrome in West Bengal* (Kolkata: Lumiere Books, 1990). *The Marginal Men* was path breaking in discussion on Partition refugees in India in many ways.
6 Ranabir Samaddar (ed.), *Refugees and the State: Practices of Asylum and Care in India, 1947–2000* (New Delhi: Sage, 2003).
7 This was surprising given the strong link between the history of European partitions and forced population flows. For wider accounts of partitions and migration in Europe, Stefano Bianchini, *Liquid Nationalism and State Partitions in Europe* (Cheltenham: Edward Elgar Publishing, 2017).
8 Paula Banerjee, Sabyasachi Basu Ray Chaudhuri, and Samir K. Das (eds.), *Internal Displacement in South Asia: The Relevance of the UN Guiding Principles* (New Delhi: Sage, 2005).
9 See in particular, B.S. Chimni, "The Geopolitics of Refugee Studies: A View from the South", *Journal of Refugee Studies*, Volume 11 (4), 1998, pp. 354–374; "Globalization, Humanitarianism and the Erosion of Refugee Protection", *Journal of Refugee Studies*, Volume 13 (3), 2000, pp. 243–64; "The Reform of the International Refugee Regime: A Dialogic Model", *Journal of Refugee Studies*, Volume 14 (2), 2001, pp. 151–161.
10 One of the notables among the new breed of postcolonial scholarship on borders, Paula Banerjee, *Borders, Histories, Existences: Gender and Beyond* (New Delhi: Sage, 2009); see also the report of a discussion on the concepts of border and crisis among others in critical migration studies, *Thinking Beyond the Border: A Critical Appraisal of Migration Research in North America*, by LIDC (London: International Development Centre) Migration Leadership Team, Global Migration Conversation, New York, 6 June 2019, www.soas.ac.uk/lidc-mlt/outputs/file141862.pdf (accessed on 5 September 2019).
11 R. Samaddar, *The Marginal Nation: Transborder Migration from Bangladesh to West Bengal* (New Delhi: Sage, 1999).
12 B.S. Chimni (ed.), *International Refugee Law: A Reader* (New Delhi: Sage, 2000).

13 *Voices of the Internally Displaced in South Asia: A Report by the Calcutta Research* Group, Calcutta Research Group, Kolkata, 2006 – http://www.mcrg.ac.in/Voices.pdf (accessed on 2 March 2020).
14 Essential for such an understanding are Walter Fernandes' decades long research, for instance, "Liberalisation and Development-induced Displacement", *Social Change*, Volume 36 (1), March 2006, pp. 109–123; "Development Induced Displacement and Sustainable Development", *Social Change*, Volume 31(1–2), March 2001, pp. 87–103; also with Gita Bharali, *Uprooted for Whose Benefit? Development-Induced Displacement in Assam 1947–2000* (Guwahati: North Eastern Social Research Centre, 2011).
15 For a broad compilation of studies based on this concept, see Paula Banerjee (ed.), *Unstable Populations, Anxious States: Mixed and Massive Population Flows in South Asia* (Kolkata: Samya, 2013); on this see also UNHCR's ten point plan of action on refugee protection and mixed migration (2006) – UNHCR, Plan of Action on Refugee Protection and Mixed Migration, revision 1, January 2007; see also, Cristophe Tometten, "Juridical Response to Mixed and Massive Population Flows", *Refugee Watch*, Volume 39–40, June–December 2012, pp. 125–140.
16 On this, see the exhaustive study by Paula Banerjee, *Borders, Histories, Existences: Gender and Beyond* (New Delhi: Sage, 2010); also on borders and migration, William Walters, "The Frontiers of European Union: A Geostrategic Perspective", *Geopolitics*, Volume 9, pp. 674–698.
17 To get an idea of the range of themes, see the volumes of *Refugee Watch: A South Asian Journal on Forced Migration*, all available online, www.mcrg.ac.in/ci.asp and www.mcrg.ac.in/ct.asp (accessed on 22 February 2018); also Tapan K. Bose, "The Rohingya: Rejected by the Country They Call Home and Unwanted by its Neighbours", *Alternatives International*, 24 October 2017, www.alterinter.org/spip.php?rubrique2 (accessed on 1 November 2017); Omprakash Mishra (ed.), *Forced Migration in the South Asian Region: Displacement, Human Rights, and Conflict Resolution* (New Delhi: Centre for Refugee Studies, Jadavpur University, Brookings Institution, and Manak Publications, 2004).
18 Paula Banerjee, Atig Ghosh, and Anasua Basu Ray Chaudhury (eds.), *The State of Being Stateless in South Asia* (Hyderabad: Orient Blackswan, 2015); see also, www.mcrg.ac.in/Statelessness/Statelessness_Concept.asp (accessed on 22 February 2015); see also, Paula Banerjee, "Women, Trafficking, and Statelessness in South Asia", *Refugee Watch*, Volume 27, June 2006, www.mcrg.ac.in/cata.htm (accessed on 22 February 2018).
19 Etienne Balibar, "Historical Dilemmas of Democracy and Their Contemporary Relevance to Citizenship", *Rethinking Marxism*, Volume 20 (4), 2008, pp. 522–538. In this essay, Balibar discusses the dialectical relationship between the concepts of democracy and citizenship by considering aporias of democracy as a model or an ideology. He argues that these closures can be overcome if we define democracy as a process of permanent anti-oligarchic "insurrection" in place of treating democracy as a stable regime. It is not the spread of democracy, therefore, that constitutes the primordial object of political theory, but the democratization of democracy itself, especially in the form of the elimination of its internal exclusions.
20 For a detailed illustration of this point, see Charlotte-Anne Malischewski and Shuvro Prosun Sarker, "Stateless in Law: Two Assessments", CRG Paper Series, *Policies and Practices*, 60 (Kolkata: Calcutta Research Group, March 2014).
21 This is more because India is not a signatory to the 1951 *Convention on Refugees*, and there is no national refugee protection Act. Refugee protection is guided by government decisions under immigration, citizenship, and foreigners' laws, though courts play a vital function – often in congruity of international law. See, Arjun Nair, *National Refugee Law for India: Challenges and Roadblocks*, ICPS Research Paper 11, December 2007; Ranabir Samaddar, *Refugees and the State: Practices of Asylum and Care in India, 1947–2000* (New Delhi: Sage, 2003); Rajeev Dhavan, "India's Refugee Law and Policy", *The Hindu*, 25 June 2004, www.thehindu.com/2004/06/25/stories/2004062501791000.htm (accessed on 22 February 2015); "Model National Law on Refugees", *ISIL Yearbook of International Humanitarian and Refugee Law*, 2001, www.worldlii.org/int/journals/ISILYBIHRL/2001/19.html (accessed on 22 February, 2016).

22 The debate summed up in the context of forced migration and security in R. Samaddar and Paula Banerjee, *Migration and Circles of Insecurity*, Revisioning and Engendering Security Series, WISCOMP (New Delhi: Rupa & Co., 2010).
23 Ranabir Samaddar, "Introduction: Power and Care – Building the New Indian State", *Refugees and the State*, pp. 21–68; the discussion on the ethical debate around the concepts of care in recent times begins with Jacques Derrida, *Of Hospitality*, trans. Rachel Bowlby (Stanford: Stanford University Press, 2000); *On Cosmopolitanism and Forgiveness*, trans. Mark Dooley and Richard Kearney (New York: Routledge, 2005).
24 Jacques Derrida, *Adieu*, trans. Pascale-Anne Brault and Michael Naas (Stanford: Stanford University Press, 1999), p. 51; read also, Mark W. Westmoreland, "Interruptions: Derrida and Hospitality", *Kritike*, Volume 2 (1), June 2008, pp. 1–10.
25 Classic in this perspective has been the debates over protection to Bangladeshi immigrants – illegal and asylum seekers. See on this debate, Sujata Ramachandran, "Indifference, Impotence, and Intolerance: Transnational Bangladeshis in India", *Global Migration Perspectives*, vol. 42 (Geneva: Global Commission on International Migration, 2005).
26 In this case, the best is to go through any related work on key concepts. For instance, David Betram, Maritsa V. Poros, and Pierre Monforte, *Key Concepts in Migration* (London: Sage, 2014), where 39 such concepts share the field.
27 Apart from Refugees and the State, which interrogated the ethical claims of the new Indian state regarding protection of refugees, readers have to read the exhaustive survey of refugee literature in India between 1996–2006 (plus the extensive bibliography) that touches on several issues raised here, by Pradip K. Bose, "Refugee, Memory, and the State: A Review of Research in Refugee Studies", *Refugee Watch*, 36, December 2010, pp. 1–30; see also, Matthew J. Gibney, *The Ethics and Politics of Asylum* (Cambridge: Cambridge University Press, 2004); Stephen John Stedman and Fed tanner (eds.), *Refugee Manipulation – War, Politics, and the Abuse of Human Sufferings* (Washington, DC: Brookings Institution, 2003) based on studies of refugees in Pakistan, Cambodia, and Zaire.
28 On the idea of the abnormal in modern societies, see Michel Foucault, *Abnormal*, Lectures at the College de France, 1974–75, trans. Graham Burchell (New York: Picador, 2003); on the idea of the migrant as the abnormal figure of our time, R. Samaddar, "Returning to the Histories of the Late 19th and Early 20th Century Immigration", *Economic and Political Weekly*, Volume L (2), 10 January 2015, pp. 49–55; also, R. Samaddar, *Emergence of the Political Subject* (New Delhi: Sage, 2010), Chapter 10, "Empire, Globalisation, and the Subject", In *Emergence of the Political Subject* (New Delhi: Sage, 2010), pp. 267–291.
29 See for instance, Simpreet Singh, "The Emergence of the Migrant as a Problem Figure in Contemporary Mumbai: Chronicles of Violence and Issues of Justice", in R. Samaddar, *Migrant and the Neoliberal City* (Hyderabad: Orient Blackswan, 2018), pp. 147–169; Saskia Sassen, *Expulsions: Brutality and Complexity in the Global Economy* (Cambridge, MA: Harvard University Press, 2014).
30 See Chapter 3; also, Rana P. Behel and Marcel van der Linden (eds.), *Coolies, Capital, and Colonialism – Studies in Indian Labour History* (New Delhi: Oxford University Press, 2007); Jan Breman, *Taming the Coolie Beast – Plantation Society and the Colonial Order in Southeast Asia* (New Delhi: Oxford University Press, 1989).
31 Loren Landau, "Communities of Knowledge or the Tyrannies of Partnership: Reflections on North-South Research Networks from a South African University on Research Networks and the Dual Imperative", *Journal of Refugee Studies*, Volume 25 (4), 2012, pp. 555–570; Landau argued that the field of refugee research often produces hierarchies both of knowledge and resources. South-based researchers find themselves in a dual imperative – that is, whereas research should be about refugees, they have to justify their work in scholarly terms and to their funding bodies. He argued that partnerships should produce research that could be used for policy purposes across regions in the North/South, but also building capacity in the South, in order to have greater influence at the policy level. Often partnerships worked against these objectives. Partnerships generated knowledge but how they generated this knowledge, who benefited from it and how was it used was questionable. The reality, he argued, was that academics in Africa must

supplement their income with consultancy work, whereby critical theorising worked directly against the academic because it alienated them from the funding they were trying to acquire. The result of this culture of consultancy was that people tried to own a field – this suppressed the work of collaborating with students or others.
32 A recent study by the Calcutta Research Group, Madhurilata Basu, Rajat Ray, and R. Samaddar (eds.), *Political Ecology of Survival – Life and Labour in the River Lands of East and North-East India* (Hyderabad: Orient Blackswan, 2018) bring out the link between resources, conflict, and displacement in details. See also, http://mcrg.ac.in/IUCN/IUCN_Report.asp (accessed on 24 February 2014); the classic study on the links between resources, ecology, and migration is however, Mike Davis, *El Nino Famines: Late Victorian Holocausts and the Making of the Third World* (London: Verso, 2002); see also Subhas Ranjan Chakrabarty, "Colonialism, Resource Crisis, and Forced Migration", CRG Research Paper Series, *Policies and Practices*, 42, 2011, www.mcrg.ac.in/PP42.pdf (accessed on 24 February 2015).
33 Paula Banerjee, "Response to Landau", *Journal of Refugee Studies*, Volume 25 (4), 2012, pp. 570–573; Banerjee in a critique of Landau argued that researchers in the South were not passive agents in collaboration, and based on their locations, they had the capacity to bring critical orientation to forced migration studies, and they had done so.
34 On this the best discussion to date is, Pradip K. Bose, "Refugee, Memory, and the State: A Review of Research in Refugee Studies", *Refugee Watch*, 36, December 2010; see also R. Samaddar (ed.), *Reflections on Partition in the East* (New Delhi: Vikas, 1997).
35 On this see the report brought by Calcutta Research Group on river erosion and displacement, authored by Krishna Bandopadhyay, Soma Ghosh, and NIlanjan Dutta, *Eroded Lives* (Kolkata: Calcutta Research Group, 2006), also www.mcrg.ac.in/Eroded_Lives.pdf (accessed on 25 February 2015). The report was an in-depth study of the conditions of the people devastated by erosion of the banks of River Ganga in the districts of Malda and Murshidabad. Riverbank erosion had over the years become a "natural" and almost regular phenomenon in the places under study. With extensive field study and study of Census reports, the researchers gave a vivid account of the district-wise displacement scenario, including the number of displaced people, their present condition, the available alternatives of livelihood that they had been forced into, etc. The report concluded with recommendations, though finally closing with a not-so-optimistic note on the chances of the administration taking any step towards the fulfillment of any of the recommended proposals. The report along with *Voices* (n 7), which studied the victims of the tsunami in 2004, became landmark documents in the evolution of critical consciousness on forced migration. See also in this connection, the report on the tsunami, forced migration, and the political economy of resettlement, Nirmal Kumar Mahato, "Environment and Migration: Purulia, West Bengal", CRG Research Paper Series, *Policies and Practices*, 30, 2010, www.mcrg.ac.in/PP30.pdf (accessed on 14 February 2015); Nirekha de Silva, "Protecting the Rights of the Tsunami Victims: The Sri Lanka Experience", CRG Research Paper Series, *Policies and Practices*, 28, 2010, www.mcrg.ac.in/PP28.pdf (accessed on 14 February 2015); Amitesh Mukhopadhyay, "Cyclone Aila and the Sundarbans: An Inquiry into the Disaster and Politics of Aid and Relief", CRG Research Paper Series, *Policies and Practices*, 26, 2009, www.mcrg.ac.in/PP26.pdf (accessed on 14 February 2015); for a collection of various studies of ecology and migration in the postcolonial context, see, *Political Ecology of Survival – Life and Labour in the River Lands of East and North-East India* (Hyderabad: Orient Blackswan, 2018).
36 Crucial in understanding this transformation is B.S. Chimni's article, "The Birth of a 'Discipline': From Refugee to Forced Migration Studies", *Journal of Refugee Studies*, Volume 22 (1), March 2009, pp. 11–29; Chimni contended that the turn from refugee studies to forced migration studies had to be viewed against the backdrop of the history and relationship of colonialism and humanitarianism. The move to forced migration studies accompanied the inauguration of a phase of political humanitarianism with a distinct accent, albeit encapsulated in new forms and issues, on "civilizing" the other. Chimni further contended that refugee studies, like forced migration studies, had served the geopolitics of hegemonic states.

37 On the Partition refugees' right to return there are several commentaries available; they show the relevance of the theme. Unfortunately, however, there is very little rigorous study on this to date. Megan Bradley's "Return of Forced Migrants" is exhaustive, but the paper is of a policy nature, and leaves the category of partition refugees out of analysis and policy prescriptions. Also, the exhaustive bibliography leaves the literature on partition refugees out. In fact there is little evidence in refugee studies literature of an awareness of the distinct position that partition refugees (in Indian sub-continent, Israel-Palestine, Korea, or erstwhile Yugoslavia occupy. For Bradley's paper see, www.forcedmigration.org/research-resources/expert-guides/return-of-forced-migrants/alldocuments (accessed on 25 February 2015); see also the comparative discussion on of various issues of right to return, http://refugeewatchonline.blogspot.in/2006/08/is-right-to-return-symbolic-right_28.html.

38 Bertolt Brecht's famous play, *Mother Courage and Her Children*, trans. Eric Bentley (New York: Doubleday, 1955); Sadat Hasan Manto, *Toba Tek Singh*, trans. Frances W. Pritchett, www.columbia.edu/itc/mealac/pritchett/00urdu/tobateksingh/translation.html (accessed on 25 February 2015); a slightly different English translation available on, www.sacw.net | February 1998.

39 For a comparative study on partitions, Stefano Bianchini, Sanjay Chaturvedi, Rada Ivekovic, and Ranabir Samaddar, *Partitions: Reshaping States and Minds* (Milton Park: Frank Cass, 2005).

40 UNHCR, *Refugee Protection and International Migration: Trends August 2013-July 2014* – Study prepared by UNHCR Division of International Protection, Geneva, November 2014, particularly pp. 17–19, www.unhcr.org/5485d2069.pdf (accessed on 25 February).

41 See the recommendations and the report of a special UNHCR assisted South Asian conference in Kolkata on the need for new protection strategies for persons in situations of protracted displacement – "Report of Dialogue on Protection Strategies for People in Situations of Forced Migration", 14–15 December 2008, http://mcrg.ac.in/UNHCRconference/home.html (accessed on 25 February 2015); for the study papers in the conference, Paula Banerjee (ed.), *Unstable Populations, Anxious States: Mixed and Massive Population Flows in South Asia* (Kolkata: Samya, 2013).

42 On the issue of responsibility, see the report, Ishita Dey and Sabyasachi Basu Ray Chaushury (eds.), *The Responsibility to Protect: IDPs and Our National and State Human Rights Commissions* (Kolkata: Calcutta Research Group, October 2007), http://mcrg.ac.in/Responsibility_to_Protect.pdf (accessed on 25 February 2015).

43 Several jurists and researchers have argued in favour of including in the category of IDPs persons affected by developmental displacement. For instance, W. Courtland Robinson, "Risks and Rights: The Causes, Consequences, and Challenges of Development Induced Displacement", Brookings Institution Occasional Paper, May 2003, www.brookings.edu/fp/projects/idp/articles/didreport.pdf (accessed on 8 June 2015). However, in the totality of the framework of the Guiding Principles, and in the perspective of massive developmental displacements throughout the developing countries of the world, the emphasis on developmental displacement remains inadequate. In the light of the researches by Walter Fernandes and others it may be safe to conclude that the number of the development-induced IDPs far outweighs that of conflict-induced IDPs. See for instance the reports by Fernandes and his collaborators on IDPs in Orissa (1997) Goa and Andhra Pradesh (2001), and West Bengal and Assam (2006) – Indian Social Institute and North Eastern Social Research Centre, New Delhi and Guwahati (mimeo).

44 Kirsten McConnachie, *Governing Refugees: Justice, Order, and Legal Pluralism* (London: Routledge, 2014); Paul Schiff Berman, "Global Legal Pluralism", *South California Review*, Volume 80, 2007, pp. 1155–1165; Paul Schiff Berman, "The New Legal Pluralism", *Annual Review of Law and Social Science*, 5, 2009, pp. 225–242; see also Nico Krisch, "The Case for Pluralismin Post-national Law", *LSE Legal Studies Working Paper*, 12, 2009.

45 The point here is that ratification of the Convention is increasingly becoming of less importance. In Africa, for instance, ratification has been higher, yet that has not desisted or reduced anti-immigrant riots, as recent (April 2015) anti-immigrant riots

in Johannesburg testify. On this, see the compilation by Madhura Chakrabarty's of several news reports, "Xenophobia in South Africa", *Refugee Watch Online,* June 5, 2015, http://refugeewatchonline.blogspot.in/2015/06/xenophobia-in-south-africa-report.html (accessed on 8 June 2015).

46 On the evolution of disability rights, Kalpana Kannabiran, *Tools of Justice: Non-discrimination and the Indian Constitution* (London: Routledge, 2012).

47 Charles Tilly, *Big Structures, Large Processes, Huge Comparisons* (New York: Russell Sage Foundation, 1994); also by Charles Tilly, *The Old New Social History and the New Old Social History*, Centre for Research and Social Organization Working Paper 218, University of Michigan, Ann Arbor, October 1980.

48 On migration data series, Chinmoy Tumbe, "Migration Persistence across Twentieth Century India", *Migration and Development*, Volume 1 (1), June 2012, pp. 87–112; on the historical continuity of migration and forced migration patterns, see R. Samaddar's *The Marginal Nation*, which discusses the historical foundations of forced migration patterns in the eastern part of South Asia.

49 Hannah Arendt, *The Origins of Totalitarianism* (New York: Meridian Books, 1951) – "It is true that the chances of the famous refugee are improved just as a dog with a name has a better chance to survive than a stray dog who is just a dog in general." p. 287.

50 Ethnographic accounts of migrants and refugees give lie to the notion of their complete helplessness. In fact the strength of the thesis of "autonomy of migration", which we shall discuss in Chapter 8, and which has its own problems, stands on an appreciation of the ability of the migrant to negotiate border controls, political vicissitudes, financial difficulty, and dominant social regulations and prohibitions. See among others an ethnography of crossing borders by Shahram Khosravi, *'Illegal' Traveller: An Auto-Ethnography of Borders* (Basingstoke, Hampshire: Palgrave MacMillan, 2010); methodologically the book composed around the experiences of an Iranian migrant makes a breakthrough in refugee studies by turning an ethnographic method into a principled critique of borders and stereotyped border studies. This happened also in postcolonial studies of the refugees when historical anthropology and various narrative devices made important breakthroughs in our knowledge of forced migration.

3
MIGRANTS IN AN EARLIER AGE OF GLOBALISATION[1]

Introduction: nation-centric history and labour-centric history

Twenty years back when I published *The Marginal Nation* (1999),[2] I had remarked intuitively that national histories would have to be revised in the light of the studies on migration. But I was not sufficiently analytic. Around the same time, studies of migrants (as distinct from migration as a process) were showing how the migrant had emerged as the figure of the abnormal in the context of the circles of insecurity that make our nationalist universe. To understand fully the implications of the emergence of the migrant as the unsettling element of our time, we have to appreciate the significance of the historical question of immigration and the attending control practices. The previous chapter had spoken of the significance of historical intelligibility in understanding our age of migration. Such an understanding will be crucial also for understanding the role mobile subjectivities play in the modern imperial-national universe. Recognition of the value of two strands of research is necessary to gain such an understanding.

First, more than any other strand of history writing, labour historians have recognised the political significance of migration in the latter half of the nineteenth century and the early part of the twentieth century. Since Stephen Castles and Godula Kosack's joint work on *Immigrant Workers and Class Structure in Western Europe* (1973),[3] referred to in the previous chapter, some excellent studies have appeared on labour migration. They indicate how a different history of the nation form can be constructed. Such a history would tell us the histories of the trajectory of citizenship (including what Marshall termed as "social citizenship") along with histories of inclusion and exclusion. Second, along with the writing of general labour history we have special studies on export of indentured labour and the growth of plantation economy, which again suggests a different way of writing the history of the nation form in the last two centuries, where the extra-nationalist narrative of labour moving from one country to another constitutes a different universe. These two facts show the permanent disjuncture between the history of the nation form and that of the differentially constituted labour form.

In fact, the new crop of historical studies on various aspects of the welfare state and schemes, inspired in some cases by the Foucauldian theme of governmentality, suggests a different way of understanding modern governance, where along with a study of the nation form at the centre of our political understanding we have also the still largely unwritten history of governing a mobile, unruly world of population flows occupying a critical place of significance. These works, some referred to in course of this chapter, give us a sense of the hidden histories of conflicts, desperate survivals, and new networks as well as old ones being transplanted across great expanse and zones. Studies of hunger in the nineteenth century, of itinerant movements, transportations of unskilled Asian labourers (branded as "coolies in the colonial time and still used by the propertied classes and contractors), spread of famines, shipping of children, adult girls, trafficking in sex, labour, and human organs, and welfare legislations to cope with this great infamy tell us how actually we have arrived at our own time of subject formation under the conditions of empire. This is certainly different from the tradition of nation-centric histories.

Take the case of transportation of indentured coolie labour, or that of the children. Thanks to the writings on plantation economy, we know something about the transportation of coolie labour. But we know very little of the ways children were sent across seas and deserts as labour force. In *Uprooted: The Shipment of Poor Children to Canada, 1867 to 1917* the historian of the transportation of child labour Roy Parker gives us detailed account of exportation of hundreds of boys and girls from England to Canada in the second half of the nineteenth century and the first few decades of the twentieth century – to work in Canada, to be beaten, sexually abused, slave laboured – all to build up Canada and to rid England of its poor destitute children.[4]

This was also roughly the time, immediately after the American Civil War when Chinese labour was imported to the United States to build the Central Pacific Railway Line. People speak of the monumental engineering tunnelling feat amidst snow and rare air at the heights at Sierra Nevada (1867); there are now films, museums, and archives on the railway line construction, the companies involved, and the enterprise of the businessmen,[5] yet not much details on the immigration of labour, labour forms, labour conditions, etc., except what we get from very few books on the Irish and Chinese labour in railway construction in the United States.[6] Chinese peasants from the Canton Province began arriving on California's shores in 1850. Initially, they took five-year stints in the mines, after which they prospected or accepted jobs as labourers, domestic workers, and fishermen. They faced intense prejudice and increasingly restrictive laws limiting work opportunity. Leland Stanford, the Governor of California, promised in 1862 in his inaugural address to protect the state from "the dregs of Asia." However, in early 1865 the Central Pacific railway company started recruiting Chinese labour because of acute labour shortage. Most of the early workers were Irish immigrants. Railroad work was hard, and management was chaotic, leading to a high attrition rate. One official source tells, "The railroad lost uncounted men to snow. Avalanches could cut down dozens at a time." There was one large snow slide at Strong's Canyon known as Camp 4. Two gangs of Chinese for Tunnels 11 and 12, as well as a gang of culvert men were in this camp. The slide took it all, and one of the culvert men was not found until the following spring. Even when the tunnels were done, maintaining them was a monumental task. In the spring of 1868 most of the high-altitude tunnels were completely blocked by ice, which had to be blasted loose and shovelled out. One description says, "When snow wasn't killing men, the work was".[7] Plus we have to remember that all these were achieved by mass murdering the Native Americans so that land could be conquered by businessmen for construction of railways. Then, after the conquest, in 1876 the United States celebrated its might, gathered in part from the completion of the railroad, at the Centennial Exposition in Philadelphia. Among the exhibits one could see the "very aristocracy of the Indian nation", and the heroic feats of construction of railways. American Indian representatives invited to the Exposition found themselves a curiosity for the fair's visitors. "The struggle was over, and Native American tribes had lost it, leaving the world of the West forever changed."[8]

Again, we know very little of the resistance of the Chinese labour except the famous strike in 1876, when on 25 June the Chinese workers left their grading work along a two-mile stretch on the eastern Sierra slope and went back to their camp. They demanded USD 40 a month instead of USD 35, and a reduction in hours. A workday on the open Sierra lasted from dawn till dusk; the Chinese labourers wanted to work no more than ten hours daily. They also asked for shorter shifts in the cramped, dangerous tunnels. The company bosses responded with stopping food supply at the heights and deployed white strong men.[9] Again we do not have definite figures of how many workers died before the strike crumbled. In fact, we do not have much study on this phase of global labour immigration and the books we have of the construction of the railways in the United States are mostly celebratory. In that age of globalisation, capital and labour both were being globalised. It is difficult to tell which preceded what. Possibly these two phenomena were inter-connected.[10]

Similarly, during the mass importation of labour for mining in Australia, girls, boys, and single women would be transported in the decades of the last quarter of the nineteenth century and specially in the first quarter of the twentieth century to the stark Edwardian homes in Australia, where (for instance in Adelaide, today the building being known as the Migration Museum) it would be written on the wall by the charity institutions and city councils, "You who have no place else on earth enter this home – never to look back to the outside world, but to take this as home". There is this astonishing collection of documents and writings, done by Mary Geyer, and published by the Migration Museum on the occasion of the Women's Suffrage Centenary in South Australia (1894–1994), titled, *Behind the Wall – The Women of the Destitute Asylum, Adelaide, 1852–1918* (1994), which tells us the destitute migrants' lives behind the walls.[11] Other stories tell us of migrant farm workers – once again in Canada, United States, and in the plains of Europe.[12] Even a century later one observer wrote of the migrant farm workers in the United States,

> Migrants parents and children are fellow citizens of ours, yet in certain respects strangers, even outcasts who are utterly removed from the America everyone else can more or less take for granted. They belong to nobody, even though travel all over America to find work. . . . Those children are lucky if they are born in a hospital and get the barest minimum of medical care through infancy and beyond. Those children are even lucky . . . if they get enough food to eat. Hungry, malnourished, often sick, those children move from country to country and across state lines. As boys and girls they learn . . . how dangerous and unkind life can be . . . how hard it is now to break away and settle down and become that most important of things (it is easy to forget just how important) – a resident, which means a member of a community, a voter able to exert political leverage, a union member with job security, a person eligible for dozens of services and programs, and opportunities.[13]

Hunger marches began in the second half of the nineteenth century and continued in the twentieth century – in both new and old worlds, colonial and colonised countries – in search for food and jobs. It is important to see the exportation of coolie labour as part of this broader history of displacement (with thin line between internal and international migration), much of which is still concealed. Various works on the forms of migrant labour of that time suggest the broader connection that we must diligently pursue in the interest of understanding what is happening today.[14] This was also the time when large numbers of indentured labour were sent to various plantations in the colonies. Indeed the indentured form of labour was prevalent in the flow of labour from Europe to the United States and the early age of modern colonialism spread widely during this time.[15]

In diligently reconstructed accounts of the late nineteenth-century famines in the context of climate change and environmental disasters, we again have a different picture of the making of our time marked by famines and massive population movements induced by dry weather, floods, hunger, and the forcible exit of large peasant communities from the emerging global food market.[16] And on the top of that add the histories of formation of large armies to fight wars in distant lands on the basis of recruitment of massive number of men of various nations on earth.[17] This history is to be found in country after country, also at global level. At the same time another process began. We are referring here to the development of the basic technologies of governing population flows. One of the purposes of these governmental technologies was to achieve in each case the right composition of the population, the right mix, as it is termed now, leading to partitions and new boundary-making exercises.[18]

All these, let us not forget, happened after the manumission or abolition of slavery in British Empire, elsewhere in Europe, and the United States (1833–1865).

The post-manumission period was one of several changing modes of labour process – the slave, indentured, the contract, and the free. These modes historically never appeared as pure types, because much of the availability of labour depended on labour's mobility – making the labour mobile. Indeed, the truth is that it was largely on the condition of making labour mobile that globalisation proceeded. This was the subaltern or the primitive aspect of globalisation – the underside of the official story. This would always involve, as Marx explained, the primitive mode of capital accumulation. Therefore, mining, construction of railways, and plantation economy appeared as the primary site of mobile labour – precisely because of the particular nature of labour process in these sectors. They foreshadow our age when entire sectors such as waste processing or domestic care and even public care economy have come to depend globally on recruitment of mobile labour. Transit labour then as now occupies a crucial place in capitalist production. Our nation-centric histories give us no clue to this vast process of population formation.

Besides, the time we are speaking of here was marked by another factor, namely that to make labour mobile, the border-making exercises by colonial powers, say in Africa or Asia, were accompanied by colonial frontier policy. Frontiers meant flexible management of labour supply. New forms of labour such as indentured required a combination of border-making exercises and frontier policies. This was evident in European colonial powers' policies with regard to labour from Africa and Asia. A flexible frontier policy helped ensure labour mobility even within European borders.

Humanitarianism and the figure of the migrant

Through all these, two issues have come closer as marks of modern time – on one hand mixed up, messy, population flows provoking desperate governmental responses; on the other hand innovations at a furious pace in humanitarian methods, functions, institutions, and principles. Suddenly governments have discovered why people move: not only due to violence, threat of violence, torture, and discrimination (by now banal causes), but they move due to also natural disasters, man-made famines and floods, climate change, developmental agenda, resource crisis, environmental catastrophes, and the like. The humanitarian response has grown accordingly in range. Governments say that they have to gear up not only to emergencies but "complex emergencies" – a scenario that alludes to a complicated assemblage of factors and elements leading to an emergency situation and impeding relief measures.[19] To understand how these two issues of our time have come close, we need to go back to the histories of population movements in the second half of the nineteenth and early twentieth century. It was then that the basic control systems were put in place, such as the introduction of the passport and the visa system,[20] recording the foreigner, developing labour market management tools to use immigrant labour for a capitalist market and for control of domestic labour, and finally developing a detailed surveillance system. In this, law – but more than law, new administrative practices – proved crucial. The feature of modern democracies practising various social exclusions developed during this time, and this is how the societies of the settled populations with their pre-ordained divisions of labour wanted to return to stability, after the unsettling element had been taken care of. By controlling the abnormal, who was generally the migrant, normalcy was to be restored. It was during this time that governing the migrant became a task of attending to pathology. The discourse of abnormality was produced from real-life events.

Let us listen to a chronicle of an event recorded meticulously by a historian of immigration in France, Clifford Rosenberg, who showed how the following event in Paris produced the figure of the migrant as abnormal. On 7 November 1923, an unemployed, homeless man, a Kabyle from Algeria, Khemili Mohamed Sulimane, entered a grocery store at number 43 rue Fondary in the fifteenth arrondissement and grabbed the grocer's wife, a thirty-year-old woman, named Jeanne Billard. Sulimane dragged her out into the crowded street where he threw her to the ground. Brandishing an enormous kitchen knife, he knelt over her, tore off her right cheek, and slit her throat, severing her left carotid artery. Covered in blood, he turned next to Louise Fougere, who was calming her wailing eight-year-old grandson, Emile, on his way home from school. Sulimane stabbed her too. She collapsed, dying on the spot. The child was finally rescued by a neighbour who quickly pulled little Emile through her ground-floor window to safety. Sulimane ran across the street and slashed two more people. All this went on until a pair of police officers arrived and shot him. Rosenberg reports,

> The double murder dominated newspaper headlines and set off a series of popular disturbances. Shortly after the murders, an unruly crowd tried to lynch an unsuspecting Algerian who happened upon them. Petitions circulated demanding that 'undesirable' elements be 'expelled' from the neighbourhood.... Reporters tracked down witnesses who claimed that Sulimane took advantage of Camille Billard's absence to woo his wife, frequently stopping by the store to profess his love for her. According to the newspapers, Jeanne Billard treated Sulimane generously, sometimes giving him leftovers from her table, but she consistently rejected his advances.

Sulimane was quoted by a reporter as saying,

> My love for Mme. Billard completely changed my life. I could no longer work, eat, or sleep; my existence without her became impossible. I told her over and over again, but, each time, she burst out laughing and threw me out. Yesterday, I went again to beg her to come with me: she brutally rejected me. So I struck.

Rosenberg added the comment,

> The theme of the invading, libidinous colonial subject laying waste to "la douce France" could not be more stereotypical.... Whatever the true nature of the killer's feelings for Jeanne Billard, news that an Algerian man

had murdered two French women and wounded two others in broad daylight outraged popular opinion and inspired a tremendous response from authorities.

As Rosenberg noted, this happened at a time when the Moroccan rebel leader Abd el-Karim inflicted a series of stunning blows to the Spanish army in the Rif war, leading to a putsch and the rise of General Miguel Primo de Rivera's authoritarian regime in Spain. The French Communist Party (PCF) only became a mass party at the time of the Popular Front, but it exerted a powerful influence much earlier, especially on colonial matters. The newly formed party energetically supported Abd el-Karim's rebels, especially as it became clear that they would soon attack French positions. Against the "bankers' and capitalists war," they demanded "recognition of the independent Rif Republic." Rosenberg wrote,

> Authorities feared that Communists and nationalist revolutionaries would exploit the freedoms of the metropole to prey on Paris's growing colonial proletariat, and then export revolution overseas. Shortly after the murders, in March 1924, the . . . minister of the interior, Camille Chautemps, called together representatives from his own Department of Algerian Affairs as well as others from the Ministries of Colonies and Labour, and the Municipal Council of Paris to devise a strategy to restrict Algerian immigration. . . . The assembled officials, of various ideological orientations, voted unanimously to require all passengers travelling from Algeria to . . . obtain a contract, approved by the Ministry of Labour, undergo a physical examination from a government doctor before departing, in order to rule out tuberculosis; and to prove their identity by presenting specially created identity cards with photographs.[21]

Events like the one just described were used by colonial authorities to give shape to their immigration policies, precisely when part of the colonial political class voiced humanitarian concerns also in order to institute some protection measures for the immigrants. Drawing extensively on the police files in Paris of that time Rosenberg has presented for us a critical moment in the history of immigration control and political surveillance. He shows how in the years after the First World War the French police, terrified by the Bolshevik Revolution and the spectre of immigrant criminality, became the first major force anywhere to systematically enforce distinctions of citizenship and national origins. As the French capital emerged in the 1920s as a haven for refugees, dissidents, and workers from throughout Europe and across the Mediterranean, police officers raided immigrant neighbourhoods to scare illegal aliens into registering with authorities and arrested those whose papers were not in order. The police began to concentrate on colonial workers from North Africa, tracking these workers with a special police brigade and segregating them in their own hospital when they fell ill. Transformed by their enforcement, legal categories that had existed for hundreds of years began to matter as never before. These categories determined whether or not families could remain together and whether people could keep their jobs or were forced to flee. During World War II, identity controls marked out entire populations for physical destruction. The treatment of foreigners during the Third Republic, Rosenberg contends, shaped the subsequent treatment of Jews by the Vichy.

These new methods of identification pioneered at that time are once again relevant to our time. They created forms of inclusion and inequality, which remain pervasive as rich states of the West find themselves compelled to provide benefits to their own citizens and at the same time recruit foreign nationals to satisfy their labour needs. Modern humanitarianism has developed as part of this scenario. As a clinical task classical humanitarianism wanted to change the soul of the "abnormal", therefore there were educationists, pedagogues, missionaries, administrators, and thinkers working on the issue of how to reform the abnormal societies. Modern humanitarianism had to combine the old techniques with new ones of care, protection, information gathering, interference, intervention, and invention of a skewed theory of sovereignty, a one-sided theory of responsibility, and the gigantic humanitarian machines which can compare today with the trans-national corporations (TNCs). In practical terms this means today managing societies, which produce the obdurate refugees and migrants to stop them from leaving the shores, keep them within the national territorial confines, and eventually to govern societies in "an enlightened way".

It was the period when policies in place of laws and directions from popularly elected assemblies started to become critical in governmental functioning. Both colonial and metropolitan experiences show how in this period policies on control and management of societies were enunciated. Relief organisations emerged, which would mean technically an end to vulnerability. Managing moving population groups became the *deux ex machina* of modern governmentality. Governments began showing awareness of the paradoxical task they faced: how much to keep these groups beyond the pale of visibility and how much to allow them to be visible. Histories of immigration suggest that to the extent to which migrant labour became crucial for expansion of industries, it had become visible.[22] However, labour did not arrive in a clear and desirable form in nationally constituted polities and markets; therefore keeping immigrant groups confined to almost invisible spaces also acquired high priority. In time, governments had to deal with enormous confusion regarding following questions:

(a) Who was a refugee and who was a migrant?
(b) What to do with the displaced due to famines, disasters, and epidemics, who will now swarm the world as migrants?
(c) What was the extent of government responsibility?
(d) Was mitigating hunger a task of the government or was this a sign of inefficient and abnormal population groups?

The attempt to solve these dilemmas found expression in various law makings, regulations, directives, new manuals about care, camps, shelter, food, water, and medicine, while even more initiatives were taken to anticipate the arrival of migrants in order to keep them at bay, and therefore to build up specially trained forces to prevent the latter's entry. The main body of new humanitarianism emerged in this time. "Destitute asylums" resembling prison houses were set up by charitable institutions to welcome survivors, particularly girls and elderly female survivors. In all these one common feature appeared, possibly for the first time: that of treating the migrant as the source of insecurity. The victim of forced migration was now an active body, whose soul no longer needed to be saved because the destitute, wretched body would soon and inevitably die, but because this was now an unruly body requiring management and control. This is the point where the migrant emerged as the subject.

Let us also note one more paradoxical aspect of our time, but first noticed in this period. If the production of the labouring subject has thus its dark and illegal side, often representing what we have come to call the primitive mode of accumulation, and this complicates the scenario, there was also the fact that governments around this time started to pass laws and take steps towards making the immigrant a naturalised part of the society, because by and large the reorganisation of labour market must happen within a free juridical space. That is when various provisions for naturalisation, domicile rights, citizenship laws, etc., began to be made, and the relation between blood and territory was sought to be defined or clarified. The goal of such naturalisation was to help (a) the multiplication of labour, and (b) retain the heterogeneity of the global space of capital. Global domination of capital was impossible without these two attributes.

What all these implied in simpler terms was that labour flows, which migration flows ultimately are, had to be controlled and regulated with laws and governmental techniques. In short it was in this period that humanitarianism became part of governmental rationality. Rights and risks were combined during this time.

This was an anarchic process and not a thought out and deliberated one. Even though this period was marked by intense administrative centralisation, an administrative centre could do things only to certain extent, while police, municipal clerks, and local politicians decided at the ground level in the suburbs and distant frontier towns how and to what degree to execute those directives because they had to have always the primary task in mind – that of ensuring the society kept running. The fate of the migrant in various parts of the world was not therefore uniform. Migrant's rights did not develop primarily through any human rights norms; no guarantee was secured from an altruistic civil society and well-informed public sphere. They evolved through contentious claim makings of various collectives, and equally complex constitutional and jurisdictional battles. Refuge, refusal, discourses of security and insecurity, and consequent actions by governments and social collectives made this process extremely contingent. It happened in India also. In the period between the establishment of rule of law in the 1860s and passage of various national security provisions in the 1930s and early 1940s we have all the indications of an emerging democracy that would be marked by inclusions and exclusions, and a differentially constituted national labour market. The nationalist history we read is therefore one only in a mythical way, because this myth hides at the same times other turbulent processes of population formation and development of control techniques, only the final signs of which we get in the passage of the Citizenship Act, the Foreigners Act, and the finalisation of the immigration rules. This is perhaps to recall Theodor Adorno's phrase again, "negative dialectics" – the more we try to think of the nation form distancing ourselves from the material process of labour, the more we are hurled back to the violent history of the labour form.[23]

Empire, borders, and the migrant

There may be one more reason behind this relative neglect of labour history. We ignored the fact that a good part of the nation form we were studying had been based on imperial structure/s. And, the state, which this nation was attempting to build, leaned substantially on imperial traditions and contexts. The particular constellations of territory, authority, and rights which supported the emergence of the nation state had imperial lineages in more than one way. Empires had been characterised by several kinds of population flows. Barbarians had appeared periodically in history against empires. Barbarians represented migratory movements, and in the context of our time we may say they had a decisive impact on what Sandro Mezzadra calls "borders/confines of citizenship".[24] Thanks to recent critical investigations into the institution of border, we now have greater insights into the contemporary economy of governmental methods relating to the institution of border and its conceptual relevance in labour migration studies.[25]

As we know, the classic concept of borders arose in the wake of the emergence of the modern state and its geopolitical dimensions, within which the individual was historically constructed as a citizen. Nation, state, citizen, border – all these seemed to unite in an excellent fit. Now two things have thrown this fit into disarray: the emergence of empire and the trans-border migratory movements, which have collectively put our understanding of citizenship in doubt. Sovereignty in the beginning was not always strictly territorial. Imperial sovereignty was not so much indicative of the borders of the empire (though Hadrian was the first known ruler to have territorial markers put in place to indicate the imperial reach), but as of exceptional powers to be above the law and execute lives as and when the emperor felt necessary. However, in this case too, the power to execute was to be moderated to fit with governmental necessities of the empire – for instance in relation to the Christians in the Roman imperium. Who was Roman was a problem then too, and trans-border incursions of people into Rome made things difficult. It was these incursions and the intrinsic difficulties of defining citizenship under imperial conditions that made empire as a form of the State increasingly impossible. The problem as we know was temporarily solved with the emergence of modern political society, where citizenship, territoriality, borders, and sovereignty were combined in the form of modern nation states – but we have to note here that this was possible not only because of popular democracy (the dream of Rousseau, and which every liberal political philosopher has looked forward to), but also because of colonialism, which meant in this respect several things.

Colonialism meant (a) clear territorial distinction between the sovereign state and the subjugated areas known as colonies, (b) clear legal distinction between participants of the polity, that is citizens, and the subjects, (c) clearly demarcated sites of developed sectors of economy and the production of primary goods, and (d) finally an effective way of combining territorial conquest, subsequent annexation, and the long distance control of economies of the world.

Yet colonialism also meant specific population policies, crucial among which were the ones to make labour mobile for railways, industries, and plantations. Imperial frontier policies adopted by colonial powers were subsequently adopted by nation states too. In this mixed way the imperial form was taken over by the modern nation state. The imperial form of the nation was the historically arrived solution to the twin problems of (a) the empire needing to have borders, and (b) the need to negotiate the territorial limits of the legitimacy of the power of the State.

Yet as the preceding pages show, immigration flows in the second half of the nineteenth century and the early part of the twentieth century were possible because of colonial-imperial structures. The mixed colonial-imperial made the solution of the border question in the form of nation states only partial. Migration history is thus "the shadowy cone over the history of Europe"[26] – that contains the unreported histories of masses of errant, deported, and eradicated individuals who live in a foreign land, in countries that do not recognize their "belonging". These migratory movements have fractured the national, ethnic, and linguistic features of polities and political societies. In a defensive move the empire now speaks of meta-borders indicating the division between the imperial land and that of the barbarians, and not the boundaries between its constituent units.

As a strategy it has had mixed fortunes. While in the last fifteen years this institutionalisation of meta-borders as a strategy has served the function of locating and defining the imperial land better, it has ill served the function of stopping the raids of what the empire considers the extra-planetary animals. Thus, for instance, labour flows from "New Europe" to "Old Europe" (or, from Mexico or Puerto Rico to the United States) threaten the imperial-civilisational core of the Euro-Atlantic continent, and consequently put pressure on the internal confines of the empire. The border/confine in this way is continually under pressure, and the stress reproduces itself in the interior of the empire. In this condition, sovereignty is present, but not in one source or organ, but in the half-juridical, half economic-political space of the empire, where several actors are at work, and whose main feature is namely that more than the empire's viability depending on the presence of sovereignty, it is sovereignty that now depends on the imperial form for its relevance and legitimacy. Thus imperial confines are being reproduced by nations everywhere to locate and keep the migrants at bay. Yet, we have to remember that in this age of empire and globalisation, governing strategies must ensure that labour flows must not be directionless; they must conform to the rules the regime of division of labour will lay down. This is the governmental rationality under imperial conditions we are referring to. The reserve army or the army of surplus labour must conform to the institutional rules of the global labour market. The logic of these institutional rules was formed in the period we have referred to in this chapter.

In short, the late nineteenth and early twentieth century was another period of globalisation when migration controls were put in place. As now, then too was control of migrant labour not the concern of governments only. Employers, recruitment agents, labour brokers in sending and receiving countries, lawyers, courts, training institutes, moneylenders and other credit agencies, bureaucrats, municipal authorities, smugglers, and a wide variety of intermediaries sought to gain from the trans-national flow of workers. Networks grew up, some of them, in Charles Tilly's language, "transplanted networks". Tilly pointed out that by the early nineteenth century, evolving capitalist economic and property relations marked by the spread of wage labour, separation of households from the means of production, and the rising productivity of commercial agriculture had combined with diminishing land resources and an expanding demand for labour in urban areas to make long-distance migration a rational choice for many Europeans. Local conditions, including land-tenure patterns, agricultural requirements, and resource management profoundly influenced rates of migration and return. They also determined the kinds of people who emigrated, such as from certain parts of southern Italy, where land ownership was still possible and therefore the migrants hoped to use their American wages to purchase land upon their return. The sons of Norwegian cattle farmers shut out from ownership also left Europe. In all these acts of emigration, awareness of networks became a critical factor.[27] On the other hand, workers developed then too different means to cope with these control mechanisms, even if partially most of the time, and if possible evaded them. But vulnerability remained overwhelming.

Globalisation means globalisation of recruitment of migrant labour, even though the situation is not what it was one hundred and fifty years ago, particularly with regard to migration of skilled labour, and what may be called migration of "immaterial labour".[28] In many cases, however, the situation obtaining today reminds us of the time we have discussed in this chapter, for instance the exploitation inherent in global supply chains of labour (for instance, Burmese migrant workers in Thailand), creation of new economic space virtually out of nothing (for instance Macao or Dubai), Filipino nightclub hostesses and girls in Hong Kong or the migrant Nepali labour there, women migrant workers in Taiwan, and the massive cities of the world marked by migrant workers and trafficked labour (including sex workers) for instance of Georgian or Armenian care-giving women in Athens. The globalisation of sex work now proceeds apace with the Internet playing a critical role. Not so long ago, a study by *The Economist* (9 August 2014) discussed the entry of sex workers of different ethnic origins in a similarly differentially constituted global flesh market. Following the expansion of the European Union and the global financial crash, sex workers from Eastern Europe to older Europe and the United States or from Africa and Central Asia to different parts of Europe now feature prominently in sex trade. Internet has expanded the market, helped sex trade escape different national legislations, allowed entry of part time sex workers, and has created new gatekeepers, new forms of surveillance, new flexibility in hourly rates of the sex workers, and has made sex work decentralised.[29]

In many senses today's entertainment, care, and the construction industry represent what the plantation and railway construction industries signified in the period referred to in this article. Thousands upon thousands of migrants workers serving worldwide from the United States to the Middle East to Southeast Asia to the Far East as masons, plumbers, coolies, nurses, ayahs, sex workers, workers in entertainment, and construction industry remind us of the late nineteenth and early twentieth century. Nursing schools are booming in the developing countries to produce the necessary labour. Bangladesh has 130 such nursing-midwifery schools, Indonesia about 1400 schools, Myanmar 48 schools, Nepal 124, Thailand 80, Sri Lanka 26, and India over 4000 schools. Midwifery and ayahs constitute the bulk of the trained personnel sent abroad. All these while the weekly earnings of registered nurses in the United States for instance remained relative stagnant from 2005 to 2011, in fact suffering 5 percent decline in actual purchasing power. The number of guest nurses in the same country increased noticeably in this period. In 1994 about 9 percent of the total registered nurse force consisted of guest nurses; by 2008 the share had gone up 16.3 percent. And mark it, at the same time in one year – 2010 alone – the incidence of injury and illness due to occupational hazards increased by 6 percent. We have similar figures of immigrant labour in sex and other entertainment industries.[30] Relating to the precariousness of the situation, this piece of news from the BBC will be perhaps more revealing than the cited figures.

> Forty-six Indian nurses are stranded in a hospital in the Iraqi city of Tikrit..., and many of the nurses have said they want to return to India as soon as possible. But two other nurses, who returned home on holiday from Iraq just before trouble broke out there last week, have told the BBC that they want to go back.
>
> "We are very tense about the situation in Iraq but I want to go back to work there," said Sindhu, who is in the southern Indian state of Kerala, on leave from the hospital in the southern Iraqi town of Nasiriya. The 28-year-old returned home on 10 June – a day before the militant Sunni group ISIS began over-running northern and central Iraqi towns and cities.
>
> [...]
>
> Sindhu is aware that the situation is grim in Iraq, particularly after news came in that 40 Indian construction workers had been kidnapped in the city of Mosul.
>
> But, if she doesn't go, she is worried about defaulting on "huge loans" that she has taken to finance her education and to pay a recruitment agent to find her a job in Iraq. "My friends in Nasiriya telephone me daily and say that I should return because there is no problem there. I cannot make up my mind. We are all tense. I paid 150,000 rupees ($2,500; £1,470) to the recruitment agency to get this job," she said.
>
> "My mother has a kidney problem. She needs to undergo dialysis thrice a week. My father is a small farmer who took loans from his friends to fund my education and pay the recruitment agent. Some friends charged interest, some didn't. I still need to repay the loans," she says.[31]

BBC further reported that before leaving for Iraq, Sindhu had worked as a nurse in Delhi where she earned a monthly salary of 11,000 rupees (in 2014 it was equivalent to $183; £108). In Nasiriya, she earned $850. She told BBC that she knew of the fighting in Iraq, but she was worried about how she was going to repay a loan she has taken to fund her education.

BBC added while commenting on the possibility of return to the safety of their homes from a country in a state of war,

> Many of the nurses who are stranded in Tikrit are also faced with the dilemma of whether to return to India or stay put in Iraq. Many have borrowed money back home and say they are able to pay it back because of the higher salaries they get in Iraq.[32]

At the same time we should not forget that these new areas of labour power production had to be secured in the first phase of this round of globalisation with coercive means exactly as in the nineteenth century when colonial population had to be sent as part of the armed forces in sea voyages to the areas where plantation industry was to come up not much later. The coincidence of securing areas for occupation and production is not and was not god ordained. Premansu Kumar Bandopadhyay's account of military expeditions to Southeast Asia from India, *Sepoys in the British Overseas Expeditions* throws light on an early phase of this process. The echoes of such expeditions in the hinterlands of India or the Amazon or the forests of Indonesia or the deserts of the Middle East can be heard today. While we need not overstretch the similarities of the two ages, these similarities are remarkable though they should not astonish us. If the earlier period of globalisation marked by industrial capitalism called for massive supply of labour forming its underbelly, this period of globalisation marked by unprecedented financialisation of capital and other resources (including land) calls for similar supply of labour (for opening up forests, construction of new towns, entertainment and care industries, etc.), forming the underbelly of the beast today. Then too, as now, it was preceded by depeasantisation on wide scale. Then too as now the process was preceded by massive application of force.

The main purpose of this chapter was not to point out the similarities of our age with that age, but to suggest that it was in that age that the basis of today's principal modes of migrant labour management urban governance as migrants began crowding the cities, and practising humanitarian care and protection as part of state functions thereby contributing to the power of the state, was laid down. The foundations of a governing apparatus that would have protection and labour regulation as its two sides were secured in this age. Even the League of Nations' initiative on refugee protection would not have been possible without this basis. All these acted as a supplement to the apparatus of power that would enable the state and indeed the global system to get a grip on human mobility, direct it, and govern it. On the other hand, this power to govern migration produced in turn the migratory flows of our time, in the forms we know, such as regular, irregular, and the like.

To conclude, while various studies are focusing on the dynamics of migrant labour today,[33] it will be good to have a sense of history of empires, particularly colonial empires, their boundary-making exercises, and the bodies that repeatedly hurled themselves on these borders and boundaries, and made migration one of the most bio-political aspects of our age. Conversely, we can say that it was in that age that control of mobile bodies began constituting one of the most critical aspects of bio-power. The emergence of some of the different forms of labour subjectivities marking our world today can be traced back to that time.

This was of course not a straightforward history, as national, gender-related, race, and several other factors contributed to the making of a hugely heterogonous labour market. The subjectivities produced in that process have contributed to the contentious history of our time.

Notes

1 This chapter elaborates the arguments I made earlier in an article, "Histories of the Late Nineteenth to Early Twentieth Century Immigration and Our Time", *Current Sociology*, Volume66 (2), 2018, pp. 192–208, https://doi.org/10.1177/0011392117736308. Used with permission.
2 R. Samaddar, *The Marginal Nation: Transborder Migration from Bangladesh to West Bengal* (New Delhi: Sage, 1999).
3 Stephens Castles and Godula Kosack, *Immigrant Workers and Class Structure in Western Europe* (London: Institute of Race Relations and Oxford University Press, 1973)
4 Roy Parker, *Uprooted: The Shipment of Poor Children to Canada, 1867–1917* (Chicago: Chicago University Press and University of Bristol Press, 2008).
5 For photographs including those on the eventual exclusion of the Chinese labour by special legislation see the site, "American Experience", www.pbs.org/wgbh/americanexperience/films/tcrr/(accessed on 21 December 2017).
6 For instance, Davad Haward, *Empire Express: Building the First Transcontinental Railroad* (New York: Penguin Books, 2000); Stephen E. Ambrose, *Nothing Like It in the World: The Men Who Built the Transcontinental Railroad 1863–1869*(New York: Simon & Schuster; 2001).
7 The account taken from, www.pbs.org/wgbh/americanexperience/features/general-article/tcrr-tunnels/ (accessed on 21 December 2017).
8 On this, www.pbs.org/wgbh/americanexperience/features/general-article/tcrr-tribes/ (accessed on 21 December 2017); see also, www.pbs.org/wgbh/americanexperience/features/tcrr-reports/ (accessed on 1 February 2019).
9 On the strike, www.pbs.org/wgbh/americanexperience/features/general-article/tcrr-cprr/(accessed on 21 December 2017).
10 Historian Michael Adas has commented,

> If the period from the 1870s is included in a long twentieth century (and perhaps even if it is not), migration served as a mode of escape from oppression and poverty and, in many instances, as an avenue toward advancement for an unprecedented number of people that soared well into the hundreds of millions by century's end. But for a clear majority of these migrants, movement was coerced by flight from war and oppression or was enticed by labor recruiters who preyed on the desperately poor. The prospects for the great majority were almost invariably lives of drudge labor in urban sweatshops, on tropical plantations, or on the wharves of an expansive, global export economy.

Michael Adas (ed.), *Essays on Twentieth Century History* (Philadelphia: Temple University Press for the American University Association, 2010), p. 2; see in particular, Jose C. Moya

and Adam Mckeown, "World Migration in the Long Twentieth Century", Chapter 1, pp. 9–52.
11 Mary Geyer, *Behind the Wall – The Women of the Destitute Asylum, Adelaide, 1852–1918* and published by the (Adelaide: Migration Museum, 1994).
12 For instance Robert Coles, *Uprooted Children – The Early Life of Migrant Farm Workers* (Pittsburgh: University of Pittsburgh Press, 1970); for late nineteenth century to early twentieth century Mexican, Indian, and Black migrant farm workers in the California Valley, Donald Worster, *Rivers of Empire: Water, Aridity, and the Growth of the American West* (New York: Oxford University Press, 1985).
13 Foreword to *Uprooted Children* by Senator Robert F. Mondale, pp. xiii–xiv.
14 Apart from works on indentured labour, classic among such works is of course, by Jan Breman, *Taming the Coolie Beast – Plantation Society and the Colonial Order in Southeast Asia* (New Delhi: Oxford University Press, 1989); also Rana P. Behel and Marcel van der Linden (eds.), *Coolies, Capital, and Colonialism – Studies in Indian Labour History* (Cambridge: Cambridge University Press, 2007).
15 The literature on indentured labour is substantial; see for instance the site of "Striking Women / Migration", www.striking-women.org/module/migration/history-migration (accessed on 1 January 2019); Galutra Bahadur, *Coolie Woman: The Odyssey of Indenture* (Chicago: The University of Chicago Press, 2014); John Wareing, *Indentured Migration and the Servant Trade from London to America, 1618–1718* (Oxford: Oxford University Press, 2017); Khal Torabully and Marina Carter, *Coolitude: An Anthology of the Indian Labour Diaspora* (London: Anthem Press, 2002); Hugh Tinker, *A New System of Slavery: The Export of Indian Labour Overseas, 1830–1920* (London and Oxford: Institute of Race Relations and Oxford University Press, 1974).
16 For instance, Mike Davis, *El Nino Famines: Late Victorian Holocausts and the Making of the Third World* (London: Verso, 2002); see also, Donald Worster, *Rivers of Empire: Water, Aridity, and the Growth of the American West* (New York: Oxford University Press, 1985).
17 Again, in the Indian instance in Southeast Asia, Premansu Kumar Bandopadhyay, *Sepoys in the British Overseas Expeditions (1762–1826)*, vol. 1 (Kolkata: K.P. Bagchi, 2011).
18 Often partition has been mistakenly considered to be an exceptional event – in South Asian history or in the history of the Cold War, such as partitions of Germany and Korea. For a broader history of partitions, state makings, and migration, see for instance, Stefano Bianchini, *Liquid Nationalism and State Partitions in Europe* (Cheltenham: Edward Elgar Publishing, 2017).
19 The UNHCR defines (2001),

> A complex emergency can be defined as a humanitarian crisis in a country, region or society where there is a total or considerable breakdown of authority resulting from internal or external conflict, and which requires an international response that goes beyond the mandate or capacity of any single agency and/or the ongoing UN country programme. Likely characteristics of complex emergencies include: a large number of civilian victims, populations who are besieged or displaced, human suffering on a major scale; substantial international assistance is needed and the response goes beyond the mandate or capacity of any one agency; delivery of humanitarian assistance is impeded or prevented by parties to the conflict; high security risks for relief workers providing humanitarian assistance; and relief workers targeted by parties to the conflict.
>
> *www.unhcr.org/partners/partners/3ba88e7c6/coordination-complex-emergencies.html (accessed on 28 February 2019)*

20 John Torpey, *The Invention of Passport: Surveillance, Citizenship, and the State* (Cambridge: Cambridge University Press, 1999); see also Martin Llyod, *The Passport: The History of Man's Most Travelled Document* (Gloucestershire: Sutton Publishing, 2003); Mahmoud Keshavarz, *The Design Politics of the Passport: Materiality, Immobility, and Dissent* (London: Bloomsbury Visual Arts, 2019). Keshavarz speaks of "passport situations", which are "those situations when and where a passport is important, thus rendering it as an operative as well as illuminative agent of making relationships" (p. 13). Passport produces the

immigrant situation, and the passport situations "are experienced, confronted, contested, or negotiated." (p. 13). Keshavarz also shows how a passport becomes one of the early and through various designs one of the most effective records of a mobile body.
21 Clifford Rosenberg, *Policing Paris – The Origins of Modern Immigration Control Between the Wars* (Ithaca: Cornell University Press, 2006), pp. 141–144; all citations regarding this incident are from these pages.
22 For instance see the work of Mary Dewhurst Lewis, *The Boundaries of the Republic: Migrant Rights and the Limits of Universalism in France, 1918–1940* (Stanford, CA: Stanford University Press, 2007).
23 Theodor Adorno, *Negative Dialectics*, trans. E.B. Ashton (London: Routledge and Kegan Paul, 1973); Adorno remarked,

> Dialectics is the consistent sense of non-identity. . . . What we differentiate will appear divergent, dissonant, negative for just as long as the structure of our consciousness obliges it to strive for unity: as long as its demand for totality will be its measure for whatever is not identical with it. . . . Contradiction is non-identity under the rule of a law that affects the non-identical as well.
>
> *pp. 5–6*

24 Sandro Mezzadra, *Borders, Confines, Migrations, and Citizenship*, May 2006, http://observatorio.fadaiat.net/tiki-index.php?page=Borders%2C%20Migrations%2C%20Citizenshp) (accessed on 21 August 2017).
25 Sandro Mezzadra and Brett Neilson, *Border as Method, or, the Multiplication of Labour* (Durham, NC: Duke University Press, 2013); also Paula Banerjee, *Borders, Histories, Existences: Gender and Beyond* (New Delhi: Sage, 2010).
26 Saskia Sassen wrote,

> Part of the difficulty for old Europe is, ironically, the lack of ahistorical perspective. Europe has a barely recognised history of several centuries of internal labour migrations. This is a history that hovers in the penumbra of official European History dominated by the image of Europe as a continent of emigration, never of immigration. In the 1700s, when Amsterdam built its polders and cleared its bogs, it brought in northern German workers; when the French built up their vineyards they brought in Spaniards; when Milan and Turin developed they brought in workers from the Alps. In the 1800s, when Haussmann redid Paris, he brought in Germans and Belgians; when London built its infrastructure for water and sewage, it brought in the Irish; when Sweden decided to become a monarchy and needed handsome palaces, it brought in Italian stoneworkers; when Switzerland built the Gotthard Tunnel, it brought in Italians; and when Germany built its railroads and steel mills it brought in Italians and Poles.

"Europe's Migrations: The Numbers and the Passions Are Not New", *Third Text*, Volume 20 (6), November 2006, pp. 635–645, 644.
27 Charles Tilly, "Transplanted Networks", in Virginia Yans-McLaughlin (ed.), *Immigration Reconsidered: History, Sociology, and Politics* (New York: Oxford University Press, 1990), chapter 3, pp. 79–95; for an earlier version, https://faculty.utep.edu/Portals/1858/Tilly%201986%20Transplanted%20Networks.pdf (accessed on 25 September 2018); also Charles Tilly, "Trust Networks in Transnational Migration", *Sociological Forum*, Volume 22 (1), March 2007, pp. 3–24.
28 For instance, the collective study on migrant labour in Asia, Kevin Hewison and Ken Young (eds.), *Transnational Migration and Work in Asia* (New York: Routledge, 2006).
29 *The Economist*, "Briefing Prostitution and the Internet: More Bang for Your Buck", 9 August 2014, pp. 15–18.
30 Figures from – United Nations Population Fund, *The State of the World's Midwifery, 2011: Delivering Health, Saving Lives* (New York: United Nations Population Fund, 2011); DPE (Department of Professional Employees, AFL-CIO) Factsheet, 2012; updated by DPE research intern Charlie Fanning (mimeo); on US figures, DPE Factsheet, April 2012, http://dpeaflcio.org/wp-content/uploads/Nursing-A-Profile-of-the-Profession-2012.

pdf; on Asian figures, compilation by Prakin Suchaxaya, South East Asian Nursing Union and World Midwifery Report, 2011, www.unfpa.org/sowmy/resources/docs/main_report/en_SOWMR_Full.pdf (accessed on 29 September 2017).
31 *BBC*, 20 June 2014, report by Imran Quereshi, www.bbc.com/news/world-asia-india-27917521 (accessed on 1 December 2015).
32 *Ibid*.
33 For instance, the collective study on migrant labour in Asia, Kevin Hewison and Ken Young (eds.), *Transnational Migration and Work in Asia* (New York: Routledge, 2006).

4
THE LABOURING SUBJECT OF REFUGEE ECONOMIES

Refugee economy as a site of several interfaces

In Stephen Castles' writings the refugee economy or the immigrant economy never features directly. He refers to changes in the immigrant labour absorption policies of the West European governments. He also reviews the economic activities of the refugees and other victims of forced migration in several countries.[1] But we do not get a full picture of why capitalism in the late twentieth or early twenty-first century needs these refugee or immigrant economic actors. The idea we get is that refugees and forced migrants want to be economically viable, relevant to the host economies, and are economically relevant, but unfortunately, they are discriminated against. The organic link between the immigrant as an economic actor and the global capitalist economy seems to escape the analysis.

However, to be fair to Castles, the immigrant or the victim of forced migration as labour is present, though not centrally, in his discussions. There are however, other studies that address the issue of refugee economy more directly. They try to prove that the refugee is an economically viable actor in the market, he or she can be an entrepreneur, and an understanding of the market dynamics and its appropriate modulation with the right kind of rules and facilitating policies can be of immense help to the refugee.[2] While these writings recognise that most refugees and illegal immigrants are denizens of informal economies, the guiding thread once more is that these economies and their actors can be of relevance to market if policy makers and analysts can develop appropriate policy response based on a correct analysis of the refugee economy. In such line of thinking again, the refugee or illegal immigrant as the labouring subject is absent. Refugee is seen as an economic actor, an informal trader, an entrepreneur, but not as labour. Thus, Alex Betts' and his colleagues' recently co-published book *Refugee Economies* does not have as a cognitive category the word labour at all, at least not in a significant way.[3]

The work showcases refugees' attempts to survive meaningfully in camps, cities, and other settlements, in ethnically homogenous or mixed settings, and the ways they prove useful to market, big business, and organised trade. Several studies along this line tell us of the success stories of migrants' economic activities.[4] The message is: The refugee or the migrant as an economic actor has arrived. Do not neglect the refugee. Do not dismiss the refugee as an economic actor.

Refugees, asylum seekers, disaster victims, the internally displaced, the temporarily tolerated migrant – categories of the excluded are proliferating; yet as Michel Agier in his detailed study of several camps shows,[5] on the ground however the structure of care and protection put in place ensures that this remains a situation of permanent catastrophe and endless emergency, where undesirables are kept apart and out of sight, while the care dispensed is designed to control, filter, and confine. How can we explain this duality of care and control coupled with exclusion? Camps are transforming; likewise immigrant settlements are changing. Camps are like holding territories of mobile labour, since they hold at one place an enormous amount of reserve labour. Camps are becoming towns, and other types of big, informal-formal settlements.[6] Without a study of the immigrant as the labouring subject it is difficult to make sense of such transformation.

Even on occasions where the refugees or immigrants are considered as economic actors it is treated as a matter of labour market segmentation and differentiation. For instance, Stephen Castles and Mark Miller's *The Age of Migration* (2003 edition) has an entire chapter on migrants in the labour force.[7] They take note of the dominant presence of the migrants in the informal economy, "growing fragmentation of immigrant employment and the range and significance of immigrant labour market diversity", and "labour market segmentation leading to long term marginalisation of certain immigrant groups and immigrant women workers, and global cities and ethnic entrepreneurs".[8] Castles and Miller ask some significant questions also on issues, such as: impact of economic restructuring on migrant workers, patterns of labour market segmentation by ethnic origin and gender, scope of underground economy, strategies by the migrant such as self-employment, small business, mutual aid, ethnic niches, etc., to deal with labour market disadvantages.[9] In all these, market is the conceptual anchor, be it labour market or trade, or marketing of skills.

As a consequence, the question frequently asked is about the impact of the refugees on the host economy, and not about why economies are unable to function without the so-called refugee economies, which supply informal labour for the host economy. Our understanding of the economic interface of refugees and economies therefore does not deepen. This is also because sufficient data is not available and the question of refugee impacts does not lend itself to conventional impact evaluation methods. Some suggest comparison of impacts of cash versus in-kind refugee aid. But there is nothing special in this. Studies of poverty alleviation programmes in developing countries show specific relevance of both strategies – depending on specific time, locality, and situation. Most studies do suggest however, that despite undergoing forced migration and often living in destitute conditions, refugees have productive capacities and assets, and they actively interact with host-country economies. Some evidence suggests that a large influx of immigrants increases unemployment among the less-skilled workforce and also decreases wages among certain populations. But again, that is the general way in which an economy expands. The impact of economic expansion has been always differential. One study found that whereas increased demand may increase prices if supply does not respond, increased demand due to an additional refugee influx exerts limited upward pressure on prices around the camps where cash has been extended to the camp inmates. Economic spillover may also result as refugee households and businesses inside the camps purchase goods and services from host-country businesses outside the camps, because the agricultural, livestock, other production activities, and all retail businesses outside the camps are mostly owned by host-country households. One survey found that while refugee households accounted for 5.5 percent of total income within a 10km radius of the three camps, 17.3 percent of surveyed businesses outside the camps reported that their main customers were refugees from the camps. The increase in refugee demand raises host-country incomes and spending which, in turn, generates additional rounds of spending impacts in the local economy. This is of course a familiar story where total expenditures including savings, equalling total income for all households and activities, ensure that changes in expenditures match changes in incomes for all agents in the local economy. But the snag in the story is that the local poor households may also receive such assistance – cash or in kind or business advance – and thus generalise the problematic. Simulations are therefore not always useful tools to understand how impacts unfold in complex systems. We can also say that the economic impacts of refugees depend on the rules governing interactions between refugees and the host country, the structure of host economies, and the characteristics of refugees.[10]

This chapter refers to Castles and Miller's study and Betts' collective study in a central way as they are important to develop a critique of market-centric analysis of refugee economy. The reason is that these two studies (along with several others) deal with what can be called the internalities of the migrant or refugee economy (thus their ethnic composition, hierarchies, location, survival techniques, etc.), and leave out the externalities, by which I mean the broader forces and dynamics that compel such internal configuration and shape labour markets. A consideration of the externalities will suggest four interactive relations impacting on refugee economies:

(a) The deeply close relation between refugees, other victims of forced migration, and the illegal immigrants; likewise the interface of classic refugees and the environmental migrants as the constituting elements of an informal labour market;
(b) The similarly close relation between refugees, illegal immigrants, and the internally displaced as labouring subjects;
(c) The connection between the refugee economy and the informal economy as a whole;

(d) And finally, the incredibly dense network between formal and informal economies, shaping certain types of economic activities as in care and entertainment industry, which features the refugee and the immigrant as the labouring subject, and which borders on both formal and informal economies.

This chapter will explore these interconnections in order to suggest why we should be cautious in basing our analysis on a market centric approach, and what may be a more fruitful way to analyse the phenomenon of the refugee and the immigrant emerging as a labouring subject

Paradoxes of labour market integration

Let us begin with the implications these connections. As we know, with growing population movements from the postcolonial countries to Europe and the United States and the growing realisation that the idea of a classic refugee defined in the UNHCR statute in the context of Cold War is inadequate now,[11] the concept of forced migration has been accepted as more holistic than the concept of refugee.[12] Not that the notion of refugee was found incorrect, but with "massive and mixed population flows"[13] (discussed in the previous chapters) from the South to the North, more importantly within the South, refugee determination as the main mode of protection of the victims of forced migration was found inadequate. The present European migration crisis demonstrates this beyond doubt.[14]

In one recent European Commission study on "An Economic Take on the Refugee Crisis" it was found out that asylum seekers were heterogeneous as a group, many more were coming increasingly from countries considered unsafe, and not necessarily refugees, and,

> Estimates suggest moderate direct fiscal implications for Member States. . . . The rise in public spending comes typically for rescue operations, border protection (especially if managing an external EU border), registration of asylum seekers, and the short term provision of food, health care and shelter for transit countries. For destination countries, spending may also include elements like social housing, training, education and expenditure related to refugees' integration and welfare benefits.

The study further added,

> Estimates from the Commission's spring 2016 economic forecast suggest that the direct additional fiscal implications for the Member States most concerned is expected to fall in the range of 0.1–0.6 % of GDP, on a cumulative basis over 2015–2016.[15]

The study was candid in terms of assessing the low economic cost to Europe of the refugee crisis and predicted that the challenge lay in devising laws and rules of labour market integration on the basis of skill, education, and other factors, though it admitted that "the cost of labour market integration is not included in the analysis, due to the lack of robust information currently available on those spending programmes."[16] The study emphasised "*the importance of an appropriate policy response, notably in terms of labour market and social integration*"[17] (italics in the original).

Governments have realised that labour market integration calls for investment and viewing the arrival of refugees and other forced migrants as opportunities, triggering further growth. First of all asylum applications are rather low when we recall the commentaries of the doomsday prophets. For instance, in the summer of 2016 more than 300,000 applications for asylum in Europe were made, which was only around 600 applications for every million Europeans.[18] When asylum seekers first arrive, the host country has to spend money to process applicants, as well as for food, housing, health, and education. In the short term, the extra spending increases the country's aggregate demand or fiscal expansion. That means more goods and services are produced, resulting in more disposable income for native workers. It may well be argued that this makes up for downward pressures on wages and inflation when the asylum seekers finally enter the job market. The process can take up to two to three years depending on relevant rules of countries. Labour market integration helps fiscal sustainability for the host country, given the specific skill base of the migrants say from Syria. Companies therefore call for a more efficient refugee policy, so that admitting refugees and other forced migrants becomes a matter of both short-term and long-term investment rather than sunk cost.

In this context, it is important to note that forced migration flows overwhelm so-called pure refugee flows and are massive and mixed in nature whether they come to Europe or move within the South. In both cases migrant economies pose the issue of labour market integration, in both cases they carry the signatures of informal economy, and in both cases migrant economies, mostly informal in nature, subsume refugee economies and other labour market actors like climate migrants, illegal immigrants, economic migrants, etc. and are in turn subsumed in the dynamics of informal economy. The dynamics of Informal economy relating to types of economic activities (for instance in care and entertainment industry in countries of Europe) subsumes all distinctions between refugees and other victims of forced migration, illegal immigrants, environmental migrants, the internally displaced, the trafficked labour, and so on.

Thus, though the phenomenon of labour market segmentation of which Castles and Miller speak is true, we have to keep in mind the countervailing reality of the utmost flexibility of capitalism to create informal arrangements in production and circulation everywhere. In this connection we can refer to Michael J. Piore's classic study, *Birds of Passage*, where he argued that the conventional push and pull theory is simply wrong, and industrial development in one place always creates an informal, low-paid economy, and calls for the import of informal, low-wage labour for jobs that otherwise would not be performed.[19] Indeed, informality and segmentation go hand in hand. Between stereotyped and regularised skills and jobs, there is a range of work arrangements creating transitory forms of labour, which navigate several institutional spaces of the market. Betts and his colleagues note this in passing. They also suggest the fact, the significance of which is central to the emergence of the migrant as the labouring subject of our time, that migrant labour has the capacity to remain footloose.[20] This is what makes *transit labour*– a characteristic feature of the labour market today. The significance of the phenomenon of transit labour increases in the wake of the expansion of the logistical economies built around supply chains in the world.[21]

On the other hand, Stephen Castles' discussion on informal and hierarchised labour market proceeds, as if in an unspoken way, on the basis of the received history of nineteenth- and twentieth-century capitalism when immigrant labour was finally absorbed in formal industrial economies.[22] Yet this was also the time when immigrant workers, who had an overwhelming number of refugees among them (think of the Palestinian refugee-workers spread all over the Middle East), were made to survive in a footloose manner in coastal towns of southern France or Australia, or, say Italy, from where indeed workers moved onto France. As we suggested in the preceding chapter, this new history – the other part of the official history of expansion of industrial capitalism on the basis of an immigrant workforce – is now being made available to us by critical histories of migration. In short, the labouring subject of refugee economy remains footloose. The refugee economy is a footloose economy, whose relevance to global capitalism today lies in the salience of the informal mode of production and circulation.[23] The global now houses the informal within the formal. Thus a formal sportswear company in its production complex may engage informal makers of shoes, footballs, cricket bats, caps, etc., who are located across vast distances, or a fashion company may contract tanneries in distant countries of the South for polished leather goods including leather bags. This is possible because standards are global, and the refugee economy in order to survive has to follow the global standards and protocols. The refugee or the immigrant economy in this way becomes a part of the global supply chain of a commodity. Classic is the case of carpet making by Tibetan refugees in Nepal or Syrian refugees making leather and other garment products in Turkey or Bangladeshi immigrants in India engaged in garment making as in Kidderpore in Kolkata, or Afghan truck drivers in Pakistan, or Afghan construction workers in Iran.[24] Important also in this respect is the role of the migration system in a region in facilitating illegal trade in opium and other contraband goods.[25] Opportunities and constraints thus have a pattern.

Syrian refugees present an insightful corpus of experiences of how and when refugees become labouring subjects.[26] A report on Syrian refugees in Turkey, which does not need explication, says,

> When Remo Fouad, a 50-year-old pastry and dessert-maker, fled Aleppo three years ago, he left with little more than his family recipes. First he tried to open a sweet shop in Egypt, then in Lebanon, burning through the money he had secreted away in a Lebanese bank account. Both failed. . . . His story is far from unique. A wave of refugees is taking advantage of the opportunities

and relative ease of doing business in Turkey. . . . Since 2011, 4,000 new businesses have been set up by Syrians or Syrians with Turkish partners. . . . According to the Economic Policy Research Foundation, an Ankara-based think-tank, 1,600 were set up in 2015, with 590 more established in the first three months of this year alone.[27]

The report refers to the 2.7million-strong influx of Syrian refugees over the past half a decade to the migration of rural workers to cities – a classic stage of development often associated with a rise in countries' incomes. But, as it says, there are questions about the ability of the Turkish economy, which grew 5.7 per cent in the last quarter of 2015, to handle a demographic shift on such a scale. Added to that the report points out that the country's unemployment is already at 11 per cent, and many of the Syrian newcomers lack Turkish language skills. Some of the Syrian migrants live in abject poverty, with beggars on the streets of almost every Turkish town, and many live in camps. Some of course belong to the middleclass, with savings of their own or the ability to borrow. The report cites examples of such refugees like Mohamed Nizar Bitar, who ran ceramics factories in Syria, and then fled to Turkey in 2013. "He spent nearly $30,000 of his savings to get his family smuggled out, and then used his last $1,000 to open an Arabic food delivery service out of a basement." The report quoted him as saying, "I have started my life again twice; I can do it again." Many economists according to the report argue that Turkey will need to capitalise on such entrepreneurial drive, else the Syrian economic boost to the country would prove short lived.[28]

We can read another brief report along with the preceding one. This report is on Syrian refugees in Lebanon. It has a more complicated story, but brings out the same dynamics of informal labour and economy,

> Business has never been better at Abu Hazem's tiny grocery shop, thanks to crowds of Syrian refugees who come to use their new, UN-funded debit cards. But around the corner, Suleiman al-Sharafi's store is empty, and the future looks less bright. "I make less now than I did before the World Food Programme made contracts with Abu Hazem. All the Syrians go there," he says, slumped down in a chair behind the counter. "Only Lebanese come to my shop now, and they're all poor." Along Lebanon's impoverished rural frontiers, the main driver of business has become Syrian refugees – and the aid they bring with them. Refugees now comprise around half of the population of the northern border region of Akkar, where the two shopkeepers live. Aid organisations like the United Nations' World Food Programme (WFP) are turning to "cash aid" for refugees, hoping to support host communities too. But the programmes highlight the complex impact humanitarian crises can have on an economy already struggling to stay afloat. A 2013 World Bank report said neighbouring Syria's three-year conflict has cost Lebanon's economy about $7.5bn. Bachir el-Khoury, an independent economic researcher in Beirut, said Lebanon's debt, one of the world's biggest before the Syria

crisis, is now growing around five times faster than its economy. The IMF predicts it will reach 148 per cent of GDP this year. The presence of refugees has strained public services such as water, electricity and hospitals, which was weak even before the crisis.... Yet some businesses are profiting from the refugee tragedy. Merchants providing food and medicine have over 1m new Syrian customers – the equivalent of more than a quarter of Lebanon's population.... They help peripheral economies most at risk now, such as the poorer border regions."... In the 185 shops the WFP contracts across Lebanon, profits are sometimes doubled.... Blue WFP cards provide $30 per refugee, electronically deposited each month. They can be used only for food at contracted grocers.... The move to cash is controversial in the international aid community, where "in-kind aid" – tangible donations such as food or tents or mattresses – once dominated. But proponents argue that the refugees themselves are best placed to spend aid effectively.[29]

This of course links the management of informal economies on a global scale with the dynamics of global governance. Betts and his colleagues thus are only partly right when they say of their work,

The theoretical purpose of these three institutions of refugeehood (urban, protected camp, and emergency camp) is to highlight the ways in which refugees' different institutional contexts shape their economic opportunity structures. Rather than being inherently different from 'citizens' or 'migrants' what makes them distinct is a set of institutional features that shape their economic lives and interaction with markets.[30]

On the contrary, one may argue that global experiences of refugee and migrant economies suggest a broad uniformity of pattern in the formation of the labouring subjects from refugee and immigrant populations, namely that they form a huge dispersed population of footloose labour whose products are linked to global market chains.[31] These population groups must be made to work as per the requirements of the global supply chains of commodities and labour; on the other hand they must remain invisible from the public eye.

Borrowing from Saskia Sassen we may call this "expulsion" – exactly the dialectical opposite of the inclusion of the immigrant population in the global cities.[32] Sassen shows that soaring income inequality and unemployment, expanding populations of the displaced and imprisoned, accelerating destruction of land and water bodies can be understood in their complexity only as a type of expulsion from professional livelihood, living space, and the biosphere that makes life possible. From finance to mining, complex types of knowledge and technology are being deployed in ways that produce brutalities and result in predatory formations. Today's financial instruments are backed by engineering expertise that enables exploitation of the environment, trading in futures, also by the legal expertise that allows the world's rich countries to acquire vast stretches of territory from the poorer ones. And the brutal fact is that the sheer complexity of the global economy makes it hard to trace lines of responsibility for the displacements, evictions, and eradications it produces.

The market opportunities Betts and others speak of have to be seen in this context. In the context of their research on refugees in Uganda, Betts and his colleagues admit of "refugee economic activities being embedded in much wider Ugandan network and economies outside the settlements".[33] But this means not only network of opportunities, but also linkages of compulsions and burdens. The earlier vocabulary of "refugee burden" and the currently replacement vocabulary of "refugee asset" both hide the salient laws of the functioning of informal economy. The replacement of one phrase with another only suggests the increasing awareness of the social scientists and policy makers of the way neo-liberal global economy makes everyone a market enabled actor, though unequally.[34]

Thus, while more than thirty-five years ago ICARA 1 (International Conference on Assistance to Refugees in Africa, 1981) and ICARA 2 (1984) highlighted the "burden" that refugees placed on their hosts, such as additional costs on already hard-pressed public and social welfare budgets, arresting economic growth, distorting markets, causing environmental degradation and putting political strains on already fragile and conflict-affected countries, today several reports speak of refugees bringing in economic benefits and social capital, such as new skills and expanding market of food and building materials stimulating growth of the host economy, with the host community also benefiting from assistance programmes such as infrastructure and welfare services provided by agencies responding to refugees' needs.[35]

It is now being argued that to resolve the enigma of "refugee economy", analysts will have to ensure that, wherever possible, relevant stakeholder groups, four in particular – refugees, host population and country, area and country of origin, and providers of assistance (which will include presumably business houses providing marketing opportunities and capital advance to the displaced) – have to be incorporated into the analysis. Then quantitative parameters will have to be evolved to measure impacts (for example, income, assets, employment, and access to natural resources) together with mediating factors such as age, gender, and length of exile; also qualitative factors such as perceptions of security and protection will have to be identified. With these two methods, the goal has to be to construct an overall socio-economic profile and analyse how the profile is affected for each of the stakeholders by forced displacement. The host country's public sector fiscal costs and impacts in providing social and welfare assistance for refugees have to be measured, such as increased medical and education provision, increased demand for utilities such as water, and longer term capital costs and impacts such as infrastructure investment. And finally, while the methodology's focus will be on livelihoods and micro-economic impacts and costs, assessing the impacts at the macro-economic level will remain an equally important dimension of the analysis.[36]

All these at the end of the day are labour market analyses. They do not throw much light on the larger forces that lead to absorption or otherwise of refugee and immigrant labour in global economy.

Yet strangely, the absorption of the refugees and the migrants in the informal labour market and informal mode of production also produces the labouring subject's autonomy.[37] In their own ways both Castles and Miller and Betts and his colleagues ignore the underlying implication of autonomy of migration for the general global economy and in particular the political economy of the uprooted. Betts and his colleagues for instance point out the diversity of refugee livelihoods by type of employment arrangement.[38] They also point out the links of the refugees as economic actors with the supply chains marking the larger economy of an area.[39] Yet, they do not ask, how does this fact speak of the autonomy of migration?

Immigration and the production of precarious labour

The salience of Syrian and Iraqi refugees and asylum seekers is that they come from countries occupying the grey zone between the North and the South. With over 80 per cent literacy, a wide skill base for entrepreneurship, and high rate of women's participation in non-family forms of labour, these countries have produced refugees who have deployed knowledge in not only reaching countries where they seek asylum, they also quickly learn new skills, adapt themselves relatively quickly – in a year or two – to new requirements of language, labour protocols, self-run business rules, and learn to straddle the two different but interacting worlds of formal economy and the informal economy. The eventual absorption of current immigrant flows of skilled, semi-skilled, and unskilled labour in labour markets of Europe and countries of other regions (Brazil, South Africa, Hong Kong, the Gulf countries, etc.), albeit in differential manner, will not be much different from what had happened in Europe, United States, Canada, and Australia in the pre–Second World War years.[40] In this dense labour market scenario, pleas for labour market equality receive consideration from well-meaning economists and refugee studies specialists, but formal (political, legal) equality makes sense only if they are relevant for entry in labour markets.[41] Otherwise as labouring subject, the migrant's lack of political equality is the other side of her economic ability to enter the labour market. It is strange then that migration analysts rarely consider the two aspects together, namely lack of entry in the formal political arena accompanied by entry in the informal and sometimes formal labour market.[42] Migrant labour copes with this dichotomous world. For long, it was a case of political opportunity, but economic closure; now it is a case of economic opening (entry in the informal labour market), but political closure. Yet the migrant as the footloose labouring subject survives this upside-down world of politics/economics because he or she moves.

This return of economy to the centre stage of discussions on refugees and migrants may appear strange, but perhaps should not be so, if we recall that at the heart of the "durable solutions" debate in refugee studies circles, the issue of economic rehabilitation was always paramount. The formation of the UNHCR itself nudged by the UN Economic and Social Council was an effort towards finding out a durable solution to refugee crisis.[43] Economy buttressed by demography has been always the other scene of refugee and migration management in the modern capitalist age.

Let us go back to the issue of Syrian migrants. By December 2015, the UNHCR had registered over 4.39 million Syrian refugees (meeting the definition of a "protracted refugee situation"), with most staying in Lebanon, Jordan, Turkey, and Iraq. One of the most discussed, debated, and researched issues was the impact of Syrian refugees including the impact of Syrian child labour[44] on the labour markets of host communities. On one side, data demonstrated that the influx of Syrian refugees had stimulated host economies in the midst of a regional economic downturn by providing labour and purchasing power; on the other side, data also suggested that the large influx of refugees had negatively affected the labour market with increased competition for jobs and downward pressure on wages. The crucial thing here is that the size of the informal economy in the region made it difficult to accurately assess the true impact on regional economies. In any case Syrian labour was and became an almost permanent feature of host labour markets. In some cases, job competition was primarily between Syrian refugees and other migrant workers, not with host communities. Across the region, in particular in Lebanon and Jordan, Syrian workers were spread out. Around 160,000 Syrian migrant workers were in Jordan before the outbreak of the war, while in Lebanon estimates fluctuated around 200,000.[45] Formal labour market calculations coupled with wage increase/decrease calculations thus do not go far. *The Economist* concluded, "Evidence suggests that immigration has only a small impact on employment or wages. Unskilled workers and existing migrants are most vulnerable, as they are the closest substitutes for the new arrivals. But the effects are still measly."[46]

Given the significant economic inequalities and political polarizations around the world, refugees, asylum seekers, and other migrants have responded with their feet to large-scale conflicts in various parts of the world. Managers of global economy are now concerned with how to forge effective policy responses to protect economic institutions, prioritise budget items to maintain basic public needs, use monetary and exchange rate mechanisms and other central bank policies to shore up market confidence, and modulate access to labour markets programmes according to particular needs. There have been also thoughts on developmental aid to help rebuild infrastructure, and, more broadly, mobilise additional financing. The flurry of policy initiatives is only because immigrants have arrived at the centre of economy as labouring subjects. What to do with the migrants and how to manage and cope with migrant economies that have become almost permanent features of various parts of global economy with the arrival of the immigrants in several countries is now one of the major concerns of the IMF, ADB, World Bank, EU, and other international bodies.[47]

Policy responses concerning labour market form the other side of what has been called the autonomy of migration – a term that means among others the willingness and the capability of the migrants to move on from one condition to another, one job to another, one economic situation to another, and one economy to another. Autonomy of migration means thus heterogeneity of labour forms. This is again brought out by empirical studies, like the one conducted by Betts and his colleagues. That more than two-thirds of refugees are in protracted displacement, at times in camps and without the right to work or move freely, does not mean that they stay put in one place. As Betts and his colleagues in their research on African refugees demonstrated, despite the constraints placed on them, "vibrant economic systems often thrive below the radar, whether in the formal or informal economy".[48] Refugees are not economically isolated; they are part of complex systems that go beyond their communities and the boundaries of particular settlements. Their report tells us of maize grown in settlements then exported across borders to neighbouring countries, and Congolese jewellery and textiles imported from as far as India and China. Somali shops import tuna from Thailand, via the Middle East and Kenya. They are as a result mostly not a burden on host states. Betts' survey showed in Kampala 21 per cent of the refugees surveyed employ others, and of those, 40 per cent employ Ugandans. Refugees are also not economically homogenous. Informality produces heterogeneity. They are technologically adaptable to needs. And, they are far from uniformly dependent on international assistance. Betts's survey showed nearly all – 99 per cent– of rural refuges reported that they had at least some form of independent income-generating activity.[49] When they were asked what kind of assistance they wanted, financial assistance did not come out top. Instead, opportunities for autonomy – including education, business training, and resettlement – were valued highly. The report observed, "Refugees are part of international trade networks. They are integral parts of international, national and local value chains for commodities and services ranging from fresh farming produce, to textiles and jewellery, cosmetics, clothing, and transport."[50] Ironically, while Betts and his colleagues conclude from their findings that refugees can be made part of and are relevant to global supply chains of commodities, it is the global nature of the supply chains that produce footloose informal labour and ensure that various categories of the displaced finally add up to the reserve army of labour to be deployed where and when necessary to the extent that big refugee camps look like townships with specific economies linked to various commodity chains. And it is this condition that accounts for the relative autonomy of migration.[51] The *politics of control* produces the *politics of migration*, which is essentially one of creating and violating borders. An economy of migration and an economy of control accompany each other. It is in the control sites like camps, the refugee and migrant settlements, informal work places in cities and small towns, urban markets, transportation and construction hubs, waste processing jobs, and small-scale and artisanal mines that we find the migrant and the refugee as the labouring subject emerging. Marked by degraded work, controlled by market rules and compulsions, tied to the obligations of supply chains, subjected to low and a differential wage systems, and unregulated labour regimes characterised by violence – it is amidst this set of conditions that migration as a socio-economic and political practice realises its autonomy.

As a consequence, migrants' labour constitutes the core of many of the social, economic, and political struggles for equality, justice, and dignity. In country after country (from Singapore to the United States) migrants have formed part of the struggles for better wages, freedom, and just conditions of life. They have emerged as subjects of living labour as a constitutive and antagonistic element in capital labour relation. Exploitation of labour was and more today is a social process; and exploitation of migrants is grounded in the entire migratory process and experience, and yet as in the case of other experiences of living labour this exploitation is always confronted with migrants' agency. As Sandro Mezzadra reminds us, this confrontation is the condition of possibility of migration and the material basis of the migrant to emerge as living labour.[52]

The exploitation of migrant as labour is linked to the nature of irregularity, which marks most of migrant economy, and the migrant as a worker. Yet, it is this precariousness originating from irregular conditions that contributes to the autonomy of migration. Autonomy clearly emerges as a profoundly ambivalent condition from the point of stable, regular economy of contemporary capitalism. The autonomous migrant as the living subject of labour tells us, precisely as the reports of Betts and many others cited here show, of the common conditions of social cooperation and production. Therein is the significance of migrant labour, whose marks are irregularity, informality, subjection to unequal labour regimes, degradation of work, footloose nature, subjection to violence, and the fundamental relevance of migrant labour to the logistical aspect of neo-liberal capitalism, such as construction labour, work in supply chains, waste processing including e-waste recycling, and last but not least in the care and entertainment industries.[53]

The last area of work mentioned in the previous line is important for our discussion here, not least because in discussions on migrant economy sex work is almost absent. Yet it is in discussions on sex work and trafficking that we find all the paradoxes of the labour market reality. In fact, the trafficking framework is inadequate for the purpose of analysing the experiences of sex work and exploitation in the field of commercial sex. The problems migrants encounter in this field are more often related to the institutional structures of immigration and the implementation of prostitution policies that restrict and prevent possibilities of migration. Sex work is a migrant-dominated field throughout the world. A recent study shows that half of the sex workers in Europe are migrants, and in West Europe the percentage is much higher – nearly 60 to 75 per cent.[54] While sex work is not criminalised in many countries, migrant sex work is often regulated through immigration policies. Work permits for migrants coming from outside the country for sex work are very difficult to obtain. Yet, this situation creates "double" markets where migrants work in more precarious condition, and become footloose, and gain agency through the interface of sex work and migration.

We rarely analyse the situation from the migrant's point of view because of the dominance of the discourse on trafficking, which means that migrant sex work is seen always in the context of sex trafficking, known today as modern slavery. Once again we can refer to Stephen Castles who viewed the issue in the context of smuggling and trafficking only,[55] and put the increasing incidence of worldwide trafficking to violence, poverty, famine, war, and persecution. He and his co-author Mark Miller also related trafficking to feminisation of migration, for instance from the Philippines.[56] But, Castles and Miller were not interested in migrant sex workers, their work problems, the labour markets issues, and punitive and control measures on migrants who undertake sex work. In fact *The Age of Migration* hardly paid any serious attention to the issue of migrant sex work.

In this way we rarely take into account the struggles and negotiations on restrictions of movements and against constraints in the labour market. The trafficking discourse also takes our focus away from labour market analysis, analysis of the associated institutional and structural framework, such as border and immigration controls, visa requirements, and a discriminatory labour protection framework that can be very much racist. As one analyst has shown,

> The majority of the sex workers either migrate with help of temporary visas to do sex work, or, if they are more settled migrants, they had often initially arrived through marriage and later ended up in sex work. Marriage or other intimate arrangements with former customers are also central to the sex workers' residency strategies.[57]

She also shows how immigration policies form different opportunities of movement and income for migrants depending on their country of origin. For instance, the majority of the sex workers in Finland come from Russia and former Soviet countries. One reason for this is that it is relatively easy for Russians to get a tourist visa to the EU, unlike migrants from African or Southeast Asian countries. And thus, sex workers on arrival find themselves in different positions depending on their race or ethnicity, working environment, age, gender, income security, and support networks. Border regimes thus not so much separate but differentiate, and contemporary border and immigration controls thus have more than territorial function. These controls modulate access, in this case of the sex workers, to labour markets. The situation produces circular migrants, who would not have the protection of welfare benefits, but on the other hand face continuous deportation threats and possibilities.[58] "Hence labour market restrictions can function as an *institutional form of immobilization* of these migrants" (Emphasis in the original).[59] Yet labour market restrictions become a catalyst in producing footloose labour. Labour market restrictions have been rarely able to do away with informal work regimes. The functioning of neo-liberal economy depends on the interrelations mentioned in this chapter.

In short, immigration policies produce precarious labour. Important to note in this context – and this has general significance for the task of theorising the migrant as living labour – is that, migrants in the informal labour market are not always particularly dependent on specific employers. Often their fate depends on immigration policies, as in Canada where an expansive accommodation policy towards the migrants has resulted in greater regularisation of employment.[60] For the migrant sex workers, with lack of alternative ways of movement, residency strategies, and forms of income, patriarchal relations of dependency are created. Borders, thought to have only a distant relation with economy, come to occupy a central place of importance in the labouring lives of refugee and migrant populations. They reproduce the overall uncertain conditions of the life of labour under capitalism. In this way, they and migrant labour in general become one of the important destabilising elements in the trajectory of neo-liberal capitalism that desperately wants to stabilise and make the refugee and the migrant a natural, market-enabled actor.[61]

This calls for a rigorous analysis of the link between the refugee-like condition and capitalism, and understand thereby the reasons why refugees and migrants working for low wages are essential for capitalism. This is a complex scenario, and this chapter has tried to demonstrate that this is not a simple case of episodes of "accumulation by dispossession", a phrase made famous by David Harvey. Clearly, a deeper process of production of living labour occasioned by unequal exchange and the extraction of surplus from low-income countries and the forging of new supply chains is at work here. After all, when the capitalists cannot afford to bear the full costs of social reproduction of labour (and think of high-skilled labour and knowledge economy of the North) that most of the labouring people have to be part-time wage earners who must use family, kinship, bodies, and traditional other (relatively) non-market resources for their reproduction.[62] The social reproduction of such labour takes a variety of forms, including, say one that ensures that deported immigrants from the United States can work at call centres in new lands (Hispanic) where they have been deported because they now have the required language felicity (in this case English) to serve the call centres.[63] The interesting point about all these reports put together is that they represent a rainbow attempt – if you like a global strategy – to create a life or a global society of refugees – parallel to the life we live. Thus, policies of right to work, resettlement programmes based on economic steps, integration in labour markets, refugee doctors in host health care systems, refugee-run rural grocery stores, interface with criminal organisations and networks, digital empowerment, skill generation, validating high academic qualifications of refugees, gig economy, livestock in refugee camps, sheltering animals in refugee camps, refugee-led education, etc., – all those themes we find in the literature on refugee economies present a collective life, functioning as a collective supplement to the life of the non-refugees.[64]

To conclude, the question of the production of living labour in a study of refugee economy is important because it puts in a critical perspective the necessity of the states and the international regime of protection to synchronise the economic and the political strategies of protection. The refugees and the migrants to be treated as labour must become de jure subjects, citizens or almost citizens with proper registration, defined entitlements and rights, at times with rights-claiming voices, and right kinds of attributes and skills. Only then can they be helped to become market-enabled actors. Yet the disjuncture between the two strategies of protection is not only typical of the postcolonial parts of the globe, the disjuncture is evident in the developed countries also – in Europe and the United States.[65] The search for "economically viable" migrant labour continues both in Europe and the United States; and nearly every time the rulers in these lands deploy the language of subsistence and economic independence, they quickly recoil back to the assertion that they must also fight the external agents of violence, tighten the borders, and remain vigilant. Such a paradox calls for a policy of permanent flexibility, so that the different temporalities of migration can be made to work to suit the economic interests of the dominant classes/states. Thus, in Europe (for instance, the recent German determination) Afghanistan is now a "safe" and "stable" regime, while Syria is a "crisis", which means that in practice "crisis" in Syria allows a government to selectively accept an influx of variably skilled labour (say, Turkish or Syrian refugees) while shutting the door on unskilled migrants from slower, steadier streams (for instance, migration of the Afghans).

In this way, capital sets in motion movements of labour within a specific field of force that dictates how and why migrant labour is to be harnessed, disciplined, and governed (for instance the dominant presence of immigrant labour in logistics, health care, agriculture, etc.), and that shapes the links between "strategies" (that control migrants once they are in motion) and the mechanisms that set these movements in motion. Fostering mobile footloose labour is functional more than ever to capital's reproduction – and this "flexibility" is the dialectical other to migrants' autonomy. The resilient migrant labour is therefore an adaptive agent, and indeed, neo-liberal capitalism in order to continue has to keep on fostering these adaptive subjects.[66]

The postcolonial age of migration thus not only indicates a geopolitical and geo-economic division of the globe between countries of the North and those of the South with population flows from the latter to the former, but also the production of these relations within the countries of the South as well as within and among the countries of the North. Migration (along with forced migration) therefore indicates a relation. Today it indicates above all some of the ways labour is produced in:

(a) Commodity production such as development of sites (with constructed buildings, lines, roads, terminals, townships etc.) along with production of mining sites such as coal and mineral ores, etc., and
(b) In logistical operations like waste reprocessing, shipping, port terminals, transportation, managing supply chains of various commodities including human bodies (known among others as human smuggling and trafficking), or the laying of cables.

Most of these operations known for their extractive character require migrant labour. They speak of certain relations in global economy, which are combinations of the postcolonial relations as well as neo-liberal relations. They also show that the question of labour and thus of economic interests lies at the heart of the resolution of the refugee and the migrant question.

Notes

1 For instance, Stephen Castles, "Migration", in David Theo Goldberg and John Solomos (eds.), *A Companion to Racial and Ethnic Studies* (Oxford: Blackwell Publishers, 2002), pp. 561–579, 570–572.
2 Typical of this approach is the collection of writings and reports in *Forced Migration Review*, 58, June 2018, the theme of the issue is "Economies: Rights and Access to Work" (hereafter *ERAW*).
3 Alex Betts, Louise Bloom, Josiah Kaplan, and Naohiko Omata, *Refugee Economies: Forced Displacement and Development* (Oxford: Oxford University Press, 2017).

4 For instance, report by Naohito Omata, "Refugees' Engagement with Host Economies in Uganda", *ERAW*, pp. 19–21; also report by Martin Ledstrup and Marie Larsen, "From Refugee to Employee: Work Integration in Rural Denmark", *ERAW*, pp. 14–16.
5 Michel Agier, *Managing the Undesirables: Refugee camps and Humanitarian Government*, trans. David Fernbach (London: Polity Press, 2011).
6 Alex Betts and his colleagues also take note of this factor in their discussion of the threefold institutional context of refugee economies – urban, protected camp, and emergency camp – *Refugee Economies*, p. 202.
7 Stephen Castles and Mark J. Miller, *The Age of Migration: International Population Movements in the Modern World*, 3rd ed. (Hampshire, Basingstoke: Palgrave MacMillan, 2003), chapter 8, "Migrants and Minorities in the Labour Force", pp. 178–197.
8 *Ibid.*, p. 183.
9 Stephen Castles and Mark J. Miller, *The Age of Migration: International Population Movements in the Modern World*, 3rd ed. (Hampshire, Basingstoke: Palgrave MacMillan, 2003), p. 179. The issue of strategies by migrant such as self-employment, small business, mutual aid, ethnic niches, etc., to deal with labour market disadvantages has been dealt at length by Betts and his co-authors.
10 Many of the observations including cited figures in this paragraph are based on J. Edward Taylor, Mateusz J. Filipski, Mohamed Alloush, Anubhab Gupta, Ruben Irvin Rojas Valdes, and Ernesto Gonzalez-Estrada, "Economic Impact of Refugees", *PNAS (Proceedings of the National Academy of Sciences of the United States of America)*, Volume 113 (27), July 2016, pp. 7449–7453.
11 Margaret E. McGuiness discusses the 1951 Convention's "limited nature of the definition of a refugee" in her essay, "Legal and Normative Dimensions of the Manipulation of Refugees", in Stephen John Stedman and Fred Tanner (eds.), *Refugee Manipulation: War, Politics, and the Abuse of Human Suffering* (Washington, DC: Brookings Institution Press, 2003), Chapter 5, pp. 135–166.
12 B.S. Chimni, "The Birth of a 'Discipline' – From Refugee to Forced Migration Studies", *Journal of Refugee Studies,* Volume 22 (1), 2009, pp. 11–29.
13 The concept of "mixed and massive flows" is indirectly admitted by the UNHCR; see the UNHCR document, "Mixed Migration: A 10 Point Plan of Action", www.unhcr.org/mixed-migration.html (accessed on 19 January 2017); "Refugees' and 'Migrants' – Frequently Asked questions", question 8–9 www.unhcr.org/news/latest/2016/3/56e95c676/refugees-migrants-frequently-asked-questions-faqs.html (accessed on 14 January 2017); see also Christophe Tometten, "Judicial Response to Mixed and Massive Population Flows", *Refugee Watch*, Volume 39–40, June–December 2012, pp. 125–140, www.mcrg.ac.in/rw%20files/RW39_40/11.pdf (accessed on 1 December 2017); "The Issue: The Growing Salience of Mixed Migration", and "Mixed Migration: Policy Challenges", *The Migration Observatory*, 24 March 2011, www.migrationobservatory.ox.ac.uk/resources/primers/mixed-migration-policy-challenges/ (accessed on 15 January 2017); and Report of the UN Secretary-General, "In Safety and Dignity: Addressing Large Movements and Refugees and Migrants", 9 May 2016, www.un.org/pga/70/wp-content/uploads/sites/10/2015/08/21-Apr_Refugees-and-Migrants-21-April-2016.pdf (accessed on 29 January 2017).
14 UK is a case in point.

> In the early 2000s, in response to a rise in asylum applications, it constructed a network of detention centres, ostensibly to process applications more quickly, and made the system tougher. Asylum seekers are banned from working and must live on £36.95 a week, one of the lowest rates in Western Europe. Detainees can be locked up for unlimited periods while allegations of verbal abuse and mistreatment have been widely reported. The institutional violence of this system is hidden.

Daniel Trilling, "What to Do with the People Who Do Make It Across?" *London Review of Books*, Volume 37(19), 2015, pp. 9–12, 12, www.lrb.co.uk/v37/n19/daniel-trilling/what-to-do-with-the-people-whodo-make-it-across (accessed on 3 January 2016).

15 "An Economic Take on the Refugee Crisis: A Macroeconomic Assessment for the EU", European Commission, Directorate-General for Economic and Financial Affairs, Institutional Paper 033, July 2016, p. 3.
16 *Ibid.*, p. 17.
17 *Ibid.*, p. 19.
18 *Euronews*, 1 November 2016 -www.euronews.com/2016/11/01/refugees-in-germany-from-desperation-to-economic-fortune (accessed on 1 January 2017).
19 Michael J. Piore, *Birds of Passage: Migrant Labor and Industrial Societies* (Cambridge: Cambridge University Press, 1979). Piore argued that such low paid, informal labour from outside never comes to settle permanently in the place they migrate to, and in this connection, he analysed the migration of Afro-American labour to the north of the United States.
20 Alex Betts, Louise Bloom, Josiah Kaplan, and Naohiko Omata, *Refugee Economies: Forced Displacement and Development* (Oxford: Oxford University Press, 2017), p. 120.
21 The idea of transit labour investigates changing patterns of labour and mobility in the whirlwind of global, particularly Asian, capitalist transformation. Mindful of the view of Asia as the world's factory, the idea tells us of the new labour, largely footloose in nature, engaged in logistical enterprises such as construction of infrastructure, transportation routes like roadways and highways, handling container cargo, processing waste including e-waste, etc. See, http://transitlabour.asia/about/ (accessed on 1 December 2016).
22 In this context we can refer to Stephen Castles' own study co-authored with Godula Kosack, *Immigrant Workers and Class Structure in Western Europe* (London: Institute of Race Relations, 1973).
23 Nora Bardelli drawing on a number of studies has argued in "The Shortcomings of Employment as a Durable Solution", *ERAW*, pp. 54–55 that this approach of refugee assistance regime prevailing today, namely the "best or only solution to protracted refugee situations is firmly rooted in improving access to employment . . . inevitably favours some and excludes others, while also ignoring the deeper political and social issues at stake" (p. 54).
24 Chris Walter, "Weaving a Future for Tibetan Refugees: Tibetan Rug Weaving Project", *Cultural Survival Quarterly Magazine*, Volume 27 (2), June 2003; the report states,

> The project's first rugs concentrated primarily on Tibetan designs, but the project's participants realized that the market was much too diverse to restrict themselves in this way; the weavers now continue to weave traditional designs, but the inventory of over 250 designs contains those inspired from traditions in every part of the world as well as modern designs of weavers' own creation.

www.culturalsurvival.org/publications/cultural-survival-quarterly/weaving-future-tibetan-refugees-tibetan-rug-weaving (accessed on 20 January 2017); "Syrian Refugees in Turkish Garment Supply Chains", Report by Business and Human Rights Resource Centre, February 2016, https://business-humanrights.org/sites/default/files/160131%20Syrian%20Refugee%20Briefing%20FINAL.pdf (accessed on 19 January 2017); also "Syrian Refugees Working in Turkey's garment Sector", Report by Ethical Trading Initiative, www.ethicaltrade.org/programmes/syrian-refugees-working-in-turkeys-garment-sector (accessed on 19 January 2017). The report said, "Turkey has seen an influx of almost three million Syrian refugees. With few legal opportunities to earn money, many seek work in Turkey's 'informal' garment sector. Here, refugees – including children – can be subject to poor working conditions and very low wages. Turkey's apparel, textiles and leather industries: Turkey's popularity as an international sourcing destination has grown due to its ability to produce high-quality products quickly. It is now the third largest exporter of garments and leather goods to Europe after Bangladesh and China. However it is an industry with a large, unregulated sector. Traditionally, workers have also faced many difficulties. These include long working hours, poor wages and gender discrimination. The garment sector's share of Turkey's GDP is 7 per cent. Its export value to Turkey is USD 12 billion; there are 1.04 million of registered workers in the regulated sector, and 1 million estimated numbers of workers thought to be working informally, of whom an increasing number are Syrian refugees. . . . Significant concerns remain. So far, take up of work permits has been slow, for example. This is thought to be due to application restrictions and registration issues. Consequently, child labour and illegal working remain serious issues." See also, Shahram Khosravi, *'Illegal' Traveller: An auto-Ethnography of Borders* (Basingstoke, Hampshire: Palgrave MacMillan, 2010), pp. 18–19; on Bangladeshi immigrant workers in garment making in Kidderpore, Kolkata, see R. Samaddar, *The Marginal Nation: Transborder Migration from Bangladesh to West Bengal* (New Delhi: Sage, 1999), chapter.

25 The Afghanistan-Iran migration system is an instance of the involvement of entire migrant populations in such trade. See, *'Illegal' Traveller: An auto-Ethnography of Borders*, chapter 2; the recent Afghanistan-Iran migration history also shows how the even so-called pure "refugee" flows are often mixed. As one analyst shows, Afghan refugee flows have built on earlier migrant labour flows and even return of the refugees to Afghanistan is only a phase in a "rite of passage", in which the Hazara must go abroad, cope with the rough world of work and survival, and then return to the native land to complete the process of growing up. This return too may be a prelude to another journey to Iran or Pakistan. Refugee flows from Afghanistan built on the kinship networks in this way. See, Alessandro Monsutti, "Migration as a Rite of Passage: Young Afghans Building Masculinity and Adulthood in Iran", *Iranian Studies*, Volume 40 (2), April 2007, pp. 167–185. Monsutti wrote,

> In 2005, over one million documented Afghans were present in Iran, mostly people living in households. There were also some 500,000 undocumented labor migrants who have left their families behind in their country of origin and constantly move back and forth between Afghanistan and Iran. Most of them are working in the agriculture and construction sectors.
>
> *(p. 171)*

and further,

> The Afghan laborers live scattered in the Iranian society, moving . . . from one building site to another, following work opportunities. They form temporary groupings as the employment structures and the possibilities to find a job. . . . Social networks are only partially determined by kinship, and migration offers to young Afghans the opportunity to diversify their social relations. Certain enterprising and competent individuals are promoted to take charge of a work team. The foreman is usually an Afghan himself and has responsibility for the hiring of workers. The Iranian employer allows him considerable leeway and, so long as things are running smoothly, does little to intervene in the everyday organization of work. The laborers group around a central personality and it is the relations of each individual with that figure which are decisive. The members of the team do not necessarily know one another, since the sources of the relationship with the foreman may be sociologically diverse: paternal kinship. . ., maternal kinship. . ., kinship through marriage. . ., neighborhood circle in the village of origin, and so on.
>
> *(p. 176)*

26 A recent and exhaustive analysis of war, dispossession, and Syrian mobility, Nergis Canefe, *The Syrian Exodus in Context: Crisis, Dispossession, and Mobility in the Middle East* (Istanbul: Bilgi University Press, 2019).
27 "Syrian Refugee Entrepreneurs Boost Turkey's Economy", Report by Mehul Srivastava, *Financial Times*, 16 May 2016, www.ft.com/content/93e3d794-1826-11e6-b197-a4af20d5575e (accessed on 6 January 2017).
28 *Ibid.*
29 Erika Solomon, "Mixed Fortunes in Lebanese Refugee Economy", *Financial Times*, 11 April 2014, www.ft.com/content/c403e0a0-c098-11e3-8578-00144feabdc0 (accessed on 13 January 2017).
30 Alex Betts, Louise Bloom, Josiah Kaplan, and Naohiko Omata, *Refugee Economies: Forced Displacement and Development* (Oxford: Oxford University Press, 2017), p. 54; also read

the analytic report by Paul Collier, "Refugee Economics", *Milken Institute Review*, 2 May 2016, www.milkenreview.org/articles/refugee-economics (accessed on 18 January 2017); the report said among others,

> Jordan alone has around a million Syrian refugees. Its largest camp, Za'atari, is only minutes away from a virtually empty industrial zone large enough to employ more than the entire labour force of the camp. Jordan has over 40 such industrial zones and many camps across the country, all of which could potentially provide jobs for refugees near temporary housing. The core of the jobs strategy would be to bring new manufacturing to these zones that would employ both refugees and Jordanians. It is, of course, essential that sufficient numbers of these jobs go to Jordanians; otherwise, the host population would have good reason to be resentful and so the Jordanian government would not permit it. Over and above their economic functionality, using zones as the core of the jobs strategy is politically attractive. The process of setting up new firms in the zones and thereby creating new jobs is easily recognizable by ordinary Jordanian citizens as a positive-sum process in which Jordanian workers gain directly and indirectly along with the refugees. Politically, providing jobs in zones is sharply distinct from simply lifting the restriction on refugees competing for jobs anywhere in Jordan. Economists might like to claim that such generosity would be mutually beneficial, but try telling that to the locals.

31 The classic instance of such links will be migrant labour in extractive industries like iron ore mining linked to the fluctuations in the prices of steel. For instance, informal and artisanal mining of iron ore went up along with formal production of iron ore before the Beijing Olympic Games. In the Indian Northeast, migrant labour, including from Nepal and Bangladesh, makes coal mining in the ecologically sensitive Jaintia Hills located in the north-eastern state of India, Meghalaya, possible. The hills are pock-marked with holes. Money lies at the bottom of steep, sheer holes dug 100–180 feet deep into the ground. Sudden rain, a tipped cart, a falling rock – just about anything can mean death in the hostile pits of the Jaintia Hills. Some estimate that a staggering 70,000 children from Nepal, Bangladesh, Assam, Bihar, and Jharkhand work in these private mines. Typically, a labour camp shelters twenty-five miners. Mining is rewarding, for while a driver may not earn more than Rs 5,000, mining can fetch around Rs 8,000 to 10,000 a month. Around one hundred thousand metric tonnes of coal, worth around Rs 500 million, is extracted from the Jaintia mines every day, and the government receives a royalty of Rs 290 per tonne; the mine owners sell it for Rs 4,200 per tonne. Life is temporary in every way in the rat mines of Meghalaya. The government does not think that any special action is necessary in this situation. Meghalaya has three autonomous district councils, which by law, have the sole authority to lease and license mines. Traditional institutions openly flout mining norms, and land is let out at will to private operators. Most mine owners procure gelatine sticks and detonators on the black market from licensed contractors. Accidents often go unreported. The government collects royalties from mine operators and even issues them receipts. Figures taken from the collection of reports from the site dedicated to mining scams in India: http://bellary0.hpage.co.in/reddy-bros_1024057.html (accessed on 12 October 2016) and a report in *Tehelka Magazine* by Kunal Majumder (3 July, 2010); it is also important to note that the UN Special Rapporteur's Report on the human rights of the migrants placed distributed by the General Assembly on 3 April 2014 noted the risks of particular groups of migrant workers and reminds us of the situation described here (UN 2014).

32 Saskia Sassen, *Expulsions: Brutality and Complexity in the Global Economy* (Cambridge: Harvard University Press, 2014).

33 Alex Betts, Louise Bloom, Josiah Kaplan, and Naohiko Omata, *Refugee Economies: Forced Displacement and Development* (Oxford: Oxford University Press, 2017), p. 123; Where Betts and his colleagues admit of constraints, it is "constraints arising from refugeehood"(p. 138). They do not speak of the general linkages and constraints of the informal economy, for which refugees and migrants with their particular de-institutionalised lives and regulations become the most appropriate subjects.

34 Not unexpectedly, the UNHCR commissioned a study in 2011 for innovation that laid emphasis on the organisation's private sector engagements. The UNHCR's Innovation Unit of the UNHCR evolved in this way to become a platform for collaboration between the UNHCR Divisions, refugees, academia, and the private sector (such as Vodafone, IKEA Foundation, Microsoft, etc.) to address complex refugee challenges. See for instance, http://innovation.unhcr.org/about-us/ (accessed on 4 January 2017). Betts also mentions the collaboration between a Silicon Valley company like Samasource and the international NGO Care International for Somali refugees following Samasource's work in the Dadaab camp focusing on crowdsourcing. (Alex Betts, Louise Bloom, Josiah Kaplan, and Naohiko Omata, *Refugee Economies: Forced Displacement and Development* (Oxford: Oxford University Press, 2017), pp. 196–197.

35 For instance, a report on Dadaab refugee camp speaks of positive impact – "In Search of Protection and Livelihoods: Socio-economic and Environmental Impacts of Dadaab Refugee Camps on Host Communities", Joint Report by Government of Denmark, Government of Kenya, and Government of Norway, *Reliefweb*, September 2010, http://reliefweb.int/report/kenya/search-protection-and-livelihoods-socio-economic-and-environmental-impacts-dadaab (accessed on 1 January 2017); the report claimed the positive economic impact of the camps for the host community was USD 14 million – about 25 per cent of the per capita income of the province. Income benefits to the host community from the sale of livestock and milk alone were USD3 million, while over 1,200 local people benefited from refugee camp-related employment or trade-related work. Roger Zetter referred to the Report while discussing the issue, "Are Refugees an Economic Burden or Benefit?" *Forced Migration Review*, 41, December 2012, pp. 50–52, www.fmreview.org/preventing/zetter.html (accessed on 19 January 2017).

36 Roger Zetter, "Are Refugees an Economic Burden or Benefit?" Zetter gives the example of Afghans in truck driving business in Pakistan.

The case of Afghan refugees in Pakistan is instructive on this point. According to a report, many Afghan refugees never participated in a refugee census for fear of forced repatriation. Nasreen Ghufran, "Afghan Refugees in Pakistan Current Situation and Future Scenario", *Policy Perspectives*, Volume 3 (2), The Muslim World, Institute of Policy Studies, n.d., www.ips.org.pk/the-muslim-world/1023-afghan-refugees-in-pakistan-current-situation-and-future-scenario/(accessed on 15 march 2017). These undocumented Afghan refugees, as several reports point out, along with the documented refugees work as loaders, carriers, shopkeepers, stone crushers, agricultural labourers, and as workers in cotton, textile, and several other industries including dry fruit processing, besides working in subaltern supply chains of sex and substance. The report of a socio-economic survey of Afghan refugees in Pakistan, conducted by the Danish Refugee Council (*Socio-Economic Survey of Afghan Refugees Living in Pakistan*, Danish Refugee Council, May 2013), conducted in five districts of Khyber Pakhunkhwa province in April 2013 brought out the following aspects: Almost half of the respondents reported that they took out a loan when they did not find jobs; a majority of the respondents were working as shopkeepers, followed by carriage drivers' and tailors; a majority of the respondents believed that shop keeping was the most profitable source of income; 57 per cent of the survey respondents were unskilled, and three-fourths (75%) of the respondents reported that they considered good remuneration while opting for any jobs; the majority of the survey's respondents wanted to get vocational training related to tailoring, auto mechanic, carpentry, masonry, and furniture making. Women wanted to learn embroidery and sewing; overall 83 per cent of the survey respondents wanted to stay in Pakistan, and half of the respondents did not want to go back to Afghanistan due to lack of livelihood opportunities there (p. 3). The report recommended (once more taking us to the labour market approach) that new and sustainable employment opportunities with entrepreneurial livelihood strategies need to be created for the refugees; since shop keeping, tailoring, transport and agriculture/farming are the most engaged domains, business interventions in these areas can bring about productive results; a market assessment should be conducted in select provinces of Afghanistan to identify the most demanding skills, so that this may help in the repatriation process; identification and establishment of micro-credit resources can enhance livelihood options for refugees; small and medium enterprises should be designed for unemployed refugees; in case of decline in the availability of labor, refugees should be skilled to cope better with the needs of emerging markets and adopt more profitable diversified enterprise; and finally refugees should be facilitated to learn technical business skills and business promotion strategies. (p. 14). See also in this regard, the UNHCR report, *Solutions Strategy for Afghan Refugees, Update 2015–16*(Geneva: UNHCR, 2016). The report brings out the inadequacy of the labour market approach. The labour market approach principally implied: a proper census and registration of Afghan citizens in Pakistan; increased assistance for development and reintegration in Afghanistan; development assistance for areas affected by the long presence of large numbers of Afghans and development assistance for communities who are presently hosting Afghan Population or Refugee villages. See also for a general description of the socio-economic condition of the early phase of Afghan refugees in Pakistan, Mohammad Najim Azadzoi, *Settlements of Afghan Refugees in Pakistan: An Evaluation of Conditions and Identification of Problems*, M.Sc. dissertation, Department of Architecture, MIT, 1984.

37 Observers noted long ago that in postcolonial economies refugee resettlement through gradual absorption in national labour force resulted in a by and large supersession of refugee identity by a settler identity. See for instance, the study of refugee resettlement of Indian refugees in the Andaman Islands by Madhumita Mazumdar, "Dwelling in Fluid Places: The Matuas of the Andaman Islands", in Clare Anderson, Madhumita Mazumdar, and Vishvajit Pandya (eds.), *New Histories of the Andaman Islands: Landscape, Place and Identity in the Bay of Bengal, 1790–2012* (Cambridge: Cambridge University Press, 2016), pp. 170–200; also, Kaustabhmani Sengupta, "Taking Refuge in the City: Migrant Population and Urban Management in Post-Partition Calcutta", in R. Samaddar (ed.), *Migrants and the Neoliberal City* (Hyderabad: Orient Blackswan, 2018), Chapter 1, pp. 23–46.

38 Alexander Betts, Louise Bloom, Josiah Kaplan, and Naohiko Omata, *Refugee Economies: Rethinking Popular Assumptions*, p. 27.

39 In this context see the fascinating narration in *Refugee Economies*, chapter 9, "The Role of Business", pp. 186–199, which hints at the larger role of supply chains in shaping refugee economies, but Betts and colleagues do not explicate the implications.

40 Stephen Castles discussed the role of immigrant labour in Nazi Germany and post-war France, where immigrant workers accounted for at least 15 per cent of the work force. See his article "Migration" in David Theo Goldberg and John Solomos (eds.), *A Companion to Racial and Ethnic Studies* (Oxford: Blackwell Publishers, 2002), pp. 571–572.

41 The investigations of labour flows into the Gulf countries in West Asia bring out the interrelations between socio-political inequalities playing into structures of migrant labour market. See Malini Mittal's work, *Work, Mobility, and Changing Family Relations: A Study of a Section of South Asian Pink Collar Workers in Kuwait*, Unpublished Ph.d dissertation, Delhi School of Economics, University of Delhi, 2017.

42 In "Democracy and Multicultural Citizenship: Australian Debates and Their Relevance for Western Europe", in Rainer Baubock (ed.), *From Aliens to Citizens: Redefining the Status of Immigrants in Europe* (Aldershot: Ashgate and European Centre Vienna, 1994), pp. 3–28, Stephen Castles discusses at length the issue of political equality, particularly equality of opportunity and equality of resources (p. 12), yet leaves out the issue of entry in the labour market completely.

43 See in this context, the discussion by Peter Gatrell, *The Making of the Modern Refugee* (Oxford: Oxford University Press, 2015), chapter 3, "Europe Uprooted: Refugee Crisis in the Mid-Century and 'Durable Solutions'", pp. 89–117.

44 BBC report by Andrew Hosken, "Syrian Child Refugees 'Being Exploited in Jordan'", 4 November 2015, www.bbc.com/news/world-middle-east-34714021 (accessed on 12 May 2018)

45 Report of the International Rescue Committee (IRC), "Economic Impacts of Syrian Refugees" (n.d.), www.rescue.org/sites/default/files/document/465/ircpolicybriefeco nomicimpactsofsyrianrefugees.pdf (accessed on 18 January 2017); the same report also noted that that the vast majority of Syrian refugees who found work entered the large

informal economies characteristic of the region's host countries. Agriculture, construction, food services and retail dominate the informal labour market, and are all sectors were not typically attractive to the majority of host workers. Reliance on migrant workers was therefore necessary as a growing educated labour force in the host country refused to engage in certain sectors seen to be non-remunerative or lacking dignity. See also the report by John Cassidy, "The Economics of Syrian Refugees", *The New Yorker*, 18 November 2015, www.newyorker.com/news/john-cassidy/the-economics-of-syrian-refugees (accessed on 4 January 2017); also see in the same vein the Brookings Institution Report by Massimiliano Cali and Samia Sekkarie, "Much Ado About Nothing? The Economic Impact of Refugee 'Invasions'", 16 September 2015, www.brookings.edu/blog/future-development/2015/09/16/much-ado-about-nothing-the-economic-impact-of-refugee-invasions/ (accessed on 15 January 2017).

46 "The Economic Impact of Refugees, For Good or Ill: Europe's New Arrivals Will Probably Dent Public Finances, but Not Wages", *The Economist*, 23 January 2016, www.economist.com/news/finance-and-economics/21688938-europes-new-arrivals-will-probably-dent-public-finances-not-wages-good-or-ill (accessed on 20 January 2017).

47 For instance, see an IMF staff discussion note by Bjorn Rother, Gaelle Pierre, Davide Lombardo, Risto Herrala, Priscilla Toffano, Eric Roos, Greg Auclair, and Karina Manasseh, "The Economic Impact of Conflicts and the Refugee Crisis in the Middle East and North Africa", IMF Staff Paper, SDN/16/08, September 2016, pp. 9–18.

48 Alexander Betts, Louise Bloom, Josiah Kaplan, and Naohiko Omata, *Refugee Economies: Rethinking Popular Assumptions* (Oxford: Humanitarian Innovation Project, Refugee Studies Centre, 2014), p. 4.

49 *Ibid.*, p. 42.

50 *Ibid.*, p. 43; Ethiopian refugees also present similar situation. According to the UNHCR (2015), Ethiopia has the largest refugee population in sub-Saharan Africa, estimated at 736,000 in 2015. Ethiopia's largest refugee group is from South Sudan, with other communities from Somalia, Sudan, Congo, Uganda, Eritrea, Yemen, and Burundi. An overwhelming number is accommodated in camps, and the rest live in Addis Ababa and other smaller cities. Their work and market activities are of similar nature as evinced in the cases of other urban refugee communities worldwide. See in this context, Gairn Kibreab, "Eritrean and Ethiopian Urban Refugees in Khartoum: What the Eye Refuses to See", *African Studies Review*, Volume 39 (3), 1996, pp. 131–178; the theme of economic self-sufficiency of the refugees emerged as a discourse in refugee literature back in 1979 when R. Chambers wrote, "Rural Refugees in Africa: What the Eye Does not See", *Disasters*, Volume 3 (4), pp. 381–392; see also, Marc-Antoine Perouse de Montclos and Peter MwangiKagwanja, "Refugee Camps or Cities? Socio-economic Dynamics of the Dadaab and Kakuma Camps in Northern Kenya", *Journal of Refugee Studies*, Volume 13 (2), 2000, pp. 205–222.

51 The theorists of autonomy of migration Dimitris Papadopoulos and the co-authors argue in their work, *Escape Routes*,

> To speak of the autonomy of migration is to understand migration as a social movement in the literal sense of the words, not as a mere response to economic and social malaise. The autonomy of migration approach does not, of course, consider migration in isolation from social, cultural and economic structures. The opposite is true: migration is understood as a creative force within these structures.

D. Papadopoulos, N. Stephenson, and V. Tsianos, *Escape Routes. Control and Subversion in the 21st Century* (London: Pluto Press, 2008), p. 202.

52 Sandro Mezzadra, "The Gaze of Autonomy. Capitalism, Migration and Social Struggles", 19 September 2010, www.uninomade.org/the-gaze-of-autonomy-capitalism-migration-and-social-struggles/(accessed on 2 December 2016); reprinted in V. Squire (ed.), *The Contested Politics of Mobility: Borderzones and Irregularity* (London: Routledge, 2011), pp. 121–143, 123.

53 R. Andrijasevic, "The Difference Borders Make: (Il)legality, Migration and Trafficking in Italy among Eastern European Women in Prostitution", in S. Ahmed, C. Castaneda, A.M.

Fortier, and M. Sheller (eds.), *Uprootings/ Regroundings: Questions of Home and Migration* (New York: Berg, 2003), pp. 251–272; see also H. Bauder, *Labour Movement. How Migration Regulates Labour Markets* (New York: Oxford University Press, 2006). Bauder thinks, "'In my view, what is missing from the literature on labour migration is a comprehensive treatment of how economic, social, cultural, and institutional processes interlock in the context of social production and reproduction" (p. 8), and "Formal citizenship, for example, is a powerful category to control migrant labour in many countries" (p. 199). Autonomy of migration assumes significance in the context of the presumed strength of the institution of formal citizenship.

54 Report by TAMPEP (European Network for HIV/STI Prevention and Health Promotion Among Migrant Sex Workers), *Sex Work in Europe: A mapping of the Prostitution Scene in 25 European Countries* (Amsterdam: Tampep International Foundation, 2009), http://tampep.eu/documents/TAMPEP%202009%20European%20Mapping%20Report.pdf (accessed on 2 January 2017); The report stated,

> Overall, most of the sex workers in Europe – most prominently in the West, South and North Regions of Europe, which comprise most of the 14 old EU countries represented in the TAMPEP Network – are migrants. Throughout the old member states, an average of approximately 70% of all sex workers are migrants, while some countries such as Italy, Spain, Austria and Luxembourg report that migrants comprise 80% to90% of the sex worker population, or 60% to 75% in Finland, the Netherlands, Belgium, Germany, France, Greece, Denmark and Norway. The greatest balance between migrants and nationals is found in Portugal (56% migrants) and the UK (41%migrants; with the highest level of concentration in London (80%)). In the new EU countries, there is a far lower estimate of migrants working in the sex industry. On average, only an approximate 16% to 18% of sex workers in Central Europe are migrants. However, while the overall average is quite low, there are significant differences among new EU countries: for example, in the Baltic States the number of migrants among the sex worker population is between 5% and 10%, while Romania and Bulgaria only have an average of 2%, the majority of whom are from Moldova. The main reason for this decreasing number of migrants in the Central European Region is the implementation of harsh legal restrictions for non-EU citizens. In contrast, 41% of the Czech Republic's sex workers are migrants, and this is due not only to its geographical position in the heart of Europe with borders with some of the old EU countries, but also to its booming economy in terms of international business and tourism. Other Central European countries in the East Region with a slightly higher proportion of migrant sex workers are Poland (33%) and Hungary (25%). The lowest percentage is in Slovakia (2%). These figures may however be underestimates due to gaps in knowledge and contacts with sex workers, particularly those working in more isolated or indoor settings. With all the differences among the countries considered, the average of migrant sex workers across Europe is currently approximately 47% to 50%.
>
> *(p. 16)*

55 Stephen Castles and Mark J. Miller, *The Age of Migration: International Population Movements in the Modern World*, 3rd ed. (Hampshire, Basingstoke: Palgrave MacMillan, 2003), pp. 115–117.
56 *Ibid.*, pp. 160–161; it is the same as in the case of immigrant employment, where Castles and Miller emphasise growing fragmentation and polarisation, but overlook the opposite, namely that this fragmentation gives rise to the footloose nature of migrant labour adaptable to sundry requirements of a global capitalist labour market (pp. 182–184); part of the problem is that Castles and Miller look at migration in North-South framework only, where immigrants are arriving incessantly in the North from the South, and do not see it in a South-South framework also, where refugees and immigrants from one country of the South arrive in another country of the South. The study by Betts and his colleagues, contrary to conventional North-South framework, throws a lot of light on South-South migration, and it is one of great strengths of their book.

57 Niina Vuolajarvi, "Precarious Intimacies: The European Border Regime and Migrant Sex Work", *Viewpoint Magazine*, 31 October 2015, https://viewpointmag.com/2015/10/31/precarious-intimacies-the-european-border-regime-and-migrant-sex-work/ (accessed on 20 January 2017).
58 Nicholas De Genova, "Migrant 'Illegality' and Deportability in Everyday Life", *Annual Review of Anthropology*, No. 31, 2002, pp. 419–447. De Genova's discussion of the production of illegality through deportability is what Sassen calls "expulsion" (n 24).
59 *Ibid.*; see also Bridget Anderson, "Migration, Immigration Controls and the Fashioning of Precarious Workers", *Work, Employment, Society*, Volume 24 (2), 2010, pp. 300–317; in this context one has to add two issues: (a) the particular question of camps, which shape the work choices of the migrants (Betts' collective study, *Refugee Economies* narrates this in great details) and (b) issue of homelessness by internally displaced population groups and internal migrants, which shape the labour form of these migrants. See on this, Richard B. Freeman, *Labour Markets in Action: Essays in Empirical Economics* (Cambridge, MA: Harvard University Press, 1989), Chapter 6, "Young Blacks and Jobs", pp. 121–132.
60 Stephen Castles and Mark J. Miller, *The Age of Migration: International Population Movements in the Modern World*, 3rd ed. (Hampshire, Basingstoke: Palgrave MacMillan, 2003), p. 91.
61 On the role of migrants in the European informal labour market, see Collin C. Williams and Ioana Alexandra Horonic, "Evaluating Working Conditions in the Informal Economy: Evidence from the 2015 European Working Conditions Survey", *International Sociology*, Volume 34 (3), 2019, pp. 289–306; Williams and Horonic cited the instance of the UK food industry marked by poor working conditions among migrants in low-skilled informal jobs in the food industry; informalisation means job insecurity, work intensification, worker expendability, worker subordination and employment intermediation. See also, A. Hodosi, "Perceptions of Irregular Immigrants' Participation in Undeclared Work in the United Kingdom from a Social Trust Perspective", *International Journal of Sociology and Social Policy*, Volume 35(5–6), pp. 375–389.
62 From this angle Aihwa Ong's insights relating to the passage of refugees to citizenship and mutations in citizenship (*Buddha is Hiding: Refugees, Citizenship, the New America*, California Series in Public Anthropology (Berkeley, CA: University of California Press, 2003) need to be complicated with issues of living labour. Under neo-liberalism the refugee as an anthropological subject is once more primarily a subject of labour. See also in this connection, A. Ong, *Flexible Citizenship: The Cultural Logics of Transnationality* (Durham, NC: Duke University Press, 1999); "Making the Biopolitical Subject: Cambodian Immigrants, Refugee Medicine, and Cultural Citizenship in California", *Social Science and Medicine*, Volume 40 (9), 1995, pp. 1243–1257; see also "A Milieu of Mutations: The Pluripotency and Fungibility of Life in Asia", *East Asian Science, Technology, and Society: An International Journal*, Volume 7 (3), 2013, pp. 69–85.
63 Jonathan Blitzer, "Letter from El Salvador: The Deportees Taking Our Calls, How American Immigration Policy has Fuelled an Unlikely Industry in El Salvador", *The New Yorker*, 23 January 2017, www.newyorker.com/magazine/2017/01/23/the-deportees-taking-our-calls (accessed on 11 March 2017); see also the report by Abigali Hunt, Emma Samman, Dina Mansour-Ilie, and Henrieke Max, "The Gig Economy in Complex Refugee Situations", *ERAW*, pp. 47–49.
64 Indeed these are some of the themes covered in *ERAW* and being observed or put in practice in a range of countries wide across the globe – from Indonesia to Jordan to Ghana to Denmark.
65 One instance is the Sudanese refugee rehabilitation in the United States; Jennifer Lynn Erickson in her research thesis, *Citizenship, Refugees, and the State: Bosnians, Southern Sudanese, and Social Service Organisations in Fargo, North Dakota*, Dissertation presented to the Department of Anthropology and the Graduate School of the University of Oregon for the degree of Doctor of Philosophy, September 2010), wrote,

> economic self-sufficiency was a measure of successful refugee resettlement and social citizenship in the U.S. Regardless of prior experience or formal education the newly arrived refugees were mandated to find waged labour as soon as possible. For most

refugees in Fargo, including Sudanese, this meant working in factories, hotels, retail, and other entry level jobs. In addition to decades of war-related trauma and forced migration, lack of experience in waged labor markets resulted in barriers to Sudanese integration. As a caseworker in Sioux Falls (2001–02) with dozens of Sudanese clients, I was surprised by the variety of experiences among Sudanese when it came to resettlement, and more specifically by the vast differences in levels of formal education and experience with waged labor. There were men (and some women) who had a college education abroad (in India, Cuba, Egypt, and Kenya) and who spoke fluent English. Others had worked for large, well-paying international organizations. There were many women, and some men, who had almost no formal education and little experience in waged labor. There were men and women who suffered from psychosocial trauma and there were men of all ages who had fought in the war.

(pp. 251–252)

"In a conversation with Santino, a man in his twenties, about the challenges facing young Sudanese men in the U.S.", he said, "there is a lot of suicide going on. Some people, they feel their life's not okay.' He recounted several cases of suicide and then added that for some Sudanese, alcohol and drugs became solutions" (p. 273). Classic is the case of tens of thousands of immigrants reportedly detained by US Immigration and Customs Enforcement (ICE) who are forced to work for $1 day, or for nothing at all, which is a violation of federal anti-slavery laws, as a lawsuit claims. The lawsuit, now having class-action status filed in 2014 against one of the largest private prison companies in the country, implies that the case can involve as many as 60,000 detained immigrants. According to the same report, Under ICE's voluntary work programme, detainees sign up to work and are paid $1 a day. The nationwide program according to the, ICE says, provides detainees opportunities to work and earn money while confined, subject to the number of work opportunities available and within the constraints of the safety, security and good order of the facility." – Kristine Phillips, "Thousands of ICE Detainees Claim They Were Forced into Labor, a Violation of Anti-slavery Laws", *Washington Post*, 6 March 2017, www.washingtonpost.com/news/post-nation/wp/2017/03/05/thousands-of-ice-detainees-claim-they-were-forced-into-labor-a-violation-of-anti-slavery-laws/?utm_term=.5c796b97f65a (accessed on 8 March 2017)
66 On the theme of resilient subject of neo-liberal capitalism, Brad Evans and Julian Reid, *Resilient Life: The Art of Living Dangerously* (London: Polity Press, 2014).

5
POSTCOLONIAL FOOTPRINTS OF THE ECOLOGICAL MIGRANTS[1]

The colonial background

We shall now move on to the issue of the ecological migrant joining in hundreds and thousands the mixed and massive population flows of our time. The process of producing "surplus" populations in postcolonial countries is a consequence of ecological marginality also. Against the background of the colonial history – in this case some of the Indian accounts of resource exploitation, agrarian crisis, and displacement – the chapter will discuss the political economy of environmental displacement today. The chapter will show the links between environmental displacement and a particular model of development, the implications of the environmental and developmental displacement in terms of accumulation of capital, and the production of mobile labour.

Mike Davis in his seminal work on the El Nino famines, *Late Victorian Holocausts: El Nino Famines and the Making of the Third World* (2002), showed how in the late nineteenth century climate change, social factors, abrupt economic transitions, and particular political command structures combined with devastating effect to cause millions of deaths across large parts of the world, so much so that in the subtitle "Late Victorian Holocausts" he linked the famines to the making of the third world.[2] While Davis drew his arguments from several studies and various sources, his great merit was in synthesising the huge material and data he had collected. He drew on the works of David Arnold and several other historians to show how the colonial organisation of power was crucial in accentuating environmental impact on peasantry in the colonised countries, and the ruinous effect it had on the customary ways of providing relief to the distressed and the victims.[3] In this discussion Jean Dreze's writings on the origin of the Famine Code in India in the late nineteenth century are also of enormous help in gaining a historical understanding of the relation between ecology, politics, and survival that was structured by colonialism.[4] There is again a fascinating work by James Vernon on hunger in Great Britain which draws on several sources including Davis' to show the intimate link between hunger, migration, and the combined effects of environmental changes and a catastrophic political economy.[5] Vernon tells us of the persistence of hunger in modern Britain leading up to the fifties of the last century. He also shows that the British governmental attitude to hunger and hunger marches was shaped in the last one hundred years by the attitude it had towards hunger and famines in the colonies. In particular, policies of thrift, herding the victims of hunger in camps, villages, and small towns, restricting their movements to rationalise the work of relief as well as to stop the spread of anarchy, modes of inspection and reporting, gearing part of the governmental machinery towards conducting relief work, then gradually modelling the work of relief along military lines of a centralised command structure, and finally tackling the eternal dilemma of a budget exercise, as to whether coping with calamities should be an exceptional event of drawing on available resources or whether this should be part of a normal budgeting exercise – all these had their origin in the colonial age.[6]

In my own work (*Memory, Identity, Power*, 1998) on the frontier areas of colonial Bengal in the second half of the nineteenth century, its Southwestern frontier known as the *Junglemahals*, I was dealing with the politics of community formation. Again, what was striking in the material I was unearthing and discussing was the way in which what is called now environmental history was integral to the history of formation and survival of peasant communities, in which the history of migration was an extremely critical component.[7] Environmental events became calamities as these would cause hunger and displacements, leading in turn to unrest and revolts. I showed how pests, forest fires, droughts, and storms, marked peasant memories of why they chose to move to other places (the colonial officials used to call it the "up-stick habit" of destitute peasants), why they migrated as semi-bonded labourers to certain lands particularly as plantation labour. All in all, it turned out to be a story of environment, history, economics, and power – operating as if in a grid on the margins of a rationally governed empire. Indeed, if we follow Davis' main argument, much of the late nineteenth century migration in large parts of the peasant world (Brazil, Egypt, India, and China) had to do with environmental disasters and the vagaries of the global food market.

In India, colonial rulers intervened with several legislations in critical situations of drought, flood, famine, and hunger – the best instance of which was the Famine Act. Famine Act, Mike Davis argued, did not pose any obstacle to what Marx and Engels had called "money relation", but a tool to further it. Peasant communities crashed out of the market and became victims of hunger. Blood ties were destroyed as children and wives were sold in numbers. The enactments on personal law, alimony, property management, and measures allowing encroachments on common property resource showed how the colonial rule reinvented a money-led society. For instance, colonial Bengal presented an acute picture of famine and continuing migration of all kinds with exceptional mobility of persons belonging to particular social groups to various towns and outside the region – all of which weakened kinship. We have accounts of famines – starting from the Famine of 1770 and ending with that of 1943 and in between the account of the famine of 1873 – that tell us of scenes of animal existence of humankind and massive migrations in search of security of life. Life in these accounts is the life of the beast, as Hunter described in *Annals of Rural Bengal*.[8]

Is the situation much different today? Questions should be asked: How do various factors combine today to produce hunger marches of our time, new resource crises, new migrants and new refugees? If hunger, famines, and floods played a crucial part in the making of the colonial economy, what are the postcolonial realities of political economy, particularly in terms of primitive accumulation that globalisation requires as its fuel? How are structures of inequalities reproduced today through these environmental catastrophes? How are fringe economies emerging and in what way do they link up with what can be called for lack of better terms mainstream economy?

An inquiry into these questions will help us to understand how even today the combined force of environmental change, resource crisis, and migration act as the locomotive of accumulation and development. Colonial history is crucial, because an understanding of the colonial time helps us to see how the postcolonial destiny awaits the entire world. To demystify the phrase, "sustainability of resources", and to get a sense of the new type of bio-power and bio-politics that is emerging, a critical postcolonial sense is important. It will help (a) bring back the issue of the colonial dynamics, which continues albeit with changes; (b) point out in this context how a new science of governance tries to manage environmental migration; and (c) understand how the migrant, through the act of crossing borders and boundaries (borders of hunger, starvation, and life and death; of places and countries; of stations in life and occupations; finally borders in the discrete map of division of labour) copes with a system that teams up with nature's calamities to turn millions into perishable lives.

Two recent companion studies have explored the colonial history of migration in India, and both have brought to light environmental factors underpinning the migration process. To mention the first one:

Based on his study of the figures on emigration from various sources the historian Subhasranjan Chakrabarty observed that overall, the available data did not indicate the socioeconomic groups from which the emigrants were drawn; but he noted that historical records – particularly the observations of a number of district collectors – did suggest that many disbanded sepoys, weavers, agricultural labourers and others engaged in low-caste service occupations were among them. In his words,

> A majority of emigrants were from rural areas and from 'overcrowded agricultural districts', where 'crop failure could plunge sections of the village community into near-starvation'. In fact, there was a strong correlation between emigration and harvest conditions."[9]
>
> Chakrabarty cited the instances of acute scarcity during 1873–75 in Bihar, Oudh, and NW Provinces provoking large-scale emigration through the port of Calcutta. The famine in south India during 1874–8 also resulted in heavy emigration.

He wrote of roadblocks being hastily put up to stem the flood of "stick-thin country people" into Bombay and Pune. In Madras the police forcibly expelled some 25,000 famine escapees. Chakrabarty concluded with these remarks,

There is little doubt about the correlation between scarcity and forced migration. Most of the emigrants probably left their villages for the first time in their lives, and they were not fully aware of the hardships involved in long voyages and in living abroad. Diseases – cholera, typhoid, dysentery – were often rampant in the depots. Mortality among the emigrants was consequently high. Mortality at sea was alarmingly high. Before 1870, about 17 to twenty per cent of the labourers deported from the port of Calcutta died before they reached their destination. The data for the years 1871–90 of voyages to British Guyana suggest that the death rate on board was about 15 per 1000. . . . It is an abiding irony that the cash crop boom accompanied a decline in agrarian productivity and food security. . . . During what constituted, in the imagination of the likes of Kipling and Curzon, the 'the glorious imperial half century' (1872–1921) life expectancy of ordinary Indians fell by a staggering twenty per cent. *Pax Britannica*, it would appear, had more victims than long centuries of war.[10]

In the other study focused on one century of migration from one single district, dry and repeatedly drought prone, Purulia in West Bengal, India, the researcher Nirmal Kumar Mahato brought out the interface of scarcity, starvation, and migration. He commented,

Due to ecological degradation the *adivasi* (indigenous) society plunged into repeated crises. With the dislocation of their ecological economy it was difficult to survive. There was nutritional crisis which affected their health also. In the post-colonial period the same trend continued. Sometime the Government took developmental initiatives but it did not try to recover the lost ecosystem so that the people could survive on their own. Traditional water management and mentality to conserve water was also lost. In the district, scarcity and nutritional crisis came not as a phenomenon but as a process. Thus, people were forced to migrate for their survival. The migration had a significant gender dimension. Large number of women emigrated in the colonial period not only for economic reasons but also due to their crumbling position in their own families. Women felt insecure in their own land. They had to migrate. This also occasioned sexual exploitation which continues to date.[11]

In the perspective of earlier studies on labour migration in colonial India, which had mostly laid emphasis on different push factors to explain labour migration, the research on Purulia is important.[12] Some of the earlier researches had enquired into the agrarian perspective e to make sense of the context of labour migration.

P.P. Mohapatra in his well-known work had observed that the phenomenon of migration in Chotanagpur was both spatially and temporarily variegated. From some areas labourers went to Assam permanently while from some other areas they migrated seasonally to the coalfields. A large number of agricultural labourers or landless and small peasants migrated to the coalfields. Migration to Assam was associated with peasant household migration. Emigration from Hazaribagh or Palamau was possibly due to lack of expansion of cultivable land because of prevailing institutional arrangements. Emigration from Ranchi, Manbhum, and Singhbhum took place because in those regions further expansion of arable land was no longer possible. Under these circumstances, a number of peasants on marginal lands with limited or no irrigation facilities came under the mercy of an erratic monsoon and thus their food supply was under severe strain.[13] Nirmal Mahato's research brought out the interrelations between arid climate, decline in household economy, land question, commercial crisis, institutional deadlocks, and labour migration. Environmental crises in indigenous belts of habitation in India show why in place of a push and pull framework a relational framework may be more fruitful to understand migration in the colonial time.

Take for instance the extreme right-wing imperial administration in India headed by Lord Lytton (1876–1880), which was the time of the Second Anglo-Afghan War and the Great Famine of 1876–78. His reign became the reason for the passage of the Indian Famine Code in 1883. Lytton arrived as the Viceroy in 1876, the year when a famine broke out in South India claiming between 6.1 million and 10.3 million people. Famine continued, and his implementation of Britain's trading policy was blamed for increasing severity of the famine. Lytton was a fanatic believer in Social Darwinism and treated the plight of the starving and dying Indians as inevitable. This was the context of the first modern codification of governmental responses to famines during the colonial occupation of India by the British. The highly detailed Indian Famine Code of 1883 classified situations of food scarcity according to a scale of intensity and laid out a series of steps that governments were obliged to take in the event of a famine. While the Code continues to influence contemporary policies as well those in several succeeding debates, as Davis showed, 1870–80s also became the time of massive migrations of starving peasants.[14]

Colonial history is important because it enables us to make sense of the ways postcolonial policy regimes have facilitated and ensured labour supply in a mad rush towards what it perceives as "development". Migration control policies and mechanisms have emerged in the wake of policies and administrative measures of controlling hunger and mitigating the effects of environmental disasters, at the same time ensuring labour supply for "development" and mega projects of infrastructure.

Hunger, disasters, and new governing mechanisms

Environmental calamities have exacerbated the notion of food insecurity. Indeed the two discourses of food insecurity and disaster feed into each other. They help to de-codify the other. Thus, each calamity is followed by debates on soaring food grain prices, withdrawal by the State of food subsidies, role of government and market forces in food grain market as well as global food politics. The Indian government (the UPA I) more than a decade back had offered in place of earlier food-for-work schemes a 100-day job guarantee scheme as an improved measure. The UPA II regime then followed up the earlier measure by taking up the task of guaranteeing food security. In a vast country like India, the conceptualisation and implementation of such a massive food scheme created debates: Could such a scheme be implemented properly? Would it not give rise to greater corruption? Would this be sustainable? And, was this the best way to ensure food security, for the main task was to guarantee a greater and easier supply of grain to poor homes. While these were general concerns, the free market advocates further argued, would this not dampen prices, harm the farmers and grain trade, and thus block asset formation in the villages?

Agricultural and rural wages are depressed in the wake of disasters and calamities. The usual government reply is that if the beneficiaries do not get supplies, as pledged in the Food Security Act, there are provisions to ensure financial assistance to them for buying the staple grains from the open market. It remains debatable if the prescribed amount of financial assistance would be enough to buy rice and wheat at open market rates in markets run by their own rules, priorities, and pressures. Agricultural economists have been often asked by common people as to what is this notion of food security; India is supposedly surplus in rice, wheat, and other food items of daily consumption, and yet food insecurity hovers over large tracts of the country accompanied by nearly 300,000 farmers' suicides in nearly last two decades.[15] Each calamity brings in its wake price increases, and while production over the long run has gone up manifold, prices including the cost of production have soared correspondingly. Instances are quite frequent where a village may produce at least three times the rice needed to feed its population and yet half the village population may get to eat only one meal a day half the year, because this section does not have the money to buy rice. Besides this huge commercialisation of food, each year a large chunk of farmland is being diverted to non-farm use. Thus, a study of a comparison between the years of implementation of the WTO agreements (1990–91 to 1995–96) and the next five years (1996–97 to 2001–02) showed that barring rice and onions the production of other farm produces had declined.[16] In short, green revolution, reckless commercialisation of land and farm produce, risk-based trade of agricultural commodities, and diversion of land from farm production to non-farm use have combined to defeat the goal of food security. Natural calamity acts as a catalyst of the entire process.

Natural calamities function as a periodic rude reminder that hunger is not over and life is not assured. In this way calamities take us back to the basic question of life, and ask what hunger is, how large parts of the country remain hungry year after year, and what it means for politics when it concerns two basic issue of living, namely food and shelter. Even though we are living under democracy, which concerns freedom and promises us improved life conditions, natural calamities nonetheless force us to ask: Does democracy do away with basic challenges of living? The answer is that under conditions of political equality in a democracy there may durable inequality with differential access of groups to food and food markets.

It was not sheer coincidence that in the nineteenth century when the idea of democracy was overwhelming the European continent that reports of famines started rocking the political establishments across the continent – famines in the colonies and reports of hunger in the metropolitan countries themselves. To recall once again the colonial age, reports on Irish Famine (1845–52) tell us of deaths of approximately one million people and emigration of another million. Ireland's population in that time fell between 20 and 25 per cent. The Famine was a watershed in the history of Ireland, so much so that modern historians regard it as a dividing line in the Irish historical narrative. Charles Tilly's accounts of collective actions in seventeenth and eighteenth century Britain and France show how food riots occasioned the development of various tools of collective protest – night vigil, torchlight processions, burning, looting grain stores, sit-ins, slogan-shouting, barricading, formation of committees and vigilante groups, drawing up and submissions of memoranda, charters, and manifestos, setting up popular councils, and finally people responding to conditions of calamity and hunger with their feet. The history of disasters, hunger, collective actions, and the governmental policies of warding off violent protests with relief, rehabilitation, and resettlement programmes mark our critical understanding of democracy. Perhaps most pertinent to our theme of concern here is that these disasters were also occasions of great migrations.

Exactly as the colonial time, we can now find in India different categories of hungry people – categories created by government policies, such as BPL (below poverty line) and APL (above poverty line). Thus with the governing principle of creating a hierarchy of eligibility for food provision and assistance, the situation is like what it was after the New Poor Law of 1834, enacted in Great Britain. Like then journalists have now brought to attention the Indians' news of hunger and hunger deaths. Exactly as then new social policies are now being discussed and implemented in order to tackle hunger in the wake of the humanitarian discovery of hunger. The discovery of hunger, as the news reports testify, has led to a discovery of the "social", on the basis of which new social legislations such as the NREGA (National Rural Employment Guarantee Act) have been founded. The government can now address the social only by addressing hunger. The social discovery of hunger possible due to investigative journalism led also to the use of hunger in order to oppose government policies. Thus began the tradition of hunger strike (in India and Ireland for instance), the message being, it is better to die in starvation than to accept a wrong government. And as in Britain, in India too in the wake of protests over scarcity of food, a new form of social government emerged with the welfare of the hungry as its aim. This has required expertise in form of science and calculation of hunger so that government can devise policies and measures to assuage hunger. James Vernon tells us how nutritionists became important in this form of social governance.[17] In India in the eighties and nineties of the last century nutritionists debated the quantum of calories required to assuage hunger, and specialists argued as to who could be called fully hungry and who partially. On this depended quantum of assistance, the kind and form of assistance, the mode of supply, the budgetary requirements, and identification of most needy areas, and along with all these emerged a panoply of graded vulnerabilities. Science facilitated the administration of food provisions. The discovery of vitamins and a bio-chemical explanation of nutrition meant that social governance of hunger would now be possible. Encouraging populations to move to newer areas of work became one of the standard methods of managing a hungry population. Expanding access to food, the role of village self-rule institutions in mitigating hunger, tightening up of administrative measures for social security of migrant workers, judicial activism, and debates over the exact cause of a hunger-death – starvation, or illness, or suicide – all these have now become dimensions of this social governance. This is what Vernon calls the government of hunger.

In such time of calamity politics becomes irrevocably biological – exactly the opposite of civil politics. How to survive, how to escape, get food, how to distribute food, how to tackle hunger protests, how to die, how to escape death by fleeing zones of starvation, and finally how to explain away deaths – all these suddenly take the centre stage of politics. Migration emerges as a policy pre-occupation in this context of food insecurity, environmental calamities, and developmental disasters. Footloose life becomes the one that millions in the South of the world live and one that the managers of global governance want to incorporate in the discourse of safety and sustainability of life. Natural and social calamities have occasioned various development strategies, disaster management programmes and projects, millennium goals, climate, environment, and resource related policies, and policies of protection of the vulnerable population groups including large migrant groups.

The lineage of the interlinked discourses of precariousness, resilience, and migration is thus long. Clearly economic reason is not enough to govern society, which needs also ecological reason to be governed – because if dangers are to remain with us and if marginal existence is going to be the characteristic of our life then we need a new ecological understanding of our precarious existence.

How could the element of uncertainty become the core of the new theology of resilience? Is it then the fact that the postcolonial life now works as the spectre haunting the developed capitalist world? At least we can say this much, that there is a strange displacement of sorts in the global hall of infamous imageries: The image of Tsunami becomes that of Hurricane Katrina; twentieth century's worst cyclone that claimed uncounted lives in Bangladesh (then East Pakistan) in 1970 appears as the advancing polar chilly weather into North America, My Lai massacre becomes the ghost haunting Boston, Madrid, New York, and numerous school shootings claiming hundreds of boys and girls, the bankruptcy of Argentina (1998–2002) becomes the insolvency of Greece (2008–15), and finally the Partition exodus becomes the trek to the mainland of Europe from the southern and eastern directions and the caravans of migrants to the United States. In this series of displacements, policies are also displaced – those exclusively meant for neo-colonies are now to be applied "at home" with of course suitable modifications.

We can note at least two features of the situation: (a) the inter-linked themes of environment, precarious life, resilience, and migration have strong postcolonial resonance; and (b) neo-liberal capitalism aims at strengthening particular governmental mechanisms to deal with life on the margin – mostly life of the migrant who stands on the margin of society, economy, climate, security, market, and reproduction.

In this background this chapter now moves on to present briefly select findings of some of the recent researches in India on the emergence of the ecological migrant as the key figure of life – in the Brahmaputra and Barak Basins in Northeast India and Deltaic West Bengal and Bihar. These findings tell us of the way ecology, developmental politics, and survival migration link with each other in producing what can be called a "moving region".

Ecology, politics, and survival migration in the east and northeast

On the recurrent flood of the Kosi River in the four districts in North Bihar researches have demonstrated the intrinsic relation between ecology, politics, and survival migration in the last decade. These researches have pointed out the social, economic, and governmental dynamics in the wake of floods in the Kosi delta. They have shown the new governmental modes of encouraging the exit option for the flood-trapped hamlets and villages, the regular train journeys of the (predominantly male) migrant labour from North Bihar to the northern part of India including Delhi, the entire political economy of flood, public works on flood control, and the developed modes of relief and rehabilitation that make a government successful.[18] They have also brought out features of popular politics, resistance, and the role of caste in the making of the migrant labour in today's India.[19] In a focused study on three districts in West Bengal delta region of the river Ganga-Bhagirathi, the gendered aspects of such migration have been brought out in clearer light.[20] In Malda, it is the erosion of the Ganga riverbanks; in Murshidabad it is the erosion of the banks of Padma's tributary Jalangi and in Cooch Behar it is erosion along the sides of Saltia, a remnant of the old course of Torsha. There are differences in the impact.

> In Malda and Murshidabad, when a displaced person points to a direction and says, 'That was my home,' or, 'that was my land' one can see just plain water. In Cooch Behar, it is a barren stretch of sand. In both cases though, the loss has been the same – below the watery or sandy grave lie people's homes, lands, hopes, and dreams. In Malda, after a piece of land goes under water, a silt-bank or *char* often rises on the other side. There, the displaced people settle amidst great difficulties and somehow make the land yield to their hard toil. In case of erosion such as in Cooch Behar, however, the land just becomes a sandbank, where hardly any crop except mustard can be grown. The once-well-off peasants are now paupers. One can see almost no paddy fields, only scattered mustard patches. In Murshidabad, too, the *char* where the displaced people are being rehabilitated is very sandy, they complain. 'My

relative died a few days ago. When we dug the earth to bury him, we found no soil but only sand,' said one of them.[21]

In this, the impact on women has been loud. It is said, when men go to war, women have to maintain the families. The same is true in this case too. Losing their livelihood, most of the men are forced to migrate in search of work, while the women are left with the responsibility to feed their children. The men who just sit at home without any work also put pressure in various ways on women having less earning opportunities. Some of these women are rolling *bidis*, some fry puffed rice (*muri*), make *badis* with gram or dal paste, or do pottery, or some other work. In Maldamore than in Murshidabad and Cooch Behar there are skilled women *bidi* workers. Many are trying to pick up the skill now under economic compulsions. Most of these women get less than the rates negotiated between the *bidi* workers' unions and the owners/contractors. They are unorganised. Some of them go to work in the fields during the sowing season; they also dig and carry the soil. In these two jobs, too, they are less paid than the male workers. Women from the Bagdi community in Murshidabad go for fishing, but face complaints of harassment by securitymen. The report says that many of the women say candidly that they are engaged in an "illegal profession". In Jalangi, one can see scores of women crossing the Bangladesh borders with sugar, electronic items, cloth, etc. Besides their daily toil, some of them admit, they have to "please" the securitymen for carrying out their unlawful livelihood. Making daily visits to the newly emerged *chars* to fetch as big a load of wild grass as they can carry and selling them for a meagre Rs 5 to Rs 10 has also become a major occupation for women in Malda. They, too, have to keep people at the *ghats* "pleased". Yet amidst all these, the women show great interest in matters of education. Even the poorest of families send their girls to schools. However, though many of the women stress the need to educate their girl children – a chance they themselves did not have even if they wished to – other reasons have been heard, too. These are: "a girl's value in today's marriage market falls if she is not educated to some extent", "the boys get jobs such as handling the boulders (for embankments), girls better go to school and get mid-day meals than sit idle at home", etc. Studies are also being affected as many schools have to shut down or shift in the wake of erosion.

The displaced women face various sexual risks. We have already mentioned that they are compelled to "please" securitymen and others at the instance of those who run the smuggling rackets. There are also rackets operating which arranges the "marriage" of girls from displaced families in "Bihar" or other distant places. During our investigation, we found that this phenomenon is particularly prevalent in Murshidabad. Many of the families in Jalangi say one or two of their daughters had been married off in Bihar. In a prolonged conversation, their mothers admit that the marriage might have been only in name and that they often do not hear of their girls after that. But, they express their helplessness and defend the "marriage" saying that there was no guarantee that they would have lived a better life here. Horror stories of someone's husband returning from worksites in Mumbai or Delhi are heard, too. The panic is spreading considerably below the surface, even as there is no system of healthchecks, even irregular ones.

The people devastated and displaced by erosion have formed their own organisations in each of the three districts, such as the *Ganga Bhangan Pratirodh Nagarik Action Committee* in Malda, *Bhangan Bidhwasta Udbastu Colony O Punarbasan Samiti* in Murshidabad, and the *Saltia Bhangan Pratirodh Nagarik Committee* in Cooch Behar. These organisations have brought together people from diverse political affiliations, various communities, and age groups. Women, though fewer in number, participate actively in all of these forums. The study also found that the displaced women show remarkable forwardness in narrating their conditions and voicing their needs and demands, even to the male member of the research team. Their self-help groups exist in wide parts of the erosion-affected areas and there is no dearth of the women's enthusiasm to join them.[22]

While in North Bihar labour in order to escape flood migrates in large number to Delhi and elsewhere in Northern and Western parts of India, in West Bengal labour migrates to nearby areas. However, in both cases migrant labour creates what was described in *The Marginal Nation* as "immigrant niche".[23] It does not mean of course the immigrant niche is always a fringe existence and the immigrant economy is a fringe economy. The labour may be integrated in several ways with mainstream economy. Yet there is no doubt that the labour emanating from flood ravaged zones occupies a niche in the map of segmented labour. That niche can be best expressed by what a researcher terms as "living with the river".[24]

Indeed, flood and riverbank erosion are two of the major global environmental disasters that the world has experienced recurrently, displacing millions of people every year, destroying homesteads, wiping out cultivable lands, reducing employment opportunities, in short, putting life and livelihood at tremendous risk. South Asian countries, especially, India, Bangladesh, Pakistan, and Nepal are open to such calamities. According to a report of the National Space Research Organisation, India is not only one of the worst flood-affected countries in the world, but also it accounts for one-fifth of global death count due to floods. The same report states, "The most flood-prone areas in India are the Brahmaputra, Ganga and Meghna River basins in the Indo-Gangetic-Brahmaputra plains in North and Northeast India, which carry 60 per cent of the nation's total river flow."[25] A recent study by the Calcutta Research Group, titled, "Ecosystems for Life: A Bangladesh-India Initiative: Ecology, Politics, and Survival in India's Northeast and Deltaic Bengal" focused in West Bengal on the deltaic forests of the Sunderbans, and the districts of Nadia, Murshidabad, and Malda. The study found the Sunderbans as a contested space caught in the quagmire of fragility, resource crisis, out migration, but also new patterns of resource sharing.[26] The study brought to the fore various coping mechanisms of people in the post Aila situation in the Sundarban forest region in Southern Bengal. The situation was marked by migration of the able-bodied males of the region to other parts of the state and the country, and a decrease in agricultural activities as a result of an increase of salinity of the soil. Men migrated to South India also, especially to Chennai, Bengaluru, Hyderabad, and Thiruvananthapuram to work as construction labourers, as workers in hosiery factories and in other unskilled jobs. Strangely, this newer phenomenon of outward migration has been able to help the declining economy of the region to rejuvenate and solve the problem of seasonal unemployment. A similar trend was observed in the study conducted on the district of Murshidabad. Loss of agricultural lands as a result of encroaching Padma, Bhagirati, and Jalangi rivers had also forced many men to migrate to big cities. People living on *char*lands or sand islands, in the border areas, live a life on the edge. At times, the precarious labour faces identity crisis adding to their woes. Vulnerabilities have led to a high rate of trafficking of young girls from the district of Murshidabad. In Nadia district, extreme pollution and continuous siltation in the river Churni have forced the local fishermen to search for an alternative source of living. A study on the district as part of the same programme revealed that more than 200,000 people, residing besides the river, are searching for alternative sources of life and living. In Matiari, the people residing in the village now complain that the natural process of erosion in Ganga has been enhanced by the regular journey of the heavy coal laden barges on the Ganga. The erosion in this region threatens the thriving household industry of bell metal and brass utensils. Thus, change in livelihood, for the people associated with the household metal industry migrating to other places for work. Deltaic Bengal is also characterised by mushrooming of brick kilns along the banks of the rivers like Ganga, Bhagirati, and Padma. The brick industry attracts seasonal labourers from Bihar and Uttar Pradesh. So, while a considerable section migrates out of Bengal, a considerable section migrates into the state. Another study revealed that in Malda district, along with other problems, there was the issue of loss of identity for people residing in *char*lands. While they have access to certain amenities like drinking water or electricity, courtesy the state of Jharkhand, they are not accepted as residents by the state of West Bengal. In this light, the report "Non-existing Population in the Char lands of Malda", highlights the point that with the amendment of The West Bengal Land Reform Act (1955) in 2000, the people of *char*lands got stripped off of their rights, and became "illegal residents". Yet, in another place called Bhutni, about 100,000 people living there are now facing displacement because of riverbank erosion and the inhabitants of at least four villages were forced to leave their homes who were in turn, turned into daily wage labourers.[27]

In yet another study – this time on the Brahmaputra basin – brought out among many other things the issue of identity of *char* dwellers. In *chars* in the Goalpara district of Assam, the villagers spoke at length about the insecurity of the people about the status of their lands and their desperation for land *patta*. Flood and erosion are once again the major environmental problems in these *chars*. When the displaced person is a peasant, he loses his most precious possession – the land that he tills and his main resource of subsistence, existence, and identity. Studies bring to fore issues of arbitrary categorisation of the *char* dwellers into Doubtful Voters or D voters, raising the larger question of political justice along with the emerging question of social justice. Once again caste and gender are found to be two major fault lines in the map of vulnerability.

The study being referred to here also looked into the impact of construction of several dams also in the Northeast. It collected several local writings on how the construction of NHPC's (National Hydro-electric Power Corporation) Lower Subansiri project had repeatedly disrupted the wildlife habitation of the area. NHPC started construction activities in and near a protected forest area without necessary clearance. During the construction phase, NHPC's activities led to the disruption and destruction of habitats of endangered species, including that of the elephants, near the dam side. The project has not only affected the migratory route of the elephants but also threatens to affect the livelihoods of many people as Subansiri river, with her mineral resources alone, has supported the lives of about 20,000 people. Local people earn their livelihood either as salary or as daily wages by working under the *maholder*.[28] The free-flowing Subansiri without having any physical barrier in its course regulates the quarrying business of sand and gravels. The timbers that come floating on the river facilitate timber business. The demand for housing material is met with the wood carried by the river, and parallel to it, a business network sprang up in due course. But the construction of the dam signals a probable change in livelihood pattern, which might force people to other parts to look for jobs.

The Indian government had identified the state of Arunachal Pradesh as a potential area of hydro-power generation and sanctioned the construction of 173 dams. The areas inhabited by the Monpa community fall among these areas. Although dams account for a major cause of affecting these people, other projects like that of national highways undertaken the Ministry of Road Transport and Highways are also responsible for displacing people. Land acquisition invariably affects people by either displacing them (known as DPs or displaced persons) or affecting their movable and immovable assets. The people belonging to tribal and ethnic minorities suffering the impact of dam projects most are filled with a sense of alienation, as a result of dispossession of their land and other resources, lack of compensation or inadequate compensation, human rights abuse and a decline in living standards.[29] There is a gradual shift in the occupational pattern from agriculture and forestry to jobs offering daily wage. Now land has been taken over for dam construction. Hence, the villagers are losing out on the earlier guaranteed earning. With contractual jobs emerging as an alternative for the locals, short-term job opportunity is only what they can look for.

This research on the Northeast is additionally significant because it brings out the strong relation between development induced displacement and environmental displacement. This makes the task of estimating the number of IDPs caused by environmental degradation, i.e. flood, riverbank erosion, and landslide etc., additionally difficult, because nothing is purely environmental, and social imprints are everywhere and every time. However, some reasonable conclusions can be drawn about the enormity of the problem. As a result of continuous environmental degradation, such as flood and riverbank erosion in the plains, and landslide in the hills, exacerbated by developmental works, population displacements have become endemic. This has also caused innumerable deaths and destruction of settlements.

The intensity of flood, riverbank erosion, and landslide has increased substantially over the years in terms of area and victims. One expert on displacement in the Northeast, Monirul Hossain, has observed,

> It would be pertinent to point out that the plight of the riverbank erosion induced IDPs are much more severe than that of the victims of flood. The victims of flood at least can go back to their original land once the flood water recedes. However, the riverbank erosion induced displaced peasants cannot go back to their land. Because, their land has become a part of river's new/extended bed. It is not only the mighty river Brahmaputra but also the innumerable small and medium sized rivers are also causing havoc in the plains of Assam, i.e. the Brahmaputra Valley and the Barak Valley. . . . According an official report, the river Brahmaputra eroded 429,657 hectares of prime agricultural land. Roughly, 7% of the land in the plains has been eroded between the years of 1951–2000. This has definitely displaced at least 3 million peasants. Today they constitute the most pauperised community in Assam's plains. In the absence of proper resettlement and rehabilitation policy, most of them have experienced multiple displacements.[30]

Hossain also observed that the flood of 2004 alone affected more than ten million people in Assam valley. Excepting two hill districts, all the districts of the plains of Assam experienced devastating flood and riverbank erosion. In an unprecedented flash flood in October of 2004, nearly one thousand people died in one single district in Assam – Goalpara.

In an equally significant study on population groups living in the river islands of Assam, known as *chars*, Gulshan Parveen conducted an investigation into environment, life, migration patterns, governmental politics, and occupational patterns in these river islands. It extended the insight from the earlier mentioned study on river erosion in Murshidabad and Malda in West Bengal. Parveen showed in this study how what was earlier small peasant migration from the north eastern parts of East Bengal in the early decades of the last century to these *chars* or river islands, has now transformed in the wake of floods and river erosion into what can be called a second wave of migration – this time to petty urban jobs like rickshaw pulling, construction labour, janitors, or service employees in the dusty small and big towns of Assam. Her findings confirm those of Mithilesh Kumar who studied the ravages by floods in North Bihar, namely, the crucial role of governmental politics in regulating flood, relief, rehabilitation, and other aspects of life, particularly education and health and the role they play in the emergence of a specific migration regime and the pattern of mobility we see in India today.[31] In the background of erosion of land, livelihood opportunities, identity, voting rights, etc., Parveen Gulshan concluded her study significantly with these words,

> Where does the state situate itself in a situation where its own citizens lose their citizenship? The way the nation-state is inseparably anchored with the territory and land, citizenship too is also anchored with the hidden notion

of land. The question of land is important as it determines the citizen's access to the state. Land becomes the basis of his/her claims for rights. However, the question of land is based on the notion of ownership of land and his/her capacity to hold on to the land permanently. Loss of land impinges on his/her citizenship. One needs to understand the inseparable linkage between the displaced people on one hand and citizenship and the state on the other. This linkage is obviously unavoidable in any political study of displacement.[32]

All in all, flood and riverbank erosion are two of the major global environmental disasters the world has experienced recurrently, making the life and livelihood in flood prone areas precarious. South Asian countries, especially, India, Bangladesh, Pakistan, and Nepal are open to such calamities. According to a report of the National Space Research Organisation (NSRO), India is one of the worst flood-affected countries in the world. Roughly one-fifth of global deaths due to floods occur in India. The report adds that the most flood-prone areas in India carrying 60 per cent of the nation's total river flow are the Brahmaputra, Ganga, and Meghna River basins in the Indo-Gangetic-Brahmaputra plains in North and Northeast India.[33] The same study also looked into the impact of construction of several dams in the Northeast, where construction activities in and near protected forest areas had commenced at times without necessary clearance.[34]

In such situation, land, identity, claims, and citizenship remain crucial aspects of life. These issues even in the case of urban refugees and rural migrants in a city retain their relevance. Studying the struggles of the urban refugees and other displaced rural people for shelter in Kolkata, one researcher wrote on the lesson of her study,

> It has been my aim to highlight a very practical dimension of the refugee struggle, by taking refugees' everyday acts of building and taking shelter as a point of departure for analysing the ways in which they have acquired a (legitimate) place for themselves within the city of Kolkata. I have attempted to show that beneath the seemingly mundane and unimaginative acts of taking shelter, simmers a certain political potential that derives from the subversive act of appropriating space. In the case of Kolkata's refugees these spatial acts of appropriation seamlessly gave into more conventional ways of political action, such as marches and protests. Yet interestingly, even this outright political strive was informed by notions of necessity and practicality. In fact, it was people's everyday struggle for shelter and subsistence that provided refugees with a ground for claiming certain 'rights'. Hence, the everyday hardships that people faced in relation to the inhospitable environment that they came to inhabit cannot be disconnected from the politicized struggle that they fought for land rights (and implicitly for citizenship). In a sense, the land itself became a medium for people's claims to the State, a battleground for conflicting interests and a breeding ground for resilience. It was in and through the city spaces of the colony that people's transition from refugee to citizen gained shape.[35]

River, land, and forests still remain central to the accounts of mobility in large parts of the postcolonial world.

Return to the debate on primitive accumulation

We can now make a better sense of this incessant production of precarious labour capitalism can neither digest nor do away with – by placing the interrelations between ecology, migration, and politics at the heart of our understanding of early twenty first century capitalism. In this context we may conclude with few observations drawn from various studies mentioned in this paper.

First, our observation concerns the neo-liberal relief, rehabilitation, and resettlement agenda. Already a decade back when the new century was taking off and in India we were studying the dynamics of post-tsunami relief, rehabilitation, and of resettlement patterns, we found that not only were earlier patterns of inequality being reproduced through the governmental dynamics, but that the public-private partnership (PPP) policy on relief, rehabilitation, and resettlement facilitated by the State in India and Sri Lanka was crucial in this reproduction on an extended scale.[36] Markets were becoming crucial in the neo-liberal agenda of disaster management. Humanitarianism was strengthened – not replaced – by this neo-liberal developmental agenda. Policies assumed that markets could make population groups vulnerable to environmental disasters resilient. Thus various forms of insurance policies and programmes in the framework of PPP emerged in the last two decades of policy explosion in India with the emergence on a substantial scale policies and businesses of agricultural insurance, disaster insurance, flood insurance, communal violence insurance, earthquake loss insurance, etc. The rest of South Asia is quickly copying the Indian style. The point is: Will this enable capitalism deal with fringe economies operating in the wake of the massive transit labour? The answer seems to be that while migrant economies will remain mostly on the fringe, capitalism is also trying to link them with global and national economies. However, like the precarious labour this solution also is precarious. Long back Marx wrote on the process of labour being alienated from the means of production to inaugurate what he termed as the primitive mode of accumulation. We can now see its return aided by the new modes of governmentality fashioned as responses to disasters. The question is, will the strategy of market enablement of the denizens of fringe economies, which we discussed in the last chapter such as refugee economies and economies practised by urban migrants, escape the political turmoil of revolts and anarchy, and facilitate market expansion?

Second, what occasions the return to the primitive mode of accumulation in this age of late capitalism marked by virtual modes of accumulation such as futures, commodity pricing forecasting, hedge funds, etc.? How do disasters combine with making money and creating capital out of disasters? In other words, how do we explain the paradoxical combination of virtual and the primitive modes of accumulation? This return to the primitive mode cannot be explained without reference to the extractive methods by which capitalism operates today. The fact is that recent debates on primitive accumulation have been too mechanistic, for they have bypassed these crucial questions. Environment and ecology are double edged concepts, for if they make us wise and conservationist, they also make us aware of the economic worth of what we call resources, that is to say worthy of producing surplus value. Thus, land has come back for unprecedented attention. Rent now occupies the core of profit; land, air, water, waste, forest – everything is for extraction. Cities are now the major extractive sites. Thus while in Arunachal Pradesh in India's Northeast river water is sought to be harnessed for power generation, downstream management of the same water ensures the destruction of the lives of thousands, turning people into precarious labour. Likewise, the expansion of mobile telephony and construction of towers on a gigantic scale tell the story of extraction of air. So is the story of mining expansion with the rise in demand of iron ore, etc. All in all, it is the extractive nature of modern capitalism combined with the speculative nature of finance that encourages the dissociation of labour from means of labour. Primitive modes of accumulation have returned under this condition.

Third, this signifies a complex method of producing mobile labour in twenty-first century capitalism. In previous chapters we already referred to the work of two well-known theorists who suggest that in the overwhelming milieu of migration we must look into the institution of border as a method in the multiplication of labour.[37] They have argued that contemporary globalisation has proliferated borders, and have investigated the implications of this proliferation for migratory movements, capitalist transformations, and political life. They have also explored the violence surrounding borderlands and border struggles across various geographical scales. In their work, border is not only a research object but also an epistemic framework. Their use of the border as method enables new perspectives on the relation between migration and capitalism. Yet, while their insight helps us to have a better grasp of the phenomenon of mobility, we have to think more in terms of grids and circuits to make sense of how labour moves, causalities are connected, inter-linkages are structured, and how all these become parts of circuits of capital. This means going back to the question of mediation.

Migration mediates. The circuit of mobility is a complex grid. Flood occurs annually. We may find mobile labour from the northern districts of Bihar or the Gangetic districts of West Bengal in Kerala or the Gulf region – not through a direct, well-ordered route, but through several mediations in form of government, labour recruitment and contracting agency, wage structure, electoral politics, and equally importantly, caste, gender, age, and community structure.[38] Like all these factors disasters too work as mediating mechanisms in the transition from the moment of production of labour to the moment of its circulation. I am not speaking here of natural disasters only. Wars – the greatest of disasters – have traditionally cleared the ground of labour force expansion and a consequent capitalist boom;[39] likewise, floods and famines have been catalytic agents in the contraction and expansion of the labour market. A great instance will be the construction of the new town near Kolkata called the Rajarhat new town. By all accounts it has been an environmental disaster. Yet this disaster, as we demonstrated in our work on new towns,[40] was the pre-condition of entry of offshore funds, construction of special economic zones (SEZ), massive construction works by developmental agencies, entry of transit labour, and the emergence of what Brett Neilson and Ned Rossiter have called the logistical city.[41]

Fourth, migration has reworked the issue of identity. Many identity claims in the last three decades in India at least, and this is perhaps true of many other parts of the world, were based, or linked to, or led to various homeland claims. Now with transit labour becoming a ubiquitous phenomenon, the identity of the migrant as labour has become increasingly important, though the identity of labour is perched on the fault lines of gender, caste, tribe, race, and foreign nationality. Yet there is no doubt that the history of immigrant labour and the making of specific class structures are becoming once again significant in this age of footloose capital. Yesterday's labour, for instance in the plantation industry, mines, and railway construction, reappears today in the form of, say construction labour, labour in nursing, care, and the entertainment industry. The similarity with the history of immigration in the late nineteenth and early twentieth centuries discussed in the last chapter is too striking to be dismissed. Like then we are now witnessing a re-emergence of races and racism. Migration has brought to the fore the question of *labour as identity*. Therefore, we now find proliferation of techniques of identifying the migrant. In India this has reached almost a frenzied state.[42]

Finally, disasters are a major piece in this complex web of migration, mobility, and generation of profit, because they represent in a congealed form what Paulo Tavares calls "the contest over government of nature".[43] In 1970 a devastating tropical cyclone struck East Pakistan (now Bangladesh) and India's West Bengal. It remains to date the deadliest tropical cyclone ever recorded and one of the deadliest natural disasters in modern times. Half a million people lost their lives in the storm. This cyclone reached its peak with winds of 185 km/h on 11 November and made landfall on the coast of East Pakistan (now Bangladesh) the following afternoon. The storm surge devastated many of the offshore islands, wiping out villages and destroying crops throughout the region. In the most severely affected Upazila, Tazumuddin, over 45 per cent of the population of 167,000 was killed by the storm. We have no proper estimate until now of the extent of dispossession and migration from coastal East Pakistan (now Bangladesh) and the scores of islands there. All we know is that the handling of the disaster by the Pakistan government was severely criticised. The anger of the East Pakistan people contributed to the subsequent war of independence in 1971. There is still no written proper history of that disaster. All we can say is that given the experiences of tsunami and the Kashmir earthquake of 2005, if the disaster of 1970 were to happen today in this age of neo-liberal governmentality, the result perhaps would not have been a war of independence but emergence of fringe economies, aid, and circuits of migration in the wake of massive developmental resettlement and recovery projects.

All in all, this is a postcolonial story of migration and internal displacement, as well as the story of the return of primitive and extractive modes of accumulation to the centre of the global capitalist dynamics today. The emergence of migrant labour is a major feature of this scenario. Yet there is a strange historical irony in this process. As this chapter shows, the migrant labour is one who crosses ecological borders at the same time. The massive migration of people from the areas mentioned in this chapter and similar others elsewhere is like a delirium wave. Howsoever a government may try to put the human settlements in order it is like an unruly force of nature omnipotent in its vigorous will to move. As if the mobility of the ecologically marginalised is a ritual response in revenge against an imbalance of power. The crisis thus occurs again and again. It must occur. Even when such a disaster is a local event, it becomes a planetary phenomenon. Think of the Irish Famine and all other disasters in our contemporary history.

In all these, readers will have noticed that this chapter has eschewed the much-discussed issue of climate refugees. There are two reasons:

First, it is difficult to attribute the main reason for any displacement due to climate change solely or primarily. Jurist Walter Kälin has cautioned,

> despite its relevance for all those affected by climate change, laws and policies addressing climate related displacement should not ask whether climate change has triggered the movement. Why? At least now and in the near future, it is impossible to determine whether a particular disaster would or would not have happened without climate change. Moreover, an exclusive focus on climate change may incite us to neglect other causes of natural disasters and environmental changes such as volcano eruptions, tsunamis or earthquakes and thus amount to discrimination against persons having equally urgent protection needs. Just as we do not ask for the root causes behind the persecution of refugees (nationalism? ideologies? dissatisfaction within the army leading to a coup?), we should not ask what has caused relevant disasters. In determining whether and how to provide temporary or permanent international protection for persons fleeing their country of origin in the aftermath of a disaster, it is enough instead to consider the environmental factors combined with the temporary or permanent unwillingness or inability of the country of origin to protect affected persons. We should therefore stop talking about "climate refugees". If we need to coin a term, referring to persons forcibly displaced internally or across international borders by environmental factors would be more appropriate.[44]

Second, the phenomenon of "climate refugees" is raised often in a way which would omit labour and life from climate, as if inhospitable climate makes living labour dead. Does climate change override the fault line running through the landscape of global migration? Unfortunately, even critical commentaries on the historical knowledge of climate change and disorders do not engage in that enquiry.[45] The writings on historical sensitivities of the theme do not give us insights into how labour operates as an organising principle in reshaping societies facing environmental challenges. Indeed our historical understanding prepares the ground for a climate of fear about climate change – a fear that shuts out labour as the key source of survival.[46] Such historical intelligibility carries a strong colonial imprint.[47] This is why we should not be surprised that in discussions on ecology, environment, and climate change the figure of the footloose labour is absent. Yet it is only through various forms of labour that migration becomes a coping strategy in face of challenges like the ones we discuss here.

In the prevailing historical wisdom, disappearing islands and "climate refugees" become signifiers of the impending doom.

Notes

1 An earlier and shorter version of this chapter appeared as R. Samaddar, "The Ecological Migrant in Postcolonial Time", in Andrew Baldwin and Giovanni Bettini (eds.), *Life Adrift: Climate Change, Migration, Critique* (Lanham, MD: Rowman and Littlefield, 2017), chapter 10, pp. 177–194 and is used here with permission.
2 Mike Davis, *El Nino Famines: Late Victorian Holocausts and the Making of the Third World* (London: Verso, 2002); also on this but with somewhat different emphasis, Arup Maharatna, *The Demography of Famines: Indian Historical Perspective* (New Delhi: Oxford University Press, 1996).
3 David Arnold, "Social Crisis and Epidemic Disease in the Famines of Nineteenth Century India", *Social History of Medicine*, Volume 6 (3), pp. 385–404.
4 Jean Dreze, "Famine Prevention in India", in Jean Dreze and Amartya Sen (eds.), *The Political Economy of Hunger, Volume II, Famine Prevention* (Oxford: Clarendon Press, 1990); chapter 1; also to be found as WIDER Working Paper, 45, May 1988, www.wider.unu.edu/publications/working-papers/previous/en_GB/wp-45/ (accessed on 1 June 2015); also see, Jean Dreze and Amartya Sen, *Hunger and Public Action* (Oxford: Oxford University Press, 1989).
5 James Vernon, *Hunger: A Modern History* (Cambridge: Harvard University Press, 2007).
6 I have discussed in greater details the significance of these historical studies elsewhere; see R. Samaddar, "The Ecological Migrant in Postcolonial Time", in Andrew Baldwin and Giovanni Bettini (eds.), *Life Adrift: Climate Change, Migration, Critique* (Lanham, MD: Rowman and Littlefield, 2017), chapter 10, pp. 177–194.
7 Ranabir Samaddar, *Memory, Identity, Power: Junglemahals: 1880–1950* (Hyderabad: Orient Longman, 1998; reprint, 2013).
8 https://archive.org/stream/annalsofruralben01hunt/annalsofruralben01hunt_djvu.txt (accessed on 15 April 2015).
9 Subhas Ranjan Chakraborty, "Colonialism, Resource Crisis, and Forced Migration", CRG Research Paper Series, *Policies and Practices*, 42 (Kolkata: Calcutta Research Group, 2011), p. 13; the sources he drew from are: W.W. Hunter, *India and the Indians*, in Herbert Risley (ed.), vol. 1 (New Delhi: Cosmo Publications, 2004, reprint), p. 497; Leela Visaria and Pravin Visaria, "Population", in Dharma Kumar (ed.), *Cambridge Economic History of India*, vol. 2 (Indian Edition, Hyderabad: Orient Longman, 1984), p. 515; Mike Davis, *El Nino Famines: Late Victorian Holocausts and the Making of the Third World* (London: Verso, 2002), pp. 26–27 and 311 ff.; Hugh Tinker, *A New System of Slavery: The Export of Indian Labour Overseas, 1830–1920* (Oxford: Oxford University Press, 1974), pp. 161–166; Lance Davis and Richard Huttenback, *Mammon and the Pursuit of Empire: The Political Economy of British Imperialism, 1860–1912* (Cambridge: Cambridge University Press, 1987), chapter 3, pp. 73–118, 110.
10 Subhas Ranjan Chakraborty, "Colonialism, Resource Crisis, and Forced Migration", CRG Research Paper Series, *Policies and Practices*, 42 (Kolkata: Calcutta Research Group, 2011), p. 13.
11 Nirmal Kumar Mahato, "Environment and Migration: Purulia, West Bengal", CRG Research Paper Series, *Policies and Practices*, 30 (Kolkata: Calcutta Research Group, 2010), p. 2.

12 For instance, H. Chottopadhaya, *Indians in Sri Lanka, A Historical Study* (Kolkata: O.P.S. Publishers, 1979); Lalita Chakraborty, "Emergence of an Industrial Labour Force in a Dual Economy: British India, 1880–1920", *The Economic and Social History Review*, Volume 10, 1978, pp. 249–328.
13 P.P. Mohapatra, "Coolies and Colliers: A Study of the Agrarian Context of Labour Migration from Chotanagpur 1880–1920", *Studies in History*, Volume 1 (20), 1985, pp. 297–298.
14 Besides, *El Nino Famines*, see also Jean Dreze, "Famine Prevention in India", in Jean Dreze and Amartya Sen (eds.), *The Political Economy of Hunger, Volume II, Famine Prevention* (Oxford: Clarendon Press, 1990).
15 According to the National Crime Records Bureau, between 2010 and 2014, the number of farmers (including agrarian labourers) committing suicides was 79,967, https://data.gov.in/resources/details-farmers-suicides-2010-2014-ministry-agriculture-farmers-welfare (accessed on 3 October 2019); from 1995 by a conservative estimate the number should be around 300,000. The National Crime Records Bureau has not released relevant figures since 2016.
16 Policy Paper 19, National Centre for Agricultural Economics and Policy Research, New Delhi, 2003.
17 James Vernon, *Hunger: A Modern History* (Cambridge: Harvard University Press, 2007).
18 Mithilesh Kumar, "Governing Flood, Migration, and Conflict in North Bihar", in R. Samaddar (ed.), *Government of Peace: Social Governance, Security, and the Problematic of Peace* (Furnham, Surrey: Ashgate, 2015), chapter 7, pp. 206–226; Manish K. Jha, "Disasters: Experiences of Development during the Embankment Years in Bihar", in R. Samaddar and Suhit K. Sen (eds.), *New Subjects and New Governance in India* (London and New Delhi: Routledge, 2012), chapter 3, pp. 109–153.
19 On the relation between migration, labour, and primitive accumulation of capital, see R. Samaddar, "Primitive Accumulation and Some Aspects of Work and Life in India", *Economic and Political Weekly*, Volume 44 (18), 2 May 2009.
20 Krishna Bandopadhyay, Soma Ghosh, and Nilanjan Dutta, *Eroded Lives* (Kolkata: Calcutta Research Group, 2006).
21 *Ibid.*, p. 16.
22 This is a summary of the report, Krishna Bandopadhyay, Soma Ghosh, and Nilanjan Dutta, *Eroded Lives* (Kolkata: Calcutta Research Group, 2006), pp. 17–20; the quoted phrases and words are also taken from these pages.
23 R. Samaddar, *The Marginal Nation: Transborder Migration from Bangladesh to West Bengal* (New Delhi and London: Sage, 1999), p. 150.
24 Madhurilata Basu, "Living with the River: Glimpses from Murshidabad", *Rivista di Studi sulla Sostenibilita*, Volume 2, 2014, pp. 105–124. The study brings out the details of the sociality created in the wake of regular floods and that binds labour to it; also see her, "Rivers, River Bank Erosion and Survival in Murshidabad", in Madhurilata Basu, Rajat Ray, and Ranabir Samaddar (eds.), *Political Ecology of Survival: Life and Labour in the River Lands of East and North East India* (Hyderabad: Orient Blackswan, 2018), pp. 84–106.
25 www.nrsc.gov.in/Earth_Observation_Applications_Disaster_Management_Floods.html (accessed on 15 May 2015).
26 www.mcrg.ac.in/IUCN/IUCN_Executive_Summary.pdf (accessed on 1 March 2018); the detailed report, "Ecosystem for Life – A Bangladesh-India Initiative – Ecology, Politics and Survival in the India Northeast and Deltaic Bengal", Calcutta Research Group archive – (CD/IUCN/MCRG/005).
27 The description is drawn from Milan Datta, "The Non-existent Population in the *Chars* of Malda", in Madhurilata Basu, Rajat Ray, and Ranabir Samaddar (eds.), *Political Ecology of Survival – Life and Labour in the River Lands of East and North-East India* (Hyderabad: Orient BlackSwan, 2018), pp. 107–120.
28 *Maholders* are those who take lease in the queries.
29 www.culturalsurvival.org/publications/cultural-survival-quarterly/brazil/world-commission-dams-review-hydroelectric-projects – The report referred to is cited and discussed in K.K. Chatradhara, "A Valley of Death: The Golden River Subansiri", in

Political Ecology of Survival – Life and Labour in the River Lands of East and North-East India (Hyderabad: Orient Blackswan, 2018), pp. 142–167.

30 Monirul Hossain, "Status Report on the IDP Situation in Assam", in Monirul Hossain and Pradip Phanjoubham, "A Status Report on Displacement in Assam and Manipur", CRG Research Paper Series, *Policies and Practices*, 12, February 2007, pp. 18–19, www.mcrg.ac.in/pp12.PDF (accessed on 8 February 2017).

31 Gulshan Parveen, "Watery Zones of Refuge: State Practices, Popular Politics and Land in the *Chars* of Assam", in Madhurilata Basu, Rajat Ray, and Ranabir Samaddar (eds.), *Political Ecology of Survival: Life and Labour in the River Lands of East and North-East India* (Hyderabad: Orient BlackSwan, 2018), pp. 121–141; the historical background and consequences of peasant migration to these river islands of Assam is well researched. The most well known is Amalendu Guha, *Planters Raj to Swaraj: Freedom, Struggle, and Electoral Politics in Assam, 1826–1947* (New Delhi: People's Publishing House); see also, Amalendu Guha, "East Bengal Immigrants and Bhasani in Assam Politics: 1928–47", *Indian Historical Congress Proceedings 35th Session*, Jadavpur, Calcutta 1974; MonirulHussain, *The Assam Movement: Class, Ideology and Identity* (New Delhi: Manak Publications, 1993); Sanjib Baruah, "Clash of Resource Use Regimes in Colonial Assam: A Nineteenth-century Puzzle Revisited", *Journal of Peasant Studies*, Volume 28 (3), 2000, pp. 109–124.

32 Gulshan Parveen, "Watery Zones of Refuge: State Practices, Popular Politics and Land in the *Chars* of Assam", in Madhurilata Basu, Rajat Ray, and Ranabir Samaddar (eds.), *Political Ecology of Survival: Life and Labour in the River Lands of East and North-East India* (Hyderabad: Orient BlackSwan, 2018), pp. 138–139.

33 www.nrsc.gov.in/Earth_Observation_Applications_Disaster_Management_Floods.html (accessed on 15 May 2015).

34 *Financing Dams in India: Risks and Challenges*, report by International Rivers Network, February 2005, www.internationalrivers.org/sites/default/files/attached-files/financingdams2005_text.pdf (accessed on 1 September 2015), p. 6. During the construction phase, these activities led in the words of *The International Rivers Network* "to the disruption and destruction of habitats of endangered species".

35 Annemiek Prins, "The Plight of Dwelling: East-Bengali Refugees and the Struggle for Land in Kolkata", *Refugee Watch*, Volume 43–44, June–December 2014. pp. 32–52, 48–49.

36 *Report on a Symposium on Tsunami and the Issues of Relief, Rehabilitation and Resettlement*, prepared by Paula Banerjee and Sabyasachi Basu Ray Chaudhury, 2005, Calcutta Research Group, www.mcrg.ac.in (accessed on 20 June 2015), a summary of the findings to be found also in *Forced Migration Review*, June 2005, www.fmreview.org/tsunami (accessed on 21 June 2015); also Nirekha De Silva, "Protecting the Rights of the Tsunami Victims: The Sri Lanka Experience", CRG Research Paper Series, *Policies and Practices*, 28; Ratna Mathai Luke, "HIV and the Displaced: Deconstructing Policy Implementation in Tsunami Camps in Tamil Nadu", *Refugee Watch*, Volume 32, December 2008, pp. 38–63; Dinusha Pathiraja, "Compare and Contrast the Situation of Conflict Related IDPs and Tsunami Related IDPs in Sri Lanka", October 2005, www.mcrg.ac.in/DP.pdf (accessed on 20 June 2015); also see various entries in the special issue of *Refugee Watch*, 24–26, October 2005.

37 Sandro Mezzadra and Brett Neilson, *Border as Method, or, the Multiplication of Labour* (Durham, NC: Duke University Press, 2013).

38 These mediations come out vividly in the Ph.d dissertation by Malini Mittal, *Mobility and Changing Family Relations: A Study of a Section of Pink- Collar Workers in Kuwait*, Delhi School of Economics, Delhi University, 2019.

39 In Chapter 4 we had referred to Syrian refugees; on war, disaster, and refugee flows from Syria, for one of the exhaustive studies, Nergis Canefe, *The Syrian Exodus in Context: Crisis, Dispossession and Mobility in the Middle East* (Istanbul: Bilgi University Press, 2018). Canefe writes of "exodus" as a tool of managing disasters and discontent.

40 Ishita Dey, Ranabir Samaddar, and Suhit Sen, *Beyond Kolkata: Rajarhat and the Dystopia of Urban Imagination* (London and New Delhi: Routledge, 2013).

41 Ned Rossiter, "The Logistical City: Software, Infrastructure, Labour", Paper presented at Cities and Materialities Workshop, Institute for Culture and Society, University of Western Sydney, 11 April 2012, http://nedrossiter.org/?p=324 (accessed on 15 June 2015); also, Steven P. Erie, *Globalizing L.A.: Trade, Infrastructure and Regional Development* (Stanford, CA: Stanford University Press, 2004); Reinhold Martin, *The Organizational Complex: Architecture, Media and Corporate Space* (Cambridge, MA: MIT Press, 2003); Ranabir Samaddar, "Rajarhat, the Urban Dystopia", *Transit Labour: Circuits, Regions, Borders*, 29 July 2011, http://transitlabour.asia/blogs/dystopia (accessed on 12 June 2014); Ishita Dey, "New Town and Labour in Transit", *Transit Labour: Circuits, Regions, Borders*, 29 July 2011, http://transitlabour.asia/blogs/newtown (accessed on 12 June 2014).

42 For the contemporary policies of identifying the migrant in India, see Atig Ghosh (ed.), *Branding the Migrant: Arguments of Rights, Welfare and Security* (Kolkata: Frontpage, 2012); see also, Manish K. Jha, P.K. Shajahan, and Mouleshri Vyas, "Biopolitics and Urban Governmentality in Mumbai", in Sandro Mezzadra, Julien Reid, and Ranabir Samaddar (eds.), *The Biopolitics of Development: Reading Michel Foucault in the Post-Colonial Present* (New Delhi and Dordrecht: Springer, 2013), Chapter 4, pp. 45–66.

43 One of the best studies on this theme is by Paulo Tavares, "Lines of Siege: The Contested Government of Nature", in *The Biopolitics of Development: Reading Michel Foucault in the Post-Colonial Present*, chapter 8, pp. 123–164.

44 Walter Kälin, "Climate Change Induced Displacement: A Challenge for International Law", Distinguished Lecture Series, 3, Calcutta Research Group, March 2011, pp. 33–34, www.mcrg.ac.in/DL3.pdf (accessed on 3 November 2018); also see Walter Kälin, "Conceptualizing Climate Induced Displacement", in Jane McAdam (ed.), *Climate Change and Displacement – Multidisciplinary Perspectives* (Oxford: Hart Publishing, 2010), pp. 81–103.

45 To give two of the finest instances of such writings, Dipesh Chakrabarty, "The Climate of History: Four Theses", *Critical Inquiry*, Volume 35, Winter 2009, pp. 197–222; Amitav Ghosh, *The Great Derangement: Climate Change and the Unthinkable* (University of Chicago Press, 2017). These writings are valuable in telling us of the historical intelligibility of climate change, but they leave labour out of the ambit of discussion.

46 Mike Hulme, "The Conquering of Climate: Discourses of Fear and Their Dissolution", *The Geographical Journal*, Volume 174 (1), March 2008, pp. 5–16; Hulme wrote, "We are living in a climate of fear about our future climate. The language of the public discourse around global warming routinely uses a repertoire which includes words such as 'catastrophe', 'terror', 'danger', 'extinction' and 'collapse'." – p. 5

47 Kate Manzo, "Imaging Vulnerability: The Iconography of Climate Change"; *Area*, 2009, *Journal Compilation, Royal Geographical Society*, pp. 1–11, doi:10.1111/j.1475-4762.2009.00887.x; see also, Carol Farbotko, "Wishful Sinking: Disappearing Islands, Climate Refugees, and Cosmopolitan Experimentation", *Asia Pacific Viewpoint*, Volume 51 (1), April 2010, pp. 47–60.

6
THE SPECTRAL PRESENCE OF THE MIGRANT

Two figures of visibility: refugee and the migrant

There is something more to the ecological marginality of select population groups. Ecological disasters strike us as cataclysmic events; whatever happens to the uprooted recedes soon from our thoughts. In South Asia, we still remember the Partition and the partition refugees, likewise in Europe wars and refugee flows. But we rarely remember the migrants due to natural calamities, developmental disasters, infrastructural madness, and economic collapses.[1] They are immigrant labour belonging to "normal" happenings of society. Refugees belong to politics, visibility, civil society, rights, and humanitarian protection. Migrants, particularly immigrant labour, belong to economics, invisibility, market, wages, and governmental welfare. The migrant remains the other of the refugee, and the humanitarian expressions about protection of the refugees have their counterpart in the stately silence about migrant labour. The writings of theorists and philosophers, such as Hannah Arendt, Edward Said, Giorgio Agamben, and others about the refugee condition have added to the visibility/invisibility syndrome. These writings also give us a clue to how population movements are managed by modern governments and the captains of industry.

This perhaps should not surprise us, as politics has been always the area of visibility while economy has been the area of unspoken laws of accumulation, production, and labour. Politics is the sphere of deliberation, ideology, arguments, and rule, while economics is about silently, "without fuss", managing the production of wealth. Laws, administrative procedures, and parliamentary confabulations will have little to say on extraction, accumulation, logistics, and wealth. Refugees belong to the former. Migrants belong to the latter. The preceding chapters tried to bring out this duality and invoked the categories of the displaced – refugee and the migrant – alternatively and interchangeably. There was, readers may think, some arbitrariness in this. That charge has to be partially admitted.

Yet the task is not to delink the two as is conventionally done (think of two separate Global Compacts on which we shall come back in details in the last chapter), or state merely that the two are interlinked, but to investigate the nature of the migrant's invisibility. We have already referred to the logistical expansion of economies and their extractive turn that increase the demand for the migrant – but remember, only as labour, and not as a political subject. In this chapter we shall explore those conditions of invisibility – the invisibility of the migrant in the process of accumulation. For that we shall have to take into account the recent transformation of global economy – in particular postcolonial economy.

Migrant labour as the vanishing mediator of economic transformation

Let us think of the urban economy with which migrant labour is closely linked. Four pillars of this transformation are: infrastructure, extraction, rent, and migrant labour. Infrastructure lends the economy the nature of a network of logistical practices. It calls for greater extractive function of economy. This makes rent one of the important sources of wealth. And transit or migrant labour makes the infrastructural and rental transformation of economy, particularly the city, possible.

One of the main dimensions of the contemporary turn towards neo-liberal urbanisation in developing countries is that it compels the city to be a logistical hub, which requires a certain mode of infrastructural reordering and expansion of the city. The crucial thing to note is that in the process of morphing into a logistical hub, the city also becomes a site of extraction. It thereby becomes a rental site. Such a city survives on the extraction of physical capacity, air, waste, soil, water, and other conceivable resources. At the same time, investment in land becomes an important outlet of capital. The postcolonial milieu of this double transformation makes more acute the contradictions between urban policy regime and neo-liberal urbanity as a whole. These contradictions revolve around two crucial issues: (a) the relation between labour and urban space in this transformation, and (b) the transformation of the city to a rental outlet, based on localised concentrations of migrant labour, a complex of place-based services to support the logistical economy, and a mad rush for extraction. The migrant stands at the centre of these relations.

We can refer to one of the most fundamental of the extractive activities in urban economy, viz., waste disposal or reprocessing, and the urban infrastructure ordered around it. In recent times, the logistics of waste has attained political significance, whether in the form of managing population segments or reprocessing the elements of waste back into the production process, such as reprocessing e-waste. Waste has acquired a contradictory character. At one level waste with its chief function of engaging migrant labour for reprocessing will appear as a marginal element in urban economy. Yet, at another level, waste reprocessing as an industry occupies a central role in the contemporary logic of capital accumulation. The logistics of waste collection, clearance, vending, reprocessing, and disposal are issues pertaining to the circulation of commodity, transportation, organising, and institutionalising the sites of reprocessing and venues of sale of commodities (from cots, furniture, paper, battery, transistor sets, shoes, flower pots, dress, clothing, books, scrap metals, to human hair, mother's milk, human womb, and all that surround us in our daily lives). The logistical organisation of waste reprocessing occupies the margin of neo-liberal modernity; yet it symbolises in this way a complex, and, ironically, a central place in the city of our time.[2]

The preceding chapters had raised the question of visibility of the migrant as labour. Indeed one can note that the ways in which the migrant emerges as a labouring subject also scripts its spectral presence in the politics and economics of the bourgeois world. As we have already noted, much of the mobile labour is involved in processing, re-processing, and particularly logistical processes. Financial processes and data economy just like waste processing play a significant role in the marginalisation of mobile labour. This is now witnessed in the backdrop of a tidal wave of bankruptcies and closures of monetary institutions, which threaten to submerge global labour market in a backlash against neo-liberal market economics. The entire logistical process in the economy also creates waste, which involves a lot of logistical labour for the reprocessing of waste. Thus waste of money, conduct, material, organic elements, biological remains, e-waste, etc., becomes a permanent feature of capitalist circuits, and the capitalist circuit in one form or another must include processing waste also, so that the circuit does not come to abrupt end, and the logic of circuit can proceed.[3] Waste appears in this way as the other form of value. Waste must now produce value. Postcolonial labour is the guarantee that nothing will be an irretrievable waste for the global commodity chain.[4] It is not surprising that migrant (including refugee) labour is heavily deployed in the processing of waste that characterises urban economy. Not without reason, contemporary global capitalism is marked by increasing production of waste, recycling of waste, an ever-increasing waste reprocessing economy, and a rapidly expanding and largely impoverished global labour force involved in waste recycling.[5]

What, then, is waste? What is reprocessing? The answers in short will be: Waste is that product that will not enter into the value chain any more. Reprocessing is that logistical dynamic which brings the so-called non-productive back into the production chain. Waste reprocessing is the eternal deferral of the end of the production chain.

This logistical organisation, of course, has a profound territorial aspect. What does it mean when we say that certain areas in the city are polluted, or some people live near or even inside a dump or in a cement or iron pipe, or that certain areas in the city are known for cheap, second-hand goods (perhaps old mobile handsets, DVD players, computers, printers or hi-fi stereos), or certain areas must be free from industrial and chemical effluents, and such a site of pollution must be shifted somewhere else? What does it mean to say that the city produces waste which must be managed, if the city has to live and reproduce itself? In other words, what is the implication of waste on space and management of the circulation of a commodity called waste? In the background of neo-liberal restructuring of the city, these questions reflect on the links between urban policy, governance, forms of labour, migration, and urban rent. They also tell us of places populated by migrant and refugee labour. If we look at Kolkata, at one level we can simply say that the problem reflects the relationship between ecological space, economic space and political space, but at another, perhaps deeper level, the problem tells of the way capital operates by first colonising a space and then making the unproductive a productive element of economy. These sites of extraction, thus, are not wastelands of capital as the late economist Kalyan Sanyal (2007) would have described them,[6] but marks of a circulation economy that a city has come to represent. Recycling, simply put, is valorising. It is, if you like, the urban image of a centuries-old process of extracting minerals.

Chandni Chowk, at the heart of Kolkata, is a site of reprocessing of several forms of waste. To quote one observer,

> Rows of sweatshops, thin benches outside these shops, on the side of the streets, and thousands of workers disassembling, and re-assembling, old electronic devices and household appliances of every sort mark the place. A newspaper remarked of the activity, 'What is trash in the West is cash east of the Hooghly'.[7]

Thin shops, narrow lanes, busy labour, and exchange of cash will tell you of the circulation of commodities coming from China or Korea (television sets, refrigerators or mobile phones), which now get their second life. They also speak of circulation of labour. But Chandni Chowk is not the only such place in Kolkata. There is Bagri Market, Chor Bazar, and then scores of places where newspapers and several other discarded things are being brought, sifted, categorised, reprocessed, repackaged, and sold. These are also places of transferring goods from wholesale to retail sale. Likewise, new flesh reprocessing areas crop up, which are places of sex industry and trading in flesh and human organs. In the areas adjoining the Kolkata port, the city has other earmarked places for trading in, and circulation of, various types of commodities, including care and service as commodity. Delhi has service villages as does Kolkata in the new town of Rajarhat. Care centres supplying caregivers (*ayahs*) too have their logistical emplacement in the city. These places tell us of the city as a grid of movements, bodies, and services – a logistical grid. They also tell us of certain kinds of supply chains subaltern in nature. Thus, trafficking of flesh and goods, for which Kolkata like Mumbai and all other port cities has been long infamous, requires its logistical set up involving reconnaissance, knowledge of routes, supply depots, consumption chains, exchange points, and an involvement with the legal surface of the activity (including stations of policing and surveillance, and posts of excise and customs inspection).[8]

An enormous amount of energy is spent on passing appropriate laws, formulating policies, setting up boards and committees, imagining a city as a region like the national capital region or the greater Kolkata vision of KMDA (Kolkata Metropolitan Development Authority, *Vision 2020*), and the migrant as an integral part of such a city.[9] Thus, consider this select list of Indian enactments and policies, a severely selected list, towards this urban restructuring towards a logistical entity, whose raison d'être will be to facilitate transportation, communication, and the circulation of men (and now women also), money, credit, information, and goods: Delhi Master Plan; Standard Operating Procedures (SOP) for Child Protection by Indian Railways; Calcutta 300: Plan for Metropolitan Development; Manual Scavengers and Construction of Dry Latrine (Prohibition) Act; Building and Other Construction Workers Welfare Act (1996); *Samajik Mukti* Card for Building and Other Construction Workers; Unorganised Sector Social Security Act; Maharashtra Slum Areas Act, Second Amendment; The Maharashtra Private Security Guards (Registration of Employment and Welfare) Act; Jawaharlal Nehru National Urban Renewal Mission; Mumbai Urban Transport Project; Mumbai Urban Infrastructure Project; Revised Development Plan of Greater Bombay; Smart Cities Mission; New Towns (in contrast to ghost towns) policy; National Policy for Hawkers; and several others. This vast range of policies, measures, acts, and plans backed by money, and to be implemented mostly in the mode of private-public partnership (PPP) necessitates one thing which is constant (besides raw material like cement, steel, glass, electronics material, and financial and credit infrastructure), and that is migrant labour, or what we described earlier as transit labour.[10]

The phenomenon of transit labour becomes comprehensible when we keep in mind the conjunction of infrastructure, logistics, and labour at which the postcolonial economy stands today. Hundreds of projects involving construction of the special economic zones (SEZs), power plants, airports, railway corridors, highways, bridges, new towns, new buildings and houses, flyovers, IT parks, data centres, various real estate such as residential and commercial projects, need not only among others steel, cement, aluminium, and fibre glass but also labour, particularly in the construction and mining sectors.

The construction industry is one of India's largest employers. Thousands of construction workers build new apartments and offices while living in squalor in roadside tents along the new buildings that come up in due course. They are like the informal miners of the country: migrants from the decimated agricultural sector, escaping poverty and disease at home, only to be sucked into a labour market characterised by exploitative labour practices, hazardous work conditions and environment, and almost complete social exclusion with almost no, or little, labour security and their income varying in response to various sorts of fluctuations (seasonal or otherwise) in the demand for labour. Migrant workers move from one construction site to another, labour camp to labour camp. At times the entire family moves, at times the male members only. According to one report, on an average, one labourer dies in the city of Bangalore every day.[11] In all these sites, as in West Bengal, a local contact in the village supplies workers to the contractor. Both extract cuts from the wages paid to the labourers. There is no direct transaction between the builder and the labourers, and this system of sub-contracting frees the actual employers of all responsibilities towards the labour. In Mumbai, consider the Bandra–Worli bridge that links Bandra and the western suburbs of Mumbai with Worli and downtown Mumbai; or the Thakur Village, a new residential township, which stands apart from other planned localities in Mumbai due to its spectacular skyline, with mostly upper-middle-class citizens living there; or the Bandra–Kurla Commercial Complex under construction, which is to be the first of a series of what is called growth centres; the National Stock Exchange building at the Bandra–Kurla Complex; and ICICI Bank headquarters. In Bangalore, consider the Brigade Metropolis, an integrated enclave located on Whitefield Road; the flyover to Electronic City to connect the city centre of Bangalore with the Electronic City, an industrial park which houses more than 100 industries, with around 60,000 employees; or in Delhi with thousands of labourers building the Airport City, the national highway leading to Gurgaon – these are all parables of the current phenomenon of transit labour, because these places symbolise the conjunction of infrastructure, logistics, and labour. Add to that the construction of several fast corridors, smart cities and SEZs in various parts of the country and we get a fair idea of the conjunction earlier mentioned.

What happens to the rent of buildings, of mines, and the price of land? What happens to the rent of bridges, highways, houses, steel and glass buildings, shopping malls, gigantic showrooms, multiplexes, airport cities, studios, cables, poles, transmission towers, dish antennas, ATM kiosks, data centres like Belapur in Mumbai, and other creations of developers and financiers? What happens to the interface of rent and interest (with interest rate becoming crucial to developers)? They show that the question here relates to "excess" – excess of what we may call average profit, excess of the surplus-value characteristic of a particular sphere of production; in other words, not the net product, but the excess of the net product in this sector over the net product of other branches of industry. In other words, the boundaries of postcolonial accumulation, though made by the fundamental dynamics of capital, are influenced to a great extent by the illusions that the same process of accumulation creates. We have indicated already what informal labour means in the context of the neo-liberal transformation of the city into a rental outlet, such as a forcible increase in surplus labour time (through unregulated long working hours, increasingly dense physical labour, the relative absence of labour laws and labour security, labour deregulation, discriminations on the basis of caste and gender, etc.). It produces not only surplus value, but also at times surplus profit in as much as we have seen that at times without much increase in constant capital, surplus profit is created through the dynamics of rent and interest.

The city will now survive on the basis of rental income, and modes of distribution of this income among public institutions, private individuals, banks and other lending agencies, and the extent to which part of this will be spent on retaining and reinforcing the public character of the city. Yet the migrant who will make such transformation possible will be there in the city life only invisibly. Migrant labour is the vanishing mediator in this neo-liberal metamorphosis. The neo-liberal city encapsulates the central social contradiction of modern global capitalism, viz., increased return from global connectedness accompanied by hyper-commodification and financialisation of land and new forms of social marginalisation, most notably the increasing informality and precarious nature of labour and life. Migrant labour represents this contradiction. The infrastructural transformation (including financial and informational infrastructure) of the city we have spoken of is not possible without migrant labour, and yet infrastructural transformation requires migrant labour to be invisible, dispensable, but ready at hand. Recall the classic study by Arjan De Hann (1997) on migrant jute workers in Kolkata[12] and contrast it with an exhaustive report on Kolkata slums;[13] we shall then understand the transformation of the migrant question. The scale and form of migration have changed. Informalisation of work is linked to the availability of migrant labour – whether in the scrap metal industry, or waste-processing zones, including processing of e-waste, or the care and entertainment industry that has expanded enormously, or the rental economy that has grown exponentially, requiring all kinds of new services to be performed by migrant labour. Yet what is important to remember is that migrant labour, with construction labour as the classic case, never settles. Rather, it unsettles the city. Roving bands of labour moving from one construction site to another remind us of the late nineteenth century phenomenon of destitute labour. At the same time, they indicate that the neo-liberal city is based on a combination of the most virtual and primitive forms of accumulation. In this paradoxical combination, migrant labour becomes *transit labour*.

We can think also of the conditions under which labour migrates from work to work, and the peasant becomes a semi-worker to become a full worker only to return to till his/her small parcel of land or work in others' fields when industrial or semi-industrial or semi-manufacturing, or even extractive jobs (like small-scale and artisanal mining or sand mining, or stone crushing) become scarce. Researches on transformations of agrarian society throw some light on transformation of labour. The un-remunerative rural small-scale economy, the impact of neo-liberal governance, massive migration, and consequent multiplication of labour forms – all these were already in evidence a decade back, for instance in India, when the *Report on Conditions of Work and Promotion of Livelihoods in the Unorganised Sector* came out in August 2007.[14] Migrant work in various logistical processes brought back the focus on studying interchangeable labour forms. In this context, it is important to note that the footloose postcolonial labour is also a consequence of international investment chains in countries like India, Bangladesh, Pakistan, Jordan, Turkey, Egypt, Colombia, Panama, Cambodia, Mexico, etc., in garment production, iron ore mining, manufacturing of ancillary parts and instruments in industries such as automobile, electronic production such as mobile telephony, leather products, toy industry, etc. These are overwhelmingly export oriented with the production sites being often special zones. Wages are often low, the work force is markedly female, and the labour supervision rules strict and marked with violence.

Think of the supreme logistical sites, such as building financial corridors or special economic zones, upgrading ports for greater container handling capacity, creating seamless multi-modal transport hubs, building new towns, reprocessing e-waste, constructing highways, airports, and logistical cities, all these requiring and creating footloose labour – the latter forever remaining in the shadows of the logistical sites, but moving on from construction work to plumbing to driving transportation vehicles, to perhaps quarrying or reprocessing urban e-waste. Profit is never derived from these logistical activities directly. For instance, in a new town where land prices will soar, built-in environment will rake in money, financial hubs will be established, BPOs will populate the town, and new steel and glass buildings will come up, the immediate revenue will be in form of rent and interest, whereas without labour the soil could not have been ready, bridges could not have been built, airports could not have been constructed, additional iron ore supply would have been impossible, and steel and glass buildings could not have come up, etc. Yet, in this circuit of commodity circulation, capital will continuously change form, and value-producing labour will be more and more distant from the final stage when the profit will be realised from the capital invested, and revenue will be shared. For capital, this is the desirable history of labour – labour at work but not visible, ready at hand but not always necessary, labour living but whenever required must soon be dead.[15] Everywhere this strategy seems to be successful only to fail at the most unexpected hour of collapse of the circulation-centric economy.

Without migrant labour deployable in sectors dependant on extraction, the expansion of the goods and services market would not have taken place. And, in all these cases, labour become available through a combination of means ranging from violence, dispossession, legislative measures, footloose or informal arrangements, and a modicum of protection. The policy explosion in India at the turn of the century and continuing through the next decade concerned precisely these aspects involving food, work, education, disaster protection, crop insurance, information, and made labour available necessary for the expansion of economy.[16]

A series of laws and illegalities made the availability of migrant labour possible. Labour became free to join these sectors as it tore away from an un-free situation marked by stagnant agriculture and long duration agrarian crisis, though the leap into freedom and back into un-freedom kept on following with each other in close succession. This is a situation that allows us to think of the plough and pick in the same breath.

Migrant labour and the black hole of ecology[17]

The migrant is invisible as it works in dark mines, which are also ecological disasters. Take the infamous case of the Bellary mines near the ruins of Vijayanagara, the former capital of the Vijayanagara Empire (14th–16th centuries) in Karnataka. The international boom for iron ore made India at the dawn of the new century the third largest exporter of iron ore in the world, and a third of the exports came from the Bellary area. The rush for the iron ore there was comparable to the gold rush in the nineteenth century. According to one source based on the Mining and Geology Department records, Bellary region alone exported 15 million tonnes of high-quality iron ore worth $67 million overseas, mainly to China. The boom in the construction industry happened in the wake of the 2008 Olympic Games in Beijing. The international price of iron ore from USD 17 per tonne in 2000–2001 rose to its peak USD 75 in 2005–2006.

Around this time the demand from the Indian steel giants also grew. Thus export, which was earlier 75 per cent of the total production, came down to 60 per cent, and the mined iron ore began to be supplied in greater volume to the Indian market. The giants of the industry – Arcelor Mittal, Posco, Tata Steel, Jindal Steel and Power – all wanted to build steel plants. In 2008 steel prices doubled surpassing $700 per ton. In view of the abnormal rise in demand for iron world over,[18] several countries banned or regulated exports in order to keep domestic prices at reasonable levels. Bellary mining symbolised the surge in demand for iron ore and the accompanying shift to privatisation and open market economy in India. Women and children were pushed into the informal labour market, especially in sectors like mining where deregulation of laws was aimed at attracting direct and private investments. Meanwhile agrarian stagnation forced the landless agricultural labourers and marginal peasantry to look for other means of wage earnings. Migrant labour "floated from mining plot to mining plot searching for sustenance in an informal system of contract labour in the mining triangle."[19] By 2005, the hectic scramble for iron ore led to an uncontrollable social and ecological chaos in the Bellary–Hospet-Sandur district. Most of the mining operations were done by small illegal mining companies, which did not follow any environmental or social regulation. The working and living conditions of the workers were highly exploitative, there was lack of even basic facilities, high level of insanitation led to ill health. Bellary recorded the highest incidence of HIV in Karnataka. Mining dust affected mine workers, who developed serious and chronic illnesses like tuberculosis, silicosis, cancer, and other respiratory illnesses. Ill workers gave place to children and youngsters into this hazardous industry. The same estimate put the number of daily wage labourers there around 60,000, half of them children under the age of 14 and around 20,000 women. The daily wages paid for men was around 110 rupees, for women around 75 rupees, children 50 rupees, and on an average a family earning about 180–200 rupees. Uncontrolled mining led to serious consequences, from the illegal exploitation of forestlands to widespread pollution, rampant corruption to child labour exploitation. Bellary "once famous for its sandalwood forests and abundant wildlife now trembled with the blasting of ore-laden hillsides and the rumble of lorries transporting rock from the mines to ports around India".[20] The entire mining operation was illegal and informal. The profits of the Bellary brothers G. Karuna Karunakara Reddy, G. Janadhana Reddy, and G. Somashekhara Reddy were stupendous, and their control over Karnataka politics became legendary. The mining boom that began by the end of 2003 (when the price of iron ore rose from Rs 200 per metric tonne to Rs 2700 per metric tonne) made the Bellary Brothers the "mining czars" of the state.[21] The scandal finally forced the Supreme Court to intervene. It appointed a Central Empowered Committee (CEC) and said that large-scale illegal mining was on in Karnataka particularly in Bellary district in connivance with officials and public representatives. A special forest bench headed by Chief Justice S.H. Kapadia issued notice to the State government and sought its response on various findings in the CEC's interim report including the export of 304.91 lakh metric tonnes of iron ore without valid permit between 2003 to 2009–10. The report, which was placed before the bench, said that there had been illegal mining on colossal scale in the state, particularly in Bellary district with active connivance of officials of the departments concerned and public representatives. The Court first banned mining in the region in 2011, and then considering the impact of the ban on mining business and livelihoods softened its stand later. The economic and ecological looting was pointed out in the five-volume report of the Justice M.B. Shah Commission. The Central Government had appointed Justice M.B. Shah as the head of a one-man panel in November, 2010. The two interim reports submitted by the Commission earlier had led the Supreme Court to impose a temporary ban on mining activities in Goa, the largest exporter of iron-ore in the country. On 21 April 2014, Supreme Court of India lifted the ban on mining in Goa with a temporary annual cap of 20 million tonnes (MT) of iron ore excavation, which was 40 MT earlier. The Court also stayed the order of the Bombay High Court directing the filing of FIRs since investigation by the state government was already underway. It also stated that several conclusions drawn by the M B Shah Commission Report were incorrect, most notably, those on legality of leases granted in 1988 and alleged encroachment.

Like iron ores mining activities for coal and sand also increased the demand for footloose labour. Illegal mining and stone crushing on the Ganges riverbed continued in the Haridwar district in Uttarakhand, this despite the fact that quarrying had been banned in the Kumbhmela area zone. An ascetic monk fasting since 19 February 2011 against illegal mining and stone crushing along the river Ganges died at the Himalayan Hospital in Dehradun, after being allegedly poisoned by stone-crushing mafia.[22] In this infrastructural expansion and the necessary logistical planning massive extraction and the availability of labour proved crucial.

Migrant labour including workers from Nepal makes coal mining in the Jaintia hills in Meghalaya possible. Money lies at the bottom of steep, sheer holes dug 100–180 feet deep into the ground. Sudden rain, a tipped cart, a falling rock – just about anything can mean death in the hostile pits of the Jaintia hills, called the rat mines. The hills are now pock-marked with sudden, unannounced holes, and these hills were known for their illegal and unscientific mining. Today as the demand for coal has shot up the mines are now increasingly being served by a workforce of children mostly between 7–17 years in age. Some estimate that a staggering 70,000 children from Nepal, Bangladesh, Assam, Bihar, and Jharkhand work in these private mines. There are about one lakh quarries in the region. Typically a labour camp shelters twenty-five miners, many of them minors. A camp is a hut located in dense forests or just in the middle of nowhere. Juvenile crime is on the rise in the district. Child miners spend days alone in dark, low tunnels, and nights spent far away from family. Yet mining is rewarding, for while a driver may not earn more than Rs 5,000 mining can fetch around Rs 8,000 to 10,000 a month. Incessant rain brings in collapse of a pit and death of a miner.[23]

The Mines Act of 1952 forbids anyone below age eighteen to be employed in mines, while the Labour Law fixes the permissible employment age at fourteen. The government seems to have no qualms about child labour as long as it gets part of the spoils. According to a report, around one lakh metric tonnes of coal, worth around Rs 50 crore, is extracted from the Jaintia mines every day. The government gets a royalty of Rs 290 per tonne; the mine owners sell it for Rs 4,200 per tonne. Most of this low-grade coal is transported to different parts of the country and to the Bangladesh border. Child labour is crucial for handling and loading also in the coal depots. The breaking of coal is the end point of the tortuous mining work by the migrant labourers from nearby areas or the distant villages of Bihar, Nepal, Bangladesh, or Assam. Life is temporary in every way in the rat mines of Meghalaya.[24]

In Meghalaya there are 300 to 500 rat-hole coal mines. A miner before entering the mine has to put a piece of cloth over his head and a rubber tire tube is secured to his back to shield him in the pit. Another piece of tube attaches a torch to his forehead as the guiding light. Hills of Meghalaya are strewn with thousands of mines of this kind, and not one of them is legal. Meghalaya as a Sixth Schedule state has three autonomous district councils with which the government by law the sole authority to lease and license mines. Traditional institutions openly flout mining norms, and land is let out at will to private operators. Most mine owners procure gelatine sticks and detonators on the black market from licensed contractors. Hence, accidents in the rat-hole mines go unreported. According to another report, unregulated mining activity has led to illegal mining of uranium also there. The government keeps on collecting royalties from illegal mine operators and even issues them receipts.[25]

Sand mining closely follows coal mining in its illegal life. Sand is a sediment brought from the area through which the river flows and gets deposited downstream. The process continues in every rainy season which means the soil gets eroded throughout the course of river and deposited as sediments depending up on the size of sand particles. The last tail end of the river carries tiny particles which flow into the sea. Himalayan rivers carry more sand than the Western Ghat ones as the soil and rock surface is softer than the Western Ghat surface. Hence the sand deposits in northern rivers are much more to the extent that the river courses change yearly due to sand deposit. In the sixties and seventies of the last century efforts were made to retain the course of the river by construction of barriers/check dams across the river. The removal of sand from the river is a necessity to keep the river bottom intact so much so that the carrying capacity of the river is maintained. The riverbed is the layer devoid of any sand particles that get deposited over riverbed. Hence the quantum of sand that should be removed is the sand deposited over the riverbed. Removal of sand deposited above the riverbed is highly needed to maintain the river intact. To call the sand removal a mining operation may not be literally correct as the same does not involve any mining process proper. The government of the day has always claimed that it seeks to balance construction needs and environmental concerns while allowing sand mining to continue illegally in many places. The euphemism is in the form of detailed guidelines on sustainable sand mining in the country and strict monitoring and crackdown against illegal mining rampant in many states. The draft guidelines also suggest increasing penalties against the illegal miners which may include confiscation of vehicles carrying illegally mined sand, recovering huge amount (five to ten times of the market value of the seized minerals), and seizures of all the equipment or machineries involved in mining in non-leased areas. The ministry has also advised use of technology like android application (App), GPS, and unique bar-coding system to track the vehicles of illegal miners and those who indulge in exploiting the natural resources beyond permissible limit. Extraction of ordinary clay or sand manually by potters and earthen tile makers, removal of sand deposited in agricultural field after flood by farmers and dredging and de-silting of dams, reservoirs, barrage, and canals are kept under the "exempt" categories in the draft. The guidelines also provide criteria for sustainable sand mining, both in-stream and off-channel extraction of sand, and detailed parameters that can be used by state and central agencies for issuing mining lease for smaller and bigger tracts. Yet the fact is that the ministry has at the same time made an exemption list where certain categories of users may be allowed sand mining keeping in view maintenance of infrastructure, abatement of disasters and property rights.[26] These guidelines mean only streamlining what is already under way and make it more profitable. Reports also tell of the ways in which illegal and informal sand mining business extracts governmental protection or informal license on the ground that if sand mining is closed, thousands of migrant labourers will become unemployed and prices of building material will shoot up affecting housing costs. The economy of small-scale and artisanal mining besides politics involves money. It is now a blood sport.

These black holes of ecology (which the rat holes of Meghalaya are) are like vampires sucking migrant labour into their unreachable depth. Not visibility, but utility to the economy ordains the migrant's presence in society. In this game of visibility/invisibility, factors of race and gender are always present. Labour in the artisanal and small-scale mines, waste processing, care, entertainment, and other allied activities, is marked by gender, age, and race. These are "dangerous" occupations that call for the presence of migrant labour of specific types.[27] Specific bodies are needed to service some of the activities of production and reproduction – yet the servicing must be done "naturally", "unnoticeably"; as if the social machine of reproduction is functioning well, smooth, oiled, properly greased. The migrant workers will be of course neither here nor there.[28]

The invisibility of migrant labour is perched on the isolation of the migrant (and the refugee) in his or her own migrant state, which will be a guarantee that there will be no corrosive effect of the presence of the migrant on the society. There will be no contagion. The purpose of the camp – housing and secluding the asylum seekers and illegal aliens – is thus met within the economy. The dynamics of invisibility thus serves the purpose of three apparatuses. First, invisibility maintained and guaranteed through surveillance ensures security of the society (think of Rohingya informal labour in Jammu). Second, seclusion in economy, maintained by law, thus "normalises" the migrant's presence. Third, if we think of this globally, it ensures a new system of power to control migrants, distribute them "evenly", and put them in their proper place in society.[29]

Notes

1 Set in the context of Great Depression *Grapes of Wrath* (1939) and other literary creations are like exceptions.
2 Part of the material in this section of the chapter dealing with the deployment of migrant labour in logistical services and leading to a logistical reorientation of the city, is drawn from my "The Logistical City", in Sujata Patel and Omita Goyal (eds.), *India's Contemporary Urban Conundrum*, India International Centre (London: Routledge, 2019).
3 On this see the interesting discussion by Vinay Gidwani, *Capital Interrupted: Agrarian Development and Politics of Work in India* (Minneapolis: University of Minnesota Press, 2008), chapter one, "Waste", pp. 1–31.
4 J. Bennett, *Vibrant Matter: A Political Ecology of the Thing* (Durham, DC: Duke University Press, 2010); see also Friends of the Earth Report, *The Policy Study Report on the Waste Electrical and Electronic Equipment Directive* (2011), www.foe.co.uk/.../report-influence-eu-policies-environment-9392 (accessed on 13 March 2016); J. Gabrys, *Digital Rubbish : A Natural History of Electronics* (Ann Arbor, MI: University of Michigan Press, 2013); S. Graham and N. Thrift, "Out of Order: Understanding Repair and Maintenance", *Theory, Culture & Society*, Volume 24 (3), 2007, pp. 1–25; J. Lepawsky, "Composing Urban Orders from Rubbish Electronics: Cityness and the Site Multiple", *International Journal of Urban and Regional Research*, Volume 39 (2), 2014, pp. 185–199; and the significant essay on labour and waste, N. Rossiter, "Translating the Indifference of Communication: Electronic Waste, Migrant Labour and the Informational Sovereignty of Logistics in China", *International Review of Information Ethics*, Volume 11, 2009, pp. 35–44.
5 Singapore, Hong Kong, Dubai, and several other metropolitan centres of global economy call for permanent presence of migrant labour for their waste process industries. One report from Bangladesh states,

> Sixty per cent of iron used in the construction business in Bangladesh comes from the ship-breaking industry, earning the state-capitalist apparatus annual revenue of US$900 million. It employs 30,000 people directly and 250,000 people indirectly. Yet the labour laws in the sector are not applied to protect the workers from grievous injury. In the last decade 250 workers have died and more than 800 have been handicapped for life. Hulking steel remains of ships that took part in maritime trade across the earth's ocean spaces in the last century undergo radical transformation, reverting from ship back to steel. The process of breaking down the massive ocean liners uses a mixture of acetylene and muscular power. Within the rusting structural frames lie the secrets of steel reclaiming its form. Here is the inverse of the shipyards of northern maritime powers, where steel, through the power of capital infrastructure, was reshaped into objects that would produce the conditions for capital to reorganize itself. The long stretching beach and the bay provide the scenography as the labourers struggle to dismember rusting leviathans in the oily mud. The bosses of the ship-breaking yards of Chittagong have an appalling human rights record despite global media coverage and impose a notorious no-photography rule.

Nabil Ahmed, "Entangled Earth", *Third Text*, Volume 27 (1), January 2013, pp. 44–53, 50.
6 Kalyan Sanyal, *Rethinking Capitalist Development: Primitive Accumulation, Governmentality, and Postcolonial Capitalism* (New Delhi: Routledge, 2007).
7 Giorgio Grappi, "Kolkata as Extraction Site", www.academia.edu/8938818/Kolkata_as_Extraction_Site (accessed on 1 October 2016).
8 For a detailed account of the role of migrants in the processing and recycling economy of Johannesburg, Yordanos Almaz Seifu, *Wayferers: Travel Journal*, trans. Hiwot Tadesse (Addis Ababa: Friedrich Ebert Stiftung, 2018), which, and for the same in Karachi and Delhi, Shahram Khosravi, *'Illegal' Traveller: An Auto-Ethnography of Borders* (Basingstoke, Hampshire: Palgrave Macmillan, 2010).
9 For such laws on Delhi, Amit Prakash, "The Capital City: Discursive Dissonance of Law and Policy", in R. Samaddar (ed.), *Migrant and the Neoliberal City* (Hyderabad: Orient Blackswan, 2018), pp. 225–257.

10 By transit labour we mean labour is in transit form: labour engaged in producing places of transit like roads, ports, flyovers, tunnels, ATM kiosks; transit towns like Cyberabad in Hyderabad; warehouses, truck terminals, IT networks, including cables and poles; also engaged in waste processing and reprocessing, in short, labour engaged in transitory activities, in one phrase, the circulation economy.
11 See http://msrelli.com/migrant-workers-in-india/ (accessed on 12 October 2015).
12 Arjan De Hann, "Unsettled Settlers: Migrant Workers and Industrial Capitalism in Calcutta", *Modern Asian Studies*, Volume 31 (4), 1997, pp. 919–949.
13 Kolkata Metropolitan Development Authority, *Vision 2020*, www.hindustantimes.com/kolkata/civic-bosses-lay-out-vision-2020-for-city/story-eoIhGUvZAG2fmuL6OEg7iK.html (accessed on 23 September 2017); also see "Urban Slum Reports: The Case of Kolkata", 2003, www.ucl.ac.uk/dpu-projects/Global_Report/pdfs/Kolkata.pdf (accessed on 1 October 2016).
14 National Commission for Enterprises for the Unorganised Sector, *Report on Conditions of Work and Promotion of Livelihoods in the Unorganised Sector* (New Delhi: Government of India, August 2007), http://dcmsme.gov.in/Condition_of_workers_sep_2007.pdf (accessed on 21 September 2018).
15 One aspect of this transformation is that besides the conditional visibility of labour in the logistical milieu, labour's individuality (product of visibility) is over as the infrastructural turn of capitalism overwhelms the society. In the logistical milieu, infrastructure is able to present labour as a necessary coordinate to the universal future made of mobility. The sacrifice of labour as individual to a projected digital future signals the transition of industrial capitalism to postcolonial capitalism, from the factory to the imperium of roads, airport cities, ports, containers, special freight corridors, Uber taxis, fast transmission cables, auto-rickshaws, and trucks.
16 Alpa Shah and Barbara Harriss-White estimated four years back that 50 to 100 million wage labourers circulate in the Indian labour market – see, "Resurrecting Scholarship on Agrarian Transformations", *Economic and Political Weekly*, Volume 46 (39), 24–30 September 2011, pp. 13–18, p. 15; On the theme of policy explosion in India, see also Madhuresh Kumar, "Globalisation, State Policies, and Sustainability of Rights", *Policies and Practices* 6, March 2005, Kolkata, www.mcrg.ac.in/pp6.pdf (accessed on 2 September 2019).
17 For details of migrant labour in small-scale and artisanal mining in India, see my "Theorising Transit Labour in Informal Mineral Extraction Processes", in Kuntala Lahiri-Dutta (ed.), *Between the Plough and the Pick: Informal, Artisanal and Small-Scale Mining in the Contemporary World* (Canberra: Australian National University Press, 2018); I am grateful to Kuntala Lahiri-Dutta for giving me access to her writings, which have been of enormous help in writing this section.
18 On the China-led global demand for iron and steel and the general commodity boom in the last ten years and the subsequent decline, the report by John W. Miller and Juliet Samuel, "Mining Companies Bury Dividends", *The Wall Street Journal* (section, Business and Tech.), 10 December 2016, pp. B1–B2. The report informs, "Between 2012 and 2014, for example, Phoenix-based Freeport-McMoran Inc., the biggest US mining company paid out $4.7 billion in dividends, according to securities filings" (p. B1).
19 Report and photographs by Marco Bulgarelli, http://marcobulgarelli.com/bellarys-mines-india/ (accessed on 12 October 2015).
20 *Ibid.*
21 Taken from the collection of reports from the site dedicated to the mining scam, http://bellary0.hpage.co.in/reddy-bros_1024057.html (accessed on 12 October 2015).
22 The UN Special Rapporteur's Report on the human rights of the migrants, placed distributed by the General Assembly on 3 April 2014, noted that risks of particular groups of migrant workers and reminds us of the situation described here. See, "Report of the Special Rapporteur on the human rights of migrants, François Crépeau with special emphasis on labour exploitation of migrants" – A/HRC/26/35.
23 This section draws from a report by Kunal Majumder, "Mining Sorrows", *Tehelka Magazine*, Volume 7 (26), Dated 3 July 2010; figures and citations are from this report; in *Let*

me Speak, trans. Victoria Ortiz (New York: Monthly Review Press, 1978) Domitila Barrios describes the work of women miners knows as the "rock pile women", who were mostly widows of miners died in the Bolivian mines or killed in massacres. These women miners worked on the artificial hills of rocks that had been thrown from the pits and had some mixture of ore and stone. The women had to break the rocks and separate the two (pp. 104–106).

24 "Mining Sorrows"; the observers of Meghalaya economy have long noted the way forest resources have been plundered by the local elite over the years on the ground of local autonomy and village ownership. One anthropologist wrote more than ten years ago, "Even if it is common knowledge that politicians and other people with power in the hill societies have enriched themselves through the reckless exploitation of the forest, this tends to be lost due to the stress on exploitation by outsiders" - Bengt G. Karlsson, "Politics of Deforestation in Meghalaya", CENISEAS paper 3, Centre for Northeast India, South and Southeast Asia Studies, Omeo Kumar Das Institute of Social Change and Development, Guwahati, 2004, p. 34.

25 Teresa Rehman, "Too Deep for the State", *Tehelka Magazine*, http://archive.tehelka.com/story_main41.asp?filename=Ws271208too_deep.asp (accessed on 11 October 2015).

26 Follow the discussion on IHRO@yahoogroups.com, 15–17 September 2015; "New Rules to Curb Illegal Sand Mining", www.livemint.com/Politics/lFs1vaw0PHEMHizHgMk83N/New-rules-to-curb-illegal-sand-mining.html (accessed on 13 October 2015); "Statement by Environment Minister on Notification for Sustainable Sand & Minor Mineral Mining", Press Information Bureau, Government of India, 24 September 2015 (accessed on 13 October 2015); plus see for details of the state of sand mining, "Report of the Ministry of Environment, Forests, and Climate Change", http://envfor.nic.in/public-information/report-moef-sand-mining (accessed on 10 October 2015).

27 Mouleshri Vyas speaks of dangerous lives of migrant labour in waste processing work in Mumbai in "The Cutting Edge: Death and Life of Safai Karmacharis and Elderly Security Guards in Mumbai", in Ranabir Samaddar (ed.), *Migrants and the Neoliberal City* (New Delhi: Orient Blackswan, 2018), pp. 170–195.

28 Jolin Joseph and Vishnu Narendran, "Neither Here nor There: An Overview of South-South Migration from both sides of the Bangladesh-India Migration Corridor", Erasmus University, ISS Working Paper General Series, No 569, pp. 1–36, May 2013.

29 Exasperated with the opaqueness of studies of migration and the migrant, Charles Tilly while interrogating work and life in modern European historical context said, finally migration inquiry boils down "to some combination of these three questions: 1. Who lives here *now*? 2. Where did they live *then*? 3. Who else lived *here* then?" (p. 48; Italics in original) Tilly ended his enquiry with this statement with saying, "The history of European migration is the history of European social life . . ." (p. 71) – Charles Tilly, "Migration in Modern European History", in W.H. McNeil and R.S. Adams (eds.), *Human Migration* (Bloomington: Indiana University Press, 1978), pp. 48–72.

7
INSECURE NATION, INSECURE MIGRANT[1]

The background

One of the reasons of the failure of *The Age of Migration* to bring out the postcolonial nature of the present age of migration is that it did not examine the internal situation of the postcolonial countries closely and kept the issue of the internally displaced population groups (IDPs) mostly out of discussion. Yet the way the issue of national security is incessantly linked to the question of migration points to the need to connect the internal with the external. How does migration appear as a threat to the security of a nation? Is the language of "doom as a result of migrant invasion", graphically invoked again and again by various nationalist leaders around the world, sudden? Is it without any colonial lineage or postcolonial effect? Apart from the obvious fact that the "invading" migrants are "barbarians", poor, primitive, aggressive, and "terroristic", and are mostly from the "South", and hence the postcolonial imprint on the global security discourse is evident, even the discourse of security is shaped by colonial history. To make sense of the link between the two discourses of migration and security, we may even leave out for the present the history of partition killings and displacements in many postcolonial countries in Asia and Africa, as other slices of postcolonial histories suffice to demonstrate the link. The following material, largely drawn from the history of the Indian Northeast, shows security and migration as inseparable twins in the colonial world and the postcolonial present.

There is however one development specific to our time. Humanitarian ideas of protection have added themselves to the notion of security. Humanitarian concerns now sit comfortably with practicalities originating from considerations of security and the imperatives of the policy makers to balance concern for the migrants with policy imperatives of the State, dominant communities, multinational corporations (MNCs), and the security lobby. Rights of the migrants are minimised in this way.

Indeed, these humanitarian ideas also serve the function of downplaying the overwhelming factor of conflict and wars in our histories. But these conflicts shape our communitarian histories because "communities must be defended" – one can say the permanent condition in which communities find themselves. We have to ask therefore: What are the conditions in which migration becomes a matter of insecurity/security? What is that point, the threshold, where these two issues intersect? What are the patterns of collective politics and collective violence that need to be studied if we are to understand the intersecting worlds of population flows and security?

Alien-hood, we must remember, everywhere begins with conquest. The modern history of immigration, insecurity, nationalism, ethnicity, and attack on the "foreigners" began almost everywhere, as in the Northeast of India, with conquest. With conquest and annexation of territory, the first seeds of racism were sown. Migration as a security problematic began in this way. Conquest, subsequent administrative reorganisation that each conquest required, and the new political-legal-administrative identity of a population made population flow an issue of security. Thus, issues of resources became matters of defending these resources against invading migrants, that is to say a matter of security, which every conquest underlined. Native/immigrant politics became a question of resource politics, race politics, and nationalist politics at the same time.

The transition from the imperial form of rule to the national form of rule has only accentuated the political problematic of immigration. The imperial form of rule in many ways had left the borders – in this case the borders in the Indian northeast – undefined and un-demarcated. But the national form of state is much more territorial. The idea of a nation, which was a weapon in the anti-colonial struggle, also made possible for the leaders of the nation to use the bureaucratic-territorial state and re-organise it on the basis of the territorial-national principle of identification of population groups, hitherto incongruent with each other. The imperial form of rule, at least the colonial rule in India, like the administration of other empires in the past, negotiated the issue of diversity of the society it was ruling with a graded form of administration, in which divide and conquer was an extremely important principle. Difference was the organising norm of the ruling political form. The national state made a switch from the norm of difference to that of homogeneity (one nation, one state), which meant among others settlement of the hitherto "unknown" frontier areas into fully politically administered areas of the national state. The constitutional deliberations in the country of the preceding ten years (about twenty years if we take Simon Commission as the starting point) of independence bear out that history of transformation of the principles of organising politics and administration from a frontier area to a fully administered part of the country.

The colonial administration had introduced the notion of an almost racialized difference between the plains and the hills. It was claimed that the hill people belonged to the Mongoloid areas; they belonged neither historically nor racially to India proper and the plains of the northeast and therefore colonial administrators like J.P. Mills and R.N. Reid contended that while power would be soon transferred to the Indians, these people of the Mongoloid areas should not be compelled to live in India. The cultural differences with mainstream Indians were obvious and needed little re-emphasis. The languages of the hills were Tibeto-Burman; the indigenous system of self-government was alive in the hills while it had disappeared from the plains – the hills were clearly different. Yet, as we know, the nationalist pressure proved too strong for the indirect and graded system of rule to continue. The 1935 Act with respect to Assam had designated the Northeast Frontier Tracts, the Naga Hills District, the Lushai Hills District, and the North Cachar Subdivision of the Cachar District as excluded areas. The Garo Hills District, the Mikir Hills in Nowgong and Sibsagar Districts, and the British portion of the Khasi and Jaintia Hills District other than Shillong Municipality and Cantonment became the partially excluded areas. A special cadre for the frontier area was created in Burma. India followed suit.[2]

By the time the Indian constitution came to be framed, continuing political exclusion of the hill areas was out of question. The main recommendation of the Constituent Assembly's sub-committee for Northeast Frontier Tribal and Excluded Areas was that while the future of these areas did not lie in absorption, it lay in political and social amalgamation. Thus, difference would remain, but political identity with the Union would be an accompanying reality.

The framing of the constitution and subsequent reorganisation of the region reflected three major developments: (a) the boundary demarcation between India and Burma was complete, dividing people into different units like the Nagas and the Mizos who by that time had started to think of themselves as distinct nationhoods; (b) the national rule in India had firmly established its hold in this area by ending the graded system of rule except what was allowed under the sixth schedule of the Indian constitution; and (c) the restructuring of the political-administrative space by creating settled and stable units of political-administrative units in form of states – a process that took full form with the North-Eastern Areas (Reorganisation) Act of 1971.

Security and the political economy of resources[3]

In the Indian Northeast the modern economy of resources began with the colonial trade of tea and timber. Besides the British-owned tea estates, gradually other estates came to be owned by various Indian groups and the Assamese groups – in the last decade of the preceding century about 150 tea estates were owned by about 130 Assamese companies in the Assam valley with the largest tea company having an annual turnover of about Rs. 50 crores. The rest of the Assamese bourgeoisie today consists of contractors, transporters, traders, and people engaged in the hotel industry and real estate business, besides engaging in LPG distribution or timber trade. An unofficial estimate puts the number of small tea growers in Assam as 500 of whom 80 per cent are Assamese. In Meghalaya the daily transaction of timber sale outside the state is nearly of the amount of Rs. 20 lakhs. The share of central grant-in-aid to total revenue receipts in Meghalaya in 1990–95 has ranged between 55 and 60 per cent. In Arunachal Pradesh it was between 64–70 per cent and in Nagaland as high as 87 per cent. Thus while the revenue-generating capacity of states in the northeast has been extremely weak, with the entire region lagging behind the rest of the country in industrial growth, power supply, fertiliser consumption, credit flow, communication facilities, and transport network, the political class survives with central aid with which it makes its nation. Besides public rent seeking activities, private rent seeking continues unabated – be it in tea industry, or in local petty trade, or in a barber's shop, in some cases the percentage of the earning given out as rent payment to private parties being as high as 25 per cent.[4] In this background of a rentier state, a parasite political class, and massive mass discontent, weak or nil growth, and absence of any appropriate policy of local development and resource generation and utilisation, the immigrants were seen as the cause of the miseries of life.

The region has a population of about 40 million, with 80 per cent of population living in rural areas, agriculture being the primary occupation of 70 per cent of population, of whom 60 per cent are cultivators, 10 per cent agricultural labourers, and 8 per cent engaging in allied farm sector. Shifting cultivation has 2.7 million hectares under it. Irrigated area as proportion of total cropped area ranges between 11 and 25 per cent as against the national average of 35 per cent. About 25 per cent of the total consumed food grain in this region is imported from outside. Agro-sector reform is almost absent while some of the big public sector enterprises marked as promising global players such as the Indian Oil Corporation, Oil Indian Limited, and Oil and Natural Gas Corporation operate in this region. Yet, notwithstanding the presence of some of the richest public sector companies in this region, the region's incapacity to generate revenue is stark – for instance although Assam produces commodities such as tea, plywood, crude oil, and jute, it gets only 5 per cent of Rs. 700 crores worth of plywood per year, and 2 per cent of tea sold through the Guwahati Tea Auction Centre. Even for the basics of flood control, the state has to depend on the centre, while the borrowing capacity of the state decreases day by day. Out of the total cess of Rs. 30,000 crores collected from the oil sector between 1984 and 1991, Rs. 26,000 crores were deposited to the Consolidated Fund of India. Thus, despite a satisfactory credit-deposit ratio (of commercial banks) in states like Tripura (61 per cent), Manipur (71 per cent), and Assam (49 per cent), the credit disbursed can be hardly properly utilised in this context. The indicators relating to small-scale industrial units and manufacturing units present an equally dismal picture.[5] The level of urbanisation in the region is quite low – only 14 per cent of the population of the region lives in towns, while density of population has increased from 57 per square kilometre in 1961 to 123 in 1991. The pressure on land has grown, and the decadal population growth rate in all the states of the region has been higher than the national average, which is 23.50 (1991 census), while non-agricultural productive activity has almost remained at the same level.[6]

At the same time, the mode of shifting agriculture has faced crisis. Shifting agriculture was a feature of a subsistence economy, and though this did not preclude trading of other products, it meant collective management of forest-land including allotment of the portion for each family, maintenance of village commons, and no accumulation of surplus for "expanded reproduction". While shifting agriculture has declined, or made impossible in a market set up, settled cultivation too has not improved. Large numbers of communities have practised settled cultivation over the ages in hill areas too, for instance Monpas of Tawang in Kameng district in Arunachal Pradesh, Khamptis of Lohit district, and Apa Tanis in Subansiri district. The Angamis and Chakesangs of Kohima district practise wet rice cultivation in form of terrace farming. In short, the principal issue of sustainability of resource use is now in question in the entire region – from the plains of Assam to the hills of Mizoram. Contrary to the popular notion of immigration as the main problem, the issue of sustainability of resources is more complicated. It is a blocked scenario, marked by inadequate formal trade and economic linkages in the east (Burma), south (the Bay), west (Bangladesh), and north (Bhutan and Tibet). Developed basically in recent history as what can be called an economy of a market along the foothills, which bears the characteristics of an extraction economy around coal and limestone, and a plantation economy around tea and timber, the scenario represents today what Dietmar Rothermund had termed long back "an enclave economy".

It is true that for the last fifteen years the Indian state has been trying to prise open the situation by its "Look East" followed by an "Act East" policy. Roads, railways, and other infrastructure of connectivity have increased, and to a certain extent therefore economy too has expanded. The expansion of connectivity is taking place in the context of a historically evolved pattern of population flows.[7] While population flows into the region and within the region keep creating insecurities of various kinds, the situation has been compounded by two factors: (a) outflow of population groups from the Northeast to other parts of the country,[8] and (b) in the wake of projects under "Look East" and "Act East" policies there is renewed labour inflow into the region. Indeed, some commentators claim that the policy of opening up the region has only aggravated the issue of insecurity.[9] In time economic insecurity has been complemented by political and existential insecurity, strengthening in the process homeland demands, and demands to expel "foreigners". The current drive to identify "aliens" in Assam, and expel them as part of the preparation of a National Register of Citizens (NRC) only testifies to the organic link between a neo-liberal development of the region and a xenophobic politics of security.[10]

In this context the mood in the Khasi and the Jaintia Hills is symptomatic of the entire region.[11] It is perhaps wrong to say that politics in the northeast is divided in two segments: the modern parliamentary politics with franchise, votes, institutions, financial agencies, education, developmental policies, etc. on one hand, and ethnicity, politics of identity, gun running, gun battles, narcotics, xenophobia, and hatred against outsiders on the other. A more circumspect view would tell us of a combined and closed world (enclave economy) of contentious politics marked by war of resources and attacks against the most immediate "enemy", the most immediate "invader", the most proximate "occupier", and the most immediate "usurper" of land. Security is intensely physical in this milieu, so is its politics, and the by-products of such politics as neo-racism. The neo-liberal policy of the region's development has not done away with enclaves of underdevelopment and depressed economy. It has only exacerbated the problem of security/insecurity.

Enclave economy is partly a product of the differential and contrasting physicality of the region. The hill ranges of Arunachal Pradesh, Nagaland, Manipur, and Mizoram belong to extra-peninsular mountains and cover approximately 60 per cent of the region. The Meghalaya-Karbi Anglong plateau sections corresponding to the peninsula account for 12 per cent of the region; and the area enclosed by the Brahmaputra plains, a continuation of Indo-Gangetic plains, and the Barak valley accounts for the rest. Similarly there are pronounced differences between the Himalayan Mountains of Arunachal Pradesh, the eastern hills such as the Naga Hills, North Cachar Hills, and Manipur ranges, and the valleys that include the Imphal valley also. The relations between the valleys and the hilly peripheries have been always unstable. Population groups have come through the passes of Arunachal Pradesh from Tibet, Nepal, and Bhutan, through the valleys of Ganga and the Brahmaputra, through the sea and the delta, and through the land routes in the Patkai range. Peasants moved in from East Bengal into Tripura along the Meghna system, indentured coolies came to the upper reaches of the region from Chotanagpur, Bengal, and Orissa, Nepalis moved in as army men and as graziers, and much before that Tais had come into Arakan and then into the Brahmaputra valley, while groups from southern and western Tibet had come to the Arakan and the eastern parts of Manipur and Mizoram. Many of these population groups besides consolidating territorially developed exclusive linkages. And, all in all a peculiar mixture of outright plunder, tribute, feudalism, slavery, several separate trade networks, and an indigenous egalitarianism prevailed, and only with the consolidation of the northern and southern Lushai Hills the region got a universal power to live under – an overarching colonial rule. Gradually administrative centres came to be established in the hills, for instance in Kohima in the Angami country in 1878, so that the entire area could now be converted to something like the status of a British district – thus the Naga Hills area came to be established quickly thereafter in 1881. Mokokchung was established in 1890, and the two parts of the Lushai Hills became a single part of Assam.

With this a definite pattern of territorial arrangements of the population groups of the region emerged: The Garos, Khasis, and Jaiantias in their hills south of the Brahmaputra valley; the Assamese in the valley along with immigrants particularly concentrated in Goalpara and Cachar areas, and the plain tribes concentrated in the lower Brahmaputra valley on the northern side of the river; Mishimis, Abors, and others in the north-eastern part of the region, now Arunachal Pradesh; Naga groups and sub-groups in the Naga Hills, Meiteis in the Imphal valley and Kuki-Chin groups in the southwestern part and Cachar; Mizo groups and sub-groups in the Mizo hills with Kuki-Chin groups in the northern parts and Reangs and others in the southwestern parts, Tripuris and Chakmas in the northeastern part of Tripura; and marking the general spatial segmentation of the region and the frontiers between prominent groups were several immigrant communities, who always disturbed the neat differences between valleys and the hills.[12] Distance factor, accessibility pattern, resource endowments such as land, water, and forests, the locative and territorial aspects of different population groups, and colonial plantation economy all contributed to the growth of "enclave existence". Lack of access to land and weak transport and communication networks reinforced in many cases the enclave pattern. And as happens everywhere in the history of the development of national and homeland politics, it was development that turned segments into enclaves and nation into homes (homelands).

Enclave economy also produced a distinct politics of security, where the immigrants quickly became the symbols of insecurity. Therefore, it should not astonish us that a discourse of security co-habits today with the discourse of retarded economy, internal colonialism, and development. Indeed, political economy (that is the political discourse of economy or politics of economy) and politics of security have always gone hand in hand. Neo-liberal expansion of economy has not done away with enclaves; enclaves are now put in service of logistical activities. The security discourse remains a constant companion.

This has been apparent in the way in which the 1,879 km. long border with Bangladesh is considered in this security discourse. Tripura's border with Bangladesh is 856 km, with Meghalaya 443 km, Mizoram 318 km, Assam 262 km, and of course West Bengal's border with Bangladesh is 2216 km long. The border with Burma is similarly treated similarly in this discourse. The border is not a site invoking commonality to share, not an opportunity to link up with others. It is seen as a threatening factor, changing the demographic complexion of these states. Tripura's indigenous population is a minority today – about 28 per cent of about 3 million population of the state. The anti-foreigner agitation in Assam from 1979 to 1985, written about since then over and over again, involved deaths (of around 7000 people), riots, massacres, forced displacement (of about 2 million), mass boycotts, paralysis of administration, and an upsurge of Assamese nationalism that required the "foreigner" to the identified as the enemy of the surging Assamese nationalism.[13] As the Assam anti-foreigner movement showed, the issue of citizenship and migration is the link between the so-called parliamentary sphere of politics and the sphere of identity politics.

Identity has little to do with looks, claims, tongues, destitution, resources, and justice, or to put it more appropriately, in the politics of identity these matters of looks, claims, tongues, and resources appear only as matter of rights – so that justice means now the expropriation of *others* and the vindication of the "politics of homeland". Because it was a matter of *citizenship*, it showed the hierarchical landscape of nationalism – foreigners could be there to keep the wheels of the tea industry running (in 1921 about one-sixth of Assam's population was engaged in tea gardens, they were from the Jharkhand region) for which the London Stock Exchange had gone mad as early as in the late nineteenth century. Similarly, they could be there to reclaim marshy lands and help the food production growing, but citizenship was for the indigenous, ethnic, and the nationals.

High population growth in Assam soon became an issue. In fifty years – 1901–51 – the growth was 138 per cent. Crop production had also increased in this period, so had increased the area under cultivation, similarly tea production had increased; but to the besieged mind, compared to labour growth all this was a minor phenomenon – be it farm labour, peasant labour, plantation labour, or labour in petty jobs. Typically, the protest of the native did not arise around the demand for jobs, but around issues of election, electoral rolls, franchise, and citizenship rights – it was a war against aliens. The citizens were prepared to remain economically impoverished, sick, and infirm, and survive on the dole handed out by the "centre", which logically, along with the tea garden owners and timber merchants should have been an equally alien presence to the natives, but it was time that the citizens had to drive out the aliens in view of the unnatural population growth in the state. It was reported that in one case 64 per cent of the total number of cases of complaints (45,000) out of a total electorate of 600,000 had been upheld against illegal immigrants.[14] The bloody anti-immigrant movement continued for five years – not only foreign immigrants were attacked; even members of the minority communities, particularly Muslims, became targets at times. Riots, torching of houses, looting, paralysing administration, civil disobedience – the war continued in all forms. War against foreigners became civil war amongst various communities. The State had to combine strong methods and persuasive techniques to administer inter-ethnic relations, and demography became one more area of governmentality, so much so that defining an Assamese – the first task of claiming a nation – became an enterprise beyond cultural articulations, it was bloody, administrative, contentious, exclusive, expelling, and an elect enterprise. From the neat writings of Assam Sahitya Sabha to anti-election agitations to the killing fields of Nellie was but a short road.[15]

On surface, it was a question of expelling or killing Muslims – at times Bengali Muslims, at times Assamese Muslims – but at the level of the physicality of nationhood, it involved the plain tribes, hill tribes, other linguistic groups such as the Nepalese, and people from other states like Nagaland, Manipur, Tripura, or West Bengal, and Bihar. Indigenous people were victims to ethnic riots in Bodoland leading to a trail of internal displacements in the area. Many organisations grew up or gathered strength and momentum in self-defence in this bloody and bloodless war, the most prominent being the United Minorities Front, which bagged seventeen out of the state's 126 Assembly seats in the Assembly elections of December 1985. The ceding of Sylhet (in form of referendum) years back in the Great Partition, as could be seen now, had done little to make Assam a pure nation,[16] even after it cut off its (East) Bengal links, for East Bengal in its different incarnations had sent in, in the words of the top ruler of Assam the Governor, Lt. General S.K. Sinha, hordes of people, in his exact words, "a silent and invidious invasion of Assam" causing the possible loss of the "geo-strategically vital districts of Lower Assam", "which would soon claim merger with Bangladesh", "the driving force of which would be the international Islamic fundamentalism". The spectre was severe: "Loss of Lower Assam will sever the entire land mass of the North East from the rest of India and the rich natural resources of that region will be lost to the nation".[17]

Because it was a war, all communities had developed strategic tools of linkages and enmities – plains/hills, valleys/hills, Hindus/Muslims, Bengalis/Assamese, Bengali Muslims/Assamese Hindus, Assamese Muslims/ Bengali Muslims, Bodos/Assamese, Bodos/Muslims, Bodos/Santhals, Assamese/Nagas, Assamese/Kukis, Karbis/Kukis, Karbis/Assamese.... It was not a case of sudden ethnic conflict, it reflected rather a condition of generalised war, because the war consisted of several battles and theatres of attrition. Insecurity from migration had created lines of all kinds, and had taken clearly military dimensions. But of that later; first let us see a little more how this condition engulfed other areas in the Northeast.

In Tripura long back in 1876–77 the indigenous people were more than two-thirds of the total population of 91,759. More than hundred years later in 1991, they counted for less than one-third of the state's population of 2,757,205. It was again roughly the same story. The Maharaja of Tripura had enacted legislation in 1917 and 1925 to acquire land for tea cultivation, which encouraged migration. Moreover, Bengali being the language of administration, immigration from East Bengal increased. Besides peasants, artisans also joined the golden trek driven from native land by recurrent famines, usury, and landlords' oppression. By 1930, the number of migrants had risen remarkably, and now for the first time land had to be reserved by measures decreed in 1931 and 1943 for the Tripuris, Jamatias, Reangs, Noatias, and the Halams. Massive internal displacements took place in the first half of the forties of the last century, when Reangs, the second largest indigenous community in Tripura, revolted against the Maharaja of Tripura and the movement was brutally suppressed. Reangs in large number left Amarpur and Udaipur in South Tripura and emigrated in thousands to the North, also towards the Chittagong Hill Tracts and the Lushai Hills. Thus Udaipur's population remained almost stagnant between 1931 (Reang population 2151) and 1961 (Reang population 2374), while in the same thirty years the Reang population of Dharmanagar rose from 735 to 18,834. The population of Belonia similarly increased, while in Kailasahar it decreased from 11,218 to 6283.[18] With the Great Partition began waves of migration in the state, and finally in the eighties Buddhist Chakma refugees entered in sizeable numbers from the Chittagong Hill Tracts in the wake of the conflict there and army operations of the Bangladesh State against the rebellion. The Tripura Upajati Juba Samity (TUJS) was formed in 1967; it led in 1978 to the formation of the first militant movement against the immigrants, the Tripura National Volunteers, which soon started attacking settlers and symbols of government authority, including at times security forces. Land question became crucial, and with *jhum* cultivation being systematically disturbed and finally destroyed, clashes began to erupt. The June riots of 1980 were the first major signal of the troubled time. It caused enormous displacements. The Dinesh Singh Committee Report estimated that nearly 372,000 persons had been affected by the riots. Of them about 150,000 people belonged to indigenous communities. Nearly 200,000 people had to be sheltered in camps. The number of total relief camps was 141; nearly 35,000 houses were gutted; and the estimated loss of property was about Rs. 21 crores. About 1300 people died. Again, in the last two years of the last decade an estimated 2614 families were displaced from severely affected areas such Khowai, Sadar, and Bishalgarh sub-divisions due to clashes. By 2000, the civil-political-military movement of the indigenous people against the settlers or migrants had become so strong that a ragtag combination of forces under the title of Indigenous People's Front of Tripura won the elections to the 28-member Tripura Tribal Autonomous District Council. The 1980s were marked with violence, large-scale settler-native inter killings, army operations, rape of women by security forces and the militants, kidnapping, and increasing communalisation of the scene. Today one estimate says that in the nineties – from 1993 to 1999 a total of 1018 persons were killed (656 non-tribal and 362 tribal) and 2001 persons were kidnapped (1663 non-tribals and 338 tribals). And then in two years, the succeeding years of 2000 and 2001, as many as 692 civilians were killed, plus 47 security forces personnel and 87 militants also lost their lives.[19] The TUJS demanded from the Government of India more powers to the Autonomous District Council, barbed wire fencing of the entire length of the 856 km-long boundary with Bangladesh, push back of immigrants who had arrived after 1971, and the introduction of the inner-line permit system to enter the Tribal Council Area.

Clashes also began in enclaves claimed by Assam and Nagaland where each claimed that people from the other state had come in and inundated the area; in Mizoram Chins were severely discriminated, in Arunachal Pradesh the Chakmas remained non-citizens even after decades of assurance to the effect that they would become citizens, and in Manipur through the years of eighties and the nineties of the last century, something happened akin to what I had described in *The Marginal Nation*, namely the decline of mixed settlements and the emergence of broken villages along the West Bengal–Bangladesh border (such as pure Muslim or pure Hindu villages). Here too, a silent process of purifying homelands had set in.[20] The hills of Manipur became pure Naga Hills or Kuki Hills. And, the frenzy of development activities in the entire region – construction of dams, roads, pipelines, power generating centres, or reserving forests – threw up new displaced, thus new migrants, new aliens, new ethnicities, and new threats.

In the construction of the Umium hydroelectric project a large number of Khasis was displaced without any chance of resettlement. Later on similar projects caused massive displacements in Chandrapur, Namrup, and Bongaigaon in Assam. The Dumbur project displaced 5845 families (an estimated number of 40,000 people) in Tripura. Before that the Kaptai dam construction on the river Karnaphuli in the Chittagong Hill Tracts in Bangladesh had displaced Chakmas and Hajongs and forced them to move to India – and many of them decades later still lead a life of a "stateless community".[21] Similarly, the oil industry did not benefit the ousted population in Duliajan, Noonmati, Bongaigaon, Digboi, and Nazira. Paper mills came up in the late seventies of the last century in Nowgaon and Cachar, land pressure increased, and the battle over resource like land became ferocious leading at times to bloodbath as in Nellie (1983). Karbi indigenous people were similarly affected. And the construction of an IIT campus in North Guwahati caused the displacement of 35,000 people. The media (*Amar Asom*, 2 September 2001) reported that out of the central grant of 10.3 crores of rupees to the state government to pay compensation, only 4.3 crores of rupees reached people. If the Tipaimukhi multi-purpose project comes up in Manipur with an estimated cost of Rs. 2899 crores (1995 price level), it will submerge fully 16 villages and partly 51 villages affecting 15,000 people. The entire Tipaimukhi development plan presents in a congealed form the conflicts between the hill and the valley, state administration and the indigenous communities, and the ideology of development and the requirement of survival.[22] Similar development awaits Arunachal Pradesh with the two proposals of Siang dam and the Subansiri hydroelectric project. Similarly in North Bengal, contemporary observers have noted, how dispossession of resources and displacement have played a crucial role in the making of a political community and the movement for its claims.[23] The battle of resources has pitted communities against the State, the army against the people, one community against another, and in general has reconstructed relations.

The situation of a generalised war in the region finds reflection in not only war rhetoric, but in actual incidents of expulsion also. At the time of writing this book, the publication of the National Register of Citizens of Assam is rocking the country with about eighteen lakhs of people being struck off the rolls of citizens, many of whom will be expelled or interned. In many places the Nepalis have been on the run, in others Bengalees. Expulsion of Nepalis in many places in the Northeast led to an autonomy movement in the Darjeeling Hills. In North Bengal, adjoining the Bodo areas of Assam, a similar process of conflict later began with the killings and expulsion of several Northeast militant groups from Southern Bhutan. Everywhere, the immigrant, known as the settler, faces insecurity symbolised by the "native"; likewise everywhere the native, known as the "indigenous", faces insecurity appearing in form of the settler. The migrant remains forever a migrant. And altogether, the State faces insecurity from the spectre of aliens swamping the land, aliens who in league with their soulmates are conspiring with foreign countries to secede or at least make the region a hotbed of conspiracies. Long drawn-out bitter clashes and bloody internal rivalries mark day-to-day governing, which becomes a tough business, because an unlikely issue had leapt to the top of the priority list – governing population flow. In this scenario of war, no wonder military discourses flourish wildly. In the combined discourse and ideology of development-security-modernity-state-army stands against the immigrants.

We find a great reflection of this phenomenon in the fact that, army generals as defenders of societies have started taking interest in governing population flows in the region. This interest started, as we know, in the colonial period with the introduction of the "imperial warrior", the *gorkha*, to fight through the jungles and the hills of the Northeast and the formation of the Assam Rifles in order to control the rebellious territories. And then in the post-independence era came directly the army plan of regrouping of villages in Mizoram displacing scores and scores of villagers in order to control the insurgency there, and its implementation in 1967–70.[24] The regrouping of villages into larger units as a counter-insurgency measure was modelled after the 1958 regrouping strategy employed by the British in Malay in the fifties, and then copied by the US forces in South Vietnam in the form of "strategic hamlets". The immediate objective of regrouping was to establish control over the villages in the interior and far flung areas of the then Mizo district of Assam, now the state of Mizoram. The Planning Commission also became an accomplice of the military in this strategy of displacing thousands of peasants, when its study team headed by Tarlok Singh visited the area and recommended regrouping. Shifting of remote hamlets and re-organising them into larger units guarded by the armed sentries so that outsiders could not sneak in became the strategy. In this way almost 75 per cent of the population of the Mizo district was regrouped in four stages – formation of protected villages (PPV), new grouping centres (NGC), voluntary grouping centres (VGC), and extended loop areas (ELA). The security forces undertook each stage of grouping, and later these centres were handed over to civilian administration. Sociologist C. Nunthara recorded the impact of the introduction of grouping of villages, and noted the devastation of community and village life, abandoning *jhum* cultivation under duress and consequent instability, shattered agricultural work pattern, various attendant social evils, and in an ironic way the advent of several modern "towns and bazaars" with diverse social occupations.[25] As peace returned, Mizoram witnessed the second highest growth rate in the country in the decade 1991–2001 – as against the national average of 21.34 it was 29.18. The Chakma population increased significantly. Nearly 7 per cent of the Mizo population had been born outside the state, and of the immigrant population, 75 per cent were nationals and 25 per cent had come from outside the country. About 80,000 Chins had come from Burma.[26] With the rise of Mizo nationalism both the Chins (who had come from across the international border) and Reangs (who to Mizos were internal immigrants) were considered as enemies of Mizoram. The relation between Mizos and the Reangs worsened considerably; many Reangs fled, others chose to fight and formed a militant organisation. Clashes erupted, Reangs demanded autonomous district council status.

In this context, it is no surprise that security becomes a macro-question, population management becomes a matter of governing from the top, and the army becomes the most accredited institution of such management. Indeed, population flow is "geopolitics" to the army, as an ex-general put it while writing a book on the Northeast. As he further put it in the broader context of the region, the situation was quite simply one of "demographic invasion". As the Mizo experience bore out, the army thought that it could displace thousands in order to ensure security; yet the army was the one institution that needed to be most vigilant against immigrants' invasion in order to ensure security of the people. Thus to the general the region was "sensitive and susceptible to foreign influences", and there was "tribal affinity" across various borders, and alleged "Chinese supply of arms in private ships through Chittagong Port" to ULFA, as he so disingenuously wrote, "A top level ULFA functionary when captured recently, seems to have confessed" to that effect.[27]

In this discourse, population flow brings in the issue of borders, not because the flow reaches always from across borders, but mobile populations are dangerous in terms of governing and administering. The fear is that the mobile population groups can mobilise support, and support across borders will be more difficult to control. Mobile groups also occasion creation of new boundaries – boundaries of ethnicity, economy, and territory. The Indo-Burma border, first settled in 1826 in the Yandabo Treaty, later confirmed in the Nehru-U Nu agreement of 1953, and hitherto left un-administered became militarised. Thus stretching from the Namkia Mountains bordering Arunachal Pradesh, then Patkai Bum bordering Nagaland, to Hamolin bordering Manipur to the Chin Hills bordering Mizoram, administration of borders became important. Kachins, Shans, Eastern Nagas, Chins, Arakanese, plus Burmese communist rebels – all could claim links across the border to this side; hence population flow could not be allowed to be negotiated at community level, it was not simply an innocent matter. It can be seen, therefore, how the military discourse, discourse of social insecurity, physical insecurity, and the contentious politics of nationhood all combined in this political exercise of ensuring security against the aliens.

The migrant in the generalised context of conflict and civil war

To be fair to the army generals the military discourse springs not only from their minds, it has roots in the internal discourse of society's security also, on which the military discourse feeds. For instance, the Bodo student leader Upendra Brahma, an active member of Assam Agitation, pressed for implementation of Clause 10 of the Assam Accord, which said, "It will be ensured that relevant laws for prevention of encroachment of government lands and lands in tribal belts and blocks are strictly enforced and unauthorised encroachers evicted as laid down under such laws". Upendra Brahma demanded the eviction of the indigenous population from Tamalpur and the "immigrants" from the *char* areas of Brahmaputra. This was certainly the signal for attacks on the Santhal population (not considered as "tribe" in Assam) in Bodo areas. Similarly, the insistence on making Assamese virtually the language of instruction in all parts of the state became a matter of contention with the All Assam Tribal Students Union. The Karbi Autonomous Council Demand Committee complained that the leaders of Assam were taking steps to wipe out other distinct languages and cultures from the state. Specialists started saying that security could be provided now only by deployment of the army. With it began the full-scale security discourse and "securitisation" of the social mind. Hereafter tea garden owners could feel secure now that the army was there; the people bought security now that they were paying taxes to government and the rebels both; and men of property had bought security with private guards and militias.

This is the backdrop of a generalised war, which includes struggles and rebellions of the last sixty to seventy years, when one's security becomes another's insecurity. In this contentious history, politics of security may be described as the meeting point, the hinge, or one may say the moment of articulation, of the political problem of power and the historical question of race. The genealogy of racism and the construction of physical boundaries when natives will take guard against aliens begin with the historical discourse against migrants and outsiders, the discourse on all "other" groups and races, and the mutual narratives of plains and the hills, the settled peasants and the indigenous. In this historical transformation of the discourse on the alien we have the reappearance of the political discourse of war, of race struggle that traverses the field of power, leads to conflicts, decides who is an alien and therefore an enemy to be killed or to be expelled, and generates domination, rebellion, and more important, hatred that will prolong this war.

The large, looming, ill-defined, and confusing figure of the "immigrant", in which various images such as the Muslim peasant from Mymensingh who had arrived in Assam in the first two decades of the last century, the Santhal peasant and tea garden labourer in Assam, the Nepali milkman, the immigrant worker in Dimapur, the Kuki in the Naga/Manipur Hills, the Hindu Bengali settler in Tripura, the Bengali help hand from Silchar working in various petty jobs in all the towns of the region, the Chin refugee in Mizoram, or the Chakmas in Arunachal Pradesh – all are mixed up. It is a product of the discursive and institutional practices of security that have been carried on in the region for the last 150 years. The figure of the migrant is formed in correlation with the development of a set of institutions of control and surveillance developed over the last hundred years (such as the line system, areas of partial and total exclusion, Acts to detect aliens and deport them, census, electoral roll preparation and revision, rules of property in the region, arrangements of autonomy, the deployment of army in the region, organisation of violence against the alien, etc.) with harsh real effects in terms of making this figure an object of lasting fear and hatred.

We can now understand how in the twenty-first century the two discourses of the terrorist and the migrant, who is permanently a potential threat to security, have coalesced. The terrorist is never from within. There is no home-grown terrorist; they all come from outside. They are products of "external" influences. They must be prevented from coming. This is the way external threats to health appear – this time due to travelling diseases. The borders must be hence controlled and strengthened. Racial mixing must be controlled and if possible prevented. In this high-potency brew of neo-liberalism, national frenzy, border regime, and untrammelled flow of capital, the only troubling element is the migrant – the potential terrorist. Insecurity envelops the society. The policies of macro-security – the security of society – can be ensured only by creating micro-insecurities.

Yet while ending this chapter we have to state once more clearly that the question of migrant and insecurity/security is not one of identity only – national or ethnic – but one of mobile populations in general, especially mobile labour. Migrants are attacked elsewhere besides the conflict-ridden Northeast. Muslim migrant labour has been subject of killings, ransom, persecution, and expulsion from various parts of India. Workers in sex and entertainment industries have been subject to extreme harassment and exploitation with law and measures like registration cards, welfare policies, and humanitarian concerns being of little help.[28] Same has been the situation for construction workers. If this is the situation within the country, we can imagine what happens to migrant workers in the Gulf. Insecurity pervades the world of footloose labour.[29] And that is how states ensure the security of nations and polities.

We have here a historical and political discourse – and it is in this sense that the security question is anchored to the issue of migration. Migration politically decentres the security question and shows a relationship between security, history, and politics. We shall resume this discussion on security in Chapter 10 in the context of migration as a theme of transitional justice. Presently let us move on to the next chapter to examine the process in which the security discourse plays itself out globally, once again based on a combination of the discourses of immigration and terrorism.

We shall discuss now what is known as the migration crisis in Europe.

Notes

1 Part of the material in this chapter is drawn from Paula Banerjee and Ranabir Samaddar, "Why Critical Migration Studies Has to be Post-colonial by Nature", in Alice Bloch and Giorgia Dona (eds.), *Forced Migration: Current Issues and Debates* (Abingdon, Milton Park: Routledge, 2019), pp. 44–59 and is used here with permission.
2 For details of this colonial history see Paula Banerjee, *Borders, Histories, Existences: Gender and Beyond* (New Delhi and London: Sage, 2010), Chapter 4, pp. 87–136; also, Paula Banerjee, "Circles of Insecuirty", in Paula Banerjee and R. Samaddar (eds.), *Migration and Circles of Insecurity* (New Delhi: Rupa, 2010), pp. 70–122; Takeshi Fuji, *Mirrors of the Colonial State – The Frontier Areas between North East India and Burma* (New Delhi: Manohar Publishers, 2001); my debt to Paula Banerjee and Subir Bhaumik for enriching my understanding the of the "migration question" in the Northeast
3 Part of this section is based on Paula Banerjee and Ranabir Samaddar, "Why Critical Migration Studies Has to be Post-colonial by Nature", in Alice Bloch and Giorgia Dona (eds.), *Forced Migration: Current Issues and Debates* (Abingdon, Milton Park: Routledge, 2019), pp. 44–59.
4 These figures are from the various reports of the Comptroller and Auditor General of India (CAG) with respect to these states, reproduced in Gurudas Das', "Liberalisation and Internal Periphery: Understanding the Implications for India's Northeast", in Gurudas Das and R.K. Purkayastha (eds.), *Liberalisation and India's North East* (New Delhi: Commonwealth Publishers, 1998), pp. 146–149.
5 Sujit Sikdar and Devadas Bhorali, "Resource Mobilisation, Distribution Effect and Economic Development of the North-eastern Region", in Gurudas Das and R.K. Purkayastha (eds.), *Liberalisation and India's North East* (New Delhi: Commonwealth Publishers, 1998), pp. 167–172.
6 All figures relating to human development taken from J.B. Ganguly, *Sustainable Human Development in the North-Eastern Region of India* (New Delhi: Regency Publications, 1996), pp. 29–53; it is noteworthy, Ganguly does not cite immigration as obstructing factor in achieving the goal of sustainable human development in the region.
7 On this, see Sucharita Sengupta and Samir Purakayastha, "Politics of Immigration and Look East Policy: Reflections from Assam and the Northeast", in Ranabir Samaddar and Anita Sengupta (eds.), *Global Governance and India's Northeast: Logistics, Infrastructure, and Society* (London and New York: Routledge, 2019), chapter 9; R. Samaddar, "The Insecure World of the Nation", in Paula Banerjee and R. Samaddar (eds.), *Migration and Circles of Insecurity* (New Delhi: Rupa, 2010), pp. 1–69.
8 This has only exacerbated racist attacks on migrants from the Northeast in Delhi and elsewhere in the country and the relation between the Northeast and the rest of the country has taken on greater racial undertone. See Atig Ghosh's perceptive essay, "The

Postcolony and the 'Racy' Histories of Accumulation", in Iman Kumar Mitra, Ranabir Samaddar, and Samita Sen (eds.), *Accumulation in Postcolonial Capitalism* (Singapore: Springer, 2017), pp. 233–247.
9   Samir K. Das, "Ethnic Subject or Subject of Security?" in R. Samaddar (ed.), *Government of Peace: Social Governance, Security and the Problematic of Peace* (Farnham, Surrey: Ashgate Pub., 2015), Chapter 4, pp. 107–133; see also, Samir K. Das, "India's Look East Policy: Imagining a New Geography of India's Northeast", *India Quarterly,* Volume 66 (4), December 2010, pp. 343–358.
10 Arup Baisya, "Citizenship Question and Assam Politics", *Frontier,* 10 January 2018, www.frontierweekly.com/views/jan-18/10-1-18-Citizenship%20Question%20and%20 Assam%20Politics.html (accessed on 20 December 2018); more on NRC see chapter 9
11 On this, Priyankar Upadhyay and Anjoo Sharan Upadhyay, "Peacebuilding in India: Meghalaya's Experience", in J. Peter Burgess, Oliver P. Richmond, and R. Samaddar (eds.), *Cultures of Governance: A Comparison of EU and Indian Theoretical and Policy Approaches* (Manchester: Manchester University Press, 2016), Chapter 8, pp. 172–189.
12 For a discussion in details on the political geography of the area, R. Gopalakrishnan, *Ideology, Autonomy and Integration in the Northeast India* (New Delhi: Omsons Publications, 1990), pp. 21–31.
13 These figures are from Monirul Hussain, *The Assam Movement: Class, Ideology and Identity* (New Delhi: Manak Publications, 1993), p. 10.
14 Sanjay Hazarika, *Strangers in the Mist* (New Delhi: Penguin, 1994), p. 138.
15 The Nellie massacre took place in central Assam on 18 February 1983. It claimed the lives of around 2500 people (unofficial figures put the figure much higher) from fourteen villages of Nagaon district. The victims were Muslims whose ancestors came from pre-partition colonial Bengal. There were some witnesses to the massacre.
16 Indeed, as historical research into the history of Sylhet referendum of 1947 bears out, the referendum by itself was the reflection of the fault lines within the Assam society. See, for instance, the essay by Bidyut Chakrabarty, "The 'Hut' and the 'Axe' – The 1947 Sylhet Referendum", *The Indian Economic and Social History Review,* Volume 39 (4), 2002, pp. 317–350.
17 "Report on Illegal Migration into Assam" *Submitted by the Governor of Assam to the President of India,* 1998, http://old.satp.org/satporgtp/countries/india/states/assam/documents/papers/illegal_migration_in_assam.htm (accessed on 11 November 2016).
18 Figures taken from *Census of India,* 1991, series 24, Tripura.
19 Figures cited from Wasbir Hussain, "Bangladeshi Migrants in India: Towards a Practical Solution – A View from the North-eastern Frontier", in P.R. Chari, Mallika Joseph, and Suba Chandran (eds.), *Missing Boundaries – Refugees, Migrants, Stateless and Internally Displaced Persons in South Asia* (New Delhi: Manohar, 2003), p. 138.
20 For details, see Phanjoubam Tarapot, *Bleeding Manipur* (New Delhi: Har-Anand Publications, 2003).
21 On this see, Sabyasachi Basu Ray Chaudhury, "Uprooted Twice – Refugees in the Chittagong Hill Tracts", in Ranabir Samaddar (ed.), *Refugees and the State – Practices of Asylum and care in India, 1947–2000* (New Delhi: Sage Publications, 2003), pp. 249–280.
22 For details on displacement due to development activities, Monirul Hussain, "State Development and Population Displacement in Northeast India", in C.J. Thomas (ed.), *Dimensions of Displaced People in Northeast India* (New Delhi: Regency Publications, 2002, hereafter *DDP*), pp. 282–298; Monirul Hussain, "State, Identity Movements and Internal Displacement in Northeast India", *Economic and Political Weekly,* Volume 35 (51), 2000; Hiram A. Ruiz, *Northeast India's Hidden Displacement,* report of the U.S. Committee for Refugees, Washington, DC, 2000.
23 Sujata D. Hazarika, "Dispossession and Displacement – The Genesis of a People's Movement in North Bengal", *DDP,* pp. 299–315.
24 Sajal Nag, "Disciplining Villages and Restoring Peace in the Countryside", in Ranabir Samaddar (ed.), *Government of Peace: Social Governance, Security and the Problematic of Peace* (Surrey: Farnham: Ashgate Publishing Ltd.), chapter 2, pp. 57–78.

Insecure nation, insecure migrant **141**

25 C. Nunthara, *Impact of the Introduction of Grouping of Villages in Mizoram* (New Delhi: Omsons Publications, 1989), pp. 50–60; the figures are from the Assam District Gazetteers, Part 4, cited as appendix to this study, pp. 61–66.
26 C. Nunthara, *Impact of the Introduction of Grouping of Villages in Mizoram* (New Delhi: Omsons Publications, 1989), pp. 50–60.
27 Lt. General N.S. Narahari, PVSM, *Security Threats to Northeast India – The Socio-Ethnic Tensions* (New Delhi: Manas Publications, 2002), preface.
28 Flavia Agnes, "Bombay Bar Dancers and the Trafficked Migrant: Globalisation and Subaltern Existence", *Refugee Watch*, 30, December 2007, www.mcrg.ac.in/rw%20files/RW30.htm#R2 (accessed on 1 January 2019).
29 One news item said,

> There are nearly 2 million Nepali migrant workers in the Gulf and Malaysia, and another 2 million seasonal migrants in India. Between July 2014–July 2015, 1002 of them died – most of them in Malaysia. More than half the deaths are due to what is called sudden unexpected death syndrome (SUDS). The workers go to sleep and never wake up. Health experts say the cause is overwork, stress, dehydration and poor diet.

Om Astha Rai and Sonia Awale, "Killed in the Line of Duty: Nepali Migrant Workers Who Return in Coffins Are Too Young and Healthy to Die", *Nepal Times*, 8–14 January 2016, https://nepalitimes.atavist.com/nepalis-killed-in-the-line-of-duty (accessed on 5 March 2019).

See also a report by Christopher Sharma, "Gulf Crisis Frightens 400,000 Nepalese Workers in Qatar", *Asia News*, 14 June 2017, www.asianews.it/news-en/Gulf-crisis-frightens-400,000-Nepalese-workers-in-Qatar-41011.html (accessed on 5 February 2019); also see Binayak Malla and Mark S. Rosenbaum, "Understanding Nepalese Labour Migration to Gulf Countries", *Journal of Poverty*, Volume 21 (5), 2017, pp. 411–433.

8

THE POSTCOLONIAL NATURE OF EUROPE'S MIGRATION CRISIS[1]

Migrants are coming

The year of 2015, known as the year of Europe's "migration crisis", was in many ways a paradoxical one. In the wake of the arrival of thousands of refugees and migrants in Europe that year, on one hand there was frenzy in the media over the massive number of immigrants, their "sudden" and "catastrophic" arrival, the reappearance of the ghostly image of the postcolonial at Europe's borders, an atmosphere of Europe "under siege",[2] and amidst all these desperate calls for a new Marshall Plan to save Europe.[3] On the other hand, as nations of Europe vied with each other as to whose responsibility it was to be humanitarian,[4] the din and cacophony made it difficult for statesmen and analysts to make out if there was a long term logic and trend in this arrival of migrants and the reappearance of violence on Europe's borders. How was one to account for that year? Was it exceptional because of the numbers and the violence associated with immigration, or was the year one in a chain of postcolonial moments of our time? Amnesia in the continent over past waves of immigration similarly dubbed as "crises" reigned,[5] while states began building fences in frenzy. According to a report by *The Economist*, Europe would soon have more physical barriers on its national borders than it did during the Cold War, and the refugee crisis, combined with Ukraine's ongoing conflict with Russia, would see governments plan and construct border walls and security fences across Mediterranean and Eastern Europe. It pointed out that in September the same year Hungary completed a fence along its border with Serbia, a major point of entry for refugees making their way into the European Union (EU). Spain fenced off its Moroccan enclaves of Ceuta and Melilla. Earlier Greece had put fences. Romania too would build defences. All these would leave Belarus's as the only unsealed border between the Baltic and the Black sea. *The Economist* pointed out in the same report,

> Since the fall of the Berlin Wall, 40 countries around the world have built fences against 64 of their neighbours. The majority cited security concerns and the prevention of illegal migration as justifications. More than 30 of those decisions were made following 9/11, 15 of them this year. In the Middle East, the wars in Iraq, Afghanistan and Syria as well as the associated wave of refugees have prompted most countries to close borders. By the end of this year, when it completes its border-wall with Jordan, Israel will have surrounded itself entirely. In Asia, too, walls and fences have proliferated. . . . In 2013 Brazil announced a "virtual" wall, monitored by drones and satellites, around its entire, nearly 15,000 km- (9,000 mile-) long border. . . . But skeptics point out that much of Brazil's border runs through rainforest that is impassable and hard to monitor. . . . The United States, which has several times fortified its border with Mexico, and Saudi Arabia, which has shuttered five of its borders since 2003, have struggled with proposals that were either too expensive or didn't work (or both). For most countries, barbed-wire or electric fences, combined with ditches and buffer zones, are the reality.[6]

Violence is of course increasingly associated with migration. Whether this violence makes migration to Europe a crisis, or because of the crisis migration has become violent is a moot question, but one that can be answered only when we have taken into account the historical basis of the current perception of migration as "crisis". This historical basis, as this chapter will argue, is in the postcolonial nature of migratory flows as well as of the migration management regime. The return of the colonial time in our age in various forms and its spectral presence makes migration a matter of crisis. This is because all that we associated with the colonial age – such as wars and violence, making of new borders and frontiers, confining people in camps, creation of a mobile workforce that can be likened to what Sylvia Federici following Marx called an "out of law" proletariat,[7] and loosening up and dilution of all population formations due to the entry of outsiders – are now making a comeback. The old nation state formation is inadequate in the face of the massive population flows both within and from outside the borders; at the same time empire-like formations have not replaced the nation form. The crisis is in this situation of ambiguity. More than anything else migration symbolises this situation. It is like the colonial period in the late nineteenth century when nations and empires jostled for sovereign status. It is also similar to the colonial age when borders had sprung into unusual policy significance.

Europe, the last liberal empire in modern age, had sought to prolong its existence through securing borders. Yet the border in an almost surrealist way has brought it back in organic contact with the colonial past. Possibly, through the recent events in Europe, migration has emerged as the unconscious tool of history to end this last liberal empire. After the Second World War, Europe had achieved unification in successive stages through dialogues on coal and steel, peace, and economic means. It established a charter of rights, founded a European Court of human rights, curtailed the sovereign framework of nation states in Europe, broadly attained currency union, held peace and security as the goal of the union, and finally as Lord Dahrendorf remarked after the *annus mirabilis* of 1989, it encouraged everyone to be a liberal with unfettered freedom to access the market so much so that countries in the east of Europe one after another joined the union to make it a true empire two centuries after Napoleon Bonaparte had failed to create one and had provoked unwittingly the first concert of the continent in 1815.[8] Yet crucial fault lines remained. The peaceful empire of our time was built in the last fifty years on whiteness of skin, a particular faith called Christianity, anti-communism, stringent anti-immigration laws and measures for people of outside the empire, neo-liberal tools of economic coordination, massive banks, flows of capital and labour, and geopolitically what turned out to be most uncertain for the fate of the continent, that is doing away with the old fuzzy division of the continent into west, middle, and the east. The present crisis of Europe in the wake of the entry of massive numbers of migrants from the Middle East and North Africa is perched on all these fault lines. The immigrants are non-Europeans, they are predominantly Muslims, quite a lot of them are not white, and they have disturbed the seamless nature of the united space called Europe, because the old divisions into west, middle, and the east have now resurfaced in the wake of the migrant rush. The European Monetary Union could not have been achieved without defining what the borders of the Union were. While preceding empires had frontiers and subsequently nation states began having more defined borders, the empire now wanted to achieve state-like clarity of borders. Thus old historical divisions were sought to be replaced with new seamless unity. Migration to Europe hurts the core of the unification project. If the old concert vanished into history with its failure to define the respective boundaries and borders of the Great Powers and folded up after the Berlin Congress (1878) that divided Africa, the present Union is facing the same problem of settling boundaries.

Yet the pre-history of the liberal empire of our time was marked by massive migrations. Greeks travelled extensively and built cities in Asia and North Africa. The Romans created an empire stretching from England to Turkey. Europe between the fourth and seventh centuries witnessed what is called the "migration of the nations", when Huns, Goths, Franks, and Angles moved to new homelands, in the process creating the foundation of the nation states of today's Europe. Around the seventeenth century and lasting for more than 400 years Europeans moved from one part of the continent to another in no coherent pattern. In the core West European countries large parts of their working classes were formed in the nineteenth and early twentieth century by migration from the Mediterranean nations. In these two centuries migrants from all over the world also travelled to Europe with ease, and Europeans migrated to the vast lands of the Americas and Australia. In postwar years, no region was more associated with guest workers, the *gastarbeiter*, than

Europe.[9] This is indeed recorded in great details by Stephen Castles and his co-authors in *The Age of Migration*.

The population movements of an earlier era form the backdrop against which Europe's migration crisis reappears. Policies, borders, population compositions, and the nature of labour markets – all these carry strong historical determinants. They help us to ask: Is the present migration a crisis, or is population movement appearing as a crisis of Europe in the particular conjuncture of our time?

It was not that post-War Europe was facing immigration flows on a large scale for the first time. Also it was not true that the migrant flow in 2015–16 was the only big flow the continent received. After the Algerian war the Algerian population in France between 1962 and 1975 doubled from 350,000 to 700,000, and France became a country of massive immigrant population. While the headlines this time outlasted the media's usual attention span,[10] they somewhat inevitably faded in subsequent years, as they faded after the Balkan wars in the 1990s, when there were 670,000 asylum applications to fifteen EU countries. In fact in 2017 the number of applicants to the twenty-eight EU countries was 626,000 people (44,000 fewer than 1992). Also to be truthful many more refugees and shelter seekers sought and found shelter elsewhere. Turkey hosts 1.8 million Syrian refugees, Lebanon 1.2 million, and Jordan 600,000. Turkey now shelters more refugees than any other country in the world, and only four countries (Turkey, Pakistan, Lebanon, and Iran) host 36 per cent of global refugees. Europe also wants to think that Germany and other countries in Europe following Germany are helping refugees, but not only countries are deciding unilaterally the number of migrants they would accept,[11] Germany's own refugee-to-native ratio is about 40 times less than Jordan's.[12] At the same time, refugee admissions in the United States dropped to 70,000 from a peak of 122,000 in 1990.[13] And we have to remember, 25 per cent of world's refugees are in the least developed countries.

No one is asking, if many are straggling into Europe, how many are simply left behind, how many stopped, and most importantly, how many dying? Warnings of the great humanitarian disaster were aplenty in the last few years when the roulette parleys among the European powers went on with absurd regularity and monotony on stricter currency union norms. Undeterred by the Mediterranean boat tragedies, the European powers forged yet another tool against human migration. They met in Marseilles in 2017 and 2018, decided on closer European coordination on security, immigration, and the economy. True to liberal ideas, overwhelming hope was placed on well-crafted integration paths on which coping with the complexity of migration was assumed to depend. In fact, it was held crucial to reinvigorate the integration processes in European countries by finding shared answers to essential questions such as: citizenship, identity, veil, religious education, places of worship, and do not forget, terrorism. This was to be done with clarity and transparency, in an open dialogue with all the younger generations who, in an aging Europe, had become essential pillars of society. It was also admitted that Europe was loaded with a long and heavy migration history, and that at the heart of the European citizenship debates was the issue of immigration.[14] And now, continental identity was being challenged by both migrants and the nationalised discourse of citizenship, making the field of citizenship a highly contentious political question.

One of the spectres looming over the script of a twilight age, we now call the "Anthropocene", is of massive migrations to the North from the supposedly climatically inhospitable regions of the South. It seems that massive waves of population flows, pressing on the peninsula from the east and from the south, are likely to change population and settlement structures of Europe for good. Millions, we are told, will want to escape the floods, earthquakes, droughts, and famines to crowd the rich countries of Europe, Japan, North America, and Australia. These are the climate refugees. They sail through the Mediterranean, pass through the snow fields, cross barbed wires, and crawl into the bellies of ships, wagons, and aircrafts to reach the Promised Land. This will be the final disaster to strike the world marking the end of the age of human intervention in nature.

Those historically minded will remember that this was the spectre that haunted the rulers in colonial parts of the world in the last quarter of the nineteenth century when the El Niño famines struck them (including India), and became, in the words of Mike Davis, the "late Victorian holocausts".[15] In that age, climate change, social factors, abrupt economic transitions, and particular political command structures combined with devastating effect to cause millions of deaths in India, also across large parts of the world. The colonial organisation of power accentuated environmental impact on the peasantry and destroyed the customary ways of providing relief to the distressed and the victims. Famine foods (foods that rats can eat but humans cannot) and migration facilitated the spread of epidemic diseases like cholera, dysentery, malaria, and smallpox.

Similarly, the managers of global governance are now worried: How will they stop migration? How can the migrants be made resilient through modes of governance so that they stay put in face of war and climate change? How can migration be an appropriate adaptive strategy? How are the travelling diseases to be stopped from entering safe countries? These indeed are the concerns of Europe's rulers, indeed rulers of all countries.

Yet we all know that migration makes no country safe or dangerous. In the words of Daniel Warner, we are all migrants at one point in the human life.[16] Therefore we witnessed in the wake of the Paris Conference on Climate Change (2015) even more desperate efforts to regulate migratory flows of humans who are escaping not only violence, but we are told, floods, famines, and droughts also – all caused supposedly by climate change. In this scenario, migrants with skills will be admitted. They will be the good refugees. This is the prevailing EU (European Union) wisdom, while the rest will be told to move within their respective countries, learn skills, and become more adaptive. Meanwhile developing nations will be asked to reduce their emission levels, not to develop at a fast pace, and to open their economies to the more climate-hospitable technologies of the West producing cars, chemicals, leather products, engineering products, and not to forget money – the most climate friendly commodity on earth. The Marseilles and the Paris discussion took place in a milieu of boat tragedies regularly occurring in the Mediterranean and the Aegean Sea, with migrants sinking and dying.

The decade had begun with disasters. In April 2011 a boat had left Libya carrying 72 Africans, but quickly ran into trouble and began losing fuel. Using a satellite phone, the passengers contacted a priest in Italy who alerted authorities. A military helicopter dropped water to the boat and was never seen again. The boat drifted for days after, at one point nearing a French aircraft carrier. No rescue operation was mounted, despite international law dictating that any ocean-going vessel must help another in distress. All but nine of the passengers died. An inquiry by the Council of Europe blamed the disaster on a "catalogue of failures" and recommended Europe overhaul its immigration policy. The United Nations declared that all migrant vessels in the Mediterranean be considered "in distress." And again in the same year, as many as 15,000 migrants were stranded in Croatia, as the prime minister said his country could no longer accept refugees and began sending people north. The death of 800 migrants in a single accident in April 2011 had already prompted calls for Europe to do more to help, and all summer leaders had debated strategies. Next year again tragedy struck on 6 September near Greek shores, 160 feet east of Samos, when a fishing boat carrying Iraqis, Syrians, and Palestinians travelling from Turkey capsized, with sixty of them dying, nearly half of them children. The boat was only around 160 feet from shore; around forty-five people managed to swim to safety. Meanwhile the Greek police announced that they had caught tens of thousands of migrants trying to cross by boat or via the strip of land connecting the country to Turkey. Three months after the fishing boat accident, Greece completed a 6.5-mile fence along its border with Turkey with funding from FRONTEX, the European Border and Coastguard Agency. Bulgaria followed suit with a fence of its own. Human Rights Watch told the daily *The Guardian* that closing the land bridge simply forced more migrants to opt for the "most deadly route": crossing the sea. The next year, 2013, with monotonous regularity, another boat carrying 200 people capsized. Italy rescued more than 100,000 people with a special rescue programme, but 2014 was to be the deadliest year for migrants. Nearly 3500 died or went missing. In 2015, in the second week in February more than 300 migrants drowned in failed crossings. Soon after the same year, on 18 April 2015 a ship carrying an estimated 950 people sank 17 miles off the Libyan coast with 800 people on the ship drowning.[17]

Amid international outcry, European ministers agreed on a 10-point plan to address the migrant issue, which in effect meant systematic efforts to destroy smuggling boats, tighter border controls on refugee routes, and a scheme to offer migrants resettlement options. Meanwhile decomposed bodies of men, women, and children suffocating to death in the back of abandoned, unventilated trucks or trapped inside boats after the latter had capsized were being found. Newspapers regularly reported on all these disasters, the climax in coverage reaching on 2 September 2015, with photographs of Kurdish-Syrian toddler Alan Kurdi's body lying on a tourist-heavy beach.[18] It became the My Lai girl's counterpart in this crisis. As the photograph became a media sensation, politicians claimed that they would reconsider their refugee policies. The British Prime Minister and the German Chancellor promised a more open-door policy, while migrants and refugees stuck in Hungary protested against the shabby treatment by that country's government. Few forgot that only few months back the same British government had refused to accommodate migrants trapped in the English Channel tunnel.

To see the paradoxes in Europe's responses to the migrant flows in this century, we need therefore a sense of history. The combination of the humanitarian and the military has strong colonial resonance. We should also remember at the same time that when deaths were happening in the Mediterranean in course of boat crossings similar crossings and deaths were happening in the Pacific and the Indian Ocean also.[19] But because it was not Europe, attention remained far less. In the deaths of the refugees and migrants whether in the Mediterranean or the Indian Ocean or the Pacific, the postcolonial irony was not be missed.[20]

Europe's border-centric response

The first response, of course, to the "migration crisis" of 2015 was to reshuffle the degrees of attention to various zones of borders. Daniel Trilling, a close observer of the scenario, pointed out that the clandestine refugee route through the western Balkans (Greece, Macedonia, Serbia, Hungary – or now Croatia), where scenes of chaos unfolded in 2015, had in fact been used for years. In 2013, Frontex had reported a sharp increase in people taking this route. In his words,

> This summer, Greece overtook Italy as the main point of entry to Europe, the numbers swelled by the surge in Syrians leaving their country. The UNHCR estimates that around 70 per cent of arrivals in Greece this year have been Syrian; the next two largest groups are Afghan and Iraqi. At the end of August, traffic on the Balkan route intensified when Germany announced it would let all Syrians on its territory apply for asylum. The countries along this route have faced a dilemma: do they let the refugees through, or is there too great a risk that the next country along will close its borders, leaving them holding the baby? Nobody wants to become, in the words of the Croatian prime minister, a 'migrant hotspot'.[21]

If Hungary, with its hard-right government and a prime minister prone to making apocalyptic statements about the threat migrants pose to "Christian Europe", chose an extreme response by building fences, threatening refugees with imprisonment for crossing its border illegally and approving the use of "non-lethal force" to repel migrants, Trilling pointed out, it was only following a logic shared by the European system as a whole. For instance, on 9 September 2015, the European Commission announced that it had taken "decisive action" in response to the crisis. In Trilling's words,

> The proposal to resettle 120,000 refugees currently in Greece, Italy and Hungary, eventually agreed on after weeks of squabbling, is to the good, but the focus remains on reducing migration to Europe. Other measures suggested include speeding up deportation procedures, re-establishing holding camps for migrants outside EU territory and creating an EU military force to tackle

people-smuggling networks in the Mediterranean. Aside from a few humanitarian gestures the aim seemed to be to restore the pre-2011 status quo: fewer migrants reaching European shores, with deaths and human rights abuses at a level the public is largely willing to ignore. 'We need to correct our policy of open doors and windows,' Donald Tusk, president of the European council, declared, after an inconclusive leaders' summit in Brussels on 24 September.[22]

This reshuffle took place as part of a wider strategy. The strategy was to contain and seal the sea. Charles Heller and Lorenzo Pezzani in a report titled, "Forensic Oceanography: Mare Clausum" demonstrated how in its policy of stemming migrant crossings of the Mediterranean into Europe, the EU with Italy as the frontline state enacted an undeclared operation, termed as *Mare Clausum*.[23] As parts of the said policy, non-governmental organisations (NGOs) attempting to rescue the migrants and bring them ashore alive were criminalised; and Italy and the EU tasked and enabled the Libyan coast guard to intercept and pull back migrants to Libya through political agreements, the provision of material and technical support, and coordination mechanisms. Heller and Pezzani's report showed that "Italy and the EU have come to exercise both strategic and operational control over the Libyan Coast Guard, which has been made to operate *refoulement by proxy* (italics in the original – RS) on behalf of Italy and the EU."[24] The report declared,

> As a result of the Mare Clausum operation at sea, which was also combined with Italy's direct negotiations with tribal leaders and militias on firm land, crossings dropped in summer 2017: July saw a reduction in arrivals of 51% in relation to the previous year, August 82%. As more migrants were contained in Libya, they experienced even worse conditions than before, in particular in increasingly overcrowded detention centres. This was acknowledged on 14 November 2017by the UN High Commissioner for Human Rights.[25]

The report called upon

> Italy and the EU to immediately end their policy of refoulement by proxy, and suspend collaboration with LYCG (Libyan Coast Guard) for as long as the latter is responsible for grave violations. Rescue activities must be used to save lives, not as a cover-up for border control. Inasmuch as the LYCG do perform rescue operations in the future, they must not be allowed to disembark migrants on Libyan territory, where migrants' lives are endangered.... Instead of seeking to contain migrants at all cost, Italy and the EU must embark on a fundamental re-orientation of the EU's migration policies towards granting legal and safe passage to migrants. Only in this way, will the smuggling business, the daily reality of thousands of migrants in distress, and the need to rescue them, finally come to an end.[26]

The report indeed makes clear the colonial imprint on the refugee and migrant control policy. Taking the Libyan case as instance Heller and Pezzani argued that the policy of Italy and the EU to stabilise the Mediterranean was through entrusting North African countries such as Libya with the task of patrolling their maritime frontiers.[27] The report also laid bare the particular patterns of practices of the EU emerging through the last few years as a result of the policies like the aforementioned. In sum, the policies are based on various combinations of humanitarianism, security practices and military intervention, delegation of tasks and responsibility, and coordination – all in the name of ensuring efficiency in migration management. And all these we must remember speak of the long history of colonial governance. Also, we have to note that the Mediterranean had to be declared as a sea of trafficking and smuggling so that the sea could be closed to boat people and presumably the victims saved.[28] The security and military argument as in the colonial age has to ride on the back of the humanitarian.[29]

We must pay attention to the way European management of borders has evolved. As the aforementioned report brings out, European border management has taken on the shape of frontier management, which is why it has become flexible. Biometric and other technological developments have enabled this flexibility in as much these developments have forced the migrants to be more resourceful.[30] Combined with the technological mode, the humanitarian nature of the work has made an efficient security policy possible. The preceding chapter showed how colonial security policy needed frontier management. Humanitarian concerns reinforced the ideological basis of the re-emerging colonial frontier policy. Frontier was a regulatory principle of high order for colonial rule. For population to be managed and population groups to be stabilised and governed, colonial rule needed flexible border policy. Such policy allowed expansion. It included administrative policies for footloose population groups, and more importantly, measures that enabled shifting of a border in case of need, in other words establish a border that would not be restricted to a line. These policies were now brought back to operation.

Establishing a humanitarian base at Lampadusa or at Idomeni where the immigrants are herded in hundreds to suffer, become sick, or as in extreme cases die,[31] returning the detainees to homelands on the basis of a vigorous deportation policy,[32] distributing the migrants over the continent – all these have called for flexible reception modes and creation of what William Walters has called, the "humanitarian border".[33] Walters reminds his readers that the "humanitarian is a complex domain possessing specific forms of governmental reason".[34] As he says, it is thus not a second order reality. It is the field where we can find the fault lines on the smooth space of globalisation, where the terms "Global North and "Global South" meet in a "concrete and abrasive way", where the humanitarian border and the "poverty frontier" meet, and where "gradients of wealth and poverty, citizenship and non-citizenship appear especially sharply".[35] The humanitarian border thus materialises only in a certain specific way and context. It not only brings back the old frontier strategy, it also accommodates the tearing lines of conflict within the process of globalisation. In this postcolonial context values play, as in the old colonial time, a good deal of role in producing humanitarianism and protection policy. Frontier then also banked on humanitarian ethos. The values associated with care and protection were earlier associated with dispossession of the weak and taxing the poor to help the poor. This time too plans are afoot to reduce the "humanitarian load" on the state. In Denmark, for instance, the ruling party planned to seize refugees' valuables to fund part of the expenses of settlement, and use such seizure as deterrent to any inclination on the part of the migrants to disobey the directives and regulations regarding entry, accommodation, settlement, relocation, etc.[36]

One crucial fact in the remaking of boundaries within Europe is that migration is rekindling old divisions. Thus besides the divisions between Europe and Asia and Europe and Africa, we have now a re-emergence of supposed divisions between the Western Europe and Eastern Europe, and between United Kingdom and Europe. These divisions are reflected in the contentious flows of labour from Eastern Europe to the Western part of the continent.[37] They reflect the process of the production of postcolonial moment in global migration history. If we continue with the division of Europe between the east and the west, we cannot but be struck by the historical fact that a "special", "separate", "less civilised", "Asiatic" part of Europe was being produced by West European imaginary for 300 years and largely coincided with the colonial history of the West. Not only the association of the Turks and Russians with Eastern Europe through two long centuries was a critical factor in this, Western Europe's own enlightenment and colonial practices also contributed to the invention of "Eastern Europe".[38] Today's unease in UK and elsewhere in Western Europe about migration from Eastern Europe materialises in this background. Through September 2015, the high year of migration to Europe, 204,630 illegal border crossings were identified on the Balkan route, while 359,171 people attempted to cross through the Eastern Mediterranean route, and 128,619 opted for the Central Mediterranean. The EU decided to pay Turkey 4.6 billion euro to settle its borders with the latter, which implied that Turkey with that money would henceforth confine the migrants within its borders and not allow them to move into Europe. EU candidacy was also used as a bargaining chip. This is truly a "boats and camps" approach with necessary bribe to the boat and camp managers.[39] The impact of geopolitics on migratory flows and strategies to control them was evident. Cash and other financial incentives to secure borders of Europe could not of course do away with geopolitical exigencies; they created greater problems for the empire. Even though this step of cash and other incentives were seen as decisive steps towards sub-contracting and privatising security of the borders, within no time Brexit and other assertive nationalist positions were voiced by countries like the United Kingdom, Italy, Hungary, and Poland. The economic rationale never works alone. In this case also, it had to function amidst a maze of geopolitical compulsions, in which inhered old colonial histories.[40]

Through participation in US bombings and intervention campaigns in Syria and Iraq, and attempts to force regime changes in Libya, Syria, Iraq, and Iran, Europe had drawn unrest closer to its borders, which started shrinking inwards. Forgetful of all these, EU decided a 10-point action plan:

- Reinforcing Jjint operations in the Mediterranean, namely Triton and Poseidon; increasing financial resources to mount these operations; extension of the operational area of the Frontex, and allowing EU to intervene further within the mandate of Frontex;

- A systematic effort to capture and destroy vessels used by the smugglers; the results obtained with the Atlanta operation (EU Naval Force engaged in counter-piracy operations at sea off the Horn of Africa) to lead EU to similar operations against smugglers in the Mediterranean;
- EUROPOL (EU's Law Enforcement Agency), FRONTEX, EASO (European Asylum Support Office), and EUROJUST (EU's Judicial Cooperation Unit) to meet regularly and work closely to gather information on smugglers modus operandi, to trace their funds, and to assist their investigation;
- EASO to deploy teams in Italy and Greece for joint processing of asylum applications;
- Member States to ensure fingerprinting of all migrants;
- Considering options for an emergency relocation mechanism;
- An EU-wide voluntary pilot project on resettlement, offering a number of places to persons in need of protection;
- Establishment of a new return programme for rapid return of irregular migrants from frontline Member States – the process to be coordinated by Frontex;
- Engagement with countries surrounding Libya through a joint effort by the Commission and the EEAS; initiatives in Niger to be stepped up; and
- Deployment of Immigration Liaison Officers (ILO) in key third countries and collecting intelligence on migratory flows and strengthening the role of the EU Delegations.[41]

As can be seen, the 10-point Action Plan was highly militaristic. The security dimension of the plan overwhelmed the humanitarian aspect. Hence quarrels over resettlement plans soon erupted and made the plan least effective. Relocation plans became controversial. Highly complex statistical tools were deployed to determine relocation quotas.[42] When the refugee protection norms were put in place in the fifties and sixties in the last century, the context was the Cold War. European protection of refugees has now a different context. In place of Cold War, there is now a global postcolonial predicament with flows from the postcolonial world, coupled with flows from the poorer parts of Europe to its richer part. In this changed context Europe does not adhere to global protection principles anymore. European Powers are discussing today distributing the "refugee burden" among various EU members – something unthinkable under the 1951 Convention. What will be the norm of such distribution? Wealth, GDP, population, size of the country, population-wealth ratio, labour market needs, country of first, second, and then the later order of access, ethnic or other similarities with the refugee population flow? It will be like marketing commodities and distributing public goods. Germany demanded on a binding quota for all EU members for relocating around 120,000 refugees from Italy, Greece, and Hungary.[43] The demand is thus now for a continent-wide population management strategy, so that the transition to market-friendly economic policies can take place in a harmonious manner. In this background market-friendly protection and support practices are experimented in Africa. In Turkey, the refugee economy has to work as an immigrant niche in the overall national economy. The immigrant niche in the market is marked by outright plunder of labour power known. It is a process akin to what is known as primitive accumulation marked with distressful work condition, semi-free labour, old labour recruitment patterns, bank loans to entrepreneurs, etc. The products of this market are linked to global commodity chains.[44] Thus while the 10-point Action Plan seems only partially successful, it was a major thrust towards materialising a continent-wise neo-liberal strategy of population management. At the same time, it could actualise only through resurrecting the postcolonial structure of relations. All these required that the neo-liberal population management strategy use population flows of this decade as "crises". Crisis is and will be neoliberalism's mode of existence.[45]

The role of reconceptualising borders as response to migration is significant in all these. We have seen the impact of colonial knowledge of making and administering borders, and the return of a frontier strategy in this context. The neo-liberal policy of population management mobilises a certain historical repertoire of governmental forms, technologies, and identities drawn from old imperial and colonial age to give shape to today's steps.

Take the case of Italy and this story by a descendant of an immigrant family in the United States, Helene Stapinski. Twelve years ago Stapinski had begun investigating a family murder that happened in Southern Italy in the nineteenth century. In the process she uncovered facts about the daily life of her ancestors and the racism they faced even from their own countrymen – facts she found more shocking than the killing. She wrote of the condition of poor women in Italy at the time when her great-great grandmother Vita Gallitelli came to America. In Italy they were subject to the whims of their padre, the men who owned the feudal land upon which they toiled. Italian women, she reported, were commonly the victims of institutionalised, systematic rape – a practice known as *prima notted*, which allowed the landowner to sleep with the virgin bride of his worker. The practice extended into the twentieth century. Helene Stapinski wrote,

> The husbands could not protest, since they would be barred from working the farm and their families left to starve.... The itinerant workers were considered subhuman and made 40 cents a day if they were chosen by the overseer, doing backbreaking work on land that was not theirs, walking several hours back and forth to the farm each day. They were expected to offer the padrone a tribute to thank him for the work on crops, or if they had it, meat they butchered themselves.

This was the basis for the shape-up on the American docks. The generation of Stavinsky's great- and great-great grandparents came in droves from Italy scraping together the 300 lire the cost of three houses at the time to book passage of each individual, spurred on by the labour demands of the industrial barons who welcomed them with open arms to America. Menial, often dangerous jobs, awaited them. Stavinsky wrote, "Some, like my relatives, came here illegally, under false names. Or as stowaways, on one ship alone, 200 stowaways were found." Yet the irony Stavinsky found was that at the end of the high tide of immigration from Italy, the United States Immigration Commission had concluded in the infamous

1911 Dillingham report that certain kinds of criminality were inherent in the Italian race. She wrote her story in 2017; she concluded by saying, "Italian-Americans who today support the president's efforts to keep Muslims and Mexicans out of the country need to look into their own histories and deep into their hearts."[46]

Not only the report tells of the colonial relations of the past including internal colonialism in Europe, which Antonio Gramsci had described as the "southern question", it also shows the historical knowledge which today's immigration laws and practices draw upon in order to decide when to clamp down the borders.[47] Clearly, the postcolonial impact has been mainly in the form of combining a nation state's border and security strategy with old imperial-colonial strategy of maintaining expansive security lines and zones, keeping virtual borderlands, expanses of indeterminate zones, and as result of all these a flexible frontier policy. This combination, to repeat, is part of an attempt to forge a rational population management policy that will make populations efficient, optimally distributed through the continent, and at the same time, make them secure. Therefore, the concern is: how to make the immigrant population groups visible for economy but invisible for politics, integrated but not so integrated as to be "natural", ready for required labour work but can be sent back when not needed, which to repeat Marx's memorable words, would be an ideal global "reserve army of labour", that would be no threat to security. At the same time border management has become context specific.[48] Indeed, in this way the frontier policy of the EU now symbolises the application of geographical reasoning to the conduct of economy. It has to thus concern itself with issues such as, deployment of frontier guards (FRONTEX) all along the "vulnerable" borders of the continent, the defence of select zones and places, and the identification of places from where the population flows may threaten Europe's so-called demographic stability. Yet the problem remains: Europe cannot do without the migrants, but the presence of the migrants must not be unruly and unpredictable. Such an expansive population settlement policy naturally has not gone down well with several European countries, which have competing nationalist visions of population compositions for their respective lands. As a consequence, immigration has become an issue of contention between the nationalist vision and continental vision. The debate on populism has much to do with this.[49]

The situation has given rise to a call for, as some say, a "security continuum".[50] It means extendable and flexible area of security and information operations. We can see this feature each time Europe has to be defined. The intractable case of "partitioning" Ireland in the event of Brexit shows the difficulties as well as contradictions in defining the borders of Europe.[51]

In this way, contemporary events which are products of a colonial past are in turn reproducing colonial relations. Classic is the case of Syrian migration to Europe. What is now happening in the Middle East is a return of a history that goes back to the understanding between the European great powers during the First World War to divide the colonies and govern the post-war colonial world. It is a history that involves exactly the last 100 years beginning in 1916 with Sykes-Picot agreement.[52] The event of Syrian War that has killed at least 250,000 people, with roughly 11.6 million people displaced from their homes (about half of Syria's prewar population), and with 4 million of them forced out of the country has produced the particular border strategy of Europe on the east. It has led the latter into delegating some of its border functions to Turkey.[53] The lock gates then sprang down on people coming from that direction.

We are thus talking here of an ensemble of events, mechanisms, and instruments that carry imprints of a colonial past and a postcolonial present and make Europe's migration policy. Crafting an appropriate and flexible border policy is the most crucial part of this policy.

The postcolonial gradient in the neo-liberal mechanisms of governance

Saskia Sassen has asked why in earlier periods of Europe's history, such as the nineteenth century, with "so many poor in some regions" there were no comparable "massive movements from poverty to prosperity. . ., with virtually no border control."[54] She alludes to the colonial element among various factors behind the migratory flows of our time. The investigation into the repository of colonial tools of governance of populations and colonial border policies framed according to the requirements of population management is thus important. The colonial policy was to fit the "right" size of the territory with the "right" shape of population and the colonial laboratory supplied Europe with necessary knowledge. Postcolonial states, India for instance, also drew on this knowledge. Thus the internal boundaries of the states were reorganised; lines of exclusion and half-exclusion were retained with new degrees of flexibility; and most importantly, citizenship policies were gradually reshaped so that demands of nationalism and the requirement to mark the aliens could be combined. The colonial encounter of several centuries provided a corpus of tools necessary for policing of population, state-orchestrated identification practices, the making of new frontiers, and the creation of sub-populations. Adoption of multiple scales of population management through various means – such as (a) division of territories and cities while instituting norms of citizenship, (b) creating racially profiled areas and groups (think of the colonial practice of identifying areas of "tribes", "criminal tribes", and "vagrant" populations), (c) long-distance transportation of people, (d) interning large herds of population in one area in times of famines or disturbances so that people do not stray around and create trouble, and (e) policing of entire populations in all these ways – was now possible due to the historical knowledge of the colonial population management including knowledge of internal colonial management of regions and groups of populations. Federico Rahola reminds us that the colony itself was like a camp. Aime Cesaire's idea was that colonial powers had imported into Europe what had been "normal" in the colonies.[55] Referring to Cesaire, Federico Rahola has argued that this not only indicates the possibility of reading continuity in a history, but also the necessity of decentring that history and reading it according to a different set of criteria. The camp, which earlier had the status of the "normal" (in/as a colony) now emerging from colonies, became an exception (in Europe). The space of camps reflecting the double nature of sovereignty exceeded and challenged the binary logic of normal/

exception and inside/outside and reflected a principle of sovereignty.[56] Confining and interning refugees and migrants was a consequence of long historical practice of rule. Rahola concludes by saying,

> The colonial origins of the camp-form therefore point to a different and more "distant" trajectory. It is not a question about how camps can be captured in a legal system by taking exception to it, but rather understanding how they sanction the limit of the reach of that system by exceeding it, and signalling at a more mundane level a border between exclusion and inclusion, and between an inside and an outside that no longer exist. To completely accept this matrix, and therefore to write a genealogy of camps, thus means to relocate camps in a territory that exceeds every representation of modern national borders and indicates at the same time this territory's spectral artificiality and intrinsic weakness. From this perspective, camps are the symptom of a space that has always transcended the specific space of nations, within which it has been historically colonized, plundered and racialized, but never totally absorbed. It is a space (and this is the postcolonial sense of the global present) that whenever it penetrates the specific space of states, violating its borders and subverting distinctions between an inside and outside, it produces holes and abysses. And in each of these holes and abysses there sits a camp.[57]

In other words, we get a new perspective on the nature of modern migration policy of Europe by reading it against the background of various colonial practices and sensibilities.[58] As in the colonial time the duality of legality and illegality was rewritten to make the colonial world, now too the relation between legality and illegality is being rewritten to make immigration a difficult act.[59] In this way, rewriting the logic of procedures of admission of migrants also commenced in right earnest, though this practice of rewriting started some time back. Thus, as one observer noted,

> When EU officials in Brussels at 1:00 a.m. on March 8, 2016 first announced their plan to send refugees back to Turkey, they did not tell the truth to journalists about the EU's own directives on refugee deportations. Article 18 of the EU directive on asylum procedure defines the criteria for a 'safe third country' to which refugees can be sent and includes section 18.c requiring that 'the principle of *non-refoulement* [not sending refugees back into danger] in accordance with the Geneva Convention is respected.' Also, individuals sent to a "safe third country" must have the right to claim refugee status there, but in Turkey – believe it or not – only people from Europe are allowed to apply formally as refugees, despite the unofficial presence of so many Syrians inside the country. . . . There have never been so many places which were unreachable until now. This chaos will unfortunately continue. . . . The EU will not be a stability factor, but become a mere target if it does not take any measure and maintains its political ineffectiveness and lack of capacity despite being a major power in the region.[60]

Indeed, rewriting the humanitarian practices of protection through various modes, such as new border policies, fashioning of frontiers, interning population groups, etc., marked the long era of colonial governance and the subsequent phase of decolonisation. It marks a crucial phase of global history, and with their impact on human migration, migration has become to quote William Walters, a "world-making phenomenon".[61] In the unravelling of the colonial gradient in today's migration management regime, we can find out the presence of the obscure link between the figure of the modern migrant thumping on the doors of Europe (or the caravan of migrants from the south amassing before the entry gates of the United States[62]) and the abstract, objective logic of global governance.[63]

To add, network proved crucial in this process of postcolonial reorientation of global migration, while the categories and thus divisions within the migrants back home and now carried by them are reproduced. In Tilly's memorable words, "networks migrate, categories stay put".[64] Drawing on the historical literature on immigration into the United States, Tilly argued that both in slavery and post-slavery periods immigration rode on the basis of networks, and in the process divisions back in the old world were reproduced in the new world. Thus job specialisations, inequalities, and hierarchies – all these became durable through the structures immigration re-produced, though the process shattered many an old one at the same time.[65] Indeed, Tilly added a further twist to the narrative by pointing out that the immigrants, coping with the new world, discovered and created new inequalities and identities.

Yet these networks, critical migration scholars are pointing out today, also symbolise the hitherto unrealised energy and innovation of the migrants, who take unpredictable turns in their lives. Sandro Mezzadra has commented,

> The diversification of migratory patterns and experiences, the stretching of migratory networks, the multiplication of what is known in migration studies as 'new immigrant destinations'. . ., the spatial and temporal turmoil that characterize contemporary migration at the global level correspond indeed to a permanent mobilization of subjective energies and potentialities. This process radically transforms and challenges established forms of life, under the pressure of material conditions of deprivation and dispossession but at the same time of a subjective push towards the opening up of new spaces of freedom and equality.[66]

We may add to the factor of mobility of networks the still under-explored area of marriage migration. While marriage migration has recently caught the attention of scholars studying situations of internal displacement in postcolonial countries, the ways in which marriage migration sustains across borders (which involves, among various elements, sex tourism, trafficking, reproduction needs, family income, etc.) and strengthens networks has still to receive close scholarly attention. The response of immigration policies and personnel to marriage migration has been confused, to say the least, because they see in it one more sign of the postcolonial invasion of Europe. At the same time the knowledge of the governance regime of the migratory practices including marriage migration is increasingly put to use towards making the control regime more effective.[67] No one knows clearly the role of wives, husbands, and offspring in forming a migrant unit. Will they be split if and when admitted, or will the rule be same for all migrants? No one has a definite answer. The bio-political confusion is great.

In short, the historical sequences described in this and the previous chapters illustrate how the ambiguous nature of the colonial past has influenced and shaped substantially the current European migration management policy which includes managing borders and frontiers.[68] Europe-Asia relations, likewise Europe-Africa relations, have long colonial histories and are marked with often violent renegotiations of the international order. Exits rarely take place without conflicts. Trying to exit the colonial past Europe has to relive many old conflicts and experience new ones.

Yet we must not assume that the imprints of colonial history and the postcolonial present has been straightforward present. In two ways variations can be noted:

First, in relation between a national and a continental management of population mobility the relation is uneven and tumultuous. While European governance of population has exhibited a specific logic of continental economy, and of borders and boundary management in which frontier management has been a crucial component, national governance has been more focused on maintaining racial purity, guarding national borders, and keeping a "national" labour force employed. Thus Italy, Hungary, Poland, and all other countries of Europe fall in the second category. "Their" labour force is possibly most footloose in the continent. At times, however, these two perspectives mesh with one another.[69]

Second, because the management of migrant population is a complex exercise, Europe as a whole has to rely increasingly on administrative measures, policies, and local decrees than on parliamentary enactments. On one side, we witness the logic of a continent-wide management of immigrant population, which seeks to override the logic of managing a nationalised labour force, and therefore the frenetic nature of the logistical management of immigration; on the other side, we can see the immigrants disregarding every rule and category laid down for them towards entry, accommodation, relief, settlement, and perhaps inclusion. Thus, migrants are of no help to the authorities when the latter have to decide as to who belongs to which category, thus, who is a refugee and who is a migrant worker? The overall consequence is a crisis of humanitarianism, a shift in the relation between the humanitarian and the economic-political management of the migration question, and a greater emphasis on the neo-liberal truth that humanitarian management has to be efficient and must produce efficient results.[70] Or, we may put it like this: The efficient result will be also the most humanitarian one.[71]

Recall therefore the earlier references in this chapter to the technological evolution of the European border regime and protection strategy, which will make the humanitarian also the efficient. We shall return to this issue in the last chapter.

Notes

1 An earlier and shorter version of this chapter appeared as R. Samaddar, "Human Migration as Crisis of Europe", *Economic and Political Weekly*, Volume 50 (51), 19 December 2015, www.epw.in/journal/2015/51/perspectives/human-migration-crisis-europe.html.
2 Ghasan Hage, "Etat de Siege: A Dying Domesticating Colonialism?" *American Ethnologist*, Volume 43 (1), 2016, pp. 1–12; Hage wrote of a feeling in Europe "of being 'under siege' (that) has become increasingly pervasive in the contemporary Western world. . . . This feeling emerges amid what I will refer to as a colonial crisis, generated by the rise in the number of people seeking asylum in Europe, the resurgence of Western militarist interventionism in the Middle East, and the various forms of Muslim self-affirmation that have accompanied it . . . the intensity of this colonially derived sense of besiegement cannot be fully understood without taking into account a similar sense of besiegement generated by the ecological crisis. . . . 'More Evidence of Europe under Siege by the Flow of Illegal Migrants from Africa': so reads the headline for apiece written by Ann Corcoran (2015), a member of Refugee.

Resettlement Watch, an organisation that purports to provide the latest news on 'the invasion of Europe'; 'Germany in a State of SIEGE,' screams a UK *Daily Mail* headline. 'Merkel was cheered when she opened the floodgates to migrants," the title continues in bold, 'Now, with gangs of men roaming the streets and young German women being told to cover up, the mood's changing', pp. 1–2.
3 "Between the Devil and Deep Blue Sea", Statement of the Norwegian Refugee Council, 29 December 2015, www.nrc.no/?did=9211815#.VwyrQNR94_5 (accessed on 3 February 2017).
4 The *New York Times* ("Countries Under the Most Strain in the European Migration Crisis", 3 September 2015) quoted German Chancellor Angela Merkel as saying, "Germany is Doing What is Morally and Legally Obliged, not More, and not Less", and the Hungarian Prime Minister Viktor Orban telling back, "The Problem is not a European Problem, the Problem is a German Problem. Nobody would like to stay in Hungary." *The New York Times* also gave figures of the respective "loads" in that year on the basis of UNHCR and World Bank findings: Germany 707,116 (including applicants since 2011); Serbia and Kosovo 362,353; Sweden 308,275; Turkey 286,770; France 282,326; Hungary 236,498; Italy 193,514; Britain 140,698; Austria 128,827; Switzerland 113,471; Belgium 97,936; Netherlands 89,557; Norway 65,462; Greece 44,761; Poland 41,750; Denmark 41,124; Finland 36,244; Bulgaria 35,402; Spain 23,109; Montenegro 8,892, www.nytimes.com/interactive/2015/08/28/world/europe/countries-under-strain-from-european-migration-crisis.html?_r=0 (accessed on 1 October 2016).
5 Ruben Andersson wrote in the thickest moment of the "crisis" of 2015,

> The panicked political debates on the 'refugee crisis' this summer have displayed a fair bit of amnesia, as if our shores had suddenly been hit by an unforeseen natural disaster: a 'tide' or 'flood,' in media jargon. In fact, European leaders should have been well-prepared for the spike in arrivals, and not just because the Syria conflict has kept festering while UN humanitarian efforts for refugees have remained vastly underfunded. In fact, Europe has seen successive 'border crises' over well more than a decade now, including the first large arrivals of sub-Saharan Africans into Italy in the early 2000s, the Spanish Canary Islands 'boat crisis' of 2006, and numerous 'emergencies' announced ever since. Each crisis has spawned more investment in border security, which has in turn worsened the problem by displacing routes, triggering more risky entry methods, and feeding the smuggling networks facilitating entry via those riskier methods and routes. We face a vicious cycle at the borders where the failure of controls feeds a demand for ever more controls: a cycle where many powerful groups stand to gain, while border crossers face ever graver risks to their safety.

"The Illegality Industry: Notes on Europe's Dangerous Border Experiment", 26 October 2015, www.law.ox.ac.uk/research-subject-groups/centre-criminology/centreborder-criminologies/blog/2015/10/illegality (accessed on 7 November 2017).
6 "More Neighbours Make More Fences", *The Economist*, 15 September 2015, www.economist.com/blogs/graphicdetail/2015/09/daily-chart-10?fsrc=rss (accessed on 2 November 2015).
7 Sylvia Federici said in an interview,

> Marx emphasized how the development of capitalism led to the formation of an 'out of law' proletariat. We might say that the formation of such a proletariat is nowadays a global phenomenon systematically pursued. We can see it clearly in the case of migration. To survive, it is increasingly necessary to enter illegality and this then allows the State to act with violence on the workforce.

"The Reproduction Crisis and the Birth of a New 'Out of Law' Proletariat", originally published in Italian, 2017, *LeftEast*, 10 July 2017, www.criticatac.ro/lefteast/the-reproduction-crisis-and-the-birth-of-a-new-out-of-law-proletariat-an-interview-with-silvia-federici/ (accessed on 19 September 2018).
8 Ralf Dahrendorf, *Reflections on the Revolution in Europe* (London: Routledge, 2017); in this context also see, Joseph Pugliese, "Embodied Economies of Colonialism and Desire in Hegel's Empire of Reason", *Social Semiotics*, Volume 4 (1–2), 1994, pp. 163–183
9 *Gastarbeiter* in German means "guest worker". It refers to foreign or migrant workers, particularly those who had moved to West Germany.
10 *International New York Times predicted*, "mass migration poised to rise", and stay that way – report by Rod Nordland, 2 November 2015, p. 8.
11 For instance, "Slovenia unilaterally imposed a daily limit of 2,500, forcing fellow European Union member Croatia to also ration entry from Serbia." – agency report, "Migrant crisis: Many stranded in Balkans", *The Statesman,* 20 October 2015, p. 8.
12 Figures are from Robert Farley, "Four Myths about the European Refugee Crisis (And Why You Need to Know the Reality)", www.lawyersgunsmoneyblog.com/2015/10/four-myths-about-the-european-refugee-crisis-and-why-you-need-to-know-the-reality#comments (accessed on 15 October 2015); another report speaks of 2,800 deaths in crossings since January 2015 – Fulya Ozerkan, "17 Migrants die Off Turkey, 500 Rescued", *Asian Age*, 27 September 2015, www.asianage.com/international/17-migrants-die-turkey-500-rescued-285 (accessed on 1 November 2015); for statistical details of refugees in Europe, see the report by Refugee Rights Europe, *The State of Refugees and Displaced People in Europe: A Summary of Research Findings Across Europe, 2017–18*, http://refugeerights.org.uk/wp-content/uploads/2018/12/RRE_SummaryReport_2017-18.pdf (accessed on 16 January 2019).
13 *Ibid.*
14 For details, "Institutional and Regulatory Framework for Migration and Asylum Policies", EU desk research, http://immigrationintegration.eu/wp-content/uploads/2017/03/FAMI2_desk-research.pdf (accessed on 1 January 2019).
15 Mike Davis, *Late Victorian Holocausts: El Nino Famines and the Making of the Third World* (London: Verso, 2002).
16 Daniel Warner, "We are all Refugees", *International Journal of Refugee Law*, Volume 4 (3), pp. 365–372.
17 News items excerpted from www.timeline.com/stories/europe-immigration-crisis?gclid=COPj3cnrtcgCFVYSjgodut4OHw (accessed on 28 October 2015).
18 *The Guardian* reported on 20 June 2018, "Since 1993, one group has kept a tally of all the migrants and refugees who died trying to reach Europe." – Report by Alex Needham, "The List: The 34,361 Men, Women and Children who Perished trying to Reach Europe", www.theguardian.com/world/2018/jun/20/the-list-34361-men-women-and-children-who-perished-trying-to-reach-europe-world-refugee-day (accessed on 1 November 2018). The report said, "The list has been compiled by United for Intercultural Action, a European network of 550 anti-racist organisations in 48 countries. The List stretches back to 1993, when Kimpua Nsimba, a 24-year-old refugee from Zaire,

was found hanged in a detention centre, five days after arriving in the UK."; see also in this connection the UNHCR report, "Desperate Journeys: Refugees and Migrants Arriving in Europe and at Europe's Borders", January-August 2018, UNHCR, Geneva, September 2018.

19 On the Indian Ocean deaths, see next chapter; on deaths in the Pacific the report by Ian Urbina, "Tricked and Indebted on Land, Abused or Abandoned at Sea", *New York Times*, 9 November 2015, www.nytimes.com/2015/11/09/world/asia/philippines-fishing-ships-illegal-manning-agencies.html?emc=edit_na_20151109&nlid=41926157&ref=cta&_r=0(accessed on 2 November 2017); it is the same narrative of mobile labour, recruitment by agencies, search for sustenance, government apathy, failed rescue missions, and other features of the scenario associated with Mediterranean instances. The deaths of Rohingya refugees in the Bay of Bengal and the Pacific also carry the same tale. Similarly neglected by international humanitarian agencies are the migrant deaths in the Americas. See the harrowing accounts in Jason de Leon, *The Land of Open Graves: Living and Dying on the Migrant Trail* (Oakland, CA: University of California Press, 2015).

20 I have elsewhere discussed in detail the implications of interpreting the dual crises of European debt and migration as a postcolonial one. See, R. Samaddar, *A Postcolonial Enquiry into Europe's Debt and Migration Crisis* (Singapore: Springer, 2016).

21 Daniel Trilling, "What to Do with the People Who Do Make It Across?" *London Review of Books*, Volume 37 (19), 8 August 2015, pp. 9–12, www.lrb.co.uk/v37/n19/daniel-trilling/what-to-do-with-the-people-who-do-make-it-across (accessed on 3 February 2019).

22 Ibid.

23 "Mare clausum" denotes closed sea. In international law it means a sea, ocean or any other navigable body of water being under the jurisdiction of a state and closed accessible to other states. It is the opposite of "mare liberum" that is free sea. Portugal and Spain in early colonial age practised a *mare clausum* policy, which was challenged by other European powers soon.

24 "A report by Forensic Oceanography by Charles Heller and Lorenzo Pezzani, affiliated to the Forensic Architecture agency, Goldsmiths, University of London, May 2018, www.forensic-architecture.org/wp-content/uploads/2018/05/2018-05-07-FO-Mare-Clausum-full-EN.pdf (accessed on 1 January 2019); I am grateful to Charles Heller for directing my attention to the report; see also "Mare Clausum: The Sea Watch vs. Libyan Coast Guard Case, 6 November 2017", www.forensic-architecture.org/case/sea-watch/ (accessed on 1 January 2019).

25 *Ibid.*, p. 14.

26 *Ibid.*, p. 15.

27 In regard to maritime policies of states the similarity with the postcolonial state of affairs in Asia is again noticeable. Reminding us of who could be the boat survivors and the boat people who died, we can note that while European Powers were playing their ping pong diplomacy around the boat survivors, similar events were taking place in the Asian part of the world. Probably it began with *Komagatamaru* ship, travelling from coast to coast for days and months and refused entry by the biggest colonial power hundred years ago in the early part of the last century. Then came the Haiti boat people, the Vietnamese boat people, and now the Rohingyas, many of whom after being pushed out of Myanmar did not have formal access to food, shelter, or work, and in search of secure life were being compelled to take to the sea in perilous journeys to Southeast Asian countries like Malaysia, with Bangladesh and Thailand being the main transits. Labelled as "Asia's new boat people" their plight has been compared to the Vietnamese exodus by boat in the 1970s. While Asia's boat people perished in the Bay of Bengal, the Strait of Malacca, and Indian Ocean, Australia denied the shelter seekers any right of entry and quarantined them in off shore islands. The next chapter discusses this in detail.

28 It is tempting to read the history of the voyages in the Indian and the Pacific Oceans in the light of the contemporary movements across the Mediterranean; see, Renisa Mawani, *Across Oceans of Law: The Komagata Maru and Jurisdiction in the Time of Empire* (Durham, DC: Duke University Press, 2018). To be truthful, the history that we know began with

Komagata Maru has continued to this day with perilous journeys by Rohingyas and others to various countries and islands and the Australian waters.
29 Report by Nourhan Abdel Aziz, Paola Monzini, and Feruccio Pastore, "The Changing Dynamics of Cross-border Human Smuggling and Trafficking in the Mediterranean", Instituto Affari Internazionali, October 2015, www.iai.it/en/pubblicazioni/changing-dynamics-cross-border-human-smuggling-and-trafficking-mediterranean (accessed on 2 February 2019).
30 Stephan Scheel, "Real Fake? Appropriating Mobility via Schengen Visa in the context of Biometric Border Controls", *Journal of Ethnic and Migration Studies*, Volume 44 (16), 2018, pp. 2747–2763; see also, Scheel, "Studying Embodied Encounters: Autonomy of Migration Beyond its Romanticisation", *Postcolonial Studies*, Volume 16 (3), 2013, pp. 279–288; for details and elaboration of his arguments on the technological impact on border regime and the autonomy of migration, see his, *Rethinking the Autonomy of Migration: On the Appropriation of Mobility within Biometric Border Regimes*, Ph.d thesis, Department of Political and International Studies, The Open University, Milton Keynes, 2016.
31 Report by Helena Smith, "Migration Crisis: Idomeni, the Train Stop that Became an 'Insult to EU Values'", *The Guardian*, 17 March 2016, www.theguardian.com/world/2016/mar/17/migration-crisis-idomeni-camp-greece-macedonia-is-an-insult-to-eu-values (accessed on 26 November 2018).
32 "Refugee Crisis: EU Deportations to Turkey from Lesbos Continue Despite Protests", *The Independent*, 8 April 2016, www.independent.co.uk/news/world/europe/refugee-crisis-eu-deportations-to-turkey-from-lesbos-continue-despite-protests-a6974266.html (accessed on 5 February 2019).
33 William Walters, "Foucault and Frontiers: Notes on the Birth of the Humanitarian Border", in U. Bröckling, S. Krasmann, and T. Lemke (eds.), *Governmentality: Current Issues and Future Challenges* (London: Routledge, 2010), pp. 138–164.
34 Ibid., p. 143.
35 Ibid., p. 146.
36 "Danish MEP Quits Ruling Party Over Plan to Seize Refugees' Valuables", *The Guardian*, 20 December 2015, www.theguardian.com/world/2015/dec/20/danish-mep-quits-ruling-party-plan-refugees-valuables (accessed on 1 November 2018).
37 József Böröcz and Mahua Sarkar, "The Unbearable Whiteness of the Polish Plumber and the Hungarian Peacock dance around 'Race'", *Slavic Review*, Volume 76 (2), Summer 2017, pp. 307–314; see also Joseph Pugliese, "Race as Category Crisis: Whiteness and the Topical Assignation of Race", *Social Semiotics*, Volume 12 (2), August 2002, pp. 149–168; see also the discussion in Chapter 1; also on globalisation and new geopolitical divisions in Europe, József Böröcz, *The European Union and Global Social Change: A Critical Geopolitical-Economic Analysis* (London: Routledge, 2010).
38 Larry Wolff, *Inventing Eastern Europe: The Map of Civilisation on the Mind of Enlightenment* (Stanford, CA: Stanford University Press, 1994); Wolff discusses in detail the roles of Rousseau and Voltaire among others in shaping the colonial discourse on Eastern Europe.
39 Hannah Postel, Matt Juden, and Owen Barder, "What the EC's 17 point Refugee Action Plan Ignores", www.cgdev.org/blog/what-ec%E2%80%99s-17-point-refugee-action-plan-ignores (accessed on 24 October 2015); also on EU's financial gesture to Turkey, Paul Taylor, "EU offers Turkey cash, closer ties", *The Canberra Times*, 17 October 2015, p. 13.
40 I have discussed this detail in R. Samaddar, *A Postcolonial Enquiry into Europe's Debt and Migration Crisis* (Singapore: Springer, 2016), chapter 4, "Human Migration Appearing as Crisis of Europe", pp. 87–116.
41 http://europa.eu/rapid/press-release_IP-15-4813_en.htm (accessed on 2 January 2019).
42 Here is one report ("EU Refugee Relocation Scheme Visualised", 2015):

> European Union Member state compliance with emergency relocation scheme: Relocation places made available as percentage of member state quota – 0.03 %, 0.20 %, 0.50 %, 0.75 %, 1.00 %, 3.00 %, 4.00 %, and 8.00 %. In response to Europe's ongoing refugee crisis, the EU parliament agreed in September to transfer 160,000 people from most affected states. EU member states have so far only made 1,418 relocation

places available and relocated even less refugees, only 116 of the total number of refugees they committed to relocating over the next two years. The proposed relocation scheme was adopted by the European Council on 14 September and 22 September and promises a significant reduction of the pressure on the most affected member states. . . . The color scale (of the map) reveals a spread of several orders of magnitude in RPA (relocation places available). Of the countries that have already made places available, Germany ranks the lowest with an RPA of 0.04 %. Romania, Sweden, Finland, and Cyprus have RPAs between 7.00 % and 10.00 %. Luxembourg's RPA (15.33 %) is only topped by Malta, whose RPA is 100.00 %. Several countries have not yet begun to create relocation places, which is why their RPA is 0.00 %. Extrapolating the visible trends into the future, countries with RPAs higher than about 7 % will be able to fulfill their quota within two years. RPA is a good indicator for fulfillment, because it takes the created relocation places into account. It is reasonable to assume that countries will relocate refugees once they have created places for them. The EU's emergency relocation mechanism is only one facet of the broader refugee crisis. Its performances serve as an indicator for how well the EU will master migration challenges to come. Germany, the country that had pushed very hard for the relocation mechanism, has not yet started to create relocation places. In its current state, it is questionable whether the mechanism is working efficiently.

Data Design Company, EU, 4 November 2015, http://datadesigncompany.com/blog/eu_refugee_relocation.php (accessed on 8 November 2017).

43 PTI report, "Germany and Austria call for EU summit on refugee crisis", *The Statesman*, 17 September 2015, www.thestatesman.com/news/world/germany-and-austria-call-for-eu-summit-on-refugee-crisis/90526.html#sauiiHlJ2ByvSe1l.99 (accessed on 30 September 2015); also "Merkel calls on Europe for joint responsibility on refugee crisis", *The Toronto Globe and Mail*, 20 September 2015, www.theglobeandmail.com/news/world/merkel-calls-on-europe-for-joint-responsibility-on-refugee-crisis/article26449744/ (accessed on 1 October 2015); observers noted that Germany's relatively open door policy had much to do with her economic needs, because as newspaper put it, "Germany's Refugee Intake Begins to Boost Economy as Settlers Soothe Country's Worker Shortage", and then, "to maintain economic well-being, country 'needs about half a million immigrants every year'" – *The Independent*, 6 May 2019 – www.independent.co.uk/news/world/europe/germany-refugee-intake-boost-economy-ageing-population-unemployment-a8901161.html?fbclid=IwAR0mGVM374B0Bh8q2GXVhMzPPNVzFmG-YiyL_cBeQ2DDHguzTik20uomTnU.

Yet the quota proposal produced only discords. See, Elspeth Guild, "Responsibility Sharing of Asylum Seekers in the EU: Good Quality First Reception is the Key", *Verfassungsblog on Matters Constitutional*, 26 August 2015, https://verfassungsblog.de/responsibility-sharing-of-asylum-seekers-in-the-eu-good-quality-first-reception-is-the-key/ (accessed on 25 January 2019); also by Cathryn Costello and Elspeth Guild, "Fixing the Refugee Crisis: Holding the Commission Accountable", *Verfassungsblog on Matters Constitutional*, 16 September 2018, https://verfassungsblog.de/fixing-the-refugee-crisis-holding-the-commission-accountable (accessed on 25 January 2019).

44 On Turkey and Middle East in the wake of the war-caused devastation and refugee flows, NergisCanafe, "Post-Colonial State and Violence: Rethinking the Middle East and North Africa Outside the Blindfold of Area Studies", *Refugee Watch*, Volume 45, June 2015, pp. 7–31.

45 On this see Phil Mirowski, *Never Let a Serious Crisis Go to Waste: How Neoliberalism Survived the Financial Meltdown* (London: Verso, 2013).

46 Helene Stapinski, "When America Barred Italians", *The New York Times*, 2 June 2017 (all cited sentences in this paragraph are from this report), www.nytimes.com/2017/06/02/opinion/illegal-immigration-italian-americans.html (accessed on 1 June 2018); on racism in the European migration crisis, Fabian Georgi, "The Role of Racism in the European 'Migration Crisis': A Historical Materialist View", in Vishwas Satgar (ed.), *Racism after Apartheid: Challenges for Marxism and Anti-Racism* (Johannesburg: University of Witwatersrand Press, 2019), Chapter 5, pp. 96–117.

47 On internal colonialism, Hanno Brankamp, "The Question of Internal Colonialism", *Pambazuka News*, 13 January 2015, www.pambazuka.org/global-south/question-%E2%80%98internal-colonialism%E2%80%99 (accessed on 5 January 2019).
48 Paolo Novak comments in "Back to Borders", *Critical Sociology*, Volume 46 (3), 2017, pp. 847–864,

> Investigating where a border manifests itself and for whom, may offer insights on the *actual* (i.e. place-specific and embodied) significance and heterogeneous configuration of the social forces, practices and relations defining borders. For example, borders between the EU and West African countries provide (abstract) socio-spatial criteria for identifying 'Spain/Morocco' or 'Italy/Tunisia' borders, and yet these borders have progressively been displaced across West Africa for the purposes of migration controls. . . . Regardless of how we conceive of its main drivers, this externalization manifests itself differently, in different places and for different individuals. It takes different forms and operates through different mechanisms, whether we are examining it in Dakar, across the Sahara desert, in Ceuta, or when a shipwreck manages to reach Lampedusa, Sicily, *or* Apulia after crossing the Mediterranean. In any of those places, furthermore, it is likely to be more or less significant, to acquire heterogeneous meanings and to produce divergent experiences, claims, and aspirations for each of the individuals and social groups involved, regardless of how they are defined by others or how they self-ascribe their identities.
>
> *(p. 858)*

49 See for instance Ruth Wodak, Majid Khosrav Nik, and Brigitte Mral (eds.), *Right-Wing Populism in Europe: Politics and Discourse* (London: Bloomsbury, 2013); what the editors call "conceptual ambivalence" (p. 6) of the term "populism" has much to do with the present indeterminacy of "nation" and "empire" as two different entities and sovereignties, and hence the ambivalent attitude of nations towards Europe as an imperial formation. The immigration debate gets louder in that context.
50 D. Bigo, "Security and Immigration: Toward a Critique of the Governmentality of Unease", *Alternatives*, Volume 27, 2002, p. 64; also, Bigo, "The European Internal Security Field: Stakes and Rivalries in a Newly Developing Area of Police Intervention", in M. Anderson and M. Den Boer (eds.), *Policing across National Boundaries* (London: Pinter, 1994). William Walters has termed the frontier management of EU as one that considers "EU's external frontier might be considered to occupy a space somewhere between the networked (non) border and the *limes*." – William Walters, "The Frontiers of the European Union: A Geostrategic Perspective", *Geopolitics*, Volume 9 (3), Autumn 2004, pp. 678–694, 693.
51 Pankaj Mishra, "The Malign Incompetence of the British Ruling Class", *The New York Times*, 17 January 2019, www.nytimes.com/2019/01/17/opinion/sunday/brexit-ireland-empire.html (accessed on 20 January 2019); Mishra wrote,

> With Brexit, the chumocrats who drew borders from India to Ireland are getting a taste of their own medicine. . . . Politicians and journalists in Ireland are understandably aghast over the aggressive ignorance of English Brexiteers. Businesspeople everywhere are outraged by their cavalier disregard for the economic consequences of new borders. But none of this would surprise anyone who knows of the unconscionable breeziness with which the British ruling class first drew lines through Asia and Africa and then doomed the people living across them to endless suffering.

See also the bells in apprehension ringing earlier: Diarmaid Ferriter, "This Brexit Plan will Divide Britain and Ireland Once More", *The Guardian*, 10 October 2016, www.theguardian.com/commentisfree/2016/oct/10/brexit-plan-divide-britain-ireland-uk-border (accessed on 8 December 2018).
52 Patrick Barnard, "Notes on Syria and the Great Refugee Crisis", *Montreal Serai*, Volume 21 (9), March 2016, http://montrealserai.com/2016/03/28/notes-on-syria-and-the-great-refugee-crisis/ (accessed on 5 April 2016).

53 In a similar vein Mark Tseng-Putterman writes of "A Century of U.S. Intervention Created the Immigration Crisis", 20 June 2018, https://medium.com/s/story/time line-us-intervention-central-america-a9bea9ebc148(accessed on 21 December 2018); Putterman lists a long series of crises caused by the US in the Latin American hemisphere following the Monroe Doctrine and comments, "Those seeking asylum today inherited a sense of crises that drove them to the border".
54 Saskia Saseen, "Europe's Migrations: The Numbers and the Passions Are Not New", *Third Text*, Volume 20 (6), 2006, pp. 634–645, 636.
55 Aime Cesaire, *Discourse on Colonialism* (New York: Monthly Review Press, 1955,1972).
56 Federico Rahola, "The Space of Camps. Towards a Genealogy of Places of Internment in the Present", in Alessandro Dal Lago and Salvatore Palidda (eds.), *Conflict, Security and the Reshaping of Society* (New York: Routledge, 2010), pp. 185–199, 198.
57 *Ibid.*, p. 198.
58 This point has been made by scholars like Nicholas De Genova who has shown how race is being reproduced in the dynamics of European reception of the immigrants. As he writes "The first intimations of a European "migrant" (or "refugee") "crisis" arose amidst the unsightly accumulation of dead black and brown bodies awash on the halcyon shores of the Mediterranean Sea." – "The 'Migrant Crisis': as Racial Crisis: Do Black Lives Matter in Europe?" *Ethnic and Racial Studies*, Volume 41 (10), 2018, pp. 1765–1782, 1765; elsewhere he has written,

> Furthermore, the border-making and border-enforcing activities of immigration enforcement have been increasingly and pervasively relocated to sites within the 'interior' of migrant-receiving states, such that illegalized migrants and refugees are made, in effect, to carry borders on their very bodies . . . as border enforcement and the prospect of deportation come to permeate the full spectrum of racialized everyday life activities and spaces.

Nicholas De Genova, "Migration and the Mobility of Labour", in Matt Vidal, Tony Smith, Tomás Rotta, and Paul Prew (eds.), *The Oxford Handbook of Karl Marx*, Oxford Handbooks Online, December 2018, p. 14, 19, doi:10.1093/oxfordhb/9780190695545.013.25.
59 Not surprisingly we shall come up with instances as this in the report by Jerry Markon, "Can a 3-year Old Represent Herself in Immigration Court? This Judge Thinks So", *Washington Post*, 5 March 2016, www.washingtonpost.com/world/national-security/can-a-3-year-old-represent-herself-in-immigration-court-this-judge-thinks-so/2016/03/03/5be59a32-db25-11e5-925f-1d10062cc82d_story.html?hpid=hp_hp-more-top-stories_immigrationkids-930am%3Ahomepage%2Fstory (accessed on 5 October 2018).
60 Patrick Barnard, "Notes on Syria and the Great Refugee Crisis", *Montreal Serai*, Volume 29 (1), March 2016, http://montrealserai.com/2016/03/28/notes-on-syria-and-the-great-refugee-crisis (accessed on 1 January 2017).
61 William Walters, "Reflections on Migration and Governmentality", *Movements: Journal for Critical Migration and Border Regime Studies*, Volume 1 (1), 2015, https://movements-journal.org/issues/01.grenzregime/04.walters--migration.governmentality.html (accessed on 2 January 2019).
62 People now waking up to the reports of the caravans reaching the southern US borders took less attention to the deaths of the migrants in the Americas on their way to the United States. Read the harrowing accounts documented in Jason de Leon, *The Land of Open Graves: Living and Dying on the Migrant Trail* (Oakland, CA: University of California Press, 2015).
63 Scholars of migration working on "root causes" argue that the pattern of the current massive global migratory flows shows, first, lack of proper methods and systems of early warning, and second, neglect of "root causes" of migration. In both these factors the postcolonial structure of the origins and dynamics of migration is evident. See for instance, Susanne Schmeidl, *From Root Cause Assessment to Preventive Diplomacy: Possibilities and Limitations of the Early Warning of Forced Migration*, Ph.d dissertation, Ohio State University, 1995.

64 Charles Tilly, "Transplanted Networks", *New School for Social Research, Centre for Studies of Social Change*, Working Paper Series, 35, October 1986, p. 3.
65 Refugee Rights Europe, *The State of Refugees and Displaced People in Europe: A Summary of Research Findings across Europe, 2017–18* (n. 8) points out the reproduction of the inequalities and many of the living conditions back home.
66 Sandro Mezzadra, "What's at Stake in the Mobility of Labour? Borders, Migration, Contemporary Capitalism", *Migration, Mobility, and Displacement*, Volume 2 (1), Winter 2016, pp. 30–43, 36; see also Marina Kaneti, "Metis, Migrants, and the Autonomy of Migration", *Citizenship Studies*, Volume 9 (6–7), 2015, pp. 620–633.
67 Stephan Scheel, "Appropriating Mobility and Bordering Europe through Romantic Love: Unearthing the Intricate Intertwinement of Border Regimes and Migratory Practices", *Migration Studies*, Volume 5 (3), 2017, pp. 389–408, 402–403.
68 The current sense of "crisis" also stems from the fact, and as Saskia Sassen points out that "Part of the difficulty of old Europe is ironically the lack of a historical perspective. Europe has a barely recognised history of several centuries of internal labour migrations. This is a history that hovers in the penumbra of official European history dominated by the image of Europe as a continent of emigration, never of immigration." – "Europe's Migrations: The Numbers and the Passions are not New", *Third Text*, Volume 20 (6), 2006, p. 644.
69 For instance, it has been argued that the German policy on migrants, the most "European" of all national polices has been geared to national necessity. See, Christophe Tometten, "Germany's 'Legal Entry' Framework for Syrian Refugees – A Tool for Containment?", *Oxford Monitor of Forced Migration*, Volume 7 (1). Tometten in this short commentary says that while the German "legal entry" framework offers more venues for protection than in any other EU Member State, it fails to provide its beneficiaries with the same status, same scope of protection, and same rights and guarantees as refugees recognised in the regular asylum procedure. It suggests that the underlying political intention for the setup of the framework is not necessarily to ensure protection but rather to facilitate efficient administrative procedures and to contain refugee movement. The design of the framework fails to align the status and rights of beneficiaries of one or the other kind of "legal entry" and thus lacks consistency. Such a fragmented framework is not an ideal model for the development of "legal entry" frameworks in other countries, nor on the EU level.
70 In the drive for efficiency, it will be thus as is sometimes the case that proceedings to determine the status of the migrant will be without due representation of the shelter or the job seeker. See the report by Oliver Laughland, "Inside Trump's Secretive Immigration Court: Far from Scrutiny and Legal Aid", *The Guardian*, 7 June 2017, www.theguardian.com/us-news/2017/jun/07/donald-trump-immigration-court-deportation-lasalle?CMP=share_btn_fb (accessed on 28 November 2018).
71 In his detailed research on Italian towns as asylum centres Paolo Novak has observed

> the evidence of the perpetuation of violent and exclusionary forms of border management and a decreasing relevance of humanitarianism in the management of EU borders, a recalibration of the kinds of activity that are feasible and appropriate for nonmarket institutions to engage in and a set of contestations.

"The Neoliberal Location of Asylum", *Political Geography*, 2019 (forthcoming); see also G. Campesi, "Seeking Asylum in Times of Crisis: Reception, Confinement, and Detention at Europe's Southern Border", *Refugee Survey Quarterly*, Volume 37(1), 2018, pp. 44–70.

9

STATELESSNESS AND THE LOST WORLD OF CITIZENSHIP

Introduction

We now move back once more to the postcolonial region and see what is happening to postcolonial citizenship in the wake of massive displacements and migratory flows. This chapter will examine the entanglements of citizenship policies and practices with the spread of statelessness today. It will begin with a brief recount of the Rohingya question in Myanmar in the broader context of citizenship policies and registration drives in some postcolonial countries, which render massive number of "illegal immigrants" stateless. Current citizenship policies in these countries reflect the desire to achieve a perfect fit between the "right" kind of population and the "right size" of territory for a nation state. These policies become significant in the background of a shift in emphasis from *jus soli* to *jus sanguinis*, existence of borderland populations and the nowhere people, population flows across (post)colonial border formations and boundary delimitations, and the growth of regional informal labour markets characterised by immigrant labour economies. The question looming large over this discussion will be: In what way is the production of statelessness in the postcolonial world different from the classical idea of statelessness originating from succession of states (for instance, Yugoslavia[1])? What are the implications of the drive for registering national citizenry we are witnessing in India and elsewhere in terms of international human rights laws and for key instruments on statelessness – the 1954 UN Convention Relating to the Status of Stateless Persons and the 1961 Convention on the Reduction of Statelessness? Will the international legal understanding of statelessness be adequate to theorise the growing phenomenon of statelessness in the postcolonial world?[2]

History of a situation

In a fascinating essay on what the East India Company called in the late eighteenth century as "Arakanese refugees" who were settled by the Company in

Chittagong-Western Burma area, Anandaroop Sen brings to light the nature of population flows in the Bengal-Burma region two centuries back – a picture that is not much different at least in some ways from what obtains in this region today.[3] Sen focused on Company's select plans of settlement whose logic was a peculiar mix of military and economic considerations of viewing space from the point of ideas of usefulness and peculiarities of "refugee" labour for military purpose. In this way Sen brought to attention the always present particular historical rendition of the meanings associated with the term "refugee", which combines notions of displaced, dispossessed, and the productive within the same analytic field. In arguing for what refugee labour implied in a land and time marked by intense war making exercises, Sen recalled the early travels of Francis Buchanan in the then lands of the Provinces of Chittagong and Tippera, and the destitution of different sections of people including the Arakanese lodged in that region. He explicitly invoked the situation of the Rohingyas and concluded his essay with asking,

> There is something else I want to gesture at here.... It has to do with the word refugee. The term has acquired particular resonances in a politics of modernity ... what happens to the figure when it is located in the early etchings of colonial empire? Deracinated from the temporal provenance of the twentieth century, how does one think of this category? What did it mean to be a refugee in Company occupied Chittagong? ... Perhaps recognizing such questions will contribute to an understanding of how the category has historically been worked out. Considering the growing numbers of Rohingya Muslims shuttling the waters of Bay of Bengal as refugees, the significance of tracing these older routes of dispossession has only become sharper.[4]

Today the Rohingyas not only bring to mind the continuities of the past and the strange (or perhaps not) ways the term "refugee" was invoked in earlier ages they also tell us of newer aspects of a situation of displacement and forced migration. If refugees were earlier a part of state-making projects – colonial or nationalist – today refugees in their condition of protracted displacement point to the possibilities of statelessness.

The ancient name for Arakan is *Rohang*, which presumably led to the word Rohingya, who historically developed from many stocks of people, including Myanmarese, Arabs, Moors, Persians, Bengalis, and others – all adhering to Islam.[5] Though the naming of *Rohingya* seems to have come about only recently, around the beginning of 1950s, the Muslims in Arakan have a long history. Arakan was occupied by the British after the first Anglo-Burmese War (1824–26). Thereafter with large scale immigration from India, the confrontation between the Muslims in the northwestern part of Arakan and the Buddhists as the majority in central and southern Arakan became tense. The defeat at the hands of the British forced Burma to sign the Treaty of Yandabo in 1826 which resulted in the absorption of Arakan into the British Empire. Eventually, Burma became a province of British India, and the easy border between Bengal and Arakan facilitated a variety of cross-border contacts.[6] Over time, numerous Bengali Muslims, some of whom were *Chittagongs*,[7] moved into northern Arakan and began to merge with the Rohingya community. In this way, the distinction between these ethnic groups was blurred following the ease of cross-border and inter-community interactions. The immigrants coming into the Arakan included many Muslims from Chittagong. The confrontation came to a head during the Japanese occupation period (1942–45), when Japan armed the Buddhist Arakanese to fight against the British and the British used Muslim forces for a counterattack. The situation did not change much after the independence of Burma in 1948.

A number of minority ethnic groups in course settled in Rakhine (then Arakan), including Chin, Mro, and Khami (mainly Christians now), Kamans in the coastal areas (largely converted to Islam), in addition to the Buddhist majority groups, and other Muslims. The Rakhine people claimed autonomy from Myanmar but without result. This conflict continues today. But we have to remember that the perceived cultural and ethnic dissimilarities between the Buddhists and Muslims were not clear in the past, and Muslims and Buddhists in the past lived on both sides of the river Naf, which marks the present border with Bangladesh; also the fact that the Buddhism of the Rakhines was of a distinct variety, *Theravada* or *Hinayana*, whose influence can be dated back to the eleventh century AD. Subsequently, the Rakhines had contested the supremacy of the Burman kings. Arakan had a series of powerful Buddhist rulers with proud cultural and political traditions similar to the Burmans, Shans, and Mons in the east.[8]

In the first Census of British Burma (1872), the Muslims were categorised either as Burman Muslims or Indian Muslims. Two-thirds of the total number of Muslims, recorded around 64,000 people, lived in the Arakan.[9] The Census of 1891 included most of the recognised territory of Myanmar today. It recorded Muslims under the categories used for the broader India census. Thus, the Muslim people were divided as Sheikhs, Sayyids, Moghuls, Pathans, and other groups, including Arakanis, Shan Muslims, Turks, Arabs, and others. Many Arakan Muslims were offspring of inter-marriages between the Indian Muslims and Burman Buddhists, and were registered as Sheikhs in the census. By 1921, there were over 500,000 Muslims in a population of over 13 million.[10] Muslims of Indian origin came from several different provinces of India.

Henceforth, there would be both regular mingling of different ethnic and religious communities as well as conflicts, especially around the Naf river border.[11] During British rule, labourers, merchants or administrators had migrated to Burma from outside. They included Hindus and Muslims, Nepalis and Tamils. Similarly, many migrated from Chittagong to the Arakan towns of Maungdaw and Sittwe or Akyab. Some of them were seasonal workers to help local rich landowners during harvest time. However, it was the activities of Chettiyar moneylenders from southern India that caused the greatest resentment amongst impoverished rural farmers in central and lower Burma. This, in turn, fuelled the growing tide of Burmese nationalism, and there were violent anti-Indian communal riots in 1930–31 and again in 1938 in which several hundred Indians were killed. As a consequence, there was a growing tendency of clubbing the Indian Muslims and the indigenous Muslims of Arakan together. Against this backdrop, during World War II, a huge number of Indians, including Muslims, fled Burma. Some followed the departing British administrators, but others were brutally chased out by the nationalists of Aung San's Burma Independence Army.[12] Thousands also died of starvation, disease, and in military attacks, accounting for one of the darkest episodes in modern Burmese history.

After Burma's independence in 1948, the government in Rangoon (now Yangon) neglected the political demands of both Muslim and Buddhist communities in Arakan, which was not granted provincial autonomy. It was under the 1974 constitution that Arakan was granted statehood and was given the official title of the Rakhine State with the name of the state capital Akyab changed to Sittwe. In 1978, a military operation combined with an unusual census operation, known as *Nagamin* or King Dragon, to check identity papers in the border region for the first time, was launched in the mountains of north Arakan. The census operation generated controversies, amidst widespread reports of army brutality, including rape, murder, and the destruction of mosques. As a result, about 200,000 Muslims took refuge elsewhere. The state-controlled media of Burma argued that many of those who had fled were in fact illegal Bengali immigrants, who had entered Burma as part of a general expansion of the Bengali population in this region of Asia. The displaced Rohingyas said they never had any national registration cards, or they had been confiscated by the immigration authorities during the 1978 operation. The discrimination became more acute after a tough Citizenship Act was passed by the Ne Win government in 1982. Under this act, three categories of citizens – national, associate, and naturalised – were created. Full citizenship in Burma was only for national ethnic groups, such as the Burmans, or those who could prove their ancestry in Burma before the first Anglo-Burmese war.

From the middle of 1991, several new regiments as well as a local border police militia known as the Na SaKa were deployed in the border region. Local Rakhine, Mro, and Chin populations began to complain of forced relocations and military harassment. Subsequently, over 250,000 Muslim refugees fled to the Cox's Bazar area of Bangladesh. The State kept on claiming that the Rohingya problem was one of unregistered illegal immigrants. The Rohingyas became a stateless population in 1982 with the revised Myanmar Citizenship Law that excluded them from the list of 135 national ethnic groups. The category of *non-state persons* had come into existence with the concept of citizenship.

Under the constitution of Burma at the time of independence, the Rohingyas had a good claim to citizenship, yet today they have become "resident foreigners", even though their families had been there for generations. The conferring of citizenship is now a matter of state privilege. And, today with the 1982 law (unlike the preceding 1948 Citizenship Act) essentially based on the principle of *jus sanguinis* very few Rohingyas have a chance of fulfilling the requirements of citizenship. In 1989, colour-coded citizens scrutiny cards (CRCs) were introduced: pink cards for full citizens, blue for associate citizens, and green for naturalised citizens. The Rohingyas were not issued any cards. In 1995, in response to UNHCR's intensive advocacy efforts to document the Rohingyas, the Burmese authorities started issuing them temporary registration cards (TRCs), a white card, pursuant to the 1949

Residents of Burma Registration Act. One has to note, the TRC does not mention the bearer's place of birth and cannot be used to claim citizenship.

If the Rohingya issue is an indication, as nationality issues get more ethnicised and securitised, we shall witness an increase of de facto statelessness in particular.[13] With the Convention on Statelessness (1954) framed in the context of postwar Europe, the question of the responsibility for production of statelessness often reflected in the form of growing de facto statelessness is becoming acute today.[14] It also throws in clear light the limits of the global protection apparatus (including Convention on the Reduction of Statelessness, 1961).[15]

At the same time we have to remember, population movements, in particular forced population movements, are seldom purely state-to-state business. They often have regional dimensions. Yet in discussions on statelessness, the regional dimension of the problem, and in this case of the Rohingya refugees, is often ignored. Commentators have noted the fluctuating attitudes and policies of great powers towards the policies of suppression of the Rohingyas by the State of Myanmar, but not its regional dimension. The regional dimension of the problem was ignored even in analyses of the Bay of Bengal crisis of 2015 involving the boat people – the Rohingyas and Bangladeshis. In recent years as Rohingyas have fled in large numbers to neighbouring Bangladesh, India, Thailand, and Malaysia, and some even tried to reach Australia, the regional dimension of the issue of statelessness has become clearer. Yet, regional and bilateral initiatives often fail. For instance, in the wake of the growing international focus on the Rohingya issue the initiative of the Thai government in May 2016 for a regional approach to address the migrant crisis did not produce much. This had followed another failed regional initiative, taken in 2002, known as the Bali Process on "People Smuggling, Trafficking in Persons and Related Transnational Crime". Several countries wanted the root causes of the flow of migrants to be taken into account as part of the initiative. However, the Myanmar government threatened to boycott the meeting and accused others of being soft on human trafficking.

As part of its "Look East Policy" India in 2008 had signed with Myanmar the Framework Agreement for facilitating the Kaladan Multi-Modal Transit Transport Project. This goal was to connect Kolkata to Sittwe port in Myanmar, via Bay of Bengal, then Sittwe port to the inland water trans-shipment terminal at Paletwa town in Myanmar through Kaladan river, connect Paletwa river terminal to the India-Myanmar border at Zorinpui at the southern tip of Mizoram in India's northeast, and finally construct the 100 km-long road from Zorinpui to the Aizawl-Saiha Highway (the Indian National Highway 54 at Lawngtlai). NH 54 is the part of the larger East-West corridor connecting the rest of India with India's northeast. Sittwe, the capital of the Rakhaine state of Myanmar in this way became a critical point of India's connectivity policy. China too got involved in the development of infrastructural facilities in Rakhine state. The CITIC (China International Trust Investment Corporation) Group Corporation Limited, a state-owned investment company, won a contract to develop the multi-billion Kyaukphyu Special Economic Zone (SEZ) that involves building a deep-sea port and an industrial park. In November 2010, the China Development Bank and Myanmar Foreign Investment Bank signed a $2.4 billion loan deal to construct the 1,060 km-long pipeline from Kyaukphyu to Kunming in the Yunnan province of China. "The loan will be mainly for the natural gas project in KyaukPhyu, which involves Myanmar, China, Korea and India, where Myanmar has 7.3 percent of the shares. Part of the loan was provided for Myanmar as an investment in the project".[16]

This is admittedly a very brief description of a local conflict growing up in history's womb, and acquiring global dimensions. At the same time it tells us how a group of population becomes stateless. But perhaps this description also throws light on the fragility of the citizenship norms of democracy. Statelessness hovers over the dark corners of the world of citizenship.

Discrimination, statelessness, and responsibility

It is important to recall at this juncture that population groups can become stateless for a variety of reasons, including inequitable laws (such as marriage laws), transfers of territory between countries, flawed or discriminatory administrative practices, lack of birth registration, and withdrawal of citizenship rights. Conservative estimates of the current number of stateless persons in the world range from about 11 to 15 million who live without a nationality – in a legal limbo.[17]

One of the main reasons why people are denied or deprived of nationality, and thus rendered stateless, is racial or ethnic discrimination. It happened in Mauritania for blacks (1989), in Estonia for ethnic Russians (after 1991), many ex-Yugoslavs (after the Balkan War in the 1990s), South Bhutanese in Bhutan (in late eighties and nineties of the last century), and now for Rohingyas.[18] In Myanmar ethnic and national identities have been effectively merged. Words such as Burmese, Burman, and Buddhist have been used interchangeably, while for decades the Muslims in Arakan, and particularly the Rohingyas have been subjected to violence, human rights abuses, and forced resettlement both within the country and across borders. Thousands of refugees and internally displaced persons (IDPs), created in the process, have led to a protracted humanitarian crisis. Myanmar's military defended its crackdown on the Rohingya Muslim minority in early March 2017 as a lawful counter-insurgency operation, adding that it was necessary to defend the country.[19] Meanwhile, from late 2016, in a return of the crisis, thousands of Rohingyas again began seeking refuge in Bangladesh, as Myanmar's forces launched a crackdown on the million-strong Muslim minority. Testimonies from refugees, satellite images compiled by human rights groups, and leaked photos and videos from inside the Rakhine state of Myanmar became available.[20] Police said three border guard posts had been attacked by Islamist militants. Interestingly, Aung Sang Suu Kyi, the symbol of the democratic upsurge in Myanmar and a Nobel Peace Prize winner, who came to power in the country after the polls in November 2015, did not show any sign of willingness to address the Rohingya issue.

In 2014, the UNHCR launched a campaign to end statelessness by 2024. Most situations of statelessness were found to be direct consequence of discrimination based on ethnicity, religion or gender. The largest stateless population of the world is in Myanmar where more than one million Rohingyas have been refused nationality. Statelessness affects the enjoyment of all the rights which most of us take for granted, for instance the right to work, the right to vote, the right to welfare benefits and a child's right to education. Statelessness exacerbates poverty, creates social tensions, breaks up families and can even fuel conflict. Stateless people are not recognised as nationals by any country and deprived of the rights most people take for granted. They often live on the margins of society where they are vulnerable to exploitation. It prevents people from moving and increases their chances of arbitrary arrest or detention with no adequate remedies. International law provides a framework for action in respect of the stateless. Despite the existence of two significant legal documents, viz., the 1954 UN Convention relating to the Status of Stateless Persons and the 1961 Convention on the Reduction of Statelessness, the situation remains grim. As referred to earlier, Article 1.1 of the 1954 UN Convention relating to the Status of Stateless Persons defines a stateless person as "a person who is not considered as a national by any State under the operation of its law." The 1954 Convention establishes minimum guarantees in areas such as education, health care, employment, and identity as well as travel documents. While it does not oblige states to provide nationality for stateless persons in its territory, it asks them to facilitate naturalisation. The 1961 Convention sets out important safeguards that can be incorporated into nationality laws to prevent statelessness, for example, in relation to acquisition of a nationality at birth or loss of nationality on marriage, or as a result of prolonged residence abroad. In addition, international human rights law plays a significant and complementary role. Its guarantees apply to all persons, with very few provisions restricted to nationals alone. Key human rights standards include the obligation to ensure birth registration, the prohibition on arbitrary deprivation of nationality, and guarantees of equal treatment for women in relation to nationality laws and protection against arbitrary detention. Yet as said, despite these and other global initiatives new risks of statelessness have emerged. The level of ratification of the UN statelessness conventions is low. The Rohingyas are continuously driven out of Myanmar; they were at times chased out of Bangladesh; some of them who reached India in phases are now on the verge of deportation. The Ministry of Home Affairs, Government of India, tells them that India is not their country, and they would be identified and sent back. Where will they go? Most of them are ignorant of laws. Countries are kicking them around. This is the position of "rightlessness" of which Hannah Arendt had talked.[21]

As one South Asian expert has pointed out, statelessness in fact points to a major weakness in international law on refugees. While massive efforts were made by the UNHCR and the global humanitarian community to help and assist the victims of forced eviction through relief, rehabilitation, and integration in host country and third-country resettlement, the problem did not go away. It increased. A major part became stateless (of nearly 43 million refugees, about 12 million were stateless). As they had no chance of going back, after protracted period of displacement they became stateless. But perhaps equally significantly, people did not have to cross the borders in order to become refugees. Losing their citizenship status or never enjoying it many became refugees even when they had not crossed international borders.

They became "refugees" in their homes, stripped of their citizenship and rendered "stateless".[22] In fact, statelessness has emerged as a serious issue in the region of South and Southeast Asia. Not just Myanmar, the citizenship laws of the postcolonial states of India, Pakistan, and Sri Lanka, moving from *jus soli* to *jus sanguinis*, are highly influenced by the self-perception of the "majority" who claimed to constitute the "nation". Ethnic bias, cultural, linguistic, religious prejudices, gender discrimination and political concerns of the emerging ruling elite shaped the policy for granting as well as denying citizenship. On the other hand the international community's engagement with the problem of statelessness is rather recent. The major weakness of international protection mechanism for the stateless persons is non-applicability of international law within the sovereign jurisdiction of sates, where the majority of stateless persons live. The states control their borders, frame the immigration policies and decide who should be allowed to enter its territory and who should be rejected. The present immigration laws, policies, and practices of most states do not make a distinction between the stateless persons and other migrants.[23] Involved in such situations like this is the issue of responsibility: responsibility of the state that forces displacement, the state that has to give shelter, the responsibility of the region (think of various regional initiatives and solutions), and the responsibility of the most powerful, that is the institutions in charge of global governance and the international legal arrangements. These failures combine to produce massive *de facto* statelessness.

This is clear as Australia continues to refuse supporting any international, and this case regional initiative, to protect the Rohingyas – particularly Rohingyas at sea – who reach various neighbouring countries of Southeast Asia. As Rohingyas fled in large numbers to neighbouring Bangladesh, India, Thailand, and Malaysia, and some even tried to reach Australia, the regional dimension of the issue of statelessness became clearer. Perhaps in regional policies for the protection of the stateless population groups part of the solution lies. In case of several stateless groups who were rehabilitated and resettled in India (or Sri Lanka in case of Tamil plantation workers or protection of Afghan escapees in India, Pakistan, and Iran) a bilateral framework and a spirit of regional understanding worked.

So, why should this not be the case for Rohingyas, and why should not states of South and Southeast Asia along with other Asia-Pacific countries deliberate on the issue of the rights of the Rohingyas, and see how the issue of statelessness can be resolved? Of course involving Myanmar will be important and essential in this exercise. We may recall how the issue of Balkan refugees and ex-Yugoslav stateless groups were resolved in the framework of Europe.

Yet, regional initiatives often fail. For instance, in the wake of the growing international focus on the Rohingya issue, the Royal Thai government called for a regional meeting to address the migrant crisis on 29 May 2016 involving fifteen nations. These included Bangladesh, Myanmar, Indonesia, Malaysia, host Thailand as well as Australia, and the United States. Several countries wanted the root causes of the flow of migrants to be discussed in the meeting. However, the Myanmar government said that it would boycott the meeting and accused others of being soft on human trafficking. This blame-game did not help. As the current migrant crisis came under further regional and international scrutiny, Myanmar was asked to recognise that its transition to democracy would be judged by how it treated its minority communities. In this connection it is important to note that the Indian Navy was involved in several relief and rescue operations in the Bay of Bengal in the past. The current humanitarian crisis in the Bay of Bengal requires from India a more pro-active policy in the sea to rescue the boat people.

Before this initiative was taken, there was another regional initiative, taken in 2002, known as the Bali Process on People Smuggling, Trafficking in Persons and Related Transnational Crime. We referred to the Bali Process earlier. It attempted to raise regional awareness of the consequences of the smuggling of people, trafficking in persons and related transnational crimes. Accordingly, it developed and implemented strategies and practical cooperation in response. More than forty-five members, including the UNHCR, the International Organization for Migration (IOM) and the United Nations Office of Drugs and Crime (UNODC), as well as a number of observer countries and international agencies participated in this voluntary forum.[24] Later, an ad hoc group was set up to develop and pursue practical measures to inform future regional cooperation on people smuggling, trafficking in persons and the irregular movement of people.[25]

In 2009, some Southeast Asian countries agreed to use the Bali process to solve the Rohingya issue. Earlier, Thailand's Prime Minister had said in February 2008 that, the issue of Rohingyas needed greater discussion in a regional forum. He told reporters in Jakarta during his visit to Indonesia then that the regional governments would take up the issue of the Rohingyas at the Bali process.[26] However, during the 2014 ASEAN Summit, in Naypyidaw, the first one to be held in the new capital of Myanmar, the plight of the Rohingya Muslims was left out of the agenda. The Government of Myanmar's decision in March 2014 to expel humanitarian groups and prevent them from providing health care and aid increased the number of the Rohingyas moving to other countries.

When the rickety boats carrying Rohingyas, with depleting food and drinking water, hit the newspaper headlines in May 2015, at least Malaysia and Indonesia responded to international pressure and said they would no longer turn away migrant boats, offering instead to take in a wave of asylum seekers, provided they could be resettled or repatriated within a year. In contrast, the Australian Prime Minister Tony Abbott said Australia wanted other countries to help with resettlement, but those seeking a better life in Australia needed only to come through the "front door". He said, "If we do the slightest thing to encourage people to get on boats, this problem will get worse, not better", and

> Australia will do absolutely nothing that gives any encouragement to anyone to think that they can get on a boat, that they can work with people-smugglers to start a new life. . . . Our role is to make it absolutely crystal clear that if you get on a leaky boat, you aren't going to get what you want. . . . This is quite properly a regional responsibility and the countries that will have to take the bulk of the responsibility are obviously the countries which are closest to the problem. . . . Australia can show leadership and compassion, just as it

did after the Tiananmen Square massacre and the Vietnam War, by authorising special intake of refugees fleeing war and persecution.[27]

We all know, what this meant in practice, basically offshore internment, known infamously as the "Pacific solution".[28]

On the other hand the Indonesians pointed out that Australia was obliged to help as a signatory to the United Nations Refugee Convention.[29] Thailand was quick to recognise the regional imperative in finding a solution to the Rohingya issue. In a meeting held as part of the Bali process (24–25 February 2009) Thailand noted the entry of Rohingyas as illegal migrants. The Thai representative noted that over 5000 boat arrivals were recorded in 2008, and the potential migrant stock would be of several hundreds of thousands. With a burden of 3 million illegal migrants, Thailand could not be either a country of transit or country of destination. Hence it pressed for a regional approach. It was

> a collective problem that the countries concerned in the region – countries of origin, transit and destination – have to collectively address, and in a comprehensive manner. We have proposed to the other affected countries (Bangladesh, India, Indonesia, Malaysia and Myanmar) to join hands with Thailand in constituting a contact group to coordinate and cooperate on this matter.

Thailand also advocated several overlapping approaches and declared its readiness to facilitate the work of a small group of relevant stakeholders towards a solution. It also declared that it was seeking cooperation of the United Nations High Commissioner for Refugees (UNHCR) and the International Organization for Migration (IOM).[30] In the same meeting at Brisbane the UNHCR representative added,

> The situation of the Rohingya, with its refugee protection and economic dimensions, therefore presents, in critical form, a case study of the broader problem of onward movement affecting the region.... The issue also needs a regional approach that can address the entire range of push and pull factors and the full cycle of displacement, which includes countries of origin, transit and destination.[31]

The presence of Rohingyas as undocumented labour migrants was also noted by the Regional Support Office of the Bali Process in a paper on "Pathways to Employment: Expanding Legal and Legitimate Labour Market Opportunities for Refugees".[32]

The Andaman Sea refugee crisis in 2015–16 finally left no one in doubt that the Rohingya crisis called for a regional approach. Sea and the oceans are always regional. Indeed they make regions. That the Andaman Sea crisis was therefore seen as a call to the region did not surprise those working for human rights and humanitarian protection. Yet little advance has been made on the issue of finding a regional solution to the Rohingya issue. The Indian and Bangladesh governments have done least in terms of forging a regional solution; and this when we know that in 2014–15 about 25,000 fled Myanmar and Bangladesh by boat, and around 8000 were stranded at sea. Around 400 possibly died. Many, fleeing, paid great deal of money for their passage. On 1 May 2015, a mass grave containing the remains of more than thirty bodies was discovered in the Sadao district of Thailand, a few hundred metres from the Malaysia border. On 5 May 2015 three Thai officials and a Myanmar national were arrested in Thailand for suspected involvement in human trafficking. Thereafter, boats began to be intercepted. Thai, Malaysian, and Indonesian authorities reportedly intercepted boats of asylum seekers and pushed them back out to sea. Consequently, boatloads of people were abandoned on the water. An estimated number of 6000 Rohingyas and Bengalis were stranded by 12 May – without food or water. Some were rescued by Indonesian and Malaysian local officials and fishermen, or they swam to shore. On 26 May, Malaysian policemen found the remains of approximately 140 bodies, perhaps of migrants from Myanmar and Bangladesh, in abandoned jungle camps near the Thai border. In short, the regional response was sorely inadequate. Policing was thought to be the main way to tackle the crisis.[33] This as in the Mediterranean aggravated the crisis. The attention of the international community remained on the Mediterranean boat crisis, and by and large the Bay of Bengal and the Indian Ocean crisis was ignored. In the din of maritime security human rights of the migrants at sea were drowned. The sovereignty games continued around the politics of boat migration. Yet the persistent attempts by the migrants to repeatedly take to the seas challenged the anonymity of death in the sea.[34]

In this situation, one-off meetings became the norm for managing mass displacement events on the Andaman Sea. Regional institutions and processes – ASEAN, the Bali Process and the Jakarta Declaration – were largely muted during the crisis. Most crucially the Bali Process did not have functioning mechanisms for officials and functionaries across the region to respond. Regional leaders made the right noises but took few concrete steps. Amidst all these came the "New York Moment" in 2016 when in September the then US President Barack Obama and UN Secretary-General Ban Ki-moon spoke in high-level discussions in New York on refugees and migrants.[35] On 19 September 2016 at the UN headquarter in New York the UN Summit for Refugees and Migrants was held. That was perhaps the last moment of attention.

Meanwhile Rohingyas in the region, including in India, became the subjects of what we may call fringe economy or refugee economy – a part of a larger informal economy, at the same time the subject of global humanitarian attention. They also became the new "boat people" of Asia and the world. Their identity was also marked by a slippage between that of a Rohingya and a Bangladeshi. As the Rohingya emerged as a stateless subject on the boat, it was difficult to say who was a Bangladeshi and who was a Rohingya.

As a group of researchers found in their study, Rohingyas took help of Bangladeshis and posed as Bangladeshis to escape to the high seas from their camps in Bangladesh, and get work after they had landed elsewhere.[36] Bangladeshis in search of work mixed with Rohingyas to get onto the boats with the help of middlemen and escape joblessness and poverty. The process of taking Bangladeshi nationals along with the Rohingyas in boats had been going on for a little more than a decade. There were police reports of young boys missing in areas adjoining Cox's Bazar. Media reports gave an idea of the extent of migration in the past ten years. The fact remained that labour migration from Bangladesh to Malaysia was a practice recognised by both governments of Malaysia and Bangladesh. Rohingyas from Bangladesh began going to Malaysia probably because the latter was a Muslim country, and they felt that there was a huge labour market with high demand for labour. Consequently, the middlemen took Rohingyas along with Bangladeshi nationals. The Bangladeshis were included as they were likely to pay more than what the Rohingyas could afford.[37] The new boat people evoked comparison with the African and West Asian groups often perishing in the Mediterranean and other seas while to trying to reach European shores.

And where else would this be found but in a boat on high sea? In the high sea desperately trying to reach Greece, who could ascertain who was a Syrian, who an Iraqi, and who was an Afghan? Or, in the Mediterranean who was a Sudanese and who was a Ugandan? On the other hand, as we know, when the captain of *Tampa* was rescuing the boatpeople in the Australian waters, he had perhaps forgotten his identity as a person of a particular national identity, and had become almost one with the survivors (Iraqis, Iranians, Afghans, and others) who had lost all national rights and their respective national identities. In fact, after attempting to rescue the boat people off the Australian shore, Captain Arne Rinnan of the *Tampa* said, "It is a terrible thing to be out there in a broken down boat. I am afraid there might be fewer rescues. It is an unwritten law of the sea to rescue people in distress. I would do it again and I hope all my seafaring colleagues would do the same". He said he was not a hero, but a simple seaman".[38] Australia in one incident closed its door to 2390 boat people with what was codenamed as "Operation Relex" at a cost of AUD 500 million. The policy coupled with deployment of army resulted in 332 deaths in the sea. Some refugees put fire to themselves. Incidentally, those in charge of Operation Relex were later given public service awards, consultancy as contractors to defence department, and one became the executive chairman and CEO of Sydney Airport.[39]

The legal limbo

We must notice several paradoxes in the situation. These paradoxes take us to the heart of the question of statelessness in the postcolonial age, namely that statelessness has as much to do with citizenship as to migration, while the conventional definition of statelessness links it to refugee-hood. Yet, as the instance of the Rohingyas showed, the situation of postcolonial statelessness cannot be understood without referring to the game of citizenship, which is acquiring greater and greater stake in the dynamics of power.

Little known outside India, there is a similar possibility of statelessness in the Indian northeast through disqualification of massive number of people (about

1.8 million) in course of a national citizenship registration drive. The final version of the National Register of Citizens (NRC) in the Indian state of Assam was published on 31 August 2019. It was a court-sanctioned registration process. The updating process was marred by controversies over what was considered arbitrary verification procedure, with extremely rigorous standards being applied on Bengali-speaking population, in particular Bengali-speaking Muslims, many of whom were immigrants from East Pakistan/Bangladesh and settled there for several decades. Disowned by India and without ties to any other country, a significant number of those excluded from the NRC are thus rendered stateless. This has created a precarious situation involving protracted detentions of those branded as "foreigners". Detention facilities have been expanded for a large number of marginalised and disenfranchised people who may have no access to effective legal aid and other constitutional guarantees, with the biggest detention centre in the country coming up soon in Assam.[40] At the same time, the Armed Forces Special Powers Act will continue for another six months in the state to quell any disturbance in the wake of the finalisation of the NRC.[41] With a policy of biometric identification energetically pursued for "suspect" foreigners, as was evident in a recent case of repatriation of a group of Rohingyas and the sharing of the data with the Myanmarese government, these possible stateless people will now live in a state of virtual detention. The NRC process has serious implications in terms of international human rights laws, while India has not signed the two key instruments on statelessness – the 1954 UN Convention Relating to the Status of Stateless Persons and the 1961 Convention on the Reduction of Statelessness.

In the Indian case of the Northeast, the original documents to prove citizenship are ironically called "legacy papers" (related to 1951 general elections when Indians as citizens had voted), which a person needed to make it to the NRC. The logic is circular, because the assumption is that if you are a citizen, you will have the legacy papers. So if you miss one or some of them you are therefore not a citizen then, and thus you cannot prove your citizenship. Even if the same documents pertaining to the period from the NRC of 1951 to the electoral rolls of March 1971 are resubmitted, they must be investigated, as the chief official of the preparation of the Register Prateek Hajela said, "from scratch", so that genuine citizenship could be established. Else, the *sans-papiers* will be sent to the district jails, which doubles up as detention centres, or other internment camps. Thus, even as 32 million people have made it to the draft NRC in Assam, about 1.8 million people's fate hangs in the balance as scraps of paper remain mute testimonies of Assam's twilight zone of citizenship.

In the legal game of citizenship the onus to prove citizenship was on the residents, not on the state. People of course could approach the NRC offices claiming that a proper examination of the individual's documents was not done, and could bring fresh evidence, either documentary or from other members of the family. Yet for women in particular it was difficult to catch this lifeline, because many of the excluded who were women were primarily married women who had submitted *gram panchayat* certificates – as a link document to prove their legacy to their original village – and those were rejected. The women had nothing left to corroborate those certificates since the village headmen did not have proper records and registers. Many more in the watery lands of Assam do not have any record of land holding and residence certificate. The net result is that a huge number of people belonging to four categories – (a) D (doubtful)-voters, (b) descendants of D voters, (c) people whose reference cases are pending at FTs (Foreigners Tribunal[42]), and (d) descendants of these persons – were kept on "hold". The circularity of the logic is clear. If you are citizen, you cannot be a doubtful voter; and you are not a citizen because you are a doubtful voter.

Yet this is not a novel situation. Even when the Indian constitution was being drafted, the search for "original" documents was exasperating. The Constituent Assembly Secretariat (CAS) was asked as to what to do about pavement dwellers, vagrants from other areas, riff-raff, and others with no papers of residence, or land ownership, or settlement certificate, and whether treat them as "citizens". From Assam itself, only one side of whose history we know – the side of landed proprietors – letters of enquiry and desperate messages seeking assurance of protection had reached the CAS. There were letters of enquiry about residents coming from other states and settled elsewhere as in the Travancore state or about foreign-returned soldiers – all without proper papers. The Assam Citizens' Association, Dhubri, had referred then, as the West Bengal Government with despair tells now, that people had the freedom to reside and settle anywhere in the country and hold or dispose of property. And then too papers were not always found in order, while states were in actual charge of enrolling citizens, and they demanded "proofs". This was probably the biggest irony. In order to be a citizen of the country, one had to now satisfy the State of one's claims and legacy. People struggled to get a place in the roll (electoral roll primarily), while not having a place there meant they were not citizens. Typical of such struggles was the efforts by the Assam Citizens' Association, Dhubri, for citizenship and voting rights of the refugees. The genealogy of Article 13 of the Indian constitution still remains hidden from the public eye. Examining that genealogy will be essential to make sense of the game of citizenship today.

In a recent study Ken MacLean has drawn on the concept of "lawfare" elucidated by Brooke Goldstein. He has shown how laws and judicial systems have been systematically used to achieve strategic military and political ends as in the Rohingya case.[43] Achieving a nationalised citizenry is one such strategic end. The Indian case, in many ways similar to the case of the Rohingyas in Myanmar, tells us that statelessness may have less to do with being a refugee rather with the politics of citizenship. It is a case of abandonment and violence. In fact, we can look at the problem in this way: Until now it was a case of citizens at home and migrants abroad with no de jure existence. Now, we may also say, citizens at home, aliens too at home at the same time. The State has abandoned some – that is to say the institution of citizenship has abandoned some, dropped some out of its world. They are a sub-class people, who must labour to exist, and must periodically undergo punitive measures like confinement to jails, detention camps, internment settlements, and if they manage to escape to a new country, then if and when they are apprehended there they will have to face deportation that is forcible return. But where will they be returned? Even this last measure cannot bring an end to the cycle of the production of statelessness, because the country to be deported to will not confer citizenship. There too they will remain a sub-class. We must therefore grasp the multi-dimensional materiality of the process of forced migration. The subject of forced migration will not be allowed any subject-hood in politics, by which we mean citizenship and rights.

In this way, the paradox becomes a significant factor in making migration a crucial question of the postcolonial age. While liberalism and classical bourgeois democracy would like all to be *de jure* subjects of society and politics, and therefore be legal economic subjects, its operation produces subjects beyond law, a process that will be essentially entangled with illegality. Therefore, the stateless migrant cannot be represented. She or he is the hysteric mode of political existence. She or he is incompatible with any position laid down by political authority, and is thus at the same time the symbol of a cathartic position in politics. Alien at "home", because citizenship norms will not allow him/her any "home", and of course alien abroad, she or he problematises both "home" and "abroad", or if we like "citizenship" and "alien-hood". There are some thinkers and activists who think that the existence of the migrant in the form of living labour solves the paradox illegality presents for our age. Unfortunately, it does not, because the stateless – the uprooted with no legal presence for society – cannot be represented. The stateless migrant has been separated from the legal world of politics and rights. She has thus externalised citizenship to the extreme, for she not only leaves the country she has lived in, she is also an immigrant who is the absolute opposite to a principle of nationality. She has also externalised the position of labour in economy. Never before was labour separated from politics in this manner.

Yet and this is the final paradox: Without her or him politics cannot be "citizenised"; the economy cannot run. This footloose subject stripped of any national identity is the ultimate figure of the impossibility of democratic politics in neo-liberal condition. The stateless migrant is the question mark before any success of bourgeois politics in the neo-liberal age. She is mobile and cannot be represented: a pure figure of mobility. In some sense only by being mobile the stateless migrant has brought to a complete extent the opposition between the form of democracy and the form of life as labour. This labour will not be represented in democracy in as much as this democracy will have no place in footloose labour.

In the production of the national space then the division between the citizens and the stateless has assumed critical importance. The national space emerges always as one of two kinds; either that of an *inside* which is to say a house for citizens or an *outside*, which is to say, an anomalous space of outsiders. The game thus at the same time interiorises and exteriorises the national space. This association of interiority with nation, life, security, and development permeates not just classical theories of citizenship, but our political life as a whole. An equally critical division of images of inside and outside accompanies the critical division of the national space. The imagination of the Rohingya as a terrorist, of a Muslim landless peasant living on the *chars* of Assam as a fundamentalist, a Bihari or Bengali living in Ahmedabad, Mumbai, or Jaipur as a suspect criminal, always seizes the space of the nation, produces this division, and delineates the difference between the interior and exterior.

The deployment of images arises from the revulsion towards an imagination of a mixed life. Thus doing away with the absolute binary of citizenship and statelessness requires doing away with our dependency on the image of a delineated interior space for its security and growth.

Therefore, it is important to note the fundamental displacement in the significance of statelessness. It is significant, not because it is a derivative of refugee-like condition, but an extension, or if you like, a subtraction of citizenship in a manner that will make the separation of the citizen and the non-citizen complete. Admittedly these two invocations are related, and the relation between being a derivative of refugee like condition and that of citizenship is complex. As a way of solving the riddle we may say, "Refugees who have a nationality at all are '*de jure* refugees', whereas refugees who do not have nationality are '*de facto* stateless'."[44] However, this chapter has shown the formula as ineffective, because even before one has moved out as a refugee, one may become stateless as in Myanmar or in the Indian Northeast or in Sri Lanka. The conditions of statelessness do not grow out of mobility, but in the production of citizenship. At the same time this is also true that the labouring poor sacrificing their citizenship rights often take to seas or deserts or snow bound routes to labour abroad and survive, and become stateless. Precarious existence devours citizenship. Yet for the rightless citizenship remains as a mirage of rights. The stateless chases the mirage eternally. It is the hope of a lost world.

The paradoxical position of a postcolonial stateless person – whether in the camp at Cox's Bazar or in Assam, or in the ghettos of Europe – brings out the dualities of politics and economics, legality and illegality, citizenship and alien-hood, and finally, visibility and non-visibility.

De facto statelessness is like a borderland existence in the planet of citizens, and it is a widespread existence. Ironically, at a time when refugee studies specialists were putting hopes on liberal norms of global governance for ensuring justice for the migrants through grant of citizenship, more and more people in this period were becoming stateless; they were being stripped of their citizenship, and/or driven out of the lands where they lived and worked, consigned to an endlessly protracted state of displacement. People, as the Rohingyas in Myanmar, became stateless even before being compelled to migrate, while at the same time a protracted state of displacement led in many cases to de facto stateless situation, such as with many South Bhutanese refugees in Nepal or Chakma refugees in India. In order to avoid international censure and disciplinary steps, a state may prevent a population group from leaving the country while at the same time will deprive the latter of full citizenship rights. Race, religion, and resource (the three R) have become factors in production of statelessness. Similar to "refugee and refugee like situation" we have now situations of "statelessness and de facto statelessness".

The trouble is: International legal wisdom emphasises definitions and the explications of said definitions. We may ask and get an answer to: *Who is a refugee?* But if we were to ask, *what is refugee-like condition* probably we shall not make much headway. The jungle in Calais, the overcrowded camps in Idomeni in Greece, or the huddled shanties in the borderlands in Turkey, or the detention camps in Assam in India for the illegal immigrants – they tell us of *situation*, a *condition*. A condition or a situation cannot be always legally defined (of course the Refugee Convention of 1951 says that a situation may be one of fear, but it leaves the matter of definition of such situation to a legal process) – in this case the de facto situation of statelessness, because such a situation can be defined only by some *lack*: lack of facilities, means of life and livelihood, lack of citizenship rights, and a lack of social entitlements, in short a lack of all that nationality would imply. In the context of the worldwide shift from *jus soli* to *jus sanguinis*, the task of giving a positive definition of statelessness (that is legally providing a positive definition of statelessness) is becoming difficult. Central Asia, West Asia, South Asia, some countries in Africa – in all these regions and places citizenship and nationality rights are increasingly under different restrictions and qualifications. Everywhere there is now a sub-population – a sub-national population consisting of disenfranchised minorities, immigrant groups, trafficked groups in labour and sex, and population groups in protracted situation of camp internment – which works as subaltern labour but without the free juridical status of citizenship. This is a fleet-footed population or a mobile labouring army, situated at one end of population distribution range, exemplifying the uneven and hierarchical situation of national populations throughout the world. As a global population group its characterisation as "stateless" tells only a formal story – that too only half – of sub-existence. It is a predatory situation causing maximum dispossession, best evidenced in lives of urban refugees, and comparable to the penal existence of groups in islands and colonies in the nineteenth century. Refracted from citizenship rights, the condition of statelessness is therefore a grey zone.

For instance, immigrants in India are declared illegal, and the Indian government may say that they are from Bangladesh, and Bangladesh refuses to take them back saying they are not citizens of Bangladesh. What happens to the rights of the migrants in such case? They lose nationality rights and other human rights. In the context of earlier discussed National Register of Citizens in Assam in India, one analyst of the Northeast Akhilranjan Dutta commented,

> The option adopted by the government, under such circumstances, has been the detention of detected illegal migrants. Assam has six detention camps so far and the state has also planned to develop a full-fledged detention centre for foreigners in Goalpara district. However, the pressing question is whether detention ought to be the solution. Can a person declared a foreigner, be detained in a camp forever? Will this not be a violation of human rights by the state, in the eyes of the international community? . . . If by amending the Citizenship Act, Hindus and other religious minorities are granted citizenship, will only illegal Muslims be forced to live in detention camps? Urgent measures need to be undertaken to avoid such eventualities.[45]

Yet with all the humanitarian anxiety, Dutta could not escape the mirage of liberal citizenship. He ended his note with these lines,

> The immediate tasks in this regard should be: the intensification of combined efforts to compel the union government to withdraw the Citizenship Act

(Amendment) Bill, 2016, in order to prevent further polarisation of the state along religious and linguistic lines; *completion of the NRC update process within a definite time frame*; and exploration of all possible means to rehabilitate the detected illegal migrants. Apart from this, *deportation through extradition*, issuing of work permits, and the possibility of engaging illegal migrants in productive labour by both by India and Bangladesh through bilateral agreement ought to be explored[46] (Italics mine).

Dutta unwittingly points towards the truth, namely that statelessness is the ever-potential world of precarious labour migrants across the borders, more within a country. Labour migrants are dispossessed of many of the citizenship rights whenever they are away from homes. Internal displacement also becomes closely related to a situation of statelessness – the glass in which the sanitised picture of migration is laid bare. The madness and the brutality marking the massive waves of migration strike one on its face. These massive waves of migration contain people who are moving due to all kinds of reasons – political persecution, statelessness, labour, environmental degradation, ecological disasters, and sexual oppression, as well as trafficking. The refugee and displacement problem becomes in this way one of the most complex humanitarian and political issues facing the world today where existing legal avenues prove woefully inadequate. The problem at one level is one of statelessness, at another level is of what Shahram Khosravi terms as "anti-citizenship". In Khosravi's words, "undocumented migrants", who often end up being stateless, languishing in jails, detention centres, and dying with no state to look for protection, and

> are seen as anti-citizens because they are considered burden on society. They are thought to have a negative effect on welfare and the economy (their only costs to society are, ironically, the costs associated with their deportation). Above all, they are portrayed as a 'labour market problem'. They *take* jobs with low wages, which *weakens* collective agreements. In the end, they *endanger* the very existence of the welfare[47] (author's italics).

Yet the borderland existence of a vast illegal population in various countries with no state to look forward to for protection indicates the possibilities of spaces other than the nationalised ones. The bilateral agreements such as the Sri Lanka-India accord on Indian Tamils of Sri Lanka (known as Srimavo-Shahstri Pact, 1964),[48] or the conferring of citizenship by the Nepal government of the foothills people of Nepal knows as Nepalis of Indian origin,[49] and several other such instances show the grey zone between citizenship and statelessness, which tell us of the possibility of other spaces. To appreciate this possibility we have to look carefully into the historical dynamics of various scales of justice – local, national, regional, and global – which can modify the flat and arid landscape of a nationalised citizenry. For that we move to the last two chapters dealing with two scales of protection and justice – the national and the global. We shall leave out the regional, as we have indicated its possibility and limits earlier in this chapter. Also, there is substantial literature on the African Charter on Human and Peoples' Rights (1981) and the Cartagena Declaration on Refugees (1984), and these have become in turn the new terrains of struggle between a regional ethos of protection and rights of the refugees and migrants backed by a spirit of solidarity and a neo-liberal politics in the region in a war like frame.[50]

The philosopher Michel Foucault called for thinking of "other spaces", which are beyond the inside/outside, beyond our comfort zone – that require continuous formation through entering into relations with new forces from the outside. Foucault concluded his essay with this rumination,

> Brothels and colonies are two extreme types of heterotopia, and if we think, after all, that the boat is a floating piece of space, a place without a place, that exists by itself, that is closed in on itself and at the same time is given over to the infinity of the sea and that, from port to port, from tack to tack, from brothel to brothel, it goes as far as the colonies in search of the most precious treasures they conceal in their gardens, you will understand why the boat has not only been for our civilization, from the sixteenth century until the present, the great instrument of economic development (I have not been speaking of that today), but has been simultaneously the greatest reserve of the imagination. The ship is the heterotopia par excellence. In civilizations without boats, dreams dry up, espionage takes the place of adventure, and the police take the place of pirates.[51]

To Foucault, the ship was thus the space of such imagination par excellence. The ship protected us from an outside which would otherwise swallow us, while at the same time delivering us to outside spaces which together constituted the voyage. In postcolonial state after state population groups have been hated, ridiculed, and deprecated by the so-called mainstream nation for having no sense of order, discipline, and national loyalty. Yet these groups, often interned or expelled, by their ambiguous existence will be now crucial in the struggle for practising the imagination of "other spaces". It is in its trait of creating the image of an anarchic space for all, which we may consider as the popular imagination of an "other space", that the postcolonial nation may discover its symbolic value. Remember, the madman aboard the ship of fools was placed on the inside of an outside as much as he was on the outside of an inside. These liminal spaces will be beyond the space of citizenship.

Notes

1 "Report on Statelessness in South-eastern Europe", UNHCR, September 2011, www.refworld.org/pdfid/514d715f2.pdf (accessed on 3 March 2018); also "Statelessness in Central Asia", Marjorie Farquharson, UNHCR, May 2011, www.unhcr.org/4dfb592e9.pdf (accessed on 3 March 2018).
2 For a variety of situations leading to statelessness, see n 18.
3 Anandaroop Sen, "A Lost Population? East India Company and Arakanese 'Refugees' in Chittagong", *Refugee Watch*, Volume 46, December 2015, pp. 1–20, www.mcrg.ac.in/rw%20files/RW46/RW46.pdf (accessed on 1 October 2017).

186 Statelessness and citizenship

4 *Ibid.*, pp. 15–16.
5 I am indebted in particular to Sabyasachi Basu Ray Chaudhury for the historical details, and this section draws substantially on the "Introduction" in Sabyasachi Basu Ray Chaudhury and Ranabir Samaddar (eds.), *Rohingya in South Asia: People without a State* (London: Routledge, 2018); The material is constructed from sources mentioned below – notes 6–12.
6 G.E. Harvey, *History of Burma: From the Earliest Times to 10 March 1824, the Beginning of the English Conquest* (London: Longmans, Green Co., 1925, reprint, New Delhi: Asia Educational Service, 2000); Nihar Ranjan Ray, *An Introduction to the Study of Theravada Buddhism in Burma: A Study in the Indo-Burmese Historical and Cultural Relations from the Earliest Times to the British Conquest*, 1946, cited in Parimal Ghosh, *Brave Men in the Hills, Resistance and Rebellion in Burma, 1825–1932* (London: C. Hurst & Co., 2000), p. 64.
7 Clive J. Christie, *A Modern History of Southeast Asia: Decolonization, Nationalism and Separation* (New York: Tauris Academic Studies and Singapore: Institute of Southeast Asian Studies, 1996), p. 164.
8 For details, see Martin Smith, *Burma: Insurgency and the Politics of Ethnicity* (London: Zed Books, 1991).
9 For further details, please see Moshe Yegar, "The Muslims of Burma", in Raphael Israeli (ed.), *The Crescent in the East: Islam in Asia Major* (London: Curzon Press, 1982), p. 102.
10 S.G. Grantham, *Census of India, 1921*, vol. X, Part I, Rangoon, 1923, cited in Swapna Bhattacharya, *India-Myanmar Relations, 1886–1948* (Kolkata: K.P. Bagchi and Co., 2007), p. 374.
11 Swapna Bhattacharya, *The Rakhine State (Arakan) of Myanmar: Interrogating History, Culture and Conflict* (New Delhi: Manohar Publishers, 2015), Chapter 2, "The Rakhine State of Myanmar in the Realm of South Asia", pp. 44–64.
12 On Aung San and the Burma Independence Army, Aung Zaw, "The Man Behind the Burma Independence Army", *The Irrawaddy*, 25 August 2017, www.irrawaddy.com/opinion/commentary/man-behind-burma-independence-army.html (accessed on 3 March 2019).
13 The difficulties and limits to the mandate of the UNHCR in tackling statelessness, particularly *de facto* statelessness, come out from the detailed analysis in Hugh Massey, "UNHCR and De Facto Statelessness", *Legal and Protection Policy Research Series*, LPPR 2010/01, April 2010, www.unhcr.org/4bc2ddeb9.pdf (accessed on 15 October 2017).
14 The difficulty of extending protection to the "stateless" becomes clear as The Convention on Statelessness (1954) states at the outset, "For the purpose of this Convention, the term 'stateless person' means a person who is not considered as a national by any State under the operation of its law." (Article 1.1).
15 Indeed, The Convention on Reduction of Statelessness (1961) is an evidence of the crucial role that blood, birth, marriage, etc. have played in the production of statelessness.
16 Juliet Shwe Gaung, "Massive Loan from China to Fund Gas Investment", *Myanmar Times*, 13 December 2010, www.mmtimes.com/business/4457-massive-loan-from-china-to-fund-gas-investment.html (accessed on 1 January 2019).
17 It will be fair to admit that the variety of situations leading to statelessness is increasingly coming to global attention. The Canadian Centre on Statelessness lists the situation as follows –

> There are several ways statelessness can occur: State Succession: Unions of countries or individual countries break apart, and the country where one resides creates new nationality laws and suddenly does not recognize a person because of her lineage, ethnicity, or perceived allegiance to other countries. Soviet Union: The dissolution of the Soviet Union in 1991 resulted in thousands of cases of statelessness in the Baltic States and in Eastern Europe. The UNHCR reports that several countries were affected, resulting in at least 680,000 people in Europe alone living without a nationality. These include "people with expired Soviet passports who have not been able to acquire the nationality of the state in which they reside since the break-up of the Soviet Union". Yugoslavia: A similar chain of events occurred after the dissolution

of Yugoslavia in 1992. The UNHCR reports that "in the countries that once made up Yugoslavia, groups of people fell between the cracks created by new nationality laws and became stateless. Though many have managed to establish their nationality, members of minority groups in south-eastern Europe, especially the Roma, continue to face difficulties accessing the documents necessary to confirm nationality. Throughout Europe, gaps in nationality legislation continue to create situations of statelessness". *Disputed Territory*: Parents who have a child in a disputed territory are often unable to register the birth of their child, and the child remains without a nationality, stateless. This can happen because government is no longer functioning. Palestinians: The most widely known example of this type of statelessness is the case of the Palestinians. According to the Canadian Council for Refugees "Palestinians represent the largest stateless community in the world: more than half of the eight million or so Palestinians are considered to be *de jure* [emphasis added] stateless persons".... Statelessness overwhelmingly affects women: *Victims of trafficking* often have their travel documents taken from them, leaving them unable to prove their identities. Many women find themselves victims of gender-based-violence and exploited into global trafficking rings, where they are often alone, prone to abuse and with little societal or legal support.... Nationality law is often discriminatory along gender lines, leaving women unable to either retain their citizenship upon *marriage* to a foreigner, or unable to acquire the citizenship of their husband's country. Many women find themselves without a nationality after marriage, and are sometimes refused access to services in both the country of their birth, and their husband's home country.... *Children:* Children are affected by statelessness in several ways. Nationality laws that dictate citizenship rules for their parents affect children. The result is that children are born limited in the services they can access, the education they will receive, and the healthcare available to them. This carries on through adulthood and affects housing, employment and virtually all aspects of their lives. Growing up without a nationality impacts the way children engage with society, and can have adverse effects on child development and family reunification.... An emerging concern is the practice of international surrogacy and the effects on children. Legal challenges are increasing as children are born in one country and adopted in another.... *Ethnic Groups*: Minority ethnic groups are particularly vulnerable to statelessness, often discriminated against as a result of nationality legislation. In addition many minority ethnic groups around the world struggle to obtain identity documents or prove their identities. Some examples are the Roma of Europe, Rohingya of Myanmar, ethnic Nepali Bhutanese of Nepal, and Haitian descendants in Dominican Republic,

www.statelessness.ca/who-is-stateless.html# (accessed on 1 January 2019).

18 For some primary idea on these cases of statelessness, such as disenfranchisement of Blacks in Mauritania by an Arab dominated state, see Sebastian Kohn, "Fear and Statelessness in Mauritania", *Open Democracy*, 3 October 2011, www.opensocietyfoundations.org/voices/fear-and-statelessness-mauritania (accessed on 1 October 2017); also by Kohn on statelessness of ethnic Russians in former Soviet Republics in Europe, "Russia and the Baltics: The Great Statelessness Game", *European Network on Statelessness*, 25 October 2012, www.statelessness.eu/blog/russia-and-baltics-great-statelessness-game (accessed on 1 October 2017); Tacita Vero, "The Grey Zone", *Slate*, 13 march 2017, www.slate.com/articles/news_and_politics/roads/2017/03/many_ethnic_russians_in_estonia_have_gray_passports_live_in_legal_limbo.html (accessed on 1 October 2017); on statelessness in the ex-Yugoslavia region, see the UNHCR report, "Report on Statelessness in South Eastern Europe", UNHCR offices in Bosnia & Herzegovina, Croatia, former Yugoslav Republic of Macedonia, Montenegro, Serbia (and Kosovo: SCR 1244), Bureau for Europe September 2011, www.refworld.org/pdfid/514d715f2.pdf (accessed on 2 October 2017); and on Bhutan, "Bhutan: Nationality, Expulsion, Statelessness, and the Right to Return", *Refworld, UNHCR and Amnesty International*, 1 September 2000, www.refworld.org/topic,50ffbce524d,50ffbce5253,,0,,COUNTRYREP,BTN.html (accessed on 2 October 2017).

19 www.abc.net.au/news/2017-03-01/myanmar-army-defends-operation-against-rohingya/8316654 (accessed on 9 March 2017).
20 http://time.com/4596937/burma-myanmar-rohingya-bangladesh-refugees-crimes-against-humanity/accessed (accessed on 2 March 2017).
21 Hannah Arendt, *The Origins of Totalitarianism* (New York: Schocken Books, 2004), pp. 353–355.
22 Tapan K. Bose, "The Rohingya: Rejected by the Country They Call Home and Unwanted by its Neighbours", *Alternatives International*, 24 October 2017, www.alterinter.org/spip.php?rubrique2 (accessed on 1 November 2017).
23 *Ibid.*
24 For details, please see www.baliprocess.net (accessed on 10 October 2015).
25 *Ibid.*
26 See *Mizzima News*, http://archive-2.mizzima.com/archive/1752-bali-process-to-take-up-rohingya-issue.html (accessed on 10 October 2015).
27 "Tony Abbott Rules out Resettling Rohingyas in Australia, Indonesia Says It Is Obliged to", *ABC News*, 21 May 2015, www.abc.net.au/news/2015-05-21/rohingyas-migrants-indonesia-says-australia-obliged-resettle/6486590 (accessed on 10 March 2019).
28 On Australia's policy of refusing asylum and interning offshore the asylum seekers who manage to reach Australian shores, known as the "pacific solution", see David Marr and Marian Wilkinson, *Dark Victory* (Crows Nest, NSW: Allen & Unwin, 2003), particularly Chapter 3, "Australia V. The Boat People", pp. 30–47; see also, Madeline Gleeson, *Offshore: Behind the Wire on Manus and Nauru* (Sydney: New South Publishing, 2016).
29 "Tony Abbott Rules Out Resettling Rohingyas in Australia, Indonesia Says It Is Obliged to", *ABC News*, 21 May 2015, www.abc.net.au/news/2015-05-21/rohingyas-migrants-indonesia-says-australia-obliged-resettle/6486590 (accessed on 10 March 2019).
30 www.baliprocess.net/UserFiles/baliprocess/File/Bali%20Process%20SOM%202009%20-%20Thailand%20Presentation%20-%20The%20Rohingya%20Situation.pdf (accessed on 29 August 2017).
31 www.baliprocess.net/UserFiles/baliprocess/File/UNHCRBalipresentation.pdf (accessed on 29 August 2017).
32 www.baliprocess.net/UserFiles/baliprocess/File/FINAL_Pathways%20Background%20Papers_050417.pdf (accessed on 26 August 2017).
33 Facts taken from, https://theconversation.com/the-andaman-sea-refugee-crisis-a-year-on-is-the-region-now-better-prepared-59687 (accessed on 28 August 2017).
34 I have been helped by Violeta Moreno-Lax and Eithymios Papastavridis, *'Boat Refugees' and Migrants at Sea: A Comparative Approach* (Leiden: Brill Nijhoff, 2017); see also, chapter 8, n 24.
35 www.odi.org/comment/10439-refugees-migrants-view-new-york-summits-un-obama (accessed on 28 August 2017).
36 The studies are presented in Sabyasachi Basu Ray Chaudhury and Ranabir Samaddar, *Rohingya in South Asia: People without a State* (London: Routledge, 2018).
37 Interview taken by Sucharita Sengupta on behalf of CRG at Cox's Bazaar on 3 July 2015.
38 David Marr and Marian Wilkinson, *Dark Victory* (Crows Nest, NSW: Allen & Unwin, 2003), p. 293.
39 *Ibid.*, pp. 287–289; the internment in Nauru caused scandal; Marr and Wilkinson wrote, "After being chastised by the Geneva headquarters, Australia cut its annual core funding to UNHCR by half" (p. 289).
40 "Biggest Detention Centre on Way in Assam", report by Prabin Kalita, *Times of India*, Kolkata, 8 September 2019, p. 9.
41 "Disturbed Area Tag in Assam Extended for another Six Month", report by Bikash Singh, *Economic Times*, 7 September 2019, https://economictimes.indiatimes.com/news/politics-and-nation/disturbed-area-tag-in-assam-extended-for-another-six-month/articleshow/71025014.cms (accessed on 8 September 2019).
42 Earlier were about 100 Foreigners Tribunal functioning in Assam. Initially, 11 Illegal Migrant Determination Tribunals (IMDT) were functioning. After the repeal of IMDT Act, the government of Assam established 21 FTs in 2005. In the year 2009, another 4

FTs were established. In 2014 additional 64 FTs were established for disposal of Pending Cases in FTs. Judges/Advocates were appointed as the members of FT under the Foreigners Tribunal Act, 1941 and Foreigners Tribunal ORDER 1964, and as per the guidelines issued by the government from time to time. The Foreigners' Tribunals are quasi-judicial courts mandated to hear appeals of those excluded from the NRC. Only Foreigner Tribunals are empowered to declare a person as a foreigner.

43 Ken MacLean, "The Rohingya Crisis and the Practices of Erasure", *Journal of Genocide Research*, Volume 21 (1), 2019, pp. 83–95.

44 Hugh Massey, "UNHCR and De Facto Statelessness", p. I; Massey's work is significant for it brings out the complexity of the interrelations between *de jure* and *de facto* statelessness, also between refugee-hood and statelessness.

45 Akhil Ranjan Dutta, "Political Destiny of Immigrants in Assam: National Register of Citizens", *Economic and Political Weekly*, Volume 53 (9), 3 March 2018, pp. 18–21.

46 *Ibid.*, p. 21.

47 Shahram Khosravi, *'Illegal' Traveller: An Auto-Ethnography of Borders* (Basingstoke, Hampshire: Palgrave MacMillan, 2010), p. 116. Khosravi records how certain perceived diseases such as repeated suicide attempts, persistent refusal syndrome, and dishonesty can disqualify someone from being given citizenship, and these can be considered as typical marks of the country of origin. An "anti-citizen" is portrayed as a criminal, as lacking identity and being irrational, irresponsible, and immoral, a risk to the well-being, virtue, values, and norms of society.

48 Indian Tamils of Sri Lanka are Tamils of Indian origin in Sri Lanka. They partly descended from workers sent from the southern part of India to Sri Lanka in the nineteenth and twentieth centuries to work in coffee, rubber, and tea plantations. They mostly live in the central highlands, also known as the Hill Country. Some have Telegu and Malayalee origins. Most are descendants of bonded labourers sent from Tamil Nadu. In 1949, the Sri Lankan government stripped the Indian Tamils of their nationality, including their right to vote. In 1964 under an agreement between the Sri Lankan and Indian governments a large percentage of the Hill Country Tamils were repatriated to India, around 30 per cent were granted Sri Lankan nationality, but the Accord left a considerable number as stateless people. By the 1990s many of them had been given Sri Lankan citizenship. By 2010 most Indian Tamils in Sri Lanka received Sri Lankan citizenship, while rest had come back to India. Some however still remained without Sri Lankan citizenship, and those who were repatriated to India and began work as plantation labour were also without substantive citizenship rights. For details of the varied map of statelessness in South Asia, Paula Banerjee, Atig Ghosh, and Anasua Basu Ray Chaudhury, *The State of Being Stateless: An Account of South Asia* (Hyderabad: Orient Blackswan, 2015).

49 The Nepal Citizenship Act was passed in 1952. It entitled immigrants staying in the country for a minimum of five years to Nepali citizenship. The Citizenship Act of 1963 entitled immigrants to Nepali citizenship if they were engaged in business and could read and write Nepali. The significant amendment came in 2006, when the Act was modified to the effect that people born before 1990 and residing permanently in the country could claim citizenship. About 2.3 million people received citizenship certificates.

50 The African Charter significantly lays down in Article 12 – (1) Every individual shall have the right to freedom of movement and residence within the borders of a State provided he abides by the law. (2) Every individual shall have the right to leave any country including his own, and to return to his country. This right may only be subject to restrictions, provided for by law for the protection of national security, law and order, public health or morality.

(3) Every individual shall have the right, when persecuted, to seek and obtain asylum in other countries in accordance with laws of those countries and International conventions. (4) A non-national legally admitted in a territory of a State Party to the present Charter, may only be expelled from it by virtue of a decision taken in accordance with the law. (5) The mass expulsion of non-nationals shall be prohibited. Mass expulsion shall be that which is aimed at national, racial, ethnic or religious groups.

It should also be noted regarding the Cartagena Declaration on Refugees that even though it is a non-binding regional, i.e. Latin American, instrument for the protection of refugees, it has since then been incorporated into the national laws and state practices of 16 countries.
51 Michel Foucault, *Of Other Spaces: Utopias and Heterotopias*, trans. Jay Miskowiec (1967, 1984), http://web.mit.edu/allanmc/www/foucault1.pdf (accessed on 8 February 2019).

10
POSTCOLONIAL MARKS ON THE PRINCIPLE OF RESPONSIBILITY[1]

Power, protection, and responsibility

The previous chapter raised the question of responsibility for the production of stateless population groups. This chapter takes the discussion on responsibility further.[2]

Through a brief study of the Indian experience of refugee protection it will pose the issue of responsibility as a critical counterpoint to the question of power. Power may produce influence and power may be an element of influence. But how do we relate power to responsibility? Given the dominant discourse of "responsibility to protect" as part of the global governance regime, this chapter will inquire, is there a different way of conceptualising the issue of responsibility in the postcolonial context? Such an inquiry will lead us to the important matter of scale – the scale of justice – since protection is almost always is seen as a global issue (indeed the Refugee Convention is an illustration of that global scale). Responsibility takes us to the perspective of the margins. Responsibility also brings in its wake the issue of providing justice to the victims of transition – a process through which postcolonial nations were born.

In any discussion on power and influence in global refugee regime, one crucial question emerging from postcolonial experiences of protection will be: What is the nature of this power and influence at the margins? This question is important because unlike the Kantian world, the world we live in is characterised by a great dissociation of power and responsibility. Wars may be imposed on countries by great powers, but the burdens of refugee flows created by wars are shouldered by countries that had little to do with the wars in question. Syria, Iraq, Yemen, Afghanistan, and Libya are some of the names that readily come to mind when we speak of wars in and population flows from countries. The Vietnam War and twenty years later disintegration of Yugoslavia at the insistence of Germany and the European

Union followed by massive refugee flows are again ready instances. Millions of Partition refugees in South Asia had little to do in making the colonial decision to divide the sub-continent. Yet through all these years the global refugee regime never questioned this dissociation of power and responsibility – primarily for two reasons. First, in the age of democracy, responsibility is considered as resting with the people; in other words they self-determine, while in reality power is exercised always by the corporate class. Second, international responsibility is exercised by the nation states, while power will be vested with transnational agencies and empires who will exercise power with little or no responsibility. In this situation of graded responsibility it is important to ask: What is the nature of power and responsibility at the margins, rather than power and influence at the centre?

It will be good to remember at the outset that in this discussion on power the context of protection is of primary importance. For we are not discussing here any sociological theory of power, we are discussing how the function of protection and the ability to protect, in other words a specific mode of care, produces power, which is both positive as well as dominating at the same time. This chapter aims to unravel this dual nature of power.

We have to remember one more point by way of introducing the issue of protection and power. Recall that the so-called global regime of protection as mandated by the Refugee Convention of 1951 is not designed and is incapable of addressing the issue of displacement due to war. The present situation of massive refugee flows is not marked by mere discrimination and limited violence, but by brutal war. The 1951 Convention barely touches the problem. The Refugee Convention's context is limited. It refers to war in the context of the World War II, and to rule out protection to persons accused of war crimes.[3] However, in the present background of massive wars in Iraq, Afghanistan, and Syria, the question of responsibility for war and displacement has assumed urgency to an altogether different degree. As we are experiencing now, in war and war-like conditions the categorical distinctions between different groups seeking shelter, assistance, and protection vanish. In such time it is important to examine the effectiveness or otherwise of the global protection apparatus for the refugees.[4]

We evaluate people and groups as responsible or not, depending on how they exercise their power. Often, we exercise moral judgment as the way. Sometimes we do this formally, for instance via legal judgement. The question will be: How do we relate moral responsibility and legal responsibility – not only of individuals but of empires, global powers, and other transnational formations or collectives? The refugee protection regime has no particular idea of (a) what we may term as *responsible agency*, whereby an institution like the state is regarded as a moral agent; or (b) *retrospective responsibility*, when a state is judged for its actions and is blamed or punished; or (c) *responsibility as a virtue*, when we praise a state as being responsible. Philosophical discussions of responsibility abound. However, in the context of postcolonial experiences, we need a wider view of responsibility in order to explore connections between moral and legal responsibility, and between global and national responsibilities. After all was it not the original philosophical invocation of the dual notions of power and responsibility, which was in political thought?[5]

Yet it is only from the margins that the contradictions and fault lines in the architecture of power, influence, and responsibility can be brought out to light, and therefore the need for a perspective "on the margins" of the global protection regime is strategic. After all one has to be aware of the asymmetries inherent in the fact that an overwhelming part (by some calculations 86 per cent) of world's refugees are hosted in the global South but an equally overwhelming part (for instance 80 per cent) of UNHCR's funding comes from states in the global North. This asymmetry means that the donors have power while host states have responsibility. The expanded mandate of the global protection regime to accommodate the needs of a wider set of "persons of concern" does not alter or significantly modify the wide divergence between the power to protect and the Refugee Convention's identification of the root causes of displacement in a "persecution-centric" approach and framing protection accordingly. This is of course not a new point. The question persists since it first appeared in the discussion in *Escape from Violence* almost thirty years back.[6] Indeed this "persecution-centric" approach carried a strong colonial legacy as the Refugee Convention had no reference to the right of the colonised to seek asylum, while the Convention on the Status of Refugees aimed to be the primary basis upon which asylum seekers were to make their claims to asylum. It was born as a key text of the human rights framework, associated with the very idea of a universalised rights-bearing subject. Yet, as Lucy Mablin has argued, Western asylum policy was marked from the early days by efforts to limit access to the right to asylum, and the exclusion of colonised peoples from access to the right to asylum. Yet asylum seekers had long existed outside of Europe, and that their exclusion from international rights was long-standing and intentional.[7]

In the context of the power of the global protection regime this chapter will therefore examine the dynamics of responsibility at the margin. It will discuss how the experience of refugee flows into India since independence conditioned her engagement with the global refugee regime, including the contradictions in the state policies towards refugees, particularly the policy of giving asylum. In the background of the Indian history of providing asylum, the chapter will argue that the relation between care and power is not a simple causal one, as if simply by caring one amasses power. The relation is complex. The arrangement of care is not simply flowing from the sovereign legal authority at the top. The heterogeneity of power builds up and draws on the heterogeneity of the act of caring. At the same time the dispersed state of responsibility not only reorients the form of power, it also orients care. This in short will be the basis of a postcolonial interrogation of the global protection regime of the refugees and the stateless. In this chapter I discuss the instance of India as a postcolonial story of protection and hospitality; the instance also tells us how postcolonial political power had had a long reciprocal relation with the notion of responsibility.[8]

The Indian story of hospitality

The Indian story is a classic case of the age-old question: How can one study the dynamics of hospitality?[9] A study of institutions of care and hospitality may imply a policy study. But can there be a policy for "hospitality" or a policy to be "kind"? If the state as an institution has to practice care and hospitality, and exercise power required for relevant practices, we have to ask: Do these two functions (providing care and exercising power), which appear as separate and distinct, build on each other?

For studying protection of refugees by the State, these questions would mean attending to the arguments and experiences relating to: (a) the definition of the term "refugee" and its scope; (b) the concept of *non-refoulement* (the principle of no forcible return) and its scope; and (c) the administrative-judicial machinery to determine the status of a shelter seeker as a refugee and once determined, the quantum of assistance the shelter seeker will need and get.[10] It also means trying to understand, where does the refugee feature in such policy formulation? We know that easy means of physical accessibility, cultural and economic networks, and political support of host government and communities are significant elements in the determination of a policy on the refugees. These elements orient care. But they also add to the power of the State to decide towards whom to extend hospitality, and whom to deny.[11] In the partitioned sub-continent of South Asia the politics of nationhood was built upon experiences of how some became citizens and some could not.[12] We know that India did not sign the Refugee Convention of 1951 or the Additional Protocol of 1967; many have therefore termed the history of how some refugees were saved, cared for, and rehabilitated in this country, while many were left out, refused, and neglected in the same period in and by the same country, by a well-known phrase from the literature of refugee studies as "calculated kindness".[13]

Refugees from Myanmar were welcomed at one point (as the Second World War ended in 1945), ignored at another (in the seventies to nineties of the last century), and prevented or obstructed from entering India at yet another point (as the new century began), and now deported. One observer has called it the "full circle".[14] Similarly, while some groups of refugees such as the Tibetans were almost allowed to be "Indianised", some other groups such as the Sri Lankan refugees spent (and still spend) their long years in India in strictly watched camps. An expert, after examining the logical structure of these contradictions and ambivalence in the Indian State's asylum policy, has termed it as "strategic ambiguity".[15] In some cases, as after the birth of Bangladesh the refugees went back quickly in 1971–72 in hundreds and thousands, while, in other cases, as in the case of the Tibetan refugees they stayed back (post 1959). The Indian State, in the latter case, did not even pursue any solution to persuade the refugees to go back. We have yet another group of cases involving the CHT (Chittagong Hill Tracts) refugees in Tripura (in the 1980s-1990s) or the Sri Lankan refugees in Tamil Nadu (from mid-1980s), whom, the State allegedly wanted to repatriate forcibly.

These cases of differential treatment of refugees and asylum seekers do not, however, exhaust the full story of the history of the hospitality of the Indian State. Many writers have chronicled how, as opposed to all these vagaries, refugee care in post-Partition Punjab and Bengal became part of building the new nation of India.

Writing of the post 1947 care and rehabilitation of the refugees from East Pakistan, one chronicler commented,

> The history of relief and rehabilitation in the east is one of gradual emplacement within a national body of those who were the victims of one of the world's worst population displacements. The travails and trauma that accompanied their emplacement are only reflective of our fledgling nationhood.[16]

The chronicler of relief and rehabilitation in the West wrote in similar vein,

> It was the characterisation of the refugee as a *critical component of nation-building* [italics author's] that marked a significant shift in conceptualisation and, consequently, in policy formulation. Linking resettlement with development, and rehabilitation with reconstruction, was a uniquely progressive and far-sighted response to a problem of crushing proportions; in this scheme of things refugees became a valuable human resource rather than, only, an onerous liability.[17]

Thus, metaphors, such as "all embracing response", "national effort", and "the desire to stretch the means of caring beyond the means" marked the scenario and were invoked again and again.

Even when one takes into reckoning the views from below, most famously expressed by Jaya Chatterjee who shows that it was not all that happy hour of nationalism, but a time marked by two contending notions of right and charity,[18] there is a fundamental agreement between all sections of the actors of that time, namely, that we/they are part of the nation, the nation must accept us/them. In this dual context of nationalism and democracy there was not only a re-emphasis on the category and role of "partition-refugees" as element of nation-building, but also a reinforcement of the duty of a state to care and the imperative to mobilise the powers at its command towards that end. Indeed to justify its status as the repository of power the state had to re-articulate its obligation to care. The birth of social security was made possible by detailed governmental policies and techniques for sheltering the refugee population, the expanding universe of nation, and the daily contest between the state that appeared as the government responsible for protection and the refugee population that became another segment of the population being governed, and demanding rights.[19]

Thus neither the security explanation, nor the kindness explanation, nor even the international law and international regime explanation will be adequate in helping us understand the mysteries behind one of the most observed and least comprehended political phenomena of our time, namely the asylum and refugee care policy of a postcolonial state. One may argue that a rights-based explanation may appear as the best route, because after all the refugees of Partition viewed their own arrival in India as a matter of right – returning home, returning to the "natural nation". Yet, we know, the situation was ambiguous: the nation was not all that "natural"; and the departure too was from a "home". Refugee protection did not evolve purely as recognition of refugee rights. It evolved to an equal degree as an ethical, humanitarian task, involving the principle of responsibility towards the subjects of the nation.

Several accounts of the Tibetan refugees in India have shown that refugees are not always a burden; they can be creative and productive.[20] In other instances refugees as guests became murderers as the history of the Taliban in Pakistan suggests. Therefore, ethics exists beyond law on refugee rights, though one can reasonably inquire as Derrida did in a lecture few years before his death, can one "cultivate an ethic of hospitality? Hospitality is culture itself and not simply one ethic among others".[21]

Against this background of several major forced population movements across the borders into India in the last seventy years and the differential attitude of the Indian State towards them, we must first summarise the main features of the situation. Only then we can begin a meaningful analysis.

- The first refugees to arrive in independent India were not the aliens who had to be given shelter; they were part of the nation;
- The first practices of refugee care and administration built up through not so much law as practices – practices of care, rehabilitation, and social security;
- Institutions are the concrete results of these practices and the few laws; they have resulted in a durable tradition of hospitality, which the State neither can fully endorse and embrace nor can reject;
- "Partition refugees" have left a deep mark on the subsequent pattern in which the state has combined care with power; this is the mark of ambiguity;
- The contest between the two notions of charity and rights that began as soon as refugees first started pouring in has influenced the subsequent discourse of "hospitality", a term that is supposed to overcome the contradiction; the current discourse of human rights on refugee protection in India takes off from this old contest between the two notions;
- The legal-administrative discourse on the refugees and foreigners were founded in a milieu of strategic ambiguity; who became alien, when, declared by whom – became a deeply circumstantial matter, never to be finally defined by law;
- Alien-hood thereby became the other part of a democratic state, which required and created at the same time the citizens as its political foundation;
- Because offering shelter and protection became deeply circumstantial, including the issue of near-permanent residence much beyond temporary visitation, local communities developed their double response of charity and fatigue, benign care and ill feeling and animosity – a response that characterised the conduct of the State also; also, local response and responsibility turned out to be important in influencing state policy on the refugees;
- Keeping the shelter-seekers in the ghetto, proscribing their movement, creating ever-new penal colonies, thus underwriting the nature of charity that the State had been providing to shelter-seekers, became in time a feature of the asylum and care practices of the State, though with some exceptions; what

began in the Andaman Islands[22] and Dandakaranya[23] continues to date – protecting and penalising have become interlinked responsibilities;
- Finally, the Convention of 1951 was powerless about how the States-system would decide the relation between visitation and residence. Thus, refugees who thought on arrival in India in 1947 that they would go back, did not, and were in all seriousness never told by the State to go back; similarly, the Tibetan refugees have not been told to go back, or repatriated; on the other hand, hundreds and thousands of refugees from East Pakistan went back as soon as the war of 1971 was over. Some of the Chakma refugees flowing into India in successive phases stayed, some went back, and some had to be induced to go back. In some cases, the State allowed the refugees to come in, and then inexplicably, shut the door on them;
- The enigma, if there is any, is therefore not so much in India's non-accession to the Convention, which in any case is inconsequential today, but in the way the State defines and configures its responsibility; and
- In brief, *responsibility* is the other great history, which runs parallel to that of rights and care, and is still largely unwritten; this history no doubt has defined the relation between care and power.

Judicial reasoning

Refugee flows to India in time became massive and mixed. Possibly it had been always so. The foundational history of care in independent India involves countless shelter-seekers, who formed part of the mixed and massive flows.[24] Two discourses are linked in this – on the illegal immigrants and that on refugees. One influences, predicates, and prejudices the other. It will be important to see: How has the justice system in India responded to this deeply equivocal relation between migrant, protection, and responsibility, and the juridical reasoning taken shape? Drawing from a larger study on this theme,[25] we shall restrict this account to the main features of judicial reasoning in India and few instances of that.

In a court decision in India, five Burmese nationals detained for entering India without any valid document and charged under relevant provisions of the Foreigners' Act of 1946 (henceforth the FA) were granted bail by the Guwahati High Court to enable them to approach the UNHCR at New Delhi for refugee status, which was subsequently granted to them, and the case was then withdrawn by the prosecution (*unreported*, State v. Khy-Htoonand 4 others, FIR No 18 (3) 89, CJM, Manipur, 1994). Similarly, in another case involving two Burmese nationals convicted for violation of the FA, the High Court ordered that the petitioners be released on an interim bail for 2 months to enable them to approach the UNHCR for grant of refugee status to them (*unreported*, State of Manipur v U MyatKyaw and Nayzin, Civil Rule No 516 of 1991, High Court of Guwahati, 1991). The Guwahati High Court had previously granted bail in 1989 to another Burmese national, Shar Aung A.K. Aung Thant Mint, also to enable him to approach the UNHCR in New Delhi. In another case an Iraqi national detained for using forged passport was authorised to stay in India and the Court ruled that with valid certification from the UNHCR with him, he could not be convicted for the offence and took a lenient view considering that he was a refugee and sentenced him to pay just a fine (*unreported*, State v Muhammad Riza Ali, FIR No 414/93, CMM New Delhi, 1995). Similarly a Sudanese woman who had come to India escaping further torture in Sudan where she had been gang-raped for converting from Islam to Christianity had been granted refugee status by the UNHCR; also her application to resettle in Canada had been accepted. In this case too, though she had been charged under relevant provisions of FA, the Court gave a light punishment – a small fine and imprisonment of 10 days already undergone by her (*unreported*, State v Eva Massur Ahmed, FIR No 278/95, MM – New Delhi 1995). In a case concerning an Afghan national, the Court similarly observed that with certification of refugee status, he could not be detained simply for not producing the valid residence permit instantly on demand; he was to be given 24 hours. But, ironically by another trial court decision, a foreign national who had similar certification and valid residence stay and had not been able to produce valid document at time of his arrest was sentenced to 6 weeks of rigorous punishment (*unreported*, State v Montasir M. Gubara, CC No 427/P/1994, ACJM, Mumbai, 1996).

In another case concerning a Burmese national who had fled to India and had been detained under the FA, and had not been able to approach the UNHCR, the Court ordered conviction and rigorous imprisonment for 6 months and deportation back to Burma. The Court also said on completion of the sentence and in response to the convict's appeal that it was not within its jurisdiction to hand over the convicted to the UNHCR (*unreported*, State v Benjamin Zang Nang, GR case no 1253 (1994), ACJM, Sealdah, West Bengal, 1996). Another case of deportation order by the Court happened when the Court sentenced an Afghan national to imprisonment for the period he had spent in jail after he had been arrested by the Border Security Force for entering the country without any valid document notwithstanding his plea that he had entered the country to save his life, and then ordered his deportation back to Afghanistan (*unreported*, State v Akhtar Muhammad, AF/6433, CJM, Amritsar, Punjab, 1997).

Can the refugees have freedom of movement? A Sri Lankan who had been granted refugee status and was staying in Chennai was arrested in Delhi for being unable to produce any valid travel document and detained under relevant provision of the FA. The Court observed that refugee status did not entitle a person to move about freely, held him guilty, and sentenced him to 6 months of rigorous imprisonment (*Unreported*, State v Hudson Vilvaraj, FIR No 583/97, MM, Delhi, 1998). This decision was in conformity with the Supreme Court judgment in State of Arunachal Pradesh v Khudiram Chakma (1994, Suppl. 1 SCC 615), where Chief Justice M.N. Venkatachaiah and Justice S. Mohan held that Chakmas were not citizens of India; they as foreigners enjoyed life and liberty only to the extent that Article 21 allowed, and this right was not extendable to Article 19. Though, in the same judgment the Court held that what was "good in terms of natural justice was hence good in law" (p. 630, paragraphs 71–72), and referred to the right to enjoy asylum in international law (paragraphs 77 and 80). And, what about refugees who forged passports or travel documents to take shelter in the country? Almost uniformly, the trial courts held that such acts constituted offence under the FA, sentenced somewhat lightly, and wherever the government had pleaded a foreigner's stay a threat to security, had ordered expulsion/deportation, or had said that further stay depended on government permission (for example, *unreported*, State v Muhammad Yashin, FIR No 289/97, SMM, Delhi, 1997).

Then there is this strange case, a case of perfect ambiguity. A woman, arrested on the ground that she was a Burmese national and had violated the FA, produced before the Court her birth certificate, residence certificate, employment certificate and a copy of the electoral roll which had her name on it as a voter. The Court ordered her free on the grounds of evidence, but observed in view of her inability to speak the Mizo language though she had claimed to be a permanent resident of Mizoram, as to how she could be so, and felt that it was strange that she had an original birth certificate, and she had been allotted permanent residence certificate in Mizoram, particularly when the issue of foreigners was a burning issue in the state (*unreported*, State v Sungenel, GR No 979/96, ADC/Judicial Officer, Aizwal, Mizoram, 1996).

By and large, trial court decisions seem to have relied upon no standard practice or law of asylum. There have been variations. When Courts have imposed fines the "refugee-offenders" in some cases have been able to pay with help from charitable organisations or NGOs. If the refugees had been fortunate to get UNHCR protection, they had been let free. In some cases, though not always, courts have allowed the persons to approach the UNHCR. But in other cases, the reasons of state in form of the FA seemed to have held sway over juridical reasoning. In several cases the High Court decisions seem to confirm the stand taken by trial courts, particularly with regard to appeals by Burmese nationals under detention and jail custody not to deport them and allow them to approach UNHCR for protection.

Thus, in sum, it can be said that the juridical reasoning to date has assumed that the burden of protecting an asylum seeker lies with the UNHCR. This includes the burden of resettlement, and the conditionality that the detained foreigner would not be able to move out to any place of choice without certification and assumption of responsibility by the UNHCR. In such reasoning the Court has held that, as much as possible under the circumstances, leniency should be shown by the State to the offenders who have violated the Foreigners Act. It has been recognised that not only persecution of a particular person, but a general atmosphere of violence and insecurity can also be grounds for asking for shelter; and if the State claims that the security of the State is in jeopardy, then expulsion or deportation has to be the norm. Granting asylum may not be an obligation of the State, and the duty of hospitality may not be legally enforceable; yet the Court expects that the State will practice hospitality as much as possible, based on its own power to determine the period of visitation according to particular circumstances.

Indeed, the Gujarat High Court summarised the position in this way (*unreported*, Kfaer Abbas Habib Al Qutaifi and Taer Ali Mansoon, Civil Rule No 3433 of 1998) in the context of India being a non-signatory to the 1951 Convention:

- *First*, the relevant international treaties and convention are not binding, but there is an obligation on the government to respect them;

- *Second*, Article 21 of the Constitution is enjoyed by also a non-citizen on Indian soil, it implies the principle of *non-refoulement*; but this does not confer on the non-citizen any right to reside and resettle, nor does it mean that if the stay of a non-national is contrary to national security, she or he can stay;
- *Third*, in case where the international covenants and treaties reinforce the fundamental rights in India, as facets of those rights they can be enforced;
- *Fourth*, the power of the government to expel a foreigner is absolute; indeed, in the last few years the court increasingly took supporting view on government's policy of deporting an asylum seeker back to his/her own country and handing over biometric information including biometric details of the asylum seeker;[26]
- *Fifth*, the work of the UNHCR in certifying refugees is humanitarian, so the government has an obligation to ensure that refugees receive international protection until their problems are solved; and
- *Finally*, in view of Article 51 that directs the State to respect international legal principles, the Courts will apply those principles in domestic law in a harmonious manner, provided such obligations are not inconsistent with domestic law.

The Supreme Court also concurred with the judicial practice of assigning the burden of protection on the UNHCR, and ruled that the issue of "reasonable procedure" in asking a non-national to leave the country arises only when there is UNHCR certification of the said non-national as refugee, and not otherwise. The Court did not lay down any standard norm in sheltering or certifying a refugee. Thus there is an unwritten division of labour: the UNHCR has exercised its mandate mainly with regard to 12,000 Afghan refugees and 1000 refugees of other nationalities; in some other cases, it has been allowed to carry out relief and settlement work; in other cases, the Government has decided the fate of the shelter seeker. Thus in case of some 100,000 Tibetan refugees, and some 65,000 Sri Lankan refugees, the UNHCR does not have a direct role. The mandate refugees assisted by the UNHCR are the Afghans, Burmese, and small number of Iranians, Sudanese, Iraqis, and others. The government issues through the Foreigners Regional Registration Office (FRRO) renewable residential permits to mandate refugees on the basis of certificates issued by the UNHCR. Yet cases before the courts continue involving refugees undergoing legal process for illegal entry. Visible and invisible frontiers have been created. The feature of these *nouvelles frontieres* is that they are being produced internally also; they are not merely vertical lines separating two spaces, but concentric circles continuously dividing and then locating these to rejoin them in the universe of the nation. Law, citizenship, rights, obligation, and morality – all are caught in this universe of concentric circles. Difference and identity – both had their place in the scheme of things.[27]

Between 1950 and 1975, the Indian government signed treaties of peace and friendship with Bhutan, Sikkim, Nepal, Burma, Sri Lanka, Bangladesh, and an odd pact with Pakistan on minorities. These treaties bore assurances of friendship on behalf of an independent and anti-colonial State. These agreements were based on and reproduced the geopolitical imaginary of an imperial nation engaged with issues of both territory and population (the agreement between India and Sri Lanka on the Indian Tamil plantation labour in Sri Lanka is an example). Territory was fixed; so also was the attempt to fix the population. Like combatting famine, combatting population instability has been a task of great magnitude. People of Indian origin who had settled overseas were to give up what we now call a "right of return", just as partition refugees once nationalised by being allowed to acquire citizenship, were to give up the "right to return". Population flow in the understanding of the modern State has queered the pitch in latter's effort to establish a singular and unitary relation between place and identity, believed to be hallmark of the modern State's existence. But as accounts of trans-border migration in South Asia demonstrate, the effort to ignore within the country the existence of people whose identities bear only faint resemblance to the professed national identity of the State has proved impossible.[28]

One more thing happened. The emphasis on partition refugees and then protection of other "refugees" so considered by the State helped the latter to be hard on the "migrants" – that is illegal migrants. The security issue became more pronounced in the State's attitude towards protecting the migrants. Courts too by and large supported the government stand. The State declined to take any responsibility of protection and respect for rights. Cases abound of hard policies and directives; push back, imprisonment, sexual exploitation, and communal treatment. The security discourse lords over all other considerations.

In sum, this discussion shows that judicial reasoning (which includes legal reasoning) is the instrument to balance power and responsibility, and as *reason* it has guided the Indian state to frame its policy of hospitality in terms of a combination of power and responsibility. Judicial reasoning is the congealed expression of the tensions central to question of power and responsibility of the State.

Forced migration and justice in the time of transition

Postcolonial existence is a permanent condition of transition. Therefore the enquiry has to be: Are there specific marks of transition in the discourse of justice for the victims of forced migration, particularly as a colonised country moves through the phase of decolonisation?

When the British left India, they left the country in ruins. The mutual killings had started in 1946 in Kolkata with the infamous Great Calcutta Riot. The riot left an estimated 10,000 dead in five days, and 100,000 displaced.[29] The government had to call the army to quell the riot, and this became the pattern both in the Punjab and Bengal. As the hour of independence approached, communities attacked each other in entire northern, western, and eastern parts of the country. Acts of killing, burning, ransacking, rape, loot, maiming, and forcibly displacing people spread like wildfire. The army had to be rushed to several places. The nation was up for grab. What did independence mean, and what was signified by freedom? What was political power, and what was sovereignty? If people were sovereign, did it mean Hindus exercising sovereignty, or Muslims, or regions? What did the idea of nation actually mean when everyone was talking of the nation gaining sovereignty? For the British, the main thing was getting out of India as fast as possible. For the Indian National Congress it meant ruling India by preventing further anarchy, re-establishing order, giving it a constitution, and holding elections to legitimise the nationalist rule. For the Muslim League the task was to build a Muslim Pakistan (that is the Muslim majority parts of India in the east and the west) out of the ruins it had inherited. But this was not enough. The way the country was partitioned left Jammu and Kashmir's fate undecided – a fate that today tells its story through thousands of deaths and displacements, and four wars between India and Pakistan. Independence also meant the obligation to define as to what would happen to areas not ruled by the British – for instance, the Naga Hills and other areas in the North-east. But there was little agreement between the concerned parties on these other claims to independence, and whatever consensus was reached quickly broke down in less than a decade. The dialogues between the imperial ruler and the colonised parties were never inclusive and federal.[30] In any case, the British left amidst the mess. The principle of "white man's burden" was over. Responsibility for the loss of lives, destruction, wars, and massive displacements fell on none. Transition had no element of justice. Natives were to now fight it out among themselves. The age of transitional justice was at least four decades away. It was the age of transitional violence or if you like civil war in the sub-continent, which in some sense still continues.

If we take the issue of displacement and refugees, as we indicated earlier, the issue of lack of responsibility becomes clear. We do not have any exact figure of the deaths and displacements that occurred in the wake of Partition – perhaps half a million died, nearly 15 million were displaced, and many were internally displaced.[31] The two young nation states – India and Pakistan – accommodated the refugees as far as possible, but differentially. Thus, refugees from East Pakistan to India were less fortunate than those from West Pakistan. Similarly, *mohajir*s from northern parts of India were less fortunate on arrival in Pakistan than the refugees from the eastern part of the Punjab. But the most scandalous part of the transition scenario was that the colonial rulers, the British, exited without even acknowledging any responsibility for the ruins in which they were leaving the country, and naturally did nothing in terms of protection and care of the displaced. The United Nations likewise did nothing, though to cope with a disaster that affected the soul of Europe it set up a special relief agency (UNRWA) in 1948 as part of its involvement in the creation of Israel, and as we know the UNHCR came up three years later. Nations of South Asia thus began their journey without any notion or mechanism of transitional justice. Also in those heady days of decolonisation they had thought, perhaps, that national independence was an accomplishment by itself and freedom primarily meant independence. Issues of moral and political satisfaction or obligation towards the people, particularly the victims of displacement, and asking for justice in the wake of transition could not be considered as question marks in the journey to independence.

The communal riots of 1946–47 that became a civil war between two religious communities in several parts of the country and led to unprecedented displacements and refugee flows for more than a decade raised the question of security. Riots became a regular feature of independent India. One community wanted security from the "invading" other community. The state wanted security from the aggressive postures, policies, and steps of the neighbouring "hostile" state. The settlers wanted security from the "natives". Natives wanted protection of their spaces from the "invading" settlers. In short security of the nation meant micro-insecurities of the people, and the nation was born with micro-insecurities all around. Laws and measures for refugee protection began to be framed in this background. The Constitutional Assembly debates leading to the provisions of the Constitution, the Foreigners Act (1946), and the Citizenship Act (1955) were framed in such milieu of insecurity. The micro-insecurities provided the building blocks of macro-security – security of the nation and the State. We discussed the issue of security at length in Chapter 7. So we shall refrain from further discussing the question save saying that security emerged as a critical issue in that time of transition and left its permanent mark on inter-community relations.

Researches also show that national independence left many areas of citizenship un-clarified. Thus questions were asked: Who were full citizens, and who were half; who were stateless, or how long the refugees could be allowed to come in from their erstwhile mother countries? Would they automatically get citizenship? Would the sons and daughters of transported labour and the survivors of the indentured labour system be able to come back from the West Indies, Guyana, countries of Africa, or Surinam, or the Fiji Islands?[32] As we know, many were not allowed to return. Many remained stateless (for instance, Indian returnees from Burma, Indian plantation workers in Sri Lanka, Chakmas from East Pakistan resettled in Arunachal Pradesh in India). Policy makers and specialists tore their hair over the aspect of justice in the Citizenship Act (Citizenship Act, 1955, sought to be amended in a Bill in 2016 to make Hindu, Sikh, Buddhist, Jain, Parsi, and Christian illegal migrants from Afghanistan, Bangladesh, and Pakistan, eligible for citizenship; Muslims or minority Muslim sects were left out) and the Foreigners Act, 1946. If these were not enough as marks of political and social injustice, as indicated earlier, citizenship in India increasingly veered towards the *jus sanguinis* principle from *jus soli*. Blood and descent (thus racial features) started playing an increasingly important role. Politics as in many other countries became bio-politics

The question, the Indian story of transition from colonialism to independence raises then is the following: If violence (and injustice connected with this) is an integral part of transition, how shall we place the principle of responsibility in the overall architecture of transition? Without enunciating a principle of restoring justice to the uprooted in the wake of transition – justice which will mean security of the victim of forced migration – can responsibility be exercised?

When we speak of overall security of the nation – an overarching security umbrella or framework – we are first of all recognising the need and the practice of a juridical structure of security that acknowledges the special claims for security of vulnerable communities, at the same time reconciles in its structure differential claims for security. Such a structure becomes *overall* by displaying three features – (a) by being legal, (b) by acknowledging special claims, and (c) by reconciling differing claims for security. In the case of India, the constitution recognised certain specific rights of the indigenous people, made room for specific provisions for those rights, provided for special security arrangements in an area such as the Northeast, tried to settle legally the international borders and boundaries as much as possible, and did away with old hierarchies in terms of political-administrative units of the Union, and made all units equal as states. Yet, as the history outlined in Chapter 7 indicated, this overall security reinforced molecular insecurity. The Indian state of Assam is the most telling case, where its international boundary, inter-state boundaries, and internal boundaries all have combined to make each fragment of the state of Assam insecure. In the region of the Northeast, probably like several others, no one can provide security at the grassroots – the rebels, the army, the ethnic home guards, the civil society, frankly no one. The special provisions only display their own inadequacy. The reconciliation mechanisms and the peace accords prove to be mere governmental exercises of rule.[33] The army and the paramilitary forces prove oppressive; and the international boundaries become the negotiating space for kin groups, kin political formations, the immigrant army of labour, and people fleeing from torture, threats of persecution, and fear. In this way borders become borderlands.[34] The overall security is reinforced by the political economy of an enclave. Such a security framework cannot fully acknowledge the figure of the immigrant except in the sense of denying or ousting the immigrant from the political universe.[35]

The reason is simple – immigrant labour upsets the private property system in whatever form it may exist – group property, nations' property, individual property, or a cartel's property. This is so because while private property requires as its political security a citizenry based on universal suffrage, a participatory system to a lesser or greater extent, a transactional mode of politics, and some sort of preferential arrangements in politics and (at times) economy based on positive discrimination, immigration breaks this framework, makes the contradiction between economics and politics acute, pitches conflict at the most fundamental levels of society, making liberal rule extremely difficult as it continues to provoke collective claims, violence, and politics to an ungovernable extent. To all these, the response of the regime of private property is to make "security" a flexible issue, which means security too has to become a theme of governmentality – a field of politics, negotiation, government, and rule.

Independence was to make the country a republic of freedom and equality of citizens. But partition made India into a collection of heterogeneous population groups with different and sometimes conflicting claims. The process of constituting the citizens and that of making the country a site of multiple types of population did not succeed one another. The two processes operated simultaneously, in the process influencing each other's mode. Hence governing population groups became increasingly difficult. Refugees, illegal immigrants, shelter-seekers, asylum applicants, stateless groups, and the internally displaced became some of the main components of the national populace aspiring to be citizens of the new nation, but who would remain always in the shadow of the rights-bearing citizenry. Governing population groups, the science of administration tells us, calls for stabilising them, regulating, and controlling their flows. This is how security became one of the essential aspects of population management.

The preceding description has tried to show the threefold component of security in relation to population management, namely: (a) the overarching sovereignty of the State (which calls for a centralised authority guarding the borders and frontiers, and maintaining police, army, administration, and laws to rule the population), (b) the disciplinary powers at all levels (which decide friend/foe distinction, make possible an economy of society, implement rules and customs, and orient mentalities), and (c) the governmental power (which regulates and controls population groups physically) that make up the triangle of security architecture. It is a triangle that reminds us of Michel Foucault, namely, that this triangle has as its primary target the population and as its essential mechanism the apparatus of security. Indeed, what needs to be added is that it is the concern for security that binds its three aspects, namely, sovereignty, disciplinary powers, and governmental functions, and brings to bear on the people a fearsome force of classification, pacification, and domestication. Transition makes the government aware of the tasks of rule, reshapes the task of governance in the structure of the triangle.

Referring back to the massive population flows in the wake of the partition of the sub-continent, the rehabilitation and resettlement of the partition refugees in two countries, India and Pakistan, were undertaken in relatively massive proportions, and not guided by any asylum laws. The task became important for the two countries because it became part of nation building in both the countries.[36] This situation left a paradoxical legacy. On one hand subsequent inflows of refugees and asylum seekers had no firm legal precedent to rely on; on the other hand the care and protection of partition refugees – at an informal and formal level – set a tradition or a benchmark guiding India's accommodation policy. It does not mean that all groups were treated equally. But Tibetans, Sri Lankan Tamils, Chakmas, East Pakistani (Bangladeshi) asylum seekers, and Burmese Indians returning to India – all were allowed visitation and stay. Thus, the first three decades after Independence became like a norm for the nation's conduct on issues of care and protection of shelter seekers. Yet, as said earlier, since the practices of the Indian state were issue-oriented, ad hoc, and pragmatic, the mechanism of transitional justice was left without any legal anchor. Courts remained to meet the legal requirements – at least partially.[37]

It has been almost a similar case with Nepal. After the civil war between the Maoists and the State ended in Nepal and the rebels entered the constitutional process, the return of the IDPs (internally displaced persons) became an important issue in the mechanism of transitional justice.[38] Much confusion remained for nearly a decade on effective return, rehabilitation, and resettlement of the IDPs given the bitterness at village level the civil war had left in its wake among people on opposite sides. However, in India no such mechanism was set up. The question of return of the refugees and rehabilitation of the IDPs in Sri Lanka after the civil war ended has been equally critical. Scores of reports and analyses testify to the significance of the issue of transitional justice including justice for the escapees of violence.

To summarise, postcolonial framing of the issue of responsibility will mean taking into account the context of decolonisation, partitions, structural reforms, environmental disasters, and neo-liberal development against which population flows continue, and important to note, in mixed and massive forms. The postcolonial reality of justice in the wake of transition is thus far removed from the cannons of transitional justice established by the liberal discourse of politics or international law and treaty obligations or settlement of disputes by international arbitration. Even the constitutional provisions of basic rights such as right to life (for all – citizens and foreigners alike) do not seem to suffice.

On the other hand, significant historical studies have shown, while borders have produced borderless and borderland people, population groups have created for themselves what can be called "borderland existence". The mainstream perception of an immigrant may not necessarily be the perception of these borderland groups, who are called immigrants. All these point towards new geographies of knowing.[39] While contemporary law, administrative practices, and mainstream economy are against such borderland existences, these existences show that the migrant refuses to be trapped in the security discourse. As a figure of autonomy (even though relative) the migrant negotiates the internal boundaries and national borders and enters giant labour markets created and recreated by global capitalism. They create borderlands everywhere.

Meanwhile, issues of rights and citizenship will not fade away, they will reappear here and there. It seems thus that the transition to citizenship will never happen or never be complete. Perhaps it is in that continuous struggle for life, minimal justice, and dignity, that justice will find its meaning. Responsibility will mean responsibility to ensure justice.

Notes

1 A shorter version of the discussion in this chapter was first made in the article, R. Samaddar, "Power and Responsibility at the Margins: The Case of India in the Global Refugee Regime", *Refuge*, Volume 33 (1), 2017, https://refuge.journals.yorku.ca/index.php/refuge/article/view/40447. Used with permission.
2 While the link between power and responsibility has been a long-standing theme in political philosophy and the literature on governance, the theme was long neglected in the protection literature.
3 The blindness of the Refugee Convention to forced population movements due to war is a matter of irony among war-fleeing asylum seekers. See the testimony by Shahram Khosravi in his *'Illegal' Traveller: An Auto-Ethnography of Borders* (Basingstoke, Hampshire: Palgrave MacMillan, 2010), where he writes of a group of asylum seekers in front of a UNHCR office in Karachi, Pakistan,

> Almost everyone had the same answer: 'There is no point in going to the UNHCR'. It was commonly believed to be a waste of time. Fleeing a war was not a good enough reason and only 'political' (*siyasi*) cases had a chance. Among the many kinds of brokers in the migration market there were even 'case dealers' who sold 'asylum cases'. In the first days I was offered 'a strong case' with 'guaranteed approval' for a hundred dollars. I made a mistake and did not buy it. My fear of being killed in a horrible war was not 'well-grounded' enough, in the view of the UNHCR officer. According to the 1951 Refugee Convention, one is a 'real' refugee only if one has

'well-founded fear of persecution' due to one's 'race, religion, nationality, political opinion, or membership in a particular social group'. So my application was easily and rapidly rejected. The 'case dealer' laughed at me when I told him that my application had been rejected. He was probably right that it was no use telling the UNHCR the truth.

(p. 33)

4 Margaret E. McGuiness discusses the 1951 Convention's "limited nature of the definition of a refugee" (p. 140) in her essay, "Legal and Normative Dimensions of the Manipulation of Refugees", in Stephen John Stedman and Fred Tanner (eds.), *Refugee Manipulation: War, Politics, and the Abuse of Human Suffering* (Washington, DC: Brookings Institution Press, 2003), Chapter 5, pp. 135–166; on the politics of encouraging secessions in former Yugoslavia, the resultant Balkan war in the 1990s, and the refugee flow, Joseph Rudolph Jr., "The Doubtful Effects of Military Intervention on Forced Migration in Yugoslavia", in Nina Nachmias and Rami Goldstein (eds.), *The Politics of Forced Migration: A Conceptual, Operational, and Legal Analysis* (Baltimore: Publish America, 2004), Chapter 7, pp. 191–224.

5 We may re-read for instance Kant's ideas of responsibility and moral responsibility forming the human being. In constituting personhood assuming responsibility becomes critically important.

6 Aristide R. Zolberg, Astri Suhrke, and Sergio Aguayo, *Escape from Violence: Conflict and the Refugee Crisis in the Developing World* (Oxford: Oxford University Press, 1989, 1992).

7 Lucy Mayblin, "Colonialism, Decolonisation, and the Right to Be Human: Britain and the 1951 Geneva Convention on the Status of Refugees", *Journal of Historical Sociology*, Volume 27 (3), September 2014, pp. 423–441.

8 T. Alexander Aleinikoff and Leah Zamore have made the most rigorous effort to circumvent the closure of the trajectory of the principle of responsibility by replacing the principle of "responsibility to protect" with "responsibility to solve". See T. Alexander Aleinikoff and Leah Zamore, *The Arc of Protection: Towards a New International Refugee Regime* (draft), chapter 4, Centre of International Cooperation, New York University, 2018, https://cic.nyu.edu/news/arc-of-protection-refugees-zamore (accessed on 30 December 2018); they argue,

> If the international system of protection is failing, whose job is it to fix it? In this chapter, we will press several arguments as to why states and international organizations have a responsibility to mend the system they have created and through which they control the movement, reception, and lives of the forcibly displaced. Our argument is to some degree a legal one, focusing on instruments and doctrines that have some force in international law. Perhaps more importantly, we make claims based on functionalism (what the protection regime requires, in a deep sense, if it is to stop failing) and on principle (one that attempts to provide a "moral fulcrum" for change).

9 In ancient philosophies the question of hospitality was significant in determining personhood. For example, Pericles said in the funeral oration speech, "Our city is thrown open to the world, and we never expel a foreigner or prevent him from seeing or learning anything of which the secret if revealed to an enemy might profit him." *The History of the Peloponnesian War in Complete Works of Thucydides*, trans. Benjamin Jowett, 2nd ed. (Oxford: Clarendon Press, 1900), Book II, paragraph 39, now available at Delphi Classics, Version I, Sussex, 2013; see also on hospitality, Cicero, *On Duties*, eds. M.T. Griffin and E.M. Atkin, Book II (Cambridge: Cambridge University Press, 1991), pp. 86–89; of the Indian classical texts the *Mahabharata* deals at length with the issue of hospitality. In this connection see the discussion by J. Derrida, *On Cosmopolitanism and Forgiveness* (London: Routledge, 2001).

10 In his address to the Roundtable Workshop on Refugees in the SAARC Region, the President of SAARCLAW (India Chapter), A.M. Singhvi admitted that these questions of state obligations needed to be viewed in the context of human rights. The debate on the need for a national refugee law in India and the work on a model law has been

conducted, however, often from a courtroom angle, and not from the perspective of massive and mixed flows – though it must be admitted that such debate represents a clear advance from the earlier state of affairs in policy matters. On the address see, "Report on Roundtable Workshop on Refugees in the SAARC Region – National Legislations on Refugees", SAARCLAW and UNHCR, New Delhi, 30 April 1999, pp. 13–18.

11 P.N. Bhagwati, *Report on Roundtable Workshop on Refugees in the SAARC Region – National Legislation on Refugees* (New Delhi: SAARCLAW and UNHCR, 1999), p. 21.

12 On this, Vazira Fazila-Yacoobali Zamindar, *The Long Partition and the Making of Modern South Asia: Refugees, Boundaries, Histories* (New York: Columbia University Press, 2007).

13 G. Loescher and J. Scanlan, *Calculated Kindness: Refugees and America's Half-Open Door, 1945-Present* (New York: Free Press, 1986).

14 S. Bhaumik, "The Returnees and the Refugees – Migration from Burma", in R. Samaddar (ed.), *Refugees and the State: Practices of Asylum and Care in India, 1947–2000* (New Delhi: Sage, 2003, hereafter *Refugees and the State*), pp. 182–210.

15 B.S. Chimni, "Status of Refugees in India – Strategic Ambiguity", in Ranabir Samaddar (ed.), *Refugees and the State: Practices of Asylum and Care in India, 1947–2000*(New Delhi: Sage, 2003), pp. 443–471.

16 S.K. Das, "State Response to the Refugee Crisis – Relief and Rehabilitation in the East", in Ranabir Samaddar (ed.), *Refugees and the State: Practices of Asylum and Care in India, 1947–2000* (New Delhi: Sage, 2003), p. 147.

17 R. Menon, "Birth of Social Security Commitments – What happened in the West", in Ranabir Samaddar (ed.), *Refugees and the State: Practices of Asylum and Care in India, 1947–2000* (New Delhi: Sage, 2003), p. 186; on the complex process of forging a new identity among refugees in the western part of India, Ravinder Kaur, *Since 1947: Partition Narratives among Punjabi Migrants of Delhi* (New Delhi: Oxford University Press, 2007).

18 J. Chatterjee, "Rights or Charity? Government and Refugees – the Debate Over Relief and Rehabilitation in West Bengal, 1947–1950", in S. Kaul (ed.), *Partitions of Memory* (New Delhi: Permanent Black, 2001).

19 The lasting significance of the Indian experiences of hosting and finally accommodating the partition refugees is embedded in the critical question of legitimacy: thus, why is the Indian state legitimate? Because it accommodates the shelter seekers, or, how long can India accommodate them? Again, India has a duty to the kin states and the other poor states. But this does not mean that that the protection policy did not change over the years. But the strategic ambiguity this chapter discusses evolved from the times of partition in 1947 and the following decade and remains notwithstanding particular differences of time.

20 See for instance, D. Norbu, "Refugees from Tibet – Structural Causes of Successful Settlements", in S.K. Roy (ed.), *Refugees and human rights* (New Delhi: Rawat Publications, 2002).

21 J. Derrida, *On Cosmopolitanism and Forgiveness* (London: Routledge, 2001), p. 16.

22 On refugee rehabilitation in the Andaman Islands, Uditi Sen, "Memories of Partition's 'Forgotten Episode': Refugee Resettlement in the Andaman Islands", *South Asia Chronicle*, 7, 2017, pp. 147–178, https://edoc.hu-berlin.de/bitstream/handle/18452/19503/07%20 -%20Focus%20-%20Sen%20-%20Memories%20of%20Partition%E2%80%99s%20 %27Forgotten%20Episode%27.%20Refugee%20Resettlement%20in%20the%20Anda man%20Islands.pdf?sequence=4&isAllowed=y (accessed on 20 October 2018); Madhumita Mazumdar, "Dwelling in fluid spaces: The Matuas of the Andaman Islands", in Madhumita Mazumdar, Clare Anderson, and Vishvajit Pandya (eds.), *New Histories of the Andaman Islands: Landscape, Place, and Identity in the Bay of Bengal, 1790–2012* (Cambridge: Cambridge University Press, 2016), Chapter 6, pp. 170–200; Sabyasachi Basu Ray Chaudhury, "Exiled to the Andamans: The Refugees from East Pakistan", in Pradip Kumar Bose (ed.), *Refugees in West Bengal: Institutional Practices and Contested Identities* (Kolkata: Calcutta Research Group, 2000), pp. 130–141.

23 On refugee rehabilitation in the Dandakaranya, Alok Ghosh, "Bengali Refugees at Dandakaranya: A Tragedy of Rehabilitation", in Pradip Kumar Bose (ed.), *Refugees in West*

Bengal: Institutional Practices and Contested Identities (Kolkata: Calcutta Research Group, 2000), pp. 106–135.
24 For a detailed account, R. Samaddar (ed.), *Refugees and the State – Practices of Asylum and Care in India, 1947–2000* (New Delhi: Sage, 2003); also see Pia Oberoi, *Exile and Belonging: Refugees and State Policy in South Asia* (New Delhi: Oxford University Press, 2006). We have to also note that the Indian story resembles greatly the refugee hosting experiences and practices of other South Asian countries, such as Bangladesh hosting the Rohingyas, Nepal hosting the Tibetan refugees, and Pakistan hosting the Afghan refugees and earlier the *Mohajirs*. Like in the Indian case in these two cases also the regime of care and protection was overwhelming informal, the dynamics of kin states operated, the states were signatories to the Refugee Convention, and by and large refugees were not forcibly repatriated. On a broad and comparative study of South Asian experiences of care and protection, Omprakash Mishra (ed.), *Forced Migration in the South Asian Region: Displacement, Human Rights, and Conflict Resolution* (New Delhi: Centre for Refugee Studies, Jadavpur University, Brookings Institution, and Manak Publications, 2004).
25 R. Samaddar, "Refugees and the Dynamics of Hospitality: The Indian Story", in Uma A. Segal, Doreen Elliott, and Nazneen S. Mayadas (eds.), *Immigration Worldwide: Policies, Practices, and Trends* (New York: Oxford University Press, 2010), Ch. 8, pp. 112–123.
26 Seven Rohingya Muslims held at a detention centre in Assam will be handed over to Myanmar after the Supreme Court today refused to stop their deportation, the first such move by the government. 'We are not inclined to interfere on the decision taken', the top court said, accepting the centre's statement that the Rohingya were illegal immigrants and Myanmar had accepted them as citizens.

Report by A. Vaidyanathan, "7 Rohingya Will be Deported, Supreme Court Says Myanmar has Accepted them", *NDTV*, 5 October 2018, www.ndtv.com/india-news/supreme-court-refuses-to-stop-deportation-of-7-rohingya-to-myanmar-today-1926544 (accessed on 5 January 2019); the decision of the Supreme Court created widespread anxiety and protest. See, for instance, the report, "Deporting Rohingya Refugees: Indian Supreme Court Violates Principle of Non-refoulement", *Oxford Human Rights Hub*, 18 October 2018, http://ohrh.law.ox.ac.uk/deporting-rohingya-refugees-indian-supreme-court-violates-principle-of-non-refoulement/ (accessed on 5 January 2019).
27 I have here summarised the conclusions of the reported and unreported cases, discussed in "Refugees and the Dynamics of Hospitality: The Indian Story", pp. 117–121.
28 For instance, the study by R. Samaddar, *The Marginal Nation* (New Delhi: Sage, 1999).
29 The actual figures of the dead and displaced may never be finally known. We have various reports of unaccounted bodies being recovered in the following days and months. On deaths: It was difficult to distinguish between deaths occurring between 16 and 20 August and in the following week. Thus, for instance, between 22 and 29 August when sporadic murders were continuing, about twenty dead bodies in various stages of decomposition were recovered from the streets. From the morgue, 100 bodies were recovered in this period, from the streets twenty, and from other places twelve. File no. 398/46, Home Political, Government of Bengal [hereafter GoB], West Bengal State Archives (hereafter WBSA), p. 8. Decomposed bodies also meant that the figures of Hindu deaths and Muslim deaths may not be correct. One note in the police file spoke of asking the Hindu Satkar Samity to recheck whether the bodies it cremated were those of Hindus in view of the high state of decomposition. File no. 398/46, Appendix A, Home Political, GoB, WBSA. We also do not have any comprehensive account of displacement, relief, and rehabilitation. In many cases Hindu and Muslim charity organisations, as well as the Hindu Mahasabha, the Congress and the Muslim League, ran their own efforts to help the distressed. On the displaced, we have this particular news item:

> The total number of destitute in Government centres in Calcutta was during the last week of November 13,800, of whom 5,000 were refugees from Bihar. In addition about 1,500 refugees had passed through Government camps to their destinations in Calcutta and elsewhere. This information was given by Sir Walter Garner, Relief

Commissioner, Bengal. Sir Walter said that the relief Department was anticipating increased pressure on its organization in Calcutta during the next few weeks, partly as a result of the influx of refugees from Bihar and partly on account of general economic conditions. The Bengal Government had made no representations to the refugees arriving from that province.

See *Calcutta Municipal Gazette* (CMG), Volume XLV, No. 1–2, 30 November – 7 December 1946, pp. 5–6. In another issue it reported on the rehabilitation situation and the works by the then Bengal government regarding rehabilitation of the citizens displaced from the city due to riots. See CMG, Volume XLV, No. 4, 21 December 1946, p. 78. The government also put 'emphasis on rehabilitation of the displaced citizens from the bustees in their previous homes'. Bihari refugees were accommodated in the Talah Park previously occupied by the military. CMG, Volume XLV, No. 18–21, 26 April 1947, p. 407.

30 The three Roundtable Conferences (1930, 1931, 1932) held by the British were marked by bickering and abstention. The Roundtable Conferences led to the Government of India Act of 1935. The Act was an evidence of the contentious nature of the deliberations, and extremely limited nature of power to be devolved on the Indians through the Act, which became in several aspects the model for the Indian Constitution.

31 Estimates of death varied – from a low of about 500,000 to a high figure of 2,000,000. Massive population exchanges took place between the two countries in the months following Partition. The population of undivided India in 1947 was approximately 390 million. At the time of Partition, 330 million people were in India, 30 million in West Pakistan, and 30 million people in East Pakistan (now Bangladesh). Once the borders were established, about 14.5 million people crossed the borders. The 1951 Census of Pakistan identified the number of displaced persons in Pakistan at 7,226,600, presumably all Muslims who had entered Pakistan from India. Similarly, the 1951 Census of India enumerated 7,295,870 displaced persons, apparently all Hindus and Sikhs moving to India from Pakistan after the Partition. Since both censuses were held about 3.6 years after the Partition, the enumeration included net population increase after the mass migration. About 11.2 million (77.4% of the displaced persons) were in the west, with the Punjab accounting for most of it: 6.5 million Muslims moved from India to West Pakistan, and 4.7 million Hindus and Sikhs moved from West Pakistan to India; thus the net migration in the west from India to West Pakistan (now Pakistan) was 1.8 million. The remaining 3.3 million (22.6% of the displaced persons) were in the east: 2.6 million moved from East Pakistan to India and 0.7 million moved from India to East Pakistan (now Bangladesh); thus net migration in the east was 1.9 million into India. On this there is a considerable amount of literature, with estimates varying. See as instances, *Ishtiaq Ahmed, The Punjab Bloodied, Partitioned and Cleaned: Unravelling the 1947 Tragedy through Secret British Reports and First Person Accounts* (Karachi: Oxford University Press, 2012); Prasant Bharadwaj, Asim Khwaja, and Atif Mian, "The Big March: Migratory Flows after the Partition of India", *Economic & Political Weekly*, Volume 43 (45), 30 August 2008, pp. 39–49; Paul R. Brass, "The Partition of India and Retributive in the Punjab, 1946–47: Means, Methods, and Purposes", *Journal of Genocide Research*, Volume 5 (1), 2003, pp. 71–101; Anita Inder Singh, *The Partition of India* (New Delhi: National Book Trust, 2006); Leszek A. Kosinski and K. Maudood Elahi (eds.), *Population Redistribution and Development in South Asia* (Dordrecht: D. Reidel Publishing Co., 1985), "Introduction", pp. 3–14; Bharadwaj and his colleagues said,

The Partition of India in 1947 along ostensibly religious lines into India, Pakistan, and what eventually became Bangladesh resulted in one of the largest and most rapid migrations in human history. In this paper district level census data from archives are compiled to quantify the scale of migratory flows across the subcontinent. We estimate total migratory inflows of 14.5 million and outflows of 17.9 million, implying 3.4 million "missing" people. The paper also uncovers a substantial degree of regional variability. Flows were much larger along the western border, higher in cities and areas close to the border, and dependent heavily on the size of the "minority" religious group. The migratory flows also display a 'relative replacement effect' with in-migrants moving to places that saw greater outmigration.

p. 39

32 On this, Paula Banerjee, "Aliens in a Colonial World", in R. Samaddar (ed.), *Refugees and the State: Practices of Asylum and care in India, 1947–2003* (New Delhi: Sage, 2003), pp. 69–105.
33 See, R. Samaddar, *The Politics of Dialogue: Living under the Geopolitical Histories of War and Peace* (Aldershot: Ashgate, 2004), chapter 6, "Governing through Peace Accords", pp. 159–196; also, R. Samaddar, "Government of Peace", in Samaddar (ed.), *Government of Peace: Social Governance, Security, and the Problematic of Peace* (Surrey, Farnham: Ashgate, 2015), Chapter 1, pp. 19–56.
34 Willem van Schendel describes the process in his *Bengal Borderlands: Beyond State and Nation in South Asia* (London: Anthem Press, 2004).
35 As indicated here if the migrant symbolises transitional violence and injustice, the question is: What does the figure of the migrant signify in different ages and systems? Thomas Nail attempts a philosophical-historical explanation in *The Figure of the Migrant* (Stanford, CA: Stanford University Press, 2015).
36 The Mohajirs in Pakistan remained an exception to the general trend of nationalisation of the refugees. Because refugees were told that they were parts of the new nation, the Mohajirs (Urdu speaking refugees from India) in Sind, Pakistan, resented the fact that they had been treated unfairly and unequally, and resources had been cornered by Sindhis and Panjabis. They resented the quota system, which facilitated Sindhis in gaining university slots and civil service jobs. The ethnic rivalry led to Mohajir political mobilisation, which was further provoked by the stagnant economy and the condition of the Biharis living in the camps in Bangladesh. The Muttahida Qaumi Movement (MQM) was born in this way in 1984. The Mohajirs claimed that they were a nation. See A.R. Siddiqi, *Partition and the Making of the Mohajir Mindset: A Narrative* (Oxford: Oxford University Press, 2008); and Nichola Khan, Mohajir Militancy, *Pakistan: Violence and Transformation in the Karachi Conflict* (London: Routledge, 2012).
37 Indian state's policy to repatriate the Rohingyas and institute countrywide a programme of NRC – both with partial judicial concurrence – suggests that perhaps the policy of hospitality is now completely predicated upon security considerations.
38 The number of IDPs in Nepal was variously put between 40,000 and 400,000, and the number of deaths 12,865. One report said,

> Conflict-induced displacement is a relatively new phenomenon in Nepal. This form of displacement started in 1996 when the internal armed conflict between the Nepal Communist Party (Maoist) and the Government of Nepal began. One estimate states that 12,865 people lost their lives in Nepal during these years due to the conflict between the Maoists and the government of Nepal (INSEC, 2006). Moreover, reports from various organizations over the last few years have quoted IDP figures that range from approximately 37,000 all the way to 400,000 – and these figures exclude those who may have crossed the border into India (SAFHR, 2005). The Inter-Agency Internal Displacement Division (IDD) Mission to Nepal reported that the most reliable estimate of IDPs in Nepal who were internally displaced by the conflict should be upwards to 200,000.

Nir Prasad Dahal, "Rethinking Nepal's IDP Policy with Reference to UN Guiding Principles", *Refugee Watch Online*, 31 March 2011, http://refugeewatchonline.blogspot.in/2011/03/rethinking-nepals-idp-policy-with.html (accessed on 17 June 2017); the figure of 200,000 was taken from another report, Anand Aditya, Bishnu Raj Upreti, and Poorna Kanta Adhikary, *Countries in Conflict and Processing of Peace: Lessons for Nepal*, 2006, Kathmandu, Friends for Peace (FFP); see also *Voices of the Internally Displaced in South Asia*, A Calcutta Research Group Report, 2006, Section III, "Nepal", pp. 49–66, www.mcrg.ac.in/Voices.pdf (accessed on 18 June 2017).

39 Foremost among such studies on South Asia are the inquiries led by Willem Van Schendel, *Bengal Borderlands: Beyond State and Nation in South Asia*; also by Schendel, "Working through Partition – Making a Living in the Bengal Borderlands", *International Review of Social History*, 46, 2000, pp. 393–421; Md. Mahbubar Rahman and Willem Van Schendel, "'I am not a Refugee' – Rethinking Partition Migration", *Modern Asian Studies*, Volume 37 (3), 2003, pp. 551–584; Willem Van Schendel, "Stateless in South Asia – The Making of India-Bangladesh Enclaves", *The Journal of Asian Studies*, Volume 61 (1), 2002, pp. 115–147.

11
THE ROADMAP OF GLOBAL POWER AND RESPONSIBILITY

The birth of a global gaze

We shall have a final engagement with the way the global figured in *The Age of Migration*. *The Age of Migration* had the great merit of presenting migration and forced migration flows on a global scale, as a global phenomenon, and not simply as an international feature. Yet as I suggest throughout this book, the systemic analysis of the global in *The Age of Migration* avoided the question of power, the scale of exercise of power, and the way management of migration became in time an essential element of global power. The systemic analysis in *The Age of Migration* proved limited because it avoided the central element in the making of the global today, namely the postcolonial question.

The preceding chapter engaged with the issue of power and responsibility at the margins by which we mean the postcolonial world. We saw the role of the postcolonial nation state in offering protection; the specific pattern in the combination of power, care, and responsibility; the customary practices of hospitality; the long-term impact of partitions, border making, and borderland violence on the postcolonial life of the nation and on the region as a whole; the history of bilateral treaties in coping with some of the impacts; a sense of the region among the countries in which the nation discovered itself, struggled, and thrived; the contending notions of security and rights, or if one wills, charity and rights; the fuzzy world of justice and jurisprudence; and an overwhelming reality of massive internal displacements and footloose labour linked to the various processes of displacement and working as the underbelly of the contemporary world. The idea was not to present the postcolonial milieu of power and responsibility as an ideal one, as a model that the structure of global governance should adopt. The idea was to give an indication of the particular realities of the postcolonial world existing under the so-called global realm of protection – existing almost as a distinctly separate realm.

Now in this concluding chapter we shall be involved with the question of the global as distinct from the local, the postcolonial local. We shall examine the roadmap of global power and responsibility, how management of population mobility figures as a crucial component of global governance. Perhaps the crucial question this chapter will pose and with which the book has to end will be: How much of the concrete practices of protection, contradictory as they are, go into the making of the global, or, does the global map of power and protection build itself by excluding these realities, which are dominantly postcolonial in nature?

The Global Compact on Refugees and *The Global Compact for Safe, Orderly, and Regular Migration*, mandated by the New York Declaration for Refugees and Migrants, 2016, and later adopted by the United Nations in 2018, have been widely considered as opportunities for the world to reconsider old approaches to refugee and migrant protection and devise a new global approach. From the time of the League of Nations and then with the beginning of the United Nations, refugee flows in Europe dominated the humanitarian anxieties of those who were managing the tasks of global governance in those days. Refugee protection from the beginning of our modern global age assumed an irreducibly international character, even though this international excluded the experiences of displacements in the vast colonial and postcolonial regions of the world.[1] The New York Declaration was part of an integrated and coordinated implementation of and follow-up to the outcomes of the major United Nations efforts in the economic, social, and other related fields. The Declaration unambiguously linked the task of protecting the migrants and refugees to a global development agenda, and said,

> In adopting the 2030 Agenda for Sustainable Development one year ago, we recognized clearly the positive contribution made by migrants for inclusive growth and sustainable development. Our world is a better place for that contribution. The benefits and opportunities of safe, orderly and regular migration are substantial and are often underestimated. Forced displacement and irregular migration in large movements, on the other hand, often present complex challenges.[2]

It was a promise of a new orientation to a global issue. In the process it gave birth to a new global developmental gaze, which connected protection, safety, and security with sustainable development.[3] In the wake of the new promise, one journal commented, "The global community should not miss the opportunity to strengthen refugee protection in an era of increased migration."[4]

Annex 1 of the Declaration spoke of a comprehensive refugee response framework (which would include improved norms of reception and admission, support for immediate and ongoing needs, support for host countries and communities, and various steps towards durable solutions) and the resolution invited the Office of the United Nations High Commissioner for Refugees (UNHCR) to engage with States and consult with all relevant stakeholders over the coming two years, with a view to evaluating the detailed practical application of the comprehensive refugee response framework and assessing the scope for refinement and further development. It also specified that the objective was to ease pressures on the host countries involved, to enhance refugee self-reliance, to expand access to third-country solutions and to support conditions in countries of origin for return in safety and dignity. The UNHCR was asked to propose a global compact on refugees in the annual report of the High Commissioner to the General Assembly in 2018, for consideration by the Assembly at its seventy-third session (Annex 1, Paragraphs 18–19). As it presented the draft of the Compact to the United Nations, the UNHCR declared, "It was a new deal for the refugees".[5]

Annex II, likewise, proposed a process of intergovernmental negotiations leading to the adoption of a global compact for safe, orderly, and regular migration. It said that the proposed global compact would set out a range of principles, commitments, and understandings among Member States regarding international migration in all its dimensions, and thus make an important contribution to global governance and enhance coordination on international migration by dealing with all aspects of international migration, including the humanitarian, developmental, human rights-related and other aspects of migration. As set out in its draft "Vision and Guiding Principles", the Migration Compact decided to focus on some of the following objectives, to be fulfilled through numerous actionable commitments, namely: collection and utilisation of accurate, disaggregated data as a basis for evidence-based policies;[6] minimisation of the adverse drivers and structural factors that compel people to leave their country of origin; providing adequate and timely information at all stages of migration, and all migrants with proof of legal identity, proper identification and documentation; enhancing availability and flexibility of pathways for regular migration; facilitating fair and ethical recruitment and safeguard conditions that ensure decent work; addressing and reducing vulnerabilities in migration; managing borders in an integrated, secure, and coordinated manner; strengthening certainty and predictability in migration procedures; using migration detention only as a measure of last resort and working towards alternatives; enhancing consular protection, assistance, and cooperation throughout the migration cycle; providing access to basic services for migrants; eliminating all forms of discrimination and promotingfact-based public discourse to shape perceptions of migration and investing in skills development and facilitate recognition of skills, qualifications, and competences; creating conditions for migrants and diasporas to fully contribute to sustainable development in all countries; promoting faster, safer, and cheaper transfer of remittances and fostering financial inclusion of migrants; and establishing mechanisms for the portability of social security entitlements and earned benefits.[7]

These two compacts together promised a new global approach to the issue of global migration including forced migration. The slogan was, "Making migration work for all." The UN Secretary-General said,

> Rather than responding to refugee displacement through a purely and often underfunded humanitarian lens, the elements of the comprehensive refugee response framework are designed to provide a more systematic and sustainable response that benefits both refugees and the communities that host them. That is advanced through the engagement of a much broader group

of stakeholders: government authorities, the United Nations and its national partners, international and regional financial institutions, and business and civil society actors. It seeks to ensure more sustainable responses by linking humanitarian and development efforts early on in a crisis and by strengthening inclusive service delivery, including through investment in national and local systems wherever possible.[8]

It did not, however, mean that this new approach would ignore security considerations. Thus, "Security matters: States and the members of the public have legitimate reasons to demand secure borders and the capacity to determine who enters and stays on in their territory", but the UN cautioned about counterproductive results from undue restriction on migration that "corrode the ability of States to deliver on these priorities, and make migrants more vulnerable." However, the

> rule of law at all levels must be strengthened. Migrants should respect the need for legal pathways, and move between countries in an orderly fashion; but to make this possible the governments need to open routes for regular migration that respond to the realities of labour demand and supply.

Further,

> Migration should never be an act of desperation: migration works for all when those who travel make an informed and voluntary choice to go abroad through legal means, but we have seen too many migrants on the move in large numbers in response to unsustainable pressures in their home countries in recent years. We should use all the developmental, governance and political tools at our disposal to prevent and mitigate the human and natural forces that drive such large movements of people, but we should also recognize that we have a duty to care for those who migrate out of desperation.[9]

The Declaration was global not only because it emanated from a global institution, but also because of the following aspects: First, a single declaration covering subjects of migration and forced migration was an acknowledgement of the reality that the two had deep relations, and that population flows were increasingly mixed and massive in nature defying neat categorisation. In this global initiative, the one on safe and orderly migration worked as the counterfoil, we can say it presented the other scene of refugee management.

Second, the Declaration also highlighted the limits and or unwillingness of States to carry primary responsibility of the refugees and migrants, and hence opened up the possibility to include, what it called the "whole of society", which is to say the "whole of globe" covering various stakeholders including business and commercial segments.

Third, the Declaration suggested uneven geographies of protection and labour market, and conceived of the globe in terms of sanctuaries, third countries, hotspots, border zones, safe corridors, legally run labour regimes, and remittance-centric segments of global economy, as well as places characterised by multi-stakeholder operations. These geographies were in part created by spatial planning for refugees and migrants, in part by financial and security operations.

Fourth, the new approach was global because refugees and migrants were conceptualised as subjects of global development.

Fifth, migration and refugee "crises" were going to be inevitable unless the world struggled for durable solutions – hence the need for globally relevant comprehensive response framework, such as the "comprehensive refugee response framework", and what IOM popularised as a "framework for effective practices with regard to management capacity building."[10]

Finally, solutions could become durable only becoming global, first as indicated earlier through practising a new geography of labour market and care, and second, by pursuing a technological mode of management that would circumvent borders and boundaries to cope with the complex reality of global migration.

A small point, perhaps not small, is that the Declaration in order to be global by and large bypassed the issue of internal displacement and addressed cross-border migration, though in few places it made references to the internally displaced. However, in strategising migration management the issue of internal displacement was not of critical importance.[11] It was a case of a new global gaze and a new design of an apparatus of power and protection. With various components in place as part of the design the idea was to create a new apparatus of protection – a new global machine greased by the ideology of humanitarianism and supremely technological in orientation in order to be efficient.

The roadmap of the global

What makes a process global? Will it be enough to say that some global institutions have participated in a process, which has made it global? Or, are there other elements and dynamics in the making of the global? It is important to examine this question while we close this book, for in some sense this is the crucial question sitting at the heart of the entire of discussion on protection today.[12]

The UNDP, to name only one institution of the many spending money on the process, spent nearly half a million dollars (USD) in 2017 in supporting the migration compact process. This was overseen by the Multi-Partner Trust Fund Office of the UNDP. Austria, Australia, Cyprus, Ireland, Norway, Slovakia, and Switzerland provided the money, with Norway putting up most of the support – USD 257,748. This was only one of the several indications of monetary and other investments to prepare consent over the global compact agenda and secure it. In this way, scores of funding agencies, countries, foundations, think tanks, and multilateral institutions got involved in the process.[13] Global conversations were initiated and held. Meetings were organised in the metropolises, mostly in the North and some in the South. The agenda of preparing the world for a new regime of protection as part of global governance was shaped through these steps. If this was only about one organisation (UNDP), one can only imagine the extent of money, number of meetings, presence of specialists, recycling of views of known specialists, and involvement of a thin layer of experts of the South that were required in the process of manufacturing consent over the idea of a global mandate. Indeed these were marks of the process. By and large human rights activists, peace activists, political parties, governments, regional associations, and critical jurists of the postcolonial world were left out. The global compact/s was/were to become a reality in a short time. A detailed work plan was chalked out for "global compact for safe, orderly and regular migration", with preparatory meetings to be held in three phases in New York, Geneva, and Vienna – the capitals of the global world. Thematic sessions, UN Regional Economic Commissions, regional consultative processes (discussions to be held in regional capital cities), multi-stakeholder meetings, global forum on migration and development, IOM conducted international dialogue on migration, and other preparatory stocktaking meetings, distribution of documents, and negotiations were steps towards building consensus on the compact.[14]

Likewise, there was a simultaneous process of a compact on refugees. The New York Declaration for Refugees and Migrants, adopted by the United Nations General Assembly in September 2016, called for the United Nations High Commissioner for Refugees, in consultation with States and other stakeholders, to develop a global compact on refugees. It was an indirect admission that the Convention of 1951 had become highly inadequate. As outlined in UNHCR's roadmap towards a global compact on refugees, the compact proposed by the High Commissioner consisted of two complementary parts: (a) a comprehensive refugee response framework (CRRF), as agreed upon by States, and (b) a programme of action setting out measures to be taken both by States and other relevant stakeholders, to "underpin the CRRF, support its application and, ultimately, ensure more equitable sharing of the responsibility for responding to large movements of refugees." The aim was to make the compact informed by the outcomes of a process that had been pursued in cooperation and consultation with Member States and other relevant stakeholders, in a number of interconnected areas. The process took special note of (a) the application of the CRRF in specific countries and situations; (b) a series of five thematic discussions, held in the second half of 2017; and (c) a stocktaking of progress made and lessons learnt. The process identified good practices in refugee responses, actions required to bring about the type of response envisaged in the New York Declaration, and areas for future development.[15] In line with the roadmap towards a compact a series of formal consultations on the draft programme of action was convened in the first half of 2018. These formal consultations (six consultations held between February and July 2018) were to be crucial steps in the development of the global compact on refugees before the compact would be proposed by the High Commissioner in his 2018 annual report the General Assembly. It was also specifically mentioned that the path of the compact would be marked by a multi-stakeholder, "whole-of-society" approach endorsed by the General Assembly in the New York Declaration that would involve "national and local authorities, international organisations, international financial institutions, regional organizations, regional coordination and partnership mechanisms, civil society partners, including faith-based organizations and academia, the private sector, media and the refugees themselves."[16]

The UNHCR was thus ambitious. On 17 May 2017 the roadmap towards a global compact on refugees was drawn. Usually nations have compacts on war, peace, cessation of hostilities, development project, regional trade, etc. Now UNHCR was embarking on achieving a compact on human beings – a group of human beings.[17] It was upheld as a political declaration (paragraph 1); member states were to reaffirm their commitments to migrants and refugees, and the UNHCR declared the need for "a framework for a comprehensive and people-centric refugee response to each situation involving large number of refugees" (paragraph 4).

Crucial in the roadmap was the "comprehensive refugee response framework" towards "a global compact for safe, orderly, and regular migration" (Annex 1 and Annex 2). The framework had four objectives:(a) ease pressures on host countries; (b) enhance refugee self-reliance;(c) expand access to third-country solutions; and (d) support conditions in countries of origin for return in safety and dignity.

We can only note here that "easing pressure on host countries" indirectly means easing pressure on countries of the North and not South (say Pakistan or Bangladesh); enhancing refugee self-reliance implies more and more dependence on the market, expanding access to third-country solutions signals shifting more burdens to countries of the South, and returning refugees has been many a time forced return or deportation as in the case of Rohingyas. These were and are time-worn policies, whose advocates never tire of repeating them, whose results have never been objectively analysed, and which now return under the call for a comprehensive refugee response framework, whose key pillars are equally time-worn, namely, reception and admission (thus they may be interned in camps and detention centres), support for immediate and ongoing needs (thus barely minimal), support for host countries and communities; and, that old pillar of protection, called "durable solutions".[18]

Added to that was the advocacy of a multi-stakeholder, which we have already mentioned, the "whole-of-society" approach that included national and local authorities, international organisations, international financial institutions, regional organisations, regional coordination and partnership mechanisms, civil society partners, including faith-based organisations and academia, the private sector, media, and the refugees themselves. The focus on a "whole of society" approach, on the level of it nothing objectionable, bypassed considering the existing protection modes in the vast postcolonial world, which we discussed in the previous chapter. The new approach takes a "modernistic" and a global governance approach, which would supposedly focus on identifying or detecting an "emergency". Thus the "whole-of-society" approach advocates,

> more sustainable refugee responses by linking humanitarian and development efforts early on in a crisis, and by strengthening sustainable approaches that invest in the resilience of both refugees and local communities, including through investment in national and local systems wherever possible.[19]

It also claims to mean understanding migration risk and resilience in the context of disasters.[20]

The global nature of the refugee response is acknowledged in this way. As said, it means three things.

First, it means a comprehensive response built around "emergency" situations, an indirect acknowledgement that migrations are becoming mixed and massive, and displacements are increasingly protracted[21] with refugees and migrants in limbo. Yet the "emergency" is not defined. What defines an emergency – the capacity of a host country, or number of escapees, or the complexity of factors contributing to an intolerable situation of not only escape but also arrival (say in Calais or Idomeni) or even passage (say through a sea), or the refusal of a state like Australia to allow the escapees to arrive to seek asylum – even sinking rickety boats on the sea and confining them to islands away from human eyes – indeed what is an emergency? What will justify global attention?

Second, it calls for widening the protection capacity through a whole of society approach, which again is an admission that states are not marshalling their protection capacity adequately – some are doing, while many are not. Therefore, societies have to be mobilised widely and deeply. This may mean putting more stress on countries already reeling under the burden of protecting and caring, while others perhaps may not share the burden at all, or share very little. In other words, the whole of society is again a global gaze that may exclude variegated approaches and experiences of care and protection, such as customary protection, bilateral treaties and other arrangements, regional initiatives,[22] local innovations, and steps to keep the borders relatively open so that refugees can come in, work, and go back in irregular manner – approaches that make stay more flexible. The whole of society approach from the beginning seems to be a captive of the myth of durable solutions, which indeed in the first place had given birth to the UNHCR.

And, third, response has to be "comprehensive", and in this way global, because other desperate attempts at durable solution have failed, and in the context of the Mediterranean crisis and the European migration crisis something had to done. Economy buttressed by demography has been always the other scene of refugee and migration management in the modern capitalist age. Yet this could be hardly acknowledged. Humanitarianism is the ground on which the new migration and refugee management mode is to be legitimised. The "whole of society" mode of management would enable the refugees and migrants to learn quickly new skills, adapt themselves relatively quickly – in a year or two – to new requirements of language, labour protocols, self-run business rules, and learn to straddle the two different but interacting worlds of formal economy and the informal economy. The eventual absorption of current immigrant flows of skilled, semi-skilled, and unskilled labour in labour markets of Europe and countries of other regions (Brazil, South Africa, Hong Kong, the Gulf countries, etc.), albeit in differential manner, will not be much different from what had happened in Europe, United States, Canada, and Australia in the pre-Second World War years.[23] "Whole of society" (that is involvement of all the "stakeholders") in a dense labour market scenario means pleas for labour market equality. But formal (political, legal) equality makes sense only if they are relevant for entry in labour markets. Otherwise as labouring subject, the migrant's lack of political equality is the other side of her economic ability to enter the labour market. Yet, the question of economy attaches itself to the humanitarian as the ever-present unbearable bug, and we recalled earlier, at the heart of the "durable solutions" debate in refugee studies circles, the issue of economic rehabilitation was always paramount. The formation of the UNHCR itself nudged by the UN Economic and Social Council was an effort towards finding out a durable solution to the refugee crisis.[24]

In short, the roadmap avoids the political question of economy, and thus the issue of financial responsibility – responsibility of global powers unleashing wars and causing population displacements, responsibility of countries embarking on citizenship drives making many people stateless and turning them into wandering hordes of protection-less subjects, and responsibility of the institutions of global governance to ensure an equitable sharing of burden. The roadmap avoids the issue of reparations – at the heart of the issue of responsibility.

But perhaps, the biggest paradox of this new global is that it treats a massive group of world population as a subject of compact as if it is a piece of land, a sea, a mineral rich territory, etc., and avoids the question of rights. But again is this not how minorities were traded as subjects of international diplomacy since the "bad" Ottoman days? Migrants and refugees have no or little rights; and there is to be no charter of rights of refugees and migrants. They are to remain as subjects of care, and hence international subjects. Thus, to be humanitarian one has to be global. And paradoxically, the global can be only humanitarian. In this way the distance between the global and the humanitarian has been bridged. And yet this can come only by erasing the contentious question of rights – a question to which we shall turn in due course.

Meanwhile this was the way the Arendtian impasse has been resolved. Hanna Arendt had raised the reality of refugees as subjects of a basic "rightlessness". Neo-liberalism resolved the problematic of a neologism. One cannot be a subject of "rightlessness", in other words in such condition one would not be a *subject* at all. Neo-liberalism has rescued the refugee as a subject – subject of economy, subject of care of the whole of society, a subject for whom politics is redundant. Rights no longer make a subject; care does, economy does, and so does global attention.

The humanitarian machine

Yet, at this point we must note that in this roadmap in which consultation was given due bureaucratic place, human rights or civil rights bodies within countries were shunned. In place were given six set of dates for six consultations within February to July 2018 to be co-chaired by a member of UNHCR's Executive Committee Bureau, together with UNHCR's Assistant High Commissioner for Protection, and to be held in private at the Palais des Nations in Geneva, Switzerland. A zero draft of the compact was shared with States and other relevant stakeholders by the end of January 2018. Following the formal consultation, UNHCR shared a revised draft of the global compact and the expected outcome at the end of the formal consultations was a non-binding document, reflecting a consensus among all UN Member States. All Member and non-Member Observer States of the United Nations, and non-governmental organisations having consultative status with the United Nations Economic and Social Council (ECOSOC) or were members of the International Council of Voluntary Agencies (ICVA), were to be invited to participate in the formal consultations.[25] Meanwhile do-gooder intellectuals were encouraged to send written contributions to the process at two UNHCR online sites.[26] Evidently, the figure of the right-bearing migrant or the refugee was a skeleton in this policy feast at Geneva. The humanitarian machine was given a new life in this way.

One telling instance of the machine being reset to work was the step to set up another bureaucratic body – an Asylum Capacity Support Group (ACSG) – by the UNHCR under the heading "Identifying International Protection Needs", as if inadequate asylum-determining capacity was the reason behind states' reluctance to take in the asylum-seeking population. Blithely the document said,

> Identifying who is in need of international protection is the first step in ensuring that refugees are properly protected, and have access to an adequate standard of treatment. The determination of refugee status is in principle the task and responsibility of States, and many States have dedicated institutions responsible for deciding on claims for refugee status. An RSD (refugee status determination) system encompasses, amongst other elements, the laws and policies, institutions, structures, and resources that, taken together, form a crucial part of a State's response to the arrival of people seeking international protection. An RSD system needs to be fair. Fairness in this context means that the outcomes of decisions on claims for international protection are in accordance with the rule of law."[27]

Four elements – fairness, efficiency, adaptability and integrity – were declared as ingredients of a quality RSD system.

The Comprehensive Refugee Response Framework (CRRF), earlier mentioned, was the keystone of the global humanitarian machine. As with all other machines, in this case also bodies were needed to feed and lubricate it. Marx spoke of human bodies and the machine in a factory. Here the bodies for the humanitarian machine were the poor states of the South, and not the reluctant countries of the North. UNHCR declared that to date the CRRF was being applied in thirteen countries and situations: Belize, Costa Rica, Guatemala, Honduras, Mexico, and Panama (who had come together under a regional approach to the Comprehensive Regional Protection and Solutions Framework) and in Africa, seven countries – Djibouti, Ethiopia, Kenya, Uganda, the United Republic of Tanzania, Somalia, and Zambia. The UNHCR further declared that the "range of situations", included "regional diversity and a variety of phases (new emergency, established situation, protracted situation)." The UNHCR also took satisfaction that important work on many of the elements of CRRF was already underway in many other contexts – for example, prevention and response to sexual and gender-based violence, or innovation in the delivery of assistance, such as cash-based interventions. It felt that the "process of assessment and refinement (was) key to the development of the global compact on refugees".[28]

The machinic nature of the CRPF devoured also the spirit of the cities. The movement, "cities of refuge" was turned into some kind of a bureaucratic appendage of a gigantic machine. Pioneered by the Rockefeller Foundation, 100 "resilient cities" were lined up.[29] Urban resilience was defined as the capacity of individuals, communities, institutions, businesses, and systems within a city to survive, adapt, and grow no matter what kinds of "chronic stresses and acute shocks" they experience. "Chronic stresses" weakened the fabric of a city on a daily or cyclical basis, and such stresses included high unemployment, inefficient public transportation systems, endemic violence, and chronic food and water shortages. "Acute shocks" such as earthquakes, floods, disease outbreaks, and terrorist attacks, were sudden and sharp events that threatened a city. A letter was sent on 4 December 2017 to Filipo Grandi, the High Commissioner for Refugees, by illustrious mayors of cities like Amman, Athens, Atlanta, Barcelona, Bristol, Chicago, District of Columbia, Dallas, Gothenburg, Los Angeles, Milan, New York City, Paris, Philadelphia, Elorza, and San Francisco. In their letter they declared,

> Cities play a central role in addressing the needs of refugees, whether they arrive independently or through formal resettlement channels, and the international system needs to keep pace with present realities. Whereas the iconic image of a refugee is a person residing in a camp, today at least 60 percent of the world's refugees reside in urban areas. Programs that provide these refugees with housing, healthcare, education, and social services are, in many cases, delivered at the local level, while designed and financed in close cooperation with the other levels of governance. For these interventions to be sustainable and efficient, they must integrate with existing city systems. Municipal authorities should be responsible for providing basic services for all residents, even when their numbers have surged unexpectedly. . . . Local authorities need approaches that benefit refugees and host communities, alike – policies and programs that build resilient, inclusive, and prosperous communities from the outset. Refugees are members of our communities, whether they stay for one year or twenty.[30]

While writing these noble lines, the illustrious mayors forgot that cities did what they could, not because their respective national governments had directed them to do so, but, as often, against respective national governments or independent of these governments, cities provided hospitality, and that these stories of hospitality were marked invariably with conflicts and contentions. Oblivious of this the mayors urged the "UNHCR to use the practical application of the Comprehensive Refugee Response Framework to further refine operational responses to urban refugee populations, and in particular, to explore the potential for durable solutions in urban areas."[31] This was the surreal voice of the "global cities", that wanted us to forget the blood and expulsion of refugees and migrants from cities,[32] and that the histories of urban openness was a not a seamless story of hospitality and kindness but one of contention. The ghost of cities like Kolkata, Karachi, Bangkok, Nairobi, Istanbul, Johannesburg, Mumbai, had effected the mythical transformation of the urban landscape into one of kindness.[33] We have to note an accompanying transformation – that of a movement inspired by thinkers like Derrida, Edward Said, Bourdieu, and others into a potential cog in the humanitarian machine.[34] Rights and justice in this way become alien cries in the world of humanitarian machines. The radical edge of the idea of "cities of refuge" rested on an acknowledgment that urban spaces were marked with the materiality of control and contests, and that space for migrants and refugees has not been given benevolently by city fathers/mothers, but that it has been an outcome of the sheer persistence of the presence of the migrant in the city. The governmentalisation of the "right to the city" movement attempts to take away that radical edge.[35]

How did this transformation come about? To understand that we must first take a look at the enormous, almost incredible, range of inputs from various institutions to the framing of the "zero draft" (at the heart of which sat the policy of a comprehensive framework). Exactly as a big factory works like an assembly of various machinic inputs, here too an assembly process could be found at work. From Council of Europe, the European Union, and the European Asylum Support Office to institutions like the Arab Regional Consultative Process on Migration and Refugee Affairs, the Vaccine Alliance, Global Youth Advisory Council, ICRC, Human Rights Council, ILO (International Labour Organisation), the UN Broadband Commission for Sustainable Development, Food and Agriculture Organization (FAO), International Fund for Agricultural Development (IFAD) and the World Food Programme (WFP), IOM (International Organisation for Migration), IPU (Inter Parliamentary Union), UN Women, World Bank, UNICEF (United Nations, UNRWA (United Nations Relief and Works Agency for Palestine Refugees in the Near East), WFP (World Food Programme), UNDP, OHCHR (The Office of the United Nations High Commissioner for Human Rights), UN Habitat, Metropolis, WHO, Asylum Access and several other international non-governmental organisations,[36] and the International Refugee Congress (IRC). Plus consider the hundreds of statements and inputs from the governments. The IRC spoke of itself as "We, 156 participants, representing 98 diverse institutions from 29 countries, including refugee led and host community civil society organisations and initiatives, academia, think tanks, municipalities, and the private sector came together in Istanbul for the International Refugee Congress on 10–11 May 2018." The gathering in Istanbul drew on the contributions of close to 600 organisations from 47 countries, which participated in consultations that were held over the past six months leading to the Congress.[37]

> This preparation process and the meeting itself provided an important platform to demonstrate our shared quest for equal participation in decision-making processes at all levels, as well as our common commitment to work together to put the voices and aspirations of refugees and host communities at the forefront of policy and program development, including the Global Compact on Refugees (GCR).[38]

To be fair, the GCR speaks of rights, but as expected is minimal in its approach. It says,

> We urge collective action to realize the following priority goals in the five thematic areas ... that were identified through our consultations: guarantees for refugee legal rights and asylum; access to quality services; durable solutions and sharing responsibilities; increased and focused support for displaced women and girls; and representation and participation at all levels of decision-making.

And further,

> Legal rights are at the core of refugee protection. Guaranteeing access to these rights would shift the dialogue from people in need to people with rights. Building structures of access to legal rights is fundamental to progressive refugee policy, the pursuit of durable solutions, the enjoyment of basic rights in asylum, and the protection of refugees, especially women and girls and marginalized groups. Whether residing in countries of first asylum, repatriating to countries of origin or resettling in other countries, refugees need guarantees for their rights and freedoms, clarity about their legal status, and access to legal recourse and assistance.[39]

One can find a pattern to the global consultations that preceded the drafting of the Compact. Most of the input providers, as evident from the preceding random list of names, were "international", the forums were "international", and UN institutions had been ploughed in – as if in an orchestrated chorus of voices in support for the need a new global compact. The UNHCR and other UN institutions could have used their country offices throughout the world, if they chose, to act as catalysts for intra-country and intra-regional discussions on what should go into a compact or what else should have been striven for towards a new global initiative, or if at all a new global compact was needed. In South Asia, the UNHCR took no such initiative; for instance, in India, none. There was very little or no discussion with rights groups, political movements, refugee advocacy platforms, scholars and their bodies, not even any discussion with humanitarian institutions providing aid and relief to the shelter seekers. And particularly the process avoided drawing any lesson from the vast corpus of experiences from the management of the fallouts from internal displacements. The UNHCR had blandly promised,

> With active assistance from the international community, UNHCR will do its utmost to mobilize support for the application of the global compact. United Nations Member States and relevant stakeholders will be invited by UNHCR to make concrete pledges, and to provide updates on their endeavours to support the application of the global compact. The United Nations High Commissioner for Refugees will include, in his annual report to the

United Nations General Assembly, information on progress made in its application. In consultation with States and relevant stakeholders, UNHCR will develop a set of key indicators to monitor and evaluate progress and outcomes of the global compact. These indicators will be measurable against the overall objectives of the global compact54 and will be aligned with and contribute to the relevant goals of the sustainable development agenda. UNHCR, with input from States and relevant stakeholders, will monitor and evaluate progress towards the achievement of these indicators. United Nations Member States could also include refugees in their progress reporting on the Sustainable Development Goals.[40]

Thus, it is a case of the "global" choosing to be global. The global is only reproducing self. Though, from some of these communiqués, statements, manifestos, declarations, and representations it seems as if the muffled voice of rights of the victims of forced migration is trying break out of the iron clad global process. The voice however is weak. It does not have the wherewithal to point out that the entire process has ignored the principle of responsibility on which the realisation of rights rests. It cannot challenge the current formulation of the "responsibility to protect" principle, which has empowered and legitimated interventions, and remained silent about any responsibility for wars, denial of asylum, structural adjustment programmes, policies of meta-borders, and regime-change campaigns that provoked in the first place the current phase of refugee and forced migration flows. The *Responsibility to Protect* (R2P) reserved all powers for the big bosses of the world and their institutions of global governance, and had tasked the hapless UN agencies with "humanitarian" responsibility.[41] Now when the R2P backfired, the global consultation process remained silent on the complicity of the global governance regime busy with humanitarian tasks. It is clearly an act of bad faith. Humanitarianism is like the food for force-feeding coming out of a machine as in the Chaplin film, *Modern Times*.

And where does the postcolonial voice figure in this cacophony of anguished statements for humanitarian protection of the victims of forced migration? Indeed if India is taken as reference, the postcolonial states were most materialistic through the consultation process, as if they had seen through the cacophony the issues at stake. Thus, the Indian concerns were anxiety about "the proposed Global Refugee Forum . . . as a global mechanism for international cooperation, implementation and follow-up of the compact in terms of its specific mandate, working modalities, funding and its relation with other extant mechanisms among others".[42] These anxieties were also about protecting sovereignty and thus India's freedom to decide on the matter of hospitality case by case – exactly as she had learnt from her erstwhile colonial master. Thus, India said,

> We recognize the fact that a number of States not parties to the international refugee instruments have shown a generous approach to hosting refugees and that the commitments and obligations of those who are party to the Refugee Convention and its protocol and those who are not, differ.

> That the broad principles contained in the 'Agenda for humanity' and the 'Grand bargain' commitments made by UNHCR, particularly those related to bringing greater transparency, progressively increasing allocation of the program resources to national and local responders, expanding investments in institutional capacity building of national partners to help reinforce them and reducing the cost of procurement and logistics are important guiding principles. . . . Further, we would like to see greater clarity and consistency in the definition and usage of important terms in the text. Like for instance, the word 'Refugees' itself.

More crucially, the compact would be legally non-binding. Thus, India appealed,

> the text could possibly be more explicit in stating that: i. The central objective of the Compact is to respond to large movements of refugees and protracted refugee situations and to ease the related burden of the host countries in most need of international support in the spirit of solidarity; ii. The national ownership of the implementation process and related capacity building and the provisioning of the requisite means and support by the international community would be critical to humanitarian action under the compact; iii. Both the implementation and follow-up of the compact would be in keeping with its apolitical and legally non-binding nature. iv. And the catalytic and supportive role of UNHCR would be consistent with its mandate on refugees.[43]

India was concerned with the realistic possibility of "the 'Grand bargain' commitments related to funding and strengthening of the institutional capacity of local responders among other", which "as endorsed by UNHCR, must be retained." This was because

> More than 4/5th of the world refugees continue to be hosted by developing countries which have constraints in terms of capacity and resource as well as pressing priorities and challenges, relating to both security and development. Some of them are not party to the international refugee law. Yet they host a large number of refugees and face protracted refugee situations.[44]

In the context of follow-up and review, India sought more detailed information on the proposed Global Refugee Forum in terms of its specific mandate, working modalities, funding and its relation with other extant mechanisms among others, and reiterated that all follow-up and review must be fully cognisant of the existing refugee burden and capacities of countries as well as their rights and obligations under international refugee law, and that the follow up must be voluntary in keeping with the "legally non-binding nature of the Compact itself."[45]

The figure of the refugee and the migrant was thus up against two realities – the reality of a global economy and the reality of sovereignty. The refugee was thus never to be a subject of maximum justice, but historically conditioned justice. We can term this as "minimal justice".

In this bleak backdrop of dissociation of power and responsibility, the UNICEF as if in a last burst of humanitarian emotion cried out,

> This is the moment for States to ensure that the provisions of the New York Declaration for Refugees and Migrants and the Convention on the Rights of the Child are fully realised for all children, especially those most at risk through no fault of their own.[46]

Towards a technocratic mode

Until now this chapter has shown how in producing a global gaze the roadmap is as important as the task of redefining and reproducing the humanitarian. However, there is another factor in producing the global. It is the vision of a technocratic mode of protection. Continuous improvements in successive drafts have been made to detail out various technocratic means and modes towards refugee protection. This is not surprising given the fact that political voices have been closed out from the beginning, diversity of experiences have been ignored, human rights have been replaced by humanitarianism, the place of claims and justice given over to pity, kindness, and compassion, and the principle of plural dialogues, decentralisation, and international legal pluralism for the task of protection has been replaced by technocratic modalities appearing as the central mode of salvation. If in the nineteenth century humanitarianism was about saving the damned souls, and in the twentieth century about saving damned bodies, in the neo-liberal twenty-first century it is going to be about finding and refining technocratic, market-based, digitally enabled modes of saving the damned world from humanitarian disasters. And this is how it will become part of a global developmental agenda. The problem now is about finding the right mode and the right instrument resilient in the face of disasters. In this technocratic turn, which is clearly away from earlier dominantly legal turn in humanitarianism post-1951, getting the right platform and the right protocol for saving the world now gets the place of honour.

One consequence of the technocratic turn is that politics is even more effaced from the refugee and migrant question. Let us take the example of race. There was only one reference to the word "race" in the final draft of the Global Compact (that too, a customary reference).[47] The deployment of the word was in the same context as in the first draft (paragraph 12), second draft (paragraph 10), and third draft (paragraph 9).[48] This singular reference in each of the three drafts, and same in nature, was in the context of non-discrimination only. The drafts never realised in their technocratic obsession that race is one of the pillars of the structure of forced migration. Same was with another key word "religion". Again the word is to be found in the same paragraph and context in the final draft and the three previous drafts. It is a stunning near-omission in the background of the global discourse on terror, which has used race and religion (often mixing them) to unleash wars on countries and peoples, and counter-terrorism logic to deny refugees and other victims of forced migration protection, and immigrant labour their rights. It is a paradox: What the philosopher calls the "colour line" is an intrinsic part of refugee experience and at the same time is pushed to the margin in the refugee protection discourse.

On the other hand, the compact almost legitimises the discourse on terror that denies the rights of the refugees and other victims. The second draft said,

> Security considerations and international protection are complementary. The primary responsibility for safety and security lies with States which can benefit from the promotion of national integrated approaches that protect refugees and their human rights, while safeguarding national security, including from a counter-terrorism perspective. The legitimate security concerns of host States are fully recognized, as well as the need to uphold the civilian and humanitarian character of asylum.[49]

The final draft stepped back from the political blunder and reformulated in the following way the point under the heading (1.3), "Safety and Security":

> Security considerations and international protection are complementary. The primary responsibility for safety and security lies with States, which can benefit from the promotion of national integrated approaches that protect refugees and their human rights, while safeguarding national security. The legitimate security concerns of host States are fully recognized, as well as the importance of upholding the civilian and humanitarian character of international protection and applicable international law, both in emergency and protracted situations. At the request of concerned States, and in full respect of national laws and policies, UNHCR and relevant stakeholders will contribute resources and expertise to support protection-sensitive arrangements for timely security screening and health assessments of new arrivals. Support will also be provided for capacity development of relevant authorities, for instance on international refugee protection and exclusion criteria; strengthening of international efforts to prevent and combat sexual and gender-based violence, as well as trafficking and smuggling in persons; capacity development for community-oriented policing and access to justice; and the identification and separation of fighters and combatants at border entry points or as early as possible after arrival in line with relevant protection safeguards. The development and implementation of programmes for protection and assistance to children formerly associated with armed groups will also be supported.
>
> *(Paragraphs 56–57)*

Yet precisely on these grounds of security, health screening, "identification and separation of fighters and combatants at border entry points or as early as possible after arrival", and "legitimate security concerns of host States", the rights of the refugees have been denied. Not incidentally, these are the marks of the fundamental phenomenological principle of race. The refugee is the carrier of race, and this is one of the ways in which migration today appears as "crisis". If blood in the not-so-ancient time determined race, religion today often acts as a determinant of race. The entire refugee protection regime from its inception has been guilty of maintaining near silence over race as a fundamental fault line in the structure of population flows, and hence has never noticed how racism has transformed over time to create newer and newer forms of boundaries that the migrants and refugees have to perpetually cross to reach the never finally reachable destinations of "safety and security" – the two words of concern of the Global Compact. The colour of the skin has been supplemented by the colour of religion today, and this became more than evident in the first full-scale race war of the neo-liberal age – the Balkan wars and the Rwandan genocide in the nineties of the last century. Race wars proliferated later under the cover of war on terror. Technocratic solutions – such as setting up a global refugee forum, support platforms, a multi-stakeholder and partnership approach, early warning system, preparedness and contingency planning, improvement of immediate reception arrangements for refugees, improved modes to monitor safety and security measures, similarly improved procedures of registration and documentation, procedures for voluntary repatriation, resettlement and complementary pathways for admission to third countries, modes of local integration along with other local solutions, intensive data collection and management, and finally better social care such as education, health, accommodation, energy needs, resource management, nutrition, etc.[50] – cannot change the facts on the ground where refugees live, say in Idomeni, Chittagong, Calais, Darfur, and other places, or the way refugees and migrants are received and detained or turned back on the borders of the metropolitan world. These technocratic solutions in an attempt to resituate in concrete terms the various historical discourses of humanitarianism from which the administrative modes of governance have emerged[51] at once introduce into our contemporary neo-liberal time the infamous figure of an alien, someone belonging to an alien race and embodying the historical facts of invasion, appropriation of lands, and the enslavement of men, women, and children.[52]

Given the reciprocity of determination of race and the status of the shelter seeker, one may ask, if the unintended fate of GCR will be the suppression of the contemporary history of racism under the discourse of care and protection. Of course we still have to locate concretely the secret relation between the ideology of humanitarianism, universalism, and the power of technological mode of care. How can humanitarianism that naturally essays into universalism become dependent on global technological power? A detailed answer is not possible here, but a short answer is necessary: Care, kindness, and hospitality form collectively the most accepted route for people's desire for justice for the wronged, deprived, and the victim (we are leaving out here the question of punishment). They belong to what can be called *sentiment*, a highly developed emotion, a "thick feeling" – a feeling without an object. Yet sentiments – powerful as they may be – are not adequate as governing tools, which we conceptualise as "applied ethics". They need a coherent formation, known as *ideology* – the ideology of going beyond boundaries, of becoming cosmopolitan in order to be humanitarian. And yet again, ideologies call for institutions – therefore global – to give shape to universalist ideologies, of which refugee care is one. Institutional power operates through specific modes that must become technological to give shape to institutional mandates and agenda. The time of the last stage in the mutation of sentiment is also the time when emotion must die.[53] The more global is the operation of ideology, the less will be the place of sentiment. Universalism must produce distinguishing categories, categories of choice, categories of determination, categories of differential care, and categories of tools meant to enable life.[54] Race and universalism or race and humanitarianism are the ever-quarrelling couple. It was true of the missionaries of the nineteenth century; it is true of the missionaries of the neo-liberal time. Humanitarian truth must find its reality in the relation it has with politics.

In this age when the range of humanitarianism extends from humanitarian bombings to humanitarian protection, responsibility and burden sharing in order to be effective has to acquire technical solutions, such as mode and determination of the quantum of monetary support to host countries and communities, providing political, material, and technical resources; help to prepare countries and agencies for large movements of refugees and to provide refugee protection; expanding access to third-country solutions including resettlement and complementary pathways,[55] such as regional mobility schemes, support to emerging resettlement countries, and identifying and involving relevant stakeholders according to their respective capacity – all these so that "burden" sharing becomes "responsibility" sharing.

In this way, the new humanitarian tools can assure that refugees will be no longer considered as burden but responsibility of the society.[56] This has been at the heart of the crucial strategy of "Comprehensive Refugee Response Framework" (CRRF), which means a globally coordinated policy involving tasks of mobilising greater resources through innovative approaches, ensuring humanitarian assistance through local systems, education to build on sustainable development goals, concrete support for national health systems, energy and environment protection, and strengthening economic opportunities for refugees and members of local communities through structural analysis of and support to local labour markets and access by refugees to financial products and services. The CRRF echoes the sustainable development goals of development.[57] This is maximum humanitarianism – when humanitarianism removes the opprobrium of "refugees as burden" and reorients the task of protection as "refugees as subjects of development". Similarly migrants also become subjects of various strategies of protection and development.[58] A cursory glance at the topics of IOM theme papers will bear this transformation of the migrant as a figure of mobility into a figure of risk, resilience, and development. Some of the topics are assisted voluntary return and reintegration, border management, climate change and environment degradation, smuggling and counter-smuggling, trafficking in persons, remittances, readmission, integration and social cohesion, expansion of mobility channels, family reunification, health, detention of immigrants, migrants from countries in crisis, management of migration statistics, responsibilities and obligations of the migrants, and facilitation of safe, orderly, and regular migration.[59] These issues mark the path of development. The migrant must negotiate these issues, and hence be resilient.

Rights and the global protection agenda

The 1951 Convention is a rights-based document, yet the Convention does not contain a charter of refugee rights or suggestion towards the formulation of any such charter. The Convention also cannot be considered as a manifesto of rights of the migrants and refugees. It is a Convention primarily enjoining certain obligations on states with regard to refugees and asylum seekers from which international law and municipal laws the world over have tried to deduce certain refugee rights. The introductory note to the text of the Convention of course says that the latter is

> Grounded in Article 14 of the Universal Declaration of Human Rights 1948, which recognizes the right of persons to seek asylum from persecution in other countries, the United Nations Convention relating to the Status of Refugees, adopted in 1951, is the centrepiece of international refugee protection today,

and further, "The Convention is both a status and rights-based instrument and is underpinned by a number of fundamental principles, most notably non-discrimination, non-penalization and non-refoulement." In scattered places in the text rights of the refugees are mentioned, such as,

> The Contracting States shall give sympathetic consideration to assimilating the rights of all refugees with regard to wage-earning employment to those of nationals, and in particular of those refugees who have entered their territory pursuant to programmes of labour recruitment or under immigration schemes.
> *(Article 17.3)*

In this situation, rights of the refugees become a matter of jurisprudence, a continuous tussle between legal and human rights activists and the states, and protection becomes a matter of following legal norms and certain protocols. In situations like the European migration "crisis" refugee rights became an anachronism. Such situation shows on one hand the ever-increasing demand on humanitarian alertness and response and on the other hand the ineffectiveness of the half-hearted approach of a global body such as the UNHCR to the issue of rights. Yet as the overwhelming presence of humanitarian approach reaches a point of emptying the approach of all humanitarian content, the rights question creeps back to the political question of migration in contemporary global history.

This was evident in the report of 2016 of the Special Rapporteur on the human rights of migrants, François Crépeau, in accordance with General Assembly resolution 70/147. The report, "Human Rights of Migrants" while concluding referred to the events in the Andaman Sea, the Asia-Pacific region, Central America, the Mediterranean Sea and the Middle East, and suggested that the

> The global compact should recognize the need for a stronger human rights-based normative and institutional framework for migration at the United

Nations, which will, in turn, have a positive effect on informal migration governance outside of the United Nations. . ., and recommended assistance to States for developing strong and effective labour law frameworks (including on labour inspection, unionization and collective bargaining), protecting the rights of all workers, including migrant workers, regardless of status, and in ensuring effective access to justice for migrants whose labour rights or human rights have been violated.[60]

It also took particular care to suggest the integration of the IOM into the United Nations system, with a process leading to the updating of its Constitution in order to include in it a strong human rights protection mandate in favour of migrants. Significantly, amidst the din over trafficking, it suggested measures to ensure a robust gender analysis of the difference in the impacts of policies on men and women, with special attention to the ways in which restrictions on women's mobility as a means of protection violate their rights and create favourable conditions for smuggling networks to thrive, including the use of a gender lens at all stages and in all aspects of the discussion as specific consideration of gender in the context of bilateral agreements, detention/deportation and readmission/repatriation is also crucial. Finally, it spoke of ensuring

> that the detention of migrants is always a measure of last resort, permissible only when reasonable, necessary and proportionate, decided on a case-by-case basis, and enforced for the shortest possible period of time; develop rights-based alternatives to detention for most cases; and ensure that migrant children and families with children are never, ever, detained for reasons relating to their administrative immigration status.[61]

Yet with all these pleas and arguments to make the rights approach central to the global compact, the global crisis of migration has been seen as a crisis of the prevailing migration management mode in the wake of massive and mixed flows. Hence, improvement of management mode and new strategies get the pride of place in the strategy laid out by the compact. The return of rights to the discourse of a global compact is thus due not to law, but to the persistence of massive and mixed migratory flows, whose unruly nature nullifies the well-laid plans for safe and orderly migration. These flows continuously pound on the walls of the protected states and regions. The displacements are now mostly protracted. It is not that the policies of the UNHCR and other similar institutions do not impact migration, but our global mandates singularly ignore the interface and entanglements of autonomy of migration, state control policies and practices, and global governance regimes. The inherently subversive and oppositional nature of migration expressed in various acts of freedom has been the greatest worry for the refugee regime, and the reactive nature of the migratory flows as resistance to control practices is also matched by the fact that the migrant resistance anticipates many of the control measures. Thus, as some have suggested, "the relation between control and escape is one of temporal difference: escape comes first".[62] Or, one can say that the migrant autonomy is already "entangled in and regulated by control".[63] Well thought out policies and measures meet as adversary migration practices; both anticipate each other; and the end result is an enormous difficulty to make migration an orderly and regulated process.[64]

Claims to justice have emerged in this situation. These claims now confront the humanitarian order. They create a new politics of rights, different from the ones recognised in the Convention of 1951 or the balancing acts of the UNHCR and the IOM. In the post–Second World War era rights were connected with welfare and a regime of Keynesianism. But Keynesianism collapsed in the 1980s. The theory of income and employment buttressed by a welfare-oriented stable state developed major cracks. Protection of citizens and aliens through welfare schemes promulgated in the global Keynesian age increasingly proved difficult. Now protection strategies have to be market enabled to save the refugees, and hence the idea of reorienting protection policies as sustainable development strategy has developed. As refugees become subjects of development, welfare declines. Wars increase. Population movements become even more daring and desperate.

Population movements as an issue of global governance acquire global importance because population movements form one of the most essential parts of population management of societies. They influence the supply of labour, its productivity, morbidity pattern, mortality rate, in short various issues affecting the reproduction of labour. They carry the ghost of Malthus. At the same time population movements can no longer be governed well by making neat distinctions between refugee and migrants; these movements are now mixed and cannot be categorised anymore. And, yet they can be governed only be being categorised according to policies and strategies.[65] It is not only a paradox, it also produces a crisis. The crisis is thus of the refugee and migration regime, which wants to put order and rules on migratory flows, while population movements are not concerned with the aims of a migration regime. It is thus a contradictory situation.[66] The dissociation of law and claims forms the context in which the rights politics reorients itself; and the GCR occupies an awkward position in this confrontation between a regulatory mode of humanitarianism and the autonomous claim to move and secure justice. The GCR is an evidence of the new situation and wants to address this new situation. That is its promise. The global humanitarian regime has been preparing for this turn for some years, particularly since 2013 when the General Assembly passed the "Declaration of the High-level Dialogue on International Migration and Development" (Resolution 68/4). But, building on humanitarian principles and a global ambition to do well for the world, it cannot venture into the *other scene* – the scene of unregulated flows, claims to autonomy and rights as the form of justice, local modes of protection, legal pluralism, scores of bilateral treaties to save refugees and restore citizenship to groups of stateless population, older histories of protection in the great decades of decolonisation, and the variegated histories of care and reconciliation. Hence the humanitarian promise appears to be limited. That is in fact the paradox. "The arc of protection" becomes increasingly narrow against which the angels of protection have to continuously fight.[67]

The paradox cannot be solved with globalisation of protection strategy, inclusion of business houses to broaden the capacity base for protection, privatisation of care, and fine tuning of strategies and policies. Indeed, one may ask, if these were the answers, what was the question? Why did we need the compacts in the first place?[68]

Notes

1 For instance, the League Covenant did not have any specific provision of international aid and protection of refugees, but political considerations of aid, expediency, conciliation, and humanitarian sympathies played crucial role in deciding the character and extent of the responsibility the League organs were to undertake for protection of refugees. This was admitted by observers even during the life of the League. See, Louise W. Holborn, "The League of Nations and the Refugee Problem", *The Annals of the American Academy of Political and Social Science*, Volume 203, May 1999, pp. 124–135. The League found its defence in its Covenant's Preamble, which declared the promotion of international cooperation through maintenance of justice as one of the goals.
2 www.un.org/en/ga/search/view_doc.asp?symbol=A/RES/71/1 (accessed on 1 July 2018), paragraph 4, pp. 1–2.
3 Already as the new century began, the UN had started looking into migration issues from the developmental angle (International Migration Report, 2002, New York: United Nations, Department of Economic and Social Affairs, Population Division, 2002, doc. ST/ESA/SER.A/220). The Report noted with satisfaction, "In his proposals for strengthening the United nations Organisation (Report of the Secretary General, A/57/387) the Secretary General of the United Nations stressed, 'it is time to take a more comprehensive look at the various dimensions of the migration issue, which now involves hundreds of millions of people and affects countries of origin, transit, and destination. We need to understand better the causes of international flows of people and their complex interrelationships with development'". – Anthony M. Messina and Gallya Lahav (eds.), *The Migration Reader: Exploring Politics and Policies* (Boulder, CO and New Delhi: Lynne Rienner Pub., and Viva Books Ltd., 2006), Chapter 2.3 (pp. 24–30, 25).
4 Kevin Appleby, "Strengthening the Global Refugee Protection System: Recommendations for the Global Compact on Refugees", *Journal on Migration and Human Security*, Volume 5 (4), 2017, pp. 780–799, 797.
5 www.unhcr.org/a-new-deal-for-refugees.html (accessed on 5 February 2019).
6 It never occurred to the IOM that data collection can be counterproductive for a large section of the migrants. See for instance, Frank Laczko of the IOM Global Migration Data Analysis Centre, "Improving Data on International Migration – Towards Agenda 2030 and the Global Compact on Migration", IOM Discussion paper, https://gmdac.iom.int/sites/default/files/presentations/Laczko.pdf (accessed on 17 August 2018); also https://migrationdataportal.org/themes/global-compact-migration (accessed on 17 August 2018).
7 Summarised, www.kaldorcentre.unsw.edu.au/publication/2018-global-compacts-refugees-and-migration (accessed on 16 August 2018).
8 "Making Migration Work for All", Report of the Secretary-General to the 72nd session of the General Assembly, 12 December 2017, https://reliefweb.int/sites/reliefweb.int/files/resources/N1743962.pdf (accesses on 20 August 2018).
9 *Ibid.*, critics however pointed out that this call for respect for borders was a false one, as the question was, "Why Should Immigrants 'Respect Our Borders'? The West Never Respected Theirs", and then, "Immigration quotas should be based on how much the host country has ruined other countries." – Suketu Mehta, *New York Times*, 7 June 2019, www.nytimes.com/2019/06/07/opinion/immigration-reparations.html?smid=nytcore-ios-share (accessed on 7 September 2019); see also, Suketu Mehta, *This Land Is Our Land: An Immigrant's Manifesto* (London: Jonathan Cape, 2019), in particular part II.
10 The Berne Initiative: International Agenda for Migration Management, www.iom.int/berne-initiative (accessed on 5 August 2018).

11 The UN Secretary General's Report, titled, "In Safety and Dignity: Addressing Large Movements and Refugees and Migrants" to the General Assembly (70th session, 21 April 2016) made considerable references to the IDPs, and had said, "To incorporate the Guiding Principles on Internal Displacement into national laws and policies and fully implement those policies to protect those who have been forced from their homes but remain within national borders", paragraph 101.2, https://refugeesmigrants.un.org/sites/default/files/in_safety_and_dignity_-_addressing_large_movements_of_refugees_and_migrants.pdf (accessed on 11 August 2018); however by the time the Declaration was finalised the issue of IDPs had receded to the margins. See on this, Elizabeth Ferris, "In Search of Commitments: The 2016 Refugee Summits", Andrew and Renata Kaldor Centre for International Refugee Law, Policy Brief 3, UNSW, November 2016; in her report on refugee summits, she rhetorically asked while noticing the absence of the issue of the IDPs, "Where, Oh, Where are the IDPs?" p. 21.
12 I have raised this question elsewhere also; see R. Samaddar, "The Global Gaze of care, Protection and Power" (*Refuge*, forthcoming, 2020–2021).
13 "Migration Compact Support MPTF: Financial Reporting on Sources and Uses of Funds for the period ending 31 December 2017", UNDP, 2018.
14 https://refugeesmigrants.un.org/sites/default/files/work_plan_gcm.pdf (accessed on 1 August 2018), p. 2.
15 As set out in the New York Declaration, the High Commissioner would include the global compact on refugees in the annual report to the General Assembly in 2018, so that it could be considered by the General Assembly during its seventy-third session, in conjunction with its annual resolution on UNHCR. See A/RES/71/1; for further information, www.unhcr.org/newyorkdeclaration; the roadmap and other background information available at www.unhcr.org/refugeecompact (accessed on 1 August 2018).
16 www.unhcr.org/newyorkdeclaration (accessed on 1 August 2018).
17 www.unhcr.org/events/conferences/58e625aa7/towards-global-compact-refugees-roadmap.html (accessed on 11 August 2018).
18 www.unhcr.org/58d135517.pdf (accessed on 15 August 2018).
19 www.unhcr.org/events/conferences/58e625aa7/towards-global-compact-refugees-roadmap.html (accessed on 11 August 2018); the concept of resilience played a big part in the framework of the compact on migration, and resilience needed technical means to build up. Thus, the IOM study paper, "Migration, Risk, and Resilience in the Context of Sudden and Slow-Onset Disaster", rolled out the technical road to build resilience of the migrants. It implied four priorities: (a) Understanding disaster risk, (b) Strengthening disaster risk governance to manage disaster risk, (c) Investing in disaster risk reduction for resilience, and (d) Enhancing disaster preparedness for effective response and to "build back better" in recovery, rehabilitation, and reconstruction (p. 2). It further meant investment in risk analysis and disaster prevention, developing disaster risk reduction policies, improving capacity to anticipate, ensuring the inclusion of international migrants in disaster preparedness for response and recovery action, and improving disaster resilience in recovery and reconstruction. (pp. 4–5), www.iom.int/sites/default/files/our_work/ODG/GCM/IOM-Thematic-Paper-Migration-Risk-and-Resilience-in-the-Context.pdf (accessed on 17 August 2018). IOM thematic papers deserve separate study in the context of this paper; however constraints of space make such an analysis here difficult.
20 "Migration, Risk, and Resilience in the Context of Sudden and Slow-Onset Disaster", p. 3.
21 Jessica Brandt and Lucy Earle commented in "The Global Compact for Refugees: Bringing Mayors to the Table", *Brookings Policy Brief*, January 2018,

> Displacement is increasingly protracted. Today, those who take flight are more likely than ever before to remain in exile for extended periods. At the end of last year, more than two-thirds of all refugees, some 11 million of them, were in a protracted refugee situation – one in which 25,000 or more refugees of the same nationality have been in exile for at least five consecutive years, with no immediate prospect of finding a durable solution.

Figures based on UNHCR, "Global Trends: Forced Displacement in 2016", UNHCR, Geneva, 2017, www.refworld.org/docid/594aa38e0.html.

22 Africa stands out as an instance the potential of regional initiatives for protection; see, Robtel Neajai Pailey, "How Africa Can Adopt a Pan-African Migration and Development Agenda", *The Africa Policy Journal*, 25 February 2019, https://apj.hkspublications.org/how-africa-can-adopt-a-pan-african-migration-and-development-agenda/ (accessed on 2 September 2019).

23 Stephen Castles discussed the role of immigrant labour in Nazi Germany and post-war France, where immigrant workers accounted for at least 15 per cent of the workforce. See his article "Migration", in David Theo Goldberg and John Solomos (eds.), *A Companion to Racial and Ethnic Studies* (Oxford: Blackwell Publishers, 2002), pp. 571–572.

24 As we showed in Chapter 4 (also n. 37, Chapter 4), for long, it was a case of political opportunity, but economic closure; now it is a case of economic opening (entry in the informal labour market), but political closure.

25 www.unhcr.org/5a60b9409.pdf (accessed on 15 August 2018).

26 refugeecompact@unhcr.org andwww.unhcr.org/fr/writtencontributions (accessed on 15 August 2018).

27 www.unhcr.org/publications/legal/5b1558104/non-paper-asylum-capacity-support-group-4-june-2018.html (accessed on 15 August 2018).

28 All citations in this paragraph are from, www.unhcr.org/dach/wp-content/uploads/sites/27/2017/07/BringingTheNewYorkDeclarationToLife.pdf (accessed on 15 August 2018).

29 "Global Migration: Resilient Cities at the Forefront", www.100resilientcities.org/turning-migration-challenges-into-opportunities-to-build-resilience/ (accessed on 15 August 2018).

30 *Ibid.*

31 All citations in this paragraph are from www.unhcr.org/5a33d4447.pdf (accessed on 11 December 2018).

32 Read, Saskia Sassen, *Expulsions: Brutality and Complexity in the Global Economy* (Cambridge: Harvard University Press, 2014).

33 On the histories of three of the well-known of postcolonial cities (Kolkata, Mumbai, Delhi) marked with massive migrant presence, R. Samaddar (ed.), *Migrant and the Neoliberal City* (Hyderabad: Orient Blackswan, 2018).

34 Costas Douzinas, "Cities of Refuge", www.opendemocracy.net/can-europe-make-it/costas-douzinas/cities-of-refuge (accessed on 12 April 2016); the idea originally comes from an ancient tale that speaks of the cities of refuge as part of the distribution of the Promised Land among the twelve tribes of Israel. Only one tribe, the Levites, was not given land to develop. The Mosaic Law stated that anyone who committed a murder was to be put to death. But for unintentional deaths, God set aside these cities to which the murderer could flee for refuge, and would be safe from the avenger, the family member charged with avenging the victim's death. The establishment of those privileged sanctuaries among the cities of the Levites is probably traceable to the idea that the Levites would be the most suitable and impartial judges. The cities of refuge were imagined in the model of Christ as places where sinners would find a refuge from the destroyer of souls. Christ provided safety to all who come to him for refuge from sin and its punishment. On the current idea and the movement of "cities of refuge", see Jonathan Mark Darling, *Cities of Refuge: Asylum and the Politics of Hospitality*, Ph.d dissertation, Durham University, 2008, http://etheses.dur.ac.uk/2228/1/2228_238.pdf (accessed on 25 July 2018); J. Derrida, *On Cosmopolitanism and Forgiveness*, trans. M. Dooley and M Hughes (London: Routledge, 2001); also K. Koser, "Social Networks and the Asylum Cycle", *International Migration Review*, Volume 31(3), 1997, pp. 591–611; on cities becoming places of refuge, Jessica Brandt and Lucy Earle, "The Global Compact for Refugees: Bringing Mayors to the Table", *Brookings Policy Brief*, January 2018.

35 Evidence of this sanitisation of the "right to the city" is to be found in the US government's move to identify cities to establish "facilities" for unaccompanied

migrant kids. CBS news, www.msn.com/en-us/news/us/government-explores-5-cities-for-new-possible-unaccompanied-migrant-kids-facilities/ (accessed on 5 September 2019).

36 Four largest international NGOs (Danish Refugee Council, Save the Children, Norwegian Refugee Council and Rescue) made a joint submission on "Key Recommendations to a Final Draft of the Global Compact on Refugees". In distinct acknowledgement of the reality, they proposed that the Global Compact should recognise that the focus has to be

> be context-specific. It would include host States; where appropriate in a solutions context, the country of origin; regional neighbours; and other cooperating States that are engaged and committed to making significant contributions (including financial, material and technical assistance, and third-country solutions) as well as representatives from the refugee and host community populations.

and further,

> The programme of action therefore envisages a mix of solutions, adapted to the specific context and circumstances of displacement and taking into account the absorption capacity, level of development and demographic situation of different countries, as well as assessed preferences of individual refugees themselves.

https://drc.ngo/media/4585168/ngo-4-recommendations-to-a-final-gcr_may18.pdf (accessed on 1 August 2018) and www.unhcr.org/5b3c8eaa7.pdf (accessed on 1 August 2018).

37 In the preparation for of the compact on safe, orderly, and regular migration, several institutions were likewise involved. However in both cases, primarily global institutions were thinking globally, and where countries were involved, mostly Ambassadors were involved in the discussions. Besides there were regional meetings where prominent NGOs were involved. All these were steps towards an intergovernmental conference to adopt the global compact. UN General Assembly Resolution at the 72nd session, 24 September 2017. Indeed the resolution (72/244) went onto extreme procedural details to make the conference for the adoption of the compact possible, www.un.org/en/ga/search/view_doc.asp?symbol=A/RES/72/244 (accessed on 16 August 2018).

38 "Shared Responsibility, Shared Humanity", *Communiqué from the International Refugee Congress*, 2018, http://jhrmk.org/index.php/2018/05/18/international-refugee-congress-2018-shared-responsibility-shared-humanity/?lang=en (accessed on 13 August 2018).

39 *Ibid.*, p. 2.

40 "The Global Compact on Refugees", Zero Draft (as at 31 January 2018), p. 14, Paragraphs 76–77, https://reliefweb.int/sites/reliefweb.int/files/resources/Zero-Draft.pdf (accessed on 13 August 2018).

41 There is a voluminous literature on the "Responsibility to Protect". On some of the reports, http://responsibilitytoprotect.org/ICISS%20Report.pdf (2001), www.files.ethz.ch/isn/181082/R2P.pdf (2011), and www.globalr2p.org/media/files/libyaandr2poccasionalpaper-1.pdf (2012).

42 "Statement by India made on Agenda item 2 (Part III.A – Programme of action: Mechanisms for burden and responsibility sharing) during the fourth round of formal consultations on the Global compact on Refugees", delivered by Sadre Alam, First Secretary, www.pmindiaun.org/pages.php?id=1648 (accessed on 12 August 2018).

43 www.unhcr.org/5b2ba4e27.pdf (accessed on 12 August 2018); indeed the scepticism of India was clear as she emphasised the need to

> follow up of the commitments of Donors to share burden and responsibility and the 'Grand Bargain' commitments endorsed by UNHCR; (and) flow up of the support provided to Countries of origin and of their commitment to share responsibility,

address the root causes and find durable solutions for voluntary return of refugees in safety and dignity.

Statement by the Indian Mission, Geneva during the Second round of formal consultations on the Global compact on refugees (Agenda item 3) – Delivered by Dr. Sadre Alam, First Secretary", www.pmindiaun.org/pages.php?id= 1627 (accessed on 12 August 2018).

44 www.pmindiaun.org/pages.php?id=1647 (accessed on 12 August 2018).
45 All citations in this paragraph are from "Statement by India made on Agenda item 6 (Part IV – Follow-up and review arrangements) during the fourth round of formal consultations on the Global compact on Refugees", Delivered by Dr. Sadre Alam, First Secretaryhttp://pmindiaun.org/pages.php?id=1790 (accessed on 12 August 2018); India's stand becomes clearer in the context of her growing activism in humanitarian assistance. See, Claudia Meier and C.S.R. Murthy, "India's Growing Involvement in Humanitarian Assistance", Berlin, Global Public Policy Institute, Research Paper 13, 2011, www.gppi.net/2011/03/14/indias-growing-involvement-in-humanitarian-assistance (accessed on 12 January 2019).
46 "The Time for Action Children Uprooted Is Now", *UNICEF*, 8 June 2018, www.unhcr.org/5a4374d47.pdf (accessed on 15 August 2018).
47 Against this background, the global compact complements ongoing United Nations endeavours in the areas of prevention, peace, security, sustainable development, migration and peacebuilding. All States and relevant stakeholders are called on to tackle the root causes of large refugee situations, including through heightened international efforts to prevent and resolve conflict; to uphold the Charter of the United Nations, international law, including international humanitarian law, as well as the rule of law at the national and international levels; to promote, respect, protect and fulfil human rights and fundamental freedoms for all; and to end exploitation and abuse, as well as discrimination of any kind on the basis of race, colour, sex, language, religion, political or other opinion, national or social origin, property, birth, disability, age, or other status. The international community as a whole is also called on to support efforts to alleviate poverty, reduce disaster risks, and provide development assistance to countries of origin, in line with the 2030 Agenda for Sustainable Development and other relevant frameworks.

Final Draft of the Global Compact on Refugees, 26 June 2018, paragraph 9, www.unhcr.org/5b3295167.pdf (accessed on 15 August 2018).

48 For the first draft, www.unhcr.org/5aa2b3287.pdf (accessed on 15 August 2018), second draft, www.unhcr.org/events/conferences/5ae758d07/official-version-draft-2-global-compact-refugees-30-april-2018.html (accessed on 15 August 2018), and third draft, www.unhcr.org/events/conferences/5b1579427/official-version-draft-3-global-compact-refugees-4-june-2018.html (accessed on 15 August 2018).
49 Second draft, paragraph 59, p. 12.
50 The changes in the successive drafts are instructive. For fine changes with regard to solutions, see, "Global Compact on Refugees: From draft 2 (30 April) to draft 3 (4 June), Explanatory Memorandum on Main Changes", www.unhcr.org/5b1579b17.pdf (accessed on 16 August 2018).
51 The IOM vision statement explicitly accords importance to a proper governance framework to realise safe and orderly migration. See, "IOM Vision on the Global Compact on Migration", paragraphs 6–10, www.iom.int/sites/default/files/our_work/ODG/GCM/IOM-vision-on-the-global-compact-on-migration-13April2017.pdf (accessed on 17 August 2018).
52 On the relation between race and alien-hood, Michel Foucault, "*Society Must be Defended*", Lectures at the College de France, 1975–76, trans. David Macey (New York:

Picador, 2003); on the relation between race, universalism, and migration, Etienne Balibar, "Is There a Neo-Racism?" and "Racism and Nationalism" in Etienne Balibar and Immanuel Wallerstein, *Race, Nation, Class: Ambiguous Identities* (London: Verso, 1991), chapter 1, pp. 17–28 and chapter 3, pp. 37–67; also, R. Samaddar, "Pangs of Ambiguity: *Race, Nation, Class* Deciphered for India", in Manuel Bojadzijev and Katrin Klingan (eds.), *Balibar / Wallertstein's "Race, nation, Class: Rereading a Dialogue for Our Times* (Hamburg and Berlin: Argument Verlagand Haus der Kulturen der Welt), pp. 171–198.

53 In the context of refugee protection, I discussed the relation in detail in *The Politics of Dialogue: Living Under the Geopolitical Histories of War and Peace* (Aldershot: Ashgate, 2004), chapter 9, "The Non-dialogic World of the Humanitarian", pp. 271–310.

54 The Summary of the High Commissioner's Dialogue on Protection Challenges 2017: "Towards a Global Compact on Refugees", 12–13 December 2017, Thematic session 4: Contemporary protection challenges, admitted the reality of the overwhelming presence of categorizing strategy, and said,

> It is important not to adopt a 'categorization' approach to addressing specific needs, or to fall into the trap of seeking to identify which groups are the 'most vulnerable'; holistic and intersectional approaches work best. At the same time, prioritization of those who are least protected, including women at risk, children and the disabled, was urged. Decisive measures to address the root causes of displacement built on cooperation, including by regional and municipal stakeholders as well as development actors, were called for. Several participants also urged more collaboration between UN agencies.

The paradox thus remains. See www.unhcr.org/5a5890137.pdf (accessed on 16 August 2018).

55 The technical nature of the idea of "complimentary pathways" will be clear from the way the concept paper for thematic discussion IV (measures to be taken in pursuit of solutions) and thematic discussion V (issues that cut across all four substantive sections of the comprehensive refugee responses, and overarching issues) in the discussion on "Towards a Global Compact on Refugees", Palais des Nations (room XIX), Geneva, 14–15 November 2017, formulated the following:

> As a complement to resettlement opportunities, safe and regulated pathways for the admission of refugees to third countries can facilitate access to protection and solutions, and are an important expression of burden- and responsibility-sharing. In line with the commitments contained in the New York Declaration, 15 this panel will consider ways that the programme of action can support the establishment or expansion of complementary pathways as part of a comprehensive refugee response, including by: (i) expanding family reunification; (ii) leveraging private and community sponsorship; (iii) increasing access to educational opportunities in third countries; (iv) facilitating labour mobility schemes; and (v) data collection on and overall monitoring of complementary pathways for admission.
> *www.unhcr.org/5a0019467.pdf (accessed on 17 August 2018)*

56 To make sense of the technical evolution one should study the UN Refugee High Commissioner's Annual Dialogues. For instance, for the 2017 dialogue where these points of emphasis were laid out, www.unhcr.org/high-commissioners-dialogue-on-protection-challenges-2017.html (accessed on 17 August 2018).

57 See paragraph 29 of "Transforming Our World: The 2030 Agenda for Sustainable Development", where the manifesto speaks of the positive contribution of refugees and migrants for "inclusive growth and sustainable development", www.un.org/ga/search/view_doc.asp?symbol=A/RES/70/1&Lang=E (accessed on 15 August 2018).

58 Volker Turk, a senior UNHCR officer speaks of the interface of humanitarian and the developmental tasks. See, Volker Turk, "Prospects for Responsibility Sharing in

the Refugee Context", *Journal on Migration and Human Security*, Volume 4 (3), 2016, pp. 45–59. In this context, Volker also noted,

> Labour mobility schemes, either within the country of asylum or a third country, are making headway in realizing the right to work and are beneficial for refugees, companies, and national and regional economies. They enable refugees to move to increase their levels of income and standard of living. They can address human resource and capital shortages as well as promote innovation and the transfer of skills. The protection benefits of labour mobility schemes are myriad, as employment and improved household income contribute to self-reliance and resilience, reduce negative coping mechanisms, prepare refugees for longer-term solutions either in or outside the country, reduce dependency on humanitarian aid and, in some cases, facilitate a path to permanent residency or naturalization. We are already starting to see this emerge in regional arrangements that may help facilitate the movement of refugees with specific skills to the countries where such skills are most needed. UNHCR has also recently entered into memoranda of understanding with the OECD and the International Labour Organization, respectively, to promote employment opportunities for refugees both within their countries of asylum and beyond.
>
> *p. 55*

59 IOM theme papers available at, www.iom.int/iom-thematic-papers (accessed on 1 August 2018).
60 Section IV, paragraphs 121–123, pp. 23–24, https://reliefweb.int/sites/reliefweb.int/files/resources/N1624876.pdf (accessed on 17 August 2018); the emphasis on rights was also in the Report of Peter Sutherland, Special Representative of the Secretary General on Migration, 2017, www.un.org/en/ga/search/view_doc.asp?symbol=A/71/728&=E%20 (accessed on 18 August 2018).
61 Paragraph 23, *ibid.*, https://reliefweb.int/sites/reliefweb.int/files/resources/N1624876.pdf (accessed on 17 August 2018).
62 Dimitris Papadopoulos, Niamh Stephenson, and Vassilis Tsianos, *Escape Routes: Control and Subversion in the Twenty-first Century* (London: Pluto Press, 2006), p. 56.
63 *Ibid.*, p. 43.
64 For a comprehensive discussion on the concept of autonomy of migration, see Stephan Scheel, "Autonomy of Migration despite Its Securitisation? Facing the Terms and Conditions of Biometric rEBORDERING", *Millennium: Journal of International Studies*, Volume 41 (3), pp. 575–600; Scheel in "Studying Embodied Encounters: Autonomy of Migration beyond its Romanticisation" speaks of the interface of the principle of autonomy and government as embodied encounters, for instance between migrant's autonomous practices of movement and myriad of regulations, including biometric surveillance. See his "Studying Embodied Encounters: Autonomy of Migration beyond its Romanticisation", *Postcolonial Studies*, Volume 16 (3), pp. 279–288.
65 The UNHCR kept on insisting that refugees were not migrants, and that its goal was to safeguard the refugee exemption from restrictive policies. As one scholar has commented,

> Sceptical media and political entrepreneurs in turn dismissively label people trying to get in as "migrants" – not "genuine refugees" with legitimate claims to enter and be protected. The notion that migrants and refugees are distinct extends throughout the academy for historical and contemporary political reasons. The great wave of transoceanic European immigration to the New World in the late nineteenth and early twentieth century took place at a time when there was no separate track for refugee admissions, nor an international refugee regime. As a result, foundational theories of immigration typically ignored the refugee question even if many of those early migratory movements, from Russian Jews fleeing pogroms to Irish escaping the Great Famine, can be reconceptualised as forced migrations. Immigration studies in the United States, Canada, and Australia address post–World War II refugee

admissions, but they easily conflate all people who moved to settler states as "immigrants," regardless of why they came.

David Scott FitzGerald and Rawan Arar, "The Sociology of
Refugee Migration", Annual Review of Sociology, Volume 44,
2018, pp. 387–406, 388.

66 The IOM vision also carries evidence of such contradiction. It states,

> The Global Compact presents an historical opportunity for achieving a world in which migrants move as a matter of choice rather than necessity, through safe, orderly, and regular channels, and in which migration is well governed and able to act as a positive force for individuals, societies, and States. IOM envisions a global compact that will place the rights, needs, capacities, and contributions of migrants at its core, with a view to ensuring their safety, dignity, and human rights. Central to this vision will be four core elements: (1) protecting the rights of migrants; (2) facilitating safe, orderly, and regular migration; (3) reducing the incidence and impacts of forced and irregular migration; and (4) addressing mobility consequences of natural and human-induced disasters.

"IOM Vision on the Global Compact on Migration", 13 April 2017,
paragraph 2, also paragraph 10, www.iom.int/sites/default/files
/our_work/ODG/GCM/IOM-vision-on-the-global-
compact-on-migration-13April2017.pdf (accessed
on 17 August 2018).

67 Alex Aleinikoff and Leah Zamore, *The Arc of Protection: Towards a New International Refugee Regime* (draft), Centre of International Cooperation, New York University, 2018, https://cic.nyu.edu/news/arc-of-protection-refugees-zamore (accessed on 30 December 2018). *The Arc of Protection* requires to be studied with close attention not because all of its formulations are correct, but because they go as far as possible towards formulating new protection principles on the basis of the old. In some cases, its formulation is instructive. For instance, Alex Aleinikoff and Leah Zamore write, No less crucially, the New Liberal Consensus says very little about enforcement of refugee rights. It emphasizes access to labour markets, to be sure; but it does so, too often, to the exclusion of refugees' welfare and labour rights – rights intended to lessen rather than increase refugees' market dependency. That omission is often defended as a matter of realpolitik, of taking seriously host states' baseline hostility toward refugees. Yet it has as much if not more to do with the supply-side preferences and pro-business policies of donors and industry: namely, that labour markets are inherently emancipatory and self-regulating; that few problems cannot be fixed with the right mix of temporary vocational training, targeted micro-lending and corporate tax concessions; that minimal safety nets are sufficient to ward 4 off abject poverty; that corporate power is benign; that wage theft and exploitation are exceptional.

Chapter 5, p. 3, www.publicseminar.org/wp-content/uploads/
2018/05/Chapter-5-1.pdf (accessed on 2 February 2019).

68 In some sense the clue to the question is in the fact that the regime of global governance adopted two compacts and not one, which would have spoken of a new meaning, a departure, and a new vision that combined the paradoxical and the intertwined realities of refugees and migrants, politics and economics, law and regulation, visibility and invisibility, specific and the global, and finally providing care and ensuring work. See in this connection the report, "Decentring the Global: A South Asian Migration Research Agenda", *Migration Leadership Team Global Migration Conversation*, Delhi, 22–23 May 2018, www.soas.ac.uk/lidc-mlt/outputs/file133830.pdf (accessed on 1 January 2019).

BIBLIOGRAPHY

Reports

Betts, Alexander, Louise Bloom, Josiah Kaplan, and Naohiko Omata. *Refugee Economies: Rethinking Popular Assumptions*. Oxford: Humanitarian Innovation Project, University of Oxford, 2014.

Calcutta Research Group and UNHCR. *Report of Dialogue on Protection Strategies for People in Situations of Forced Migration*. Kolkata: Calcutta Research Group, 2008. http://mcrg.ac.in/UNHCRconference/home.html. Accessed February 25, 2015.

Danish Refugee Council. *Socio-Economic Survey of Afghan Refugees Living in Pakistan*. Danish Refugee Council, Copenhagen, May 2013. https://adsp.ngo/wp-content/uploads/2018/12/P-14_Socio-Economic-Survey-of-Afghan-Refugees-Living-in-Pakistan.pdf Accessed March 1, 2018

Doomernik, J. *A Study of the Effectiveness of Integration*. Geneva: ILO Migration Programme Series, 1998.

Government of Bengal. File no. 398/46. West Bengal State Archives.

Government of Denmark, Government of Kenya, and Government of Norway. "In Search of Protection and Livelihoods: Socio-economic and Environmental Impacts of Dadaab Refugee Camps on Host Communities." *Reliefweb*, September 30, 2010. http://reliefweb.int/report/kenya/search-protection-and-livelihoods-socio-economic-and-environmental-impacts-dadaab. Accessed January 1, 2017.

Government of India. *1991 Census Handbook: Census of India: Tripura*. Series 24. New Delhi: Registrar General and Census Commissioner of India, 1991.

Government of India. *Report on Conditions of Work and Promotion of Livelihoods in the Unorganised Sector*. New Delhi: National Commission for Enterprises for the Unorganised Sector, 2007. http://dcmsme.gov.in/Condition_of_workers_sep_2007.pdf. Accessed September 21, 2018.

Government of India. *Slums in India: A Statistical Compendium, 2011*. New Delhi: Ministry of Housing and Urban Poverty Alleviation, National Buildings Organisation, 2011.

Government of India. *Details of Farmers Suicides from 2010 to 2014*. National Crime Records Bureau, Ministry of Home Affairs, 2014. https://data.gov.in/resources/details-farmers-suicides-2010-2014-ministry-agriculture-farmers-welfare. Accessed October 3, 2018.

Government of India. *Statement by India Made on Agenda Item 2 (Part III. A – Programme of Action: Mechanisms for Burden and Responsibility Sharing) During the Fourth Round of Formal Consultations on the Global Compact on Refugees – Delivered by Dr. Sadre Alam, First Secretary, 8–10 May 2018*. Geneva: Permanent Mission of India, 2018. www.pmindiaun.org/pages.php?id=1648. Accessed August 12, 2018.

Government of India. *Statement by India Made During the Fifth Round of Formal Consultations on the Global Compact on Refugees – Delivered by Dr. Sadre Alam, First Secretary*. Geneva, Switzerland, June 12–13, 2018. www.unhcr.org/5b2ba4e27.pdf. Accessed August 12, 2018.

Government of West Bengal. *Calcutta Municipal Gazette*. Vol. XLV, No. 1–2. November 30–December 7, 1946, Kolkata.

Government of West Bengal. *Calcutta Municipal Gazetteer*. Vol. XLV, No. 4. December 21, 1946, Kolkata.

Government of West Bengal. *Calcutta Municipal Gazetteer*. Vol. XLV, No. 18–21. April 26, 1947, Kolkata.

IOM. *Migration Governance Framework*. Geneva: IOM UN Migration, n.d. www.iom.int/sites/default/files/about-iom/migof_brochure_a4_en.pdf. Accessed March 19, 2018.

IOM. *The Berne Initiative: International Agenda for Migration Management*. Geneva: International Organization for Migration (IOM) and the Federal Office for Migration (FOM), 2005. www.iom.int/berne-initiative. Accessed August 5, 2018.

"Report on Illegal Migration into Assam." *Submitted by the Governor of Assam to the President of India*, 1998. http://old.satp.org/satporgtp/countries/india/states/assam/documents/papers/illegal_migration_in_assam.htm. Accessed November 11, 2016.

Rudiger, Anja, and Sarah Spencer. *The Economic and Social Aspects of Integration*. Brussels: OECD, 2003. www.oecd.org/migration/mig/15516956.pdf. Accessed March 21, 2018.

"The Global Compact on Refugees." *United Nations*, Zero Draft. January 31, 2018. https://reliefweb.int/sites/reliefweb.int/files/resources/Zero-Draft.pdf. Accessed August 13, 2018.

"The Global Compact on Refugees." *UNHCR*, Draft 1. March 9, 2018. www.unhcr.org/5aa2b3287.pdf. Accessed August 15, 2018.

"The Global Compact on Refugees." *UNHCR*, Draft 2. April 30, 2018. www.unhcr.org/events/conferences/5ae758d07/official-version-draft-2-global-compact-refugees-30-april-2018.html. Accessed August 15, 2018.

"The Global Compact on Refugees." *UNHCR*, Draft 3. June 4, 2018. www.unhcr.org/events/conferences/5b1579427/official-version-draft-3-global-compact-refugees-4-june-2018.html. Accessed August 15, 2018.

"The Global Compact on Refugees." *Final Draft*, June 26, 2018. www.unhcr.org/5b3295167.pdf. Accessed August 15, 2018.

"The Global Compact on Refugees." *UNHCR*, December 2018. www.unhcr.org/refugeecompact. Accessed August 1, 2018.

"The Global Compact on Refugees: From Draft 2 (30 April) to Draft 3 (4 June), Explanatory Memorandum on Main Changes." *UNHCR*, n.d. www.unhcr.org/5b1579b17.pdf. Accessed August 16, 2018.

"The State of the World's Midwifery: Delivering Health, Saving Lives." *United Nations*, 2011. www.unfpa.org/sites/default/files/pub-pdf/en_SOWMR_Full.pdf. Accessed September 29, 2017.

UNHCR. *Refugee Protection and Mixed Migration: A 10-Point Plan of Action*. Geneva: UNHCR, 2007. www.unhcr.org/protection/migration/4742a30b4/refugee-protection-mixed-migration-10-point-plan-action.html. Accessed March 12, 2018.

UNHCR. "Report on Statelessness in South-Eastern Europe." *Bureau for Europe*, September 2011. www.refworld.org/pdfid/514d715f2.pdf. Accessed March 3, 2018.

UNHCR. *Refugee Protection and International Migration: Trends August 2013-July 2014*. Geneva: UNHCR Division of International Protection, 2014. www.unhcr.org/5485d2069.pdf. Accessed February 25, 2015.

UNHCR. *Solutions Strategy for Afghan Refugees, Update 2015–16*. Geneva: UNHCR, 2016.

UNHCR. *Global Trends: Forced Displacement in 2016*. Geneva: UNHCR, 2017. www.refworld.org/docid/594aa38e0.html. Accessed November 2, 2018.

UNHCR. "Towards a Global Compact on Refugees." *Palais des Nations (Room XIX), Geneva*, November 14–15, 2017. www.unhcr.org/5a0019467.pdf. Accessed August 17, 2018.

UNHCR. "Towards a Global Compact on Refugees." *UNHCR*, The Summary of the High Commissioner's Dialogue on Protection Challenges 2017, Thematic Session, no. 4. (December 12–13, 2017). www.unhcr.org/5a5890137.pdf. Accessed August 16, 2018.

UNHCR. *Desperate Journeys: Refugees and Migrants Arriving in Europe and at Europe's Borders*. Geneva: UNHCR, 2018.

United Nations. *International Migration Report, 2002*. New York: United Nations, Department of Economic and Social Affairs, Population Division, 2002, doc. ST/ESA/SER.A/220.

United Nations. *Resolution Adopted by the General Assembly on 19 September 2016*. New York: United Nations General Assembly, 2016. www.un.org/en/ga/search/view_doc.asp?symbol=A/RES/71/1. Accessed July 1, 2018.

United Nations. "In Safety and Dignity: Addressing Large Movements and Refugees and Migrants." *UN Secretary General's Report to the General Assembly*, 70th session. April 21, 2016. https://refugeesmigrants.un.org/sites/default/files/in_safety_and_dignity_-_addressing_large_movements_of_refugees_and_migrants.pdf. Accessed August 11, 2018.

United Nations. "Making Migration Work for All." *Report of the Secretary-General to the 72nd Session of the General Assembly*, December 12, 2017. https://reliefweb.int/sites/reliefweb.int/files/resources/N1743962.pdf. Accessed August 20, 2018.

United Nations General Assembly. "Report of the Special Rapporteur on the Human Rights of Migrants, François Crépeau with Special Emphasis on Labour Exploitation of Migrants." *United Nations*, A/HRC/26/35, April 3, 2014.

United Nations Population Fund. *The State of the World's Midwifery, 2011: Delivering Health, Saving Lives*. New York: United Nations Population Fund, 2011.

United Nations Secretary General. "In Safety and Dignity: Addressing Large Movements and Refugees and Migrants." *United Nations General Assembly*, 2016. www.un.org/pga/70/wp-content/uploads/sites/10/2015/08/21-Apr_Refugees-and-Migrants-21-April-2016.pdf. Accessed January 29, 2017.

Books, articles and journals

"A History of Migration." *Striking Women: Migration*, n.d. www.strikingwomen.org/module/migration/history-migration. Accessed January 1, 2019.

"A New Deal for Refugees: What Is the Global Compact on Refugees?" *UNHCR*, December 2018. www.unhcr.org/a-new-deal-for-refugees.html. Accessed February 5, 2019.

Abraham, Itty. "Refugees and Humanitarianism." *Refugee Watch*, Special Issue no. 24–26 (October 2005). www.mcrg.ac.in/rw%20files/RW24.doc. Accessed March 12, 2018.

Adams, Simon. "Libya and the Responsibility to Protect." *Global Centre for the Responsibility to Protect*, Occasional Paper Series, no. 3 (October 2012). www.globalr2p.org/media/files/libyaandr2poccasionalpaper-1.pdf. Accessed August 12, 2018.

Adorno, Theodor. *Negative Dialectics*. Translated by E.B. Ashton. London: Routledge and Kegan Paul, 1973.

Agamben, Giorgio. *State of Exception*. Translated by Kevin Attell. Chicago: University of Chicago Press, 2005.

Bibliography

Agier, Michel. "Between War and City: Towards an Urban Anthropology of Refugee Camps." *Ethnography* 3, no. 3 (2002): 317–366.

Agier, Michel. "The Chaos and the Camps: Fragments of a Humanitarian Government." In *The Maghreb Connection: Movements of Life across North Africa*, edited by Ursula Biemann and Brian Holmes, 260–282. Barcelona: Actar, 2006.

Agier, Michel. *Managing the Undesirables: Refugee Camps and Humanitarian Government*. Translated by David Fernbach. London: Polity Press, 2011.

Agnes, Flavia. "Bombay Bar Dancers and the Trafficked Migrant: Globalisation and Subaltern Existence." *Refugee Watch*, no. 30 (December 2007). www.mcrg.ac.in/rw%20files/RW30.htm#R2. Accessed January 1, 2019.

Ahmed, Ishtiaq. *The Punjab Bloodied, Partitioned and Cleaned: Unravelling the 1947 Tragedy Through Secret British Reports and First-Person Accounts*. Karachi: Oxford University Press, 2012.

Ahmed, Nabil. "Entangled Earth". *Third Text* 27, no. 1 (January 2013): 44–53.

Alex, Aleinikoff, and Leah Zamore. *The Arc of Protection: Towards a New International Refugee Regime*. Draft. New York: Centre of International Cooperation, New York University, 2018. https://cic.nyu.edu/news/arc-of-protection-refugees-zamore. Accessed December 30, 2018.

Ambrose, Stephen E. *Nothing like It in the World: The Men Who Built the Transcontinental Railroad 1863–1869*. New York: Simon & Schuster, 2001.

Anand, Aditya, Bishnu Raj Upreti, and Poorna Kanta Adhikary. *Countries in Conflict and Processing of Peace: Lessons for Nepal*. Kathmandu: Friends for Peace, 2006.

Anderson, Bridget. "Migration, Immigration Controls and the Fashioning of Precarious Workers." *Work, Employment, Society* 24, no. 2 (2010): 300–317.

Anderson, Bridget. "Towards a New Politics of Migration?" *Ethnic and Racial Studies* 40, no. 9 (2017): 1527–1537.

Andersson, R. "Hunter and Prey: Patrolling Clandestine Migration in the Euro-African Borderlands." *Anthropological Quarterly* 87, no. 1 (2014): 119–149.

Andrew, Hosken. "Syrian Child Refugees 'Being Exploited in Jordan'." *BBC*, November 4, 2015. www.bbc.com/news/world-middle-east-34714021. Accessed May 12, 2018.

Andrijasevic, Rutvica. "The Difference Borders Make: (Il)legality, Migration and Trafficking in Italy Among Eastern European Women in Prostitution." In *Uprootings/Regroundings: Questions of Home and Migration*, edited by S. Ahmed, C. Castaneda, A.M. Fortier, and M. Sheller, 251–272. New York: Berg, 2003.

Ann, Corcoran. "More Evidence of Europe Under Siege by the Flow of Illegal Migrants from Africa." *TMA Sierra Hills*, May 31, 2015. https://tmasierrahills.blogspot.com/2015/05/rr-watch-ann-corcoran-more-evidence.html. Accessed February 3, 2017.

Appleby, Kevin. "Strengthening the Global Refugee Protection System: Recommendations for the Global Compact on Refugees." *Journal on Migration and Human Security* 5, no. 4 (2017): 780–799.

Arendt, Hannah. *The Origins of Totalitarianism*. New York: Meridian Books, 1951.

Arendt, Hannah. "We Refugees." In *Altogether Elsewhere: Writers on Exile*, edited by Marc Robinson, 110–119. London: Faber and Faber, 1994.

Arendt, Hannah. *The Origins of Totalitarianism*. New York: Schocken Books, 2004.

Arnold, David. "Social Crisis and Epidemic Disease in the Famines of Nineteenth Century India." *Social History of Medicine* 6, no. 3 (December 1993): 385–404.

Azadzoi, Mohammad Najim. "Settlements of Afghan Refugees in Pakistan: An Evaluation of Conditions and Identification of Problems." Master's dissertation, Department of Architecture, MIT, 1984.

Aziz, Nourhan Abdel, Paola Monzini, and Feruccio Pastore. "The Changing Dynamics of Cross-Border Human Smuggling and Trafficking in the Mediterranean." *Instituto Affari*

Internazionali, October 2015. www.iai.it/en/pubblicazioni/changing-dynamics-cross-border-human-smuggling-and-trafficking-mediterranean. Accessed February 2, 2019.

Bahadur, Gaiutra. *Coolie Woman: The Odyssey of Indenture.* Chicago: The University of Chicago Press, 2014.

Baisya, Arup. "Citizenship Question and Assam Politics." *Frontier,* January 10, 2018. www.frontierweekly.com/views/jan-18/10-1-18-Citizenship%20Question%20and%20Assam%20Politics.html. Accessed December 20, 2018.

Balibar, Etienne. "Is There a Neo-Racism?" In *Race, Nation, Class: Ambiguous Identities,* edited by Etienne Balibar and Immanuel Wallerstein, 17–28. London: Verso, 1991.

Balibar, Etienne. "Racism and Nationalism." In *Race, Nation, Class: Ambiguous Identities,* edited by Etienne Balibar and Immanuel Wallerstein, 37–67. London: Verso, 1991.

Balibar, Etienne. "Historical Dilemmas of Democracy and Their Contemporary Relevance to Citizenship." *Rethinking Marxism* 20, no. 4 (2008): 522–538.

Bandopadhyay, Krishna, Soma Ghosh, and Nilanjan Dutta. *Eroded Lives.* Kolkata: Calcutta Research Group, 2006.

Bandopadhyay, Premansu Kumar. *Sepoys in the British Overseas Expeditions (1762–1826).* Vol. 1. Kolkata: K.P. Bagchi, 2011.

Banerjee, Paula. "Aliens in a Colonial World." In *Refugees and the State: Practices of Asylum and Care in India, 1947–2003,* edited by Ranabir Samaddar, 69–105. New Delhi: Sage, 2003.

Banerjee, Paula. "Women, Trafficking, and Statelessness in South Asia." *Refugee Watch,* no. 27 (June 2006). www.mcrg.ac.in/cata.htm. Accessed February 22, 2018.

Banerjee, Paula. *Borders, Histories, Existences: Gender and Beyond.* New Delhi: Sage, 2010.

Banerjee, Paula. "Circles of Insecurity." In *Migration and Circles of Insecurity,* edited by Paula Banerjee and Ranabir Samaddar, 70–122. New Delhi: Rupa, 2010.

Banerjee, Paula. "Response to Landau." *Journal of Refugee Studies* 25, no. 4 (May 2012): 570–573.

Banerjee, Paula, ed. *Unstable Populations, Anxious States: Mixed and Massive Population Flows in South Asia.* Kolkata: Samya, 2013.

Banerjee, Paula, and Sabyasachi Basu Ray Chaudhury. *Report on a Symposium on Tsunami and the Issues of Relief, Rehabilitation and Resettlement.* Kolkata: Calcutta Research Group, 2005. www.mcrg.ac.in. Accessed June 20, 2015.

Banerjee, Paula, Sabyasachi Basu Ray Chaudhury, and Samir K. Das, eds. *Internal Displacement in South Asia: The Relevance of the UN Guiding Principles.* New Delhi: Sage, 2005.

Banerjee, Paula, Anasua Basu Ray Chaudhury, and Atig Ghosh. *The State of Being Stateless: An Account of South Asia.* Hyderabad: Orient Blackswan, 2015.

Banerjee, Paula, and Ranabir Samaddar, eds. *Voices of the IDPs.* Kolkata: Calcutta Research Group, 2006.

Barbora, Sanjay. "Riding the Rhino: Conservation, Conflicts, and Militarisation of Kaziranga National Park in Assam." *Antipode* 49, no. 5 (November 2017): 1145–1163.

Bardelli, Nora. "The Shortcomings of Employment as a Durable Solution." *Forced Migration Review,* Economies: Rights and Access to Work, no. 58 (June 2018): 54–55.

Barnard, Patrick. "Notes on Syria and the Great Refugee Crisis." *Montreal Serai* 29, no. 1 (March 2016).

Baruah, Sanjib. "Clash of Resource Use Regimes in Colonial Assam: A Nineteenth-Century Puzzle Revisited." *Journal of Peasant Studies* 28, no. 3 (2000): 109–124.

Basu, Madhurilata. "Living with the River: Glimpses from Murshidabad." *Rivista di Studisulla Sostenibilita,* no. 2 (2014): 105–124.

Basu, Madhurilata, Rajat Ray, and Ranabir Samaddar, eds. *Political Ecology of Survival – Life and Labour in the River Lands of East and North-East India.* Hyderabad: Orient Blackswan, 2018.

Basu Ray Chaudhury, Sabyasachi. "Exiled to the Andamans: The Refugees from East Pakistan." In *Refugees in West Bengal: Institutional Practices and Contested Identities*, edited by Pradip Kumar Bose, 130–141. Kolkata: Calcutta Research Group, 2000.

Basu Ray Chaudhury, Sabyasachi. "Uprooted Twice – Refugees in the Chittagong Hill Tracts." In *Refugees and the State – Practices of Asylum and Care in India, 1947–2000*, edited by Ranabir Samaddar, 249–280. New Delhi: Sage Publications, 2003.

Basu Ray Chaudhury, Sabyasachi, and Ranabir Samaddar. *Rohingya in South Asia: People Without a State*. London: Routledge, 2018.

Baubock, Rainer. *From Aliens to Citizens: Redefining the Status of Immigrants in Europe*. Aldershot: Ashgate and European Centre Vienna, 1994.

Bauder, H. *Labour Movement. How Migration Regulates Labour Markets*. New York: Oxford University Press, 2006.

Behel, Rana P., and Marcel van der Linden, eds. *Coolies, Capital, and Colonialism – Studies in Indian Labour History*. New Delhi: Oxford University Press, 2007.

Bennett, J. *Vibrant Matter: A Political Ecology of the Thing*. Durham: Duke University Press, 2010.

Berman, Paul Schiff. "Global Legal Pluralism." *South California Law Review* 80 (2007): 1155–1165.

Berman, Paul Schiff. "The New Legal Pluralism." *Annual Review of Law and Social Science*, no. 5 (2009): 225–242.

Betram, David, Maritsa V. Poros, and Pierre Monforte. *Key Concepts in Migration*. London: Sage, 2014.

Betts, Alexander, and Paul Collier. *Refuge: Transforming a Broken Refugee System*. London: Allen Lane, 2017.

Betts, Alexander, Josiah David Kaplan, Louise Bloom, and Naohiko Omata. *Refugee Economies: Forced Displacement and Development*. Oxford: Oxford University Press, 2017.

Bhaduri, Amit. "A Study in Development by Dispossession." *Cambridge Journal of Economics* 42, no. 1 (January 2018): 19–31. doi:10.1093/cje/bex026. Accessed February 2, 2018.

Bhagwati, P.N. *Report on Roundtable Workshop on Refugees in the SAARC Region – National Legislation on Refugees*. New Delhi: SAARCLAW and UNHCR, 1999.

Bharadwaj, Prasant, Asim Khwaja, and Atif Mian. "The Big March: Migratory Flows After the Partition of India." *Economic & Political Weekly* 43, no. 45 (August 2008): 39–49.

Bhattacharya, Swapna. "The Rakhine State of Myanmar in the Realm of South Asia." In *The Rakhine State (Arakan) of Myanmar: Interrogating History, Culture and Conflict*, edited by Swapna Bhattachary, 44–64. New Delhi: Manohar Publishers, 2015.

Bhaumik, S. "The Returnees and the Refugees – Migration from Burma." In *Refugees and the State: Practices of Asylum and Care in India, 1947–2000*, edited by Ranabir Samaddar, 182–210. New Delhi: Sage, 2003.

"Bhutan: Nationality, Expulsion, Statelessness, and the Right to Return." *Refworld, UNHCR and Amnesty International*, September 1, 2000. www.refworld.org/topic,50ffbce524d,50ffbce5253,3b83b6df7,0,,COUNTRYREP,BTN.html. Accessed October 2, 2017.

Bialasiewicz, Luiza. "Where Do We Want the EU's Borders to Lie?" *Transit Online*, November 9, 2015. www.iwm.at/transit/transit-online/want-eus-borders-lie/. Accessed March 20, 2018.

Bianchini, Stefano. *Liquid Nationalism and State Partitions in Europe*. Cheltenham: Edward Elgar Publishing, 2017.

Bianchini, Stefano, Sanjay Chaturvedi, Rada Ivekovic, and Ranabir Samaddar. *Partitions: Reshaping States and Minds*. Milton Park: Frank Cass, 2005.

Bigo, Didier. "The European Internal Security Field: Stakes and Rivalries in a Newly Developing Area of Police Intervention." In *Policing Across National Boundaries*, edited by M. Anderson and M. den Boer. London: Pinter, 1994.

Bigo, Didier. "Security and Immigration: Toward a Critique of the Governmentality of Unease." *Alternatives*27, Special Issue (2002): 63–92.
Bonjour, Saskia, and Jan Willem Duyvendak. "The 'Migrant with Poor Prospects': Racialised Intersections of Class and Culture in Dutch Civic Integration Debates." *Ethnic and Racial Studies* 41, no. 5 (2018): 882–900.
Böröcz, József. *The European Union and Global Social Change: A Critical Geopolitical-Economic Analysis*. London: Routledge, 2010.
Böröcz, József, and Mahua Sarkar. "The Unbearable Whiteness of the Polish Plumber and the Hungarian Peacock Dance around 'Race'." *Slavic Review*76, no. 2 (Summer 2017): 307–314.
Bose, Pradip K., ed. *Refugees in West Bengal: Institutional Practices and Contested Identities*. Kolkata: Calcutta Research Group, 2000.
Bose, Pradip K. "Refugee, Memory, and the State: A Review of Research in Refugee Studies." *Refugee Watch*, no. 36 (December 2010): 1–30.
Bose, Tapan K. "The Rohingya: Rejected by the Country They Call Home and Unwanted by Its Neighbours." *Alternatives International*, October 24, 2017. www.alterinter.org/spip.php?rubrique2. Accessed November 1, 2017.
Bradley, Megan. *Return of Forced Migrants: A Research Guide*. Oxford: University of Oxford, Refugee Studies Centre, 2006.
Bradley, Megan. "The International Organization for Migration (IOM): Gaining Power in the Forced Migration Regime." *Refuge* 33, no. 1 (2017): 97–106. https://refuge.journals.yorku.ca/index.php/refuge/article/view/40452/36445. Accessed March 20, 2018.
Brandt, Jessica, and Lucy Earle. "The Global Compact for Refugees: Bringing Mayors to the Table." *Brookings Policy Brief*, January 2018.
Brankamp, Hanno. "The Question of Internal Colonialism." *Pambazuka News*, January 13, 2015. www.pambazuka.org/global-south/question-%E2%80%98internal-colonialism%E2%80%99. Accessed January 5, 2019.
Brass, Paul R. "The Partition of India and Retributive in the Punjab, 1946–47: Means, Methods, and Purposes." *Journal of Genocide Research* 5, no. 1 (2003): 71–101.
Brecht, Bertolt. *Mother Courage and Her Children*. Translated by Eric Bentley. New York: Doubleday, 1955.
Breman, Jan. *Taming the Coolie Beast – Plantation Society and the Colonial Order in Southeast Asia*. New Delhi: Oxford University Press, 1989.
"Bringing the New York Declaration to Life: Applying the Comprehensive Refugee Response Framework (CRRF)." *UNHCR*, New York Declaration for Refugees and Migrants. September 19, 2016. www.unhcr.org/dach/wp-content/uploads/sites/27/2017/07/BringingTheNewYorkDeclarationToLife.pdf. Accessed August 15, 2018.
Bulmer, Martin, and John Solomos. "Migration and Race in Europe." *Ethnic and Racial Studies* 41, no. 5 (2018): 779–784.
Calcutta Research Group. "Nepal." In *Voices of the Internally Displaced in South Asia*, 49–66. Kolkata: Calcutta Research Group Report, 2006. www.mcrg.ac.in/Voices.pdf. Accessed June 18, 2017.
Cali, Massimiliano, and Samia Sekkarie. "Much Ado about Nothing? The Economic Impact of Refugee 'Invasions'." *Brookings*, September 16, 2015. www.brookings.edu/blog/future-development/2015/09/16/much-ado-about-nothing-the-economic-impact-of-refugee-invasions/. Accessed January 15, 2017.
Campesi, G. "Seeking Asylum in Times of Crisis: Reception, Confinement, and Detention at Europe's Southern Border." *Refugee Survey Quarterly* 37, no. 1 (2018): 44–70.
Canefe, Nergis. "Post-Colonial State and Violence: Rethinking the Middle East and North Africa Outside the Blindfold of Area Studies." *Refugee Watch*, no. 45 (June 2015): 7–31.

Canefe, Nergis. *The Syrian Exodus in Context: Crisis, Dispossession, and Mobility in the Middle East*. Istanbul: Bilgi University Press, 2018.

Carino, Joji. "The World Commission on Dams: A Review of Hydroelectric Projects and the Impact on Indigenous Peoples and Ethnic Minorities." *Cultural Survival Quarterly Magazine*, September 1999. www.culturalsurvival.org/publications/cultural-survival-quarterly/brazil/world-commission-dams-review-hydroelectric-projects-. Accessed February 8, 2017.

Carter, Marina, and Khal Torabully. *Coolitude: An Anthology of the Indian Labour Diaspora*. London: Anthem Press, 2002.

Castles, Stephen. "Migration." In *A Companion to Racial and Ethnic Studies*, edited by David Theo Goldberg and John Solomos, 561–579. Oxford: Blackwell Publishers, 2002.

Castles, Stephen. "Why Migration Policies Fail." *Ethnic and Racial Studies* 27, no. 2 (2004): 205–227.

Castles, Stephen. "Migration and Social Transformation." *Inaugural Public Lecture at London School of Economics Migration Studies Unit, London*, November 15, 2007. https://slideplayer.com/slide/6616392/. Accessed February 25, 2018.

Castles, Stephen. "Understanding Global Migration: A Social Transformation Perspective." *Journal of Ethnic and Migration Studies* 36, no. 10 (2010): 1565–1586.

Castles, Stephen. "Migration, Crisis, and the Global Labour Market." *Globalizations* 8, no. 3 (2011): 311–324.

Castles, Stephen. "A Response to Bridget Anderson: Migration Policies Are Problematic – Because They Are About Migration." *Ethnic and Racial Studies* 40, no. 9 (2017): 1538–1543.

Castles, Stephen, Heather Booth, and Tina Wallace. *Here for Good: Western Europe's New Ethnic Minorities*. London: Pluto Press, 1984.

Castles, Stephen, Hein de Haas, and Mark J. Miller. *The Age of Migration: International Population Movements in the Modern World*. 5th ed. New York: Palgrave Macmillan, 2015.

Castles, Stephen, and Godula Kosack. *Immigrant Workers and Class Structure in Western Europe*. London and New York: Oxford University Press for Institute of Race Relations, 1973.

Castles, Stephen, and Mark J. Miller, eds. "Migrants and Minorities in the Labour Force." In *The Age of Migration: International Population Movements in the Modern World*, 3rd ed., 178–197. Hampshire, Basingstoke: Palgrave Macmillan, 2003.

Cesaire, Aime. *Discourse on Colonialism*. New York: Monthly Review Press, 1955, 1972.

Chak, Tings. "Undocumented: The Architecture of Migrant Detention." *Migration, Mobility, & Displacement* 2, no. 1 (2016): 6–29.

Chakrabarti, Prafulla K. *The Marginal Men – The Refugees and the Left Political Syndrome in West Bengal*. Kolkata: Lumiere Books, 1990.

Chakrabarty, Bidyut. "The 'Hut' and the 'Axe' – The 1947 Sylhet Referendum." *The Indian Economic and Social History Review* 39, no. 4 (2002): 317–350.

Chakrabarty, Dipesh. "The Climate of History: Four Theses." *Critical Inquiry* 35 (Winter 2009): 197–222.

Chakrabarty, Madhura. "Xenophobia in South Africa." *Refugee Watch Online*, June 5, 2015. http://refugeewatchonline.blogspot.in/2015/06/xenophobia-in-south-africa-report.html. Accessed June 8, 2015.

Chakrabarty, Subhas Ranjan. "Colonialism, Resource Crisis, and Forced Migration." *Policies and Practices*, no. 42 (2011): 1–15. www.mcrg.ac.in/PP42.pdf. Accessed February 24, 2015.

Chakravarty, Lalita. "Emergence of an Industrial Labour Force in a Dual Economy: British India, 1880–1920." *The Economic and Social History Review* 15, no. 3 (July–September 1978): 249–326.

Chambers, Robert. "Rural Refugees in Africa: What the Eye Does not See." *Disasters* 3, no. 4 (December 1979): 381–392.

Chand, Ramesh. "Government Intervention in Foodgrain Markets in the New Context." *National Centre for Agricultural Economics and Policy Research Policy Paper*, no. 19 (2003): 1–118.

Chatterjee, J. "Rights or Charity? Government and Refugees – The Debate over Relief and Rehabilitation in West Bengal, 1947–1950." In *Partitions of Memory*, edited by S. Kaul. New Delhi: Permanent Black, 2001.

Chattopadhyaya, Haraprasad. *Indians in Sri Lanka: A Historical Study*. Kolkata: O.P.S. Publishers, 1979.

Chaudhuri, Shreyashi. "Is the Right to Return a Symbolic Right?" *Refugee Watch Online*, August 28, 2006. http://refugeewatchonline.blogspot.in/2006/08/is-right-to-return-symbolic-right_28.html. Accessed February 25, 2015.

Chimni, B.S. "The Geopolitics of Refugee Studies: A View from the South." *Journal of Refugee Studies* 11, no. 4 (1998): 354–374.

Chimni, B.S. "Globalization, Humanitarianism and the Erosion of Refugee Protection." *Journal of Refugee Studies* 13, no. 3 (2000): 243–264.

Chimni, B.S., ed. *International Refugee Law: A Reader*. New Delhi: Sage, 2000.

Chimni, B.S. "The Reform of the International Refugee Regime: A Dialogic Model." *Journal of Refugee Studies* 14, no. 2 (2001): 151–161.

Chimni, B.S. "Status of Refugees in India – Strategic Ambiguity." In *Refugees and the State: Practices of Asylum and Care in India, 1947–2000*, edited by Ranabir Samaddar, 443–471. New Delhi: Sage, 2003.

Chimni, B.S. "The Birth of a 'Discipline': From Refugee to Forced Migration Studies." *Journal of Refugee Studies* 22, no. 1 (March 2009): 11–29.

Christie, Clive J. *A Modern History of Southeast Asia: Decolonization, Nationalism and Separation*. New York: Tauris Academic Studies and Singapore: Institute of Southeast Asian Studies, 1996.

Cicero, Marcus Tullius. *On Duties*. Edited by M.T. Griffin and E.M. Atkin. Book II. Cambridge: Cambridge University Press, 1991.

Coles, Robert. *Uprooted Children – The Early Life of Migrant Farm Workers*. Pittsburgh: University of Pittsburgh Press, 1970.

Collier, Paul. "Refugee Economics." *Milken Institute Review*, May 2, 2016. www.milkenreview.org/articles/refugee-economics. Accessed January 18, 2017.

Collyer, Michael. "Steel Wheels: The Age of Migration 5.0. Review of *The Age of Migration*, by Stephen Castles, Hein de Haas, and Mark J. Miller." *Ethnic and Racial Studies* 38, no. 13 (2015): 2362–2365.

Costello, Cathryn, and Elspeth Guild. "Fixing the Refugee Crisis: Holding the Commission Accountable." *Verfassungs Blog on Matters Constitutional*, September 16, 2018. https://verfassungsblog.de/fixing-the-refugee-crisis-holding-the-commission-accountable. Accessed January 25, 2019.

Dahal, Nir Prasad. "Rethinking Nepal's IDP Policy with Reference to UN Guiding Principles." *Refugee Watch Online*, March 31, 2011. http://refugeewatchonline.blogspot.in/2011/03/rethinking-nepals-idp-policy-with.html. Accessed June 17, 2017.

Dahrendorf, Ralf. *Reflections on the Revolution in Europe*. New York: Routledge, 2017.

Darling, Jonathan Mark. "Cities of Refuge: Asylum and the Politics of Hospitality." PhD diss., Durham University, 2008. http://etheses.dur.ac.uk/2228/1/2228_238.pdf. Accessed July 25, 2018.

Das, Gurudas. "Liberalisation and Internal Periphery: Understanding the Implications for India's Northeast." In *Liberalisation and India's North East*, edited by Gurudas Das and R.K. Purkayastha, 146–149. New Delhi: Commonwealth Publishers, 1998.

Das, Samir K. "State Response to the Refugee Crisis – Relief and Rehabilitation in the East." In *Refugees and the State: Practices of Asylum and Care in India, 1947–2000*, edited by Ranabir Samaddar, 106–151. New Delhi: Sage, 2003.

Das, Samir K. "India's Look East Policy: Imagining a New Geography of India's Northeast." *India Quarterly* 66, no. 4 (December 2010): 343–358.

Das, Samir K. "Ethnic Subject or Subject of Security?" In *Government of Peace: Social Governance, Security and the Problematic of Peace*, edited by Ranabir Samaddar, 107–133. Farnham, Surrey: Ashgate Publishing, 2015.

Datta, Milan. "The Non-existent Population in the *Chars* of Malda." In *Political Ecology of Survival – Life and Labour in the River Lands of East and North-East India*, edited by Madhurilata Basu, Rajat Ray, and Ranabir Samaddar, 107–120. Hyderabad: Orient Blackswan, 2018.

Davis, Lance E., and Robert A. Huttenback. *Mammon and the Pursuit of Empire: The Political Economy of British Imperialism, 1860–1912*. Cambridge: Cambridge University Press, 1987; Chapter 3, "British Business and the Profits from Empire." In 73–118.

Davis, Mike. *El Nino Famines: Late Victorian Holocausts and the Making of the Third World*. London: Verso, 2002.

"Decentering the 'Global': A South Asian Migration Research Agenda." In *LIDC Migration Leadership Team Global Migration Conversation Delhi*, May 22–23, 2018. www.soas.ac.uk/lidc-mlt/outputs/file133830.pdf. Accessed January 1, 2019.

De Chungara, Domitila Barrios, and Moema Viezzer. *Let me Speak: Testimony of Domitila, a Woman of the Bolivian Mines*. Translated by Victoria Ortiz. New York: Monthly Review Press, 1978.

De Genova, Nicholas. "Migrant 'Illegality' and Deportability in Everyday Life." *Annual Review of Anthropology*, no. 31 (2002): 419–447.

De Genova, Nicholas, ed. *The Borders of "Europe": Autonomy of Migration, Tactics of Bordering*. Durham, NC: Duke University Press, 2017.

De Genova, Nicholas. "Migration and the Mobility of Labour." In *The Oxford Handbook of Karl Marx*, Oxford Handbooks Online, edited by Matt Vidal, Tony Smith, Tomás Rotta, and Paul Prew, December 2018. doi:10.1093/oxfordhb/9780190695545.013.25. Accessed July 3, 2019.

De Genova, Nicholas. "The 'Migrant Crisis': As Racial Crisis: Do Black Lives Matter in Europe?" *Ethnic and Racial Studies* 41, no. 10 (2018): 1765–1782.

De Hann, Arjan. "Unsettled Settlers: Migrant Workers and Industrial Capitalism in Calcutta." *Modern Asian Studies* 31, no. 4 (1997): 919–949.

de Leon, Jason. *The Land of Open Graves: Living and Dying on the Migrant Trail*. Oakland, CA: University of California Press, 2015.

"Deporting Rohingya Refugees: Indian Supreme Court Violates Principle of Non-refoulement." *Oxford Human Rights Hub*, October 18, 2018. http://ohrh.law.ox.ac.uk/deporting-rohingya-refugees-indian-supreme-court-violates-principle-of-non-refoulement/. Accessed January 5, 2019.

Derrida, Jacques. *Adieu*. Translated by Pascale-Anne Brault and Michael Naas. Stanford: Stanford University Press, 1999.

Derrida, Jacques. *Of Hospitality*. Translated by Rachel Bowlby. Stanford: Stanford University Press, 2000.

Derrida, Jacques. *On Cosmopolitanism and Forgiveness*. Translated by M. Dooley and M Hughes. London: Routledge, 2001.

Derrida, Jacques. *On Cosmopolitanism and Forgiveness*. Translated by Mark Dooley and Richard Kearney. New York: Routledge, 2005.

De Silva, Nirekha. "Protecting the Rights of the Tsunami Victims: The Sri Lanka Experience." *Policies and Practices*, no. 28 (2010): 1–55. www.mcrg.ac.in/PP28.pdf. Accessed February 14, 2015.

Dey, Ishita. "New Town and Labour in Transit." *Transit Labour: Circuits, Regions, Borders*, July 29, 2011. http://transitlabour.asia/blogs/newtown. Accessed June 12, 2014.

Dey, Ishita, and Sabyasachi Basu Ray Chaudhury, eds. *The Responsibility to Protect: IDPs and Our National and State Human Rights Commissions*. Kolkata: Calcutta Research Group, 2007. http://mcrg.ac.in/Responsibility_to_Protect.pdf. Accessed February 25, 2015.

Dey, Ishita, Ranabir Samaddar, and Suhit Sen. *Beyond Kolkata: Rajarhat and the Dystopia of Urban Imagination*. London and New Delhi: Routledge, 2013.

Don. "Review of the Fifth Edition of *The Age of Migration*, by Stephen Castles, Hein de Haas and Mark J. Miller." *Migrants' Rights Network*, March 16, 2014. www.migrantsrights.org.uk/blog... (now unavailable, originally appearing on www.goodreads.com/review/list/1478469-don?shelf=modern-society – here also now unavailable). Accessed November 20, 2017.

Dreze, Jean. "Famine Prevention in India." *Wider*, Working Paper, no. 45 (May 1988): 4–143. www.wider.unu.edu/publications/working-papers/previous/en_GB/wp-45/. Accessed June 1, 2015.

Dreze, Jean. "Famine Prevention in India." In *The Political Economy of Hunger*, edited by Jean Dreze and Amartya Sen. Vol. 2. Oxford: Clarendon Press, 1990.

Dreze, Jean, and Amartya Sen. *Hunger and Public Action*. Oxford: Oxford University Press, 1989.

D'Souza, Radha. *What Is Wrong with Rights: Social Movements, Law, and Liberal Imaginations*. London: Pluto Press, 2018.

Dutta, Akhil Ranjan. "Political Destiny of Immigrants in Assam: National Register of Citizens." *Economic and Political Weekly* 53, no. 9 (March 2018): 18–21.

"Economic Impacts of Syrian Refugees: Existing Research Review & Key Takeaways." *International Rescue Committee*, n.d. www.rescue.org/sites/default/files/document/465/ircpolicybriefeconomicimpactsofsyrianrefugees.pdf. Accessed January 18, 2017.

"Ecosystem for Life- A Bangladesh-India Initiative- Ecology, Politics and Survival in the India Northeast and Deltaic Bengal." *Calcutta Research Group* archive, n.d.

Ekelund, Helena. "Review of *The Age of Migration: International Population Movements in the Modern World* (Fourth Edition), by Stephen Castles and Mark Miller." *Journal of Contemporary European Research* 5, no. 2 (Summer 2009): 326–327.

Erickson, Jennifer Lynn. "Citizenship, Refugees, and the State: Bosnians, Southern Sudanese, and Social Service Organisations in Fargo, North Dakota." PhD diss., Department of Anthropology and the Graduate School of the University of Oregon for the Degree of Doctor of Philosophy, 2010.

Erie, Steven P. *Globalizing L.A.: Trade, Infrastructure and Regional Development*. Stanford, CA: Stanford University Press, 2004.

"EU Refugee Relocation Scheme Visualised." November 4, 2015. http://datadesigncompany.com/blog/eu_refugee_relocation.php. Accessed November 8, 2017.

European Commission. "An Economic Take on the Refugee Crisis: A Macroeconomic Assessment for the EU." *Directorate-General for Economic and Financial Affairs*, Institutional Paper, no. 33 (July 2016): 7–36.

Evans, Brad, and Julian Reid. *Resilient Life: The Art of Living Dangerously*. London: Polity Press, 2014.

"Executive Summary of the Resource Pack." In *Mahanirban Calcutta Research Group and Development Media Limited, Dhaka, Bangladesh*, n.d. www.mcrg.ac.in/IUCN/IUCN_Executive_Summary.pdf. Accessed March 1, 2018.

Faist, Thomas. "Migrants as Transnational Development Agents: An Inquiry into the Newest Round of the Migration – Development Nexus." *Population, Space and Place* 14, no. 1 (2008): 21–42.

Faist, Thomas. "The Moral Polity of Forced Migration." *Ethnic and Racial Studies* 41, no. 3 (2018): 412–423.

Farbotko, Carol. "Wishful Sinking: Disappearing Islands, Climate Refugees, and Cosmopolitan Experimentation." *Asia Pacific Viewpoint* 51, no. 1 (April 2010): 47–60.

Farquharson, Marjorie. "Statelessness in Central Asia." *UNHCR*, May 2011. www.unhcr.org/4dfb592e9.pdf. Accessed March 3, 2018.

Fazila-Yacoobali Zamindar, Vazira. *The Long Partition and the Making of Modern South Asia: Refugees, Boundaries, Histories*. New York: Columbia University Press, 2007.

Federici, Sylvia. "The Reproduction Crisis and the Birth of a New 'Out of Law' Proletariat." *Left East*, July 10, 2017. www.criticatac.ro/lefteast/the-reproduction-crisis-and-the-birth-of-a-new-out-of-law-proletariat-an-interview-with-silvia-federici/. Accessed December 15, 2017.

Fernandes, Walter. "Development Induced Displacement and Sustainable Development." *Social Change* 31, no. 1–2 (March 2001): 87–103.

Fernandes, Walter. "Liberalisation and Development-Induced Displacement." *Social Change* 36, no. 1 (March 2006): 109–123.

Fernandes, Walter, and Gita Bharali. *Uprooted for Whose Benefit? Development-Induced Displacement in Assam 1947–2000*. Guwahati: North Eastern Social Research Centre, 2011.

Ferris, Elizabeth. "In Search of Commitments: The 2016 Refugee Summits." *UNSW Andrew and Renata Kaldor Centre for International Refugee Law Policy Brief*, no. 3 (November 2016).

"Financing Dams in India: Risks and Challenges." *International River Networks*, February 2005. www.internationalrivers.org/sites/default/files/attached-files/financingdams2005_text.pdf. Accessed September 1, 2015.

FitzGerald, David Scott, and Rawan Arar. "The Sociology of Refugee Migration." *Annual Review of Sociology*, no. 44 (2018): 387–406.

Foucault, Michel. "Of Other Spaces: Utopias and Heterotopias, March 1967." In *Architecture Mouvement Continuite*, translated by Jay Miskowiec, 1984. http://web.mit.edu/allanmc/www/foucault1.pdf. Accessed February 8, 2019.

Foucault, Michel. *Abnormal, Lectures at the College de France, 1974–75*, translated by Graham Burchell. New York: Picador, 2003.

Foucault, Michel. *Society Must Be Defended, Lectures at the College de France, 1975–76*, translated by David Macey. New York: Picador, 2003.

Freeman, Richard B. "Young Blacks and Jobs." In *Labour Markets in Action: Essays in Empirical Economics*, edited by Richard B. Freeman, 121–132. Cambridge, MA: Harvard University Press, 1989.

Fuji, Takeshi. *Mirrors of the Colonial State – The Frontier Areas between North East India and Burma*. New Delhi: Manohar Publishers, 2001.

Gabrys, J. *Digital Rubbish: A Natural History of Electronics*. Ann Arbor, MI: University of Michigan Press, 2013.

Ganguly, J.B. *Sustainable Human Development in the North-Eastern Region of India*. New Delhi: Regency Publications, 1996.

Garelli, G., and M. Tazzioli. "Challenging the Discipline of Migration: Militant Research in Migration Studies." *Postcolonial Studies* 16, no. 3 (2013): 245–249.

Gatrell, Peter. "Europe Uprooted: Refugee Crisis in the Mid-Century and 'Durable Solutions'." *The Making of the Modern Refugee*, edited by Peter Gatrell, 89–117. Oxford: Oxford University Press, 2015.

Geyer, Mary. *Behind the Wall – The Women of the Destitute Asylum, Adelaide, 1852–1918*. Adelaide: Migration Museum, 1994.

Ghosh, Alok. "Bengali Refugees at Dandakaranya: A Tragedy of Rehabilitation." In *Refugees in West Bengal: Institutional Practices and Contested Identities*, edited by Pradip Kumar Bose, 106–135. Kolkata: Calcutta Research Group, 2000.

Ghosh, Amitav. *The Great Derangement: Climate Change and the Unthinkable*. Chicago: University of Chicago Press, 2017.

Ghosh, Atig, ed. *Branding the Migrant: Arguments of Rights, Welfare and Security*. Kolkata: Frontpage, 2012.

Ghosh, Atig. "The Postcolony and the 'Racy' Histories of Accumulation." In *Accumulation in Postcolonial Capitalism*, edited by Iman Kumar Mitra, Ranabir Samaddar, and Samita Sen, 233–247. Singapore: Springer, 2017.

Ghufran, Nasreen. "Afghan Refugees in Pakistan Current Situation and Future Scenario." *Policy Perspectives* 3, no. 2 (n.d.). www.ips.org.pk/the-muslim-world/1023-afghan-refugees-in-pakistan-current-situation-and-future-scenario/. Accessed March 15, 2017.

Gibney, Matthew J. *The Ethics and Politics of Asylum*. Cambridge: Cambridge University Press, 2004.

Gidwani, Vinay. "Waste." In *Capital Interrupted: Agrarian Development and Politics of Work in India*, 1–31. Minneapolis: University of Minnesota Press, 2008.

Gleeson, Madeline. *Offshore: Behind the Wire on Manus and Nauru*. Sydney: New South Publishing, 2016.

"Global Compact for Safe, Orderly and Regular Migration Development Process." In *IOM Migration Data Portal*, n.d. https://migrationdataportal.org/themes/global-compact-migration. Accessed August 17, 2018.

"Global Migration: Resilient Cities at the Forefront." In *100 Resilient Cities*. September 7–9, 2016. https://medium.com/resilient-cities-at-the-forefront/about. Accessed August 15, 2018.

Gopalakrishnan, R. *Ideology, Autonomy and Integration in the Northeast India*. New Delhi: Omsons Publications, 1990.

Government of India. *Statement by Environment Minister on Notification for Sustainable Sand & Minor Mineral Mining*. Press Information Bureau, 2015. https://pib.gov.in/newsite/PrintRelease.aspx?relid=127174. Accessed October 10, 2015.

Graham, S., and N. Thrift. "Out of Order: Understanding Repair and Maintenance." *Theory, Culture & Society* 24, no. 3 (2007): 1–25.

Grantham, S.G. *Census of India, 1921*. Vol. X, Part I, Rangoon, 1923. Cited in Swapna Bhattacharya. *India-Myanmar Relations, 1886–1948*. Kolkata: K.P. Bagchi and Co., 2007.

Grappi, Giorgio. "Kolkata as Extraction Site: E-waste and Raw Materials Circulation." *Explorations in Space and Society*, no. 29 (September 2013): 33–36. www.academia.edu/8938818/Kolkata_as_Extraction_Site. Accessed October 1, 2016.

Guha, Amalendu. "East Bengal Immigrants and Bhasani in Assam Politics: 1928–47." *Proceedings of the Indian History Congress* 35 (1974): 348–365.

Guha, Amalendu. *Planters-raj to Swaraj: Freedom, Struggle, and Electoral Politics in Assam, 1826–1947*. New Delhi: Indian Council of Historical Research, 1977.

Guild, Elspeth. "Responsibility Sharing of Asylum Seekers in the EU: Good Quality First Reception Is the Key." *Verfassungs Blog on Matters Constitutional*, August 26, 2015. https://verfassungsblog.de/responsibility-sharing-of-asylum-seekers-in-the-eu-good-quality-first-reception-is-the-key/. Accessed January 25, 2019.

Hage, Ghasan. "Etat de Siege: A Dying Domesticating Colonialism?" *American Ethnologist* 43, no. 1 (2016): 1–12.

Hampshire, Stuart. "Intention and Action." In *Thought and Action*, edited by Stuart Hampshire, new ed., 90–168. London: Chatto and Windus, 1982.

Harvey, G.E. *History of Burma: From the Earliest Times to 10 March 1824, the Beginning of the English Conquest*. London: Longmans, Green Co., 1925. Reprint. New Delhi: Asia Educational Service, 2000.

Haward, David. *Empire Express: Building the First Transcontinental Railroad*. New York: Penguin Books, 2000.

Hazarika, Sanjay. *Strangers in the Mist*. New Delhi: Penguin, 1994.

Hazarika, Sujata D. "Dispossession and Displacement – The Genesis of a People's Movement in North Bengal." *Dimensions of Displaced People in Northeast India*, 299–315. New Delhi: Regency Publications, 2002.

Heidemann, Frank, and Abhijit Dasgupta. "Learning to Live in the Colonies and Camps: Repatriates and Refugee in Tamil Nadu." *Economic and Political Weekly*, 53, no. 8 (February 24, 2018): 39–47.

Hewison, Kevin, and Ken Young, eds. *Transnational Migration and Work in Asia*. New York: Routledge, 2006.

Holborn, Louise W. "The League of Nations and the Refugee Problem." *The Annals of the American Academy of Political and Social Science* 203 (May 1999): 124–135.

Høvring, Roald, Tiril Skarstein, and Amjad Yamin. "Between the Devil and Deep Blue Sea." *Norwegian Refugee Council*, December 1, 2015. www.nrc.no/perspectives/2015/nr-4/between-the-devil-and-the-deep-blue-sea/. Accessed February 3, 2017.

Hulme, Mike. "The Conquering of Climate: Discourses of Fear and Their Dissolution." *The Geographical Journal* 174, no. 1 (March 2008): 5–16.

Hunt, Abigail, Emma Samman, Dina Mansour-Ilie, and Henrieke Max. "The Gig Economy in Complex Refugee Situations." *Forced Migration Review Economies: Rights and Access to Work*, no. 58 (June 2018): 47–49.

Hunter, W.W. *Annals of Rural Bengal*. 2nd ed. New York: Leypoldt and Holt, 1868. https://archive.org/stream/annalsofruralben01hunt/annalsofruralben01hunt_djvu.txt. Accessed April 15, 2015.

Hunter, W.W. *India and the Indians*. Edited by Herbert Risley. Vol. 1. New Delhi: Cosmo Publications, 2004.

Hussain, Monirul. *The Assam Movement: Class, Ideology and Identity*. New Delhi: Manak Publications, 1993.

Hussain, Monirul. "State, Identity Movements and Internal Displacement in Northeast India." *Economic and Political Weekly* 35, no. 51 (2000): 4519–4523.

Hussain, Monirul. "State Development and Population Displacement in Northeast India." In *Dimensions of Displaced People in Northeast India*, edited by C.J. Thomas, 282–298. New Delhi: Regency Publications, 2002.

Hussain, Monirul. "Status Report on the IDP Situation in Assam." *Policies and Practices*, no. 12 (February 2007): 18–19. www.mcrg.ac.in/pp12.PDF. Accessed February 8, 2017.

Hussain, Wasbir. "Bangladeshi Migrants in India: Towards a Practical Solution – A View from the North-eastern Frontier." In *Missing Boundaries – Refugees, Migrants, Stateless and Internally Displaced Persons in South Asia*, edited by P.R. Chari, Mallika Joseph, and Suba Chandran, 125–150. New Delhi: Manohar, 2003.

Imran, Qureshi. "Why Indian Nurses Want to go Back to Iraq." *BBC*, June 20, 2014. www.bbc.com/news/world-asia-india-27917521. Accessed December 1, 2015.

"Institutional and Regulatory Framework for Migration and Asylum Policies." *European Union*, Draft Note, n.d. http://immigrationintegration.eu/wp-content/uploads/2017/03/FAMI2_desk-research.pdf. Accessed January 1, 2019.

"Intergovernmental Conference to Adopt the Global Compact for Safe, Orderly and Regular Migration." *General Assembly Resolution*, 72nd session, September 24, 2017. www.un.org/en/ga/search/view_doc.asp?symbol=A/RES/72/244. Accessed August 16, 2018.

"IOM Vision on the Global Compact on Migration." *IOM*, April 13, 2017. www.iom.int/sites/default/files/our_work/ODG/GCM/IOM-vision-on-the-global-compact-on-migration-13April2017.pdf. Accessed August 17, 2018.

ISIL. "Model National Law on Refugees." *ISIL Yearbook of International Humanitarian and Refugee Law*, 2001. www.worldlii.org/int/journals/ISILYBIHRL/2001/19.html. Accessed February 22, 2016.

Isin, Engin. "Citizens Without Nations." *Environment and Planning D: Society and Space* 30, no. 2 (June 2012): 450–467.

Islam, Md. Kamrul. "Review of *The Age of Migration: International Population Movements in the Modern World*, by Stephen Castles, Hein de Haas and Mark Miller." *Canadian Studies in Population* 40, no. 1–2 (Spring–Summer 2013): 105–106.

Jha, Manish K. "Disasters: Experiences of Development During the Embankment Years in Bihar." In *New Subjects and New Governance in India*, edited by Ranabir Samaddar and Suhit K. Sen, 109–153. London and New Delhi: Routledge, 2012.

Jha, Manish K., P.K. Shajahan, and Mouleshri Vyas. "Biopolitics and Urban Governmentality in Mumbai." In *The Biopolitics of Development: Reading Michel Foucault in the Post-Colonial Present*, edited by Sandro Mezzadra, Julien Reid, and Ranabir Samaddar, 45–66. New Delhi and Dordrecht: Springer, 2013.

Joseph, Jolin, and Vishnu Narendran. "Neither Here nor There: An Overview of South-South Migration from Both Sides of the Bangladesh-India Migration Corridor." *Erasmus University ISS Working Paper* General Series, no. 569 (May 2013): 1–36.

Kälin, Walter. "Conceptualizing Climate Induced Displacement." In *Climate Change and Displacement: Multidisciplinary Perspectives*, edited by Jane McAdam, 81–103. Oxford: Hart Publishing, 2010.

Kälin, Walter. "Climate Change Induced Displacement: A Challenge for International Law." *Calcutta Research Group* Distinguished Lecture Series, no. 3 (March 2011): 33–34. www.mcrg.ac.in/DL3.pdf. Accessed November 3, 2018.

Kaneti, Marina. "Metis, Migrants, and the Autonomy of Migration." *Citizenship Studies* 9, no. 6–7 (2015): 620–633.

Kannabiran, Kalpana. *Tools of Justice: Non-Discrimination and the Indian Constitution*. London: Routledge, 2012.

Karlsson, Bengt G. "Politics of Deforestation in Meghalaya." *CENISEAS* (Centre for Northeast India, South and Southeast Asia Studies, Omeo Kumar Das Institute of Social Change and Development, Guwahati), Paper 3, 2004.

Kaur, Ravinder. *Since 1947: Partition Narratives among Punjabi Migrants of Delhi*. New Delhi: Oxford University Press, 2007.

Kermani, Navid. *Upheaval: The Refugee Trek through Europe*. Translated by Tony Crawford. London: Polity Press, 2017.

Keshavarz, Mahmoud. *The Design Politics of the Passport: Materiality, Immobility, and Dissent*. London: Bloomsbury Visual Arts, 2019.

"Key Recommendations to a Final Draft of the Global Compact on Refugees." In *Danish Refugee Council, Save the Children, Norwegian Refugee Council and Rescue*, n.d. https://drc.ngo/media/4585168/ngo-4-recommendations-to-a-final-gcr_may18.pdfand www.unhcr.org/5b3c8eaa7.pdf. Accessed August 1, 2018.

Khan, Nichola. *Mohajir Militancy in Pakistan: Violence and Transformation in the Karachi Conflict*. London: Routledge, 2012.

Khosravi, Shahram. *'Illegal' Traveller: An Auto-Ethnography of Borders*. Basingstoke, Hampshire: Palgrave MacMillan, 2010.

Kibreab, Gairn. "Eritrean and Ethiopian Urban Refugees in Khartoum: What the Eye Refuses to see." *African Studies Review* 39, no. 3 (1996): 131–178.

King, Russell. "Migration Comes of Age." *Ethnic and Racial Studies* 38, no. 13 (2015): 2366–2372.
Koser, K. "Social Networks and the Asylum Cycle." *International Migration Review* 31, no. 3 (1997): 591–611.
Kosinski, Leszek A., and K. Maudood Elahi, eds. "Introduction." In *Population Redistribution and Development in South Asia*, edited by Leszek A. Kosinski and K. Maudood Elahi, 3–14. Dordrecht: D. Reidel Publishing Co., 1985.
Krisch, Nico. "The Case for Pluralism in Post-national Law." *LSE Legal Studies Working Paper*, no. 12 (2009).
Kumar, Madhuresh. "Globalisation, State Policies, and Sustainability of Rights." *Policies and Practices*, no. 6 (March 2005): 5–117. www.mcrg.ac.in/pp6.pdf. Accessed September 2, 2019.
Kumar, Mithilesh. "Governing Flood, Migration, and Conflict in North Bihar." In *Government of Peace: Social Governance, Security, and the Problematic of Peace*, edited by Ranabir Samaddar, 206–226. Farnham, Surrey: Ashgate, 2015.
Kundu, Nitai. "Urban Slum Reports: The Case of Kolkata." In *United Nations Global Report on Human Settlements*, 2003. www.ucl.ac.uk/dpu-projects/Global_Report/pdfs/Kolkata.pdf. Accessed October 1, 2016.
Laczko, Frank. "Improving Data on International Migration – Towards Agenda 2030 and the Global Compact on Migration." *IOM Global Migration Data Analysis Centre*, Discussion Paper (December 2016). https://gmdac.iom.int/sites/default/files/presentations/Laczko.pdf. Accessed August 17, 2018.
Lambert, Helene. "Review of *The Age of Migration*, by Stephen Castles, Hein de Haas and Mark J. Miller." *Millennium: Journal of International Studies* 23, no. 2 (1994): 436–437.
Landau, Loren. "Communities of Knowledge or the Tyrannies of Partnership: Reflections on North-South Research Networks from a South African University on Research Networks and the Dual Imperative." *Journal of Refugee Studies* 25, no. 4 (2012): 555–570.
Ledstrup, Martin, and Marie Larsen. "From Refugee to Employee: Work Integration in Rural Denmark." *Forced Migration Review*, Economies: Rights and Access to Work, no. 58 (June 2018): 14–16.
Lepawsky, J. "Composing Urban Orders from Rubbish Electronics: Cityness and the Site Multiple." *International Journal of Urban and Regional Research* 39, no. 2 (2014): 185–199.
Lewis, Mary Dewhurst. *The Boundaries of the Republic: Migrant Rights and the Limits of Universalism in France, 1918–1940*. Stanford, CA: Stanford University Press, 2007.
Llyod, Martin. *The Passport: The History of Man's Most Travelled Document*. Gloucestershire: Sutton Publishing, 2003.
Loescher, G., and J. Scanlan. *Calculated Kindness: Refugees and America's Half-Open Door, 1945-Present*. New York: Free Press, 1986.
"Logistics, Power, Strike: Elements for the Political Infrastructure." *Logistics and the Transnational Social Strike* (Fall 2017): 5–12. www.transnational-strike.info/wp-content/uploads/Logistics-the-Transnational-Social-Strike-%E2%80%94-TSS-Journal-Fall-2017-1.pdf. Accessed January 20, 2018.
Luke, Ratna Mathai. "HIV and the Displaced: Deconstructing Policy Implementation in Tsunami Camps in Tamil Nadu." *Refugee Watch*, no. 32 (December 2008): 38–63.
MacLean, Ken. "The Rohingya Crisis and the Practices of Erasure." *Journal of Genocide Research* 21, no. 1 (2019): 83–95.
Mahato, Nirmal Kumar. "Environment and Migration: Purulia, West Bengal." *Policies and Practices*, no. 30 (2010): 1–15. www.mcrg.ac.in/PP30.pdf. Accessed February 14, 2015.
Majumder, Kunal. "Half-Life of the Coal Child." *Tehelka Magazine*, July 3, 2010.
Majumder, Kunal. "Mining Sorrows." *Tehelka Magazine* 7, no. 26 (July 2010).

Malischewski, Charlotte-Anne, and Shuvro Poasun Sarker. "Stateless in Law: Two Assessments." *Policies and Practices*, no. 60 (March 2014): 1–36.

Malla, Binayak, and Mark S. Rosenbaum. "Understanding Nepalese Labour Migration to Gulf Countries." *Journal of Poverty* 21, no. 5 (2017): 411–433.

Manto, Sadat Hasan. *Toba Tek Singh*. *Frances W. Pritchett*. Translated by Frances W. Pritchett, n.d. www.columbia.edu/itc/mealac/pritchett/00urdu/tobateksingh/translation.html. Accessed February 25, 2015.

Manzo, Kate. "Imaging Vulnerability: The Iconography of Climate Change." *Area* (January 2009): 1–12. www.katemanzo.com/wp-content/uploads/2009/04/Area-proof-2009.pdf. Accessed June 21, 2015.

Marco, Bulgarelli. "Bellary's Mines (India)." *Marco Bulgarelli* (blog), n.d. http://marcobulgarelli.com/bellarys-mines-india/. Accessed October 12, 2015.

"Mare Clausum: The Sea Watch vs. Libyan Coast Guard Case." *Forensic Oceanography, Forensic Architecture*, November 6, 2017. www.forensic-architecture.org/case/sea-watch/. Accessed January 1, 2019.

Marr, David, and Marian Wilkinson. "Australia V. The Boat People." In *Dark Victory*, 30–47. Crows Nest, NSW: Allen & Unwin, 2003.

Marrus, Michael R. *The Unwanted: European Refugees in the Twentieth Century*. New York: Oxford University Press, 1985.

Marta Foresti. "Refugees and Migrants: The View from This Week's New York Summits." *ODI*, September 22, 2016. www.odi.org/comment/10439-refugees-migrants-view-new-york-summits-un-obama. Accessed August 28, 2017.

Massey, Hugh. "UNHCR and De Facto Statelessness." *Legal and Protection Policy Research Series*, LPPR 2010/01 (April 2010): 1–66. www.unhcr.org/4bc2ddeb9.pdf. Accessed October 15, 2017.

Mazumdar, Madhumita. "Dwelling in Fluid Places: The Matuas of the Andaman Islands." In *New Histories of the Andaman Islands: Landscape, Place and Identity in the Bay of Bengal, 1790–2012*, edited by Clare Anderson, Madhumita Mazumdar, and Vishvajit Pandya, 170–200. Cambridge: Cambridge University Press, 2016.

McConnachie, Kirsten. *Governing Refugees: Justice, Order, and Legal Pluralism*. London: Routledge, 2014.

McGuiness, Margaret E. "Legal and Normative Dimensions of the Manipulation of Refugees." In *Refugee Manipulation: War, Politics, and the Abuse of Human Suffering*, edited by Stephen John Stedman and Fred Tanner, 135–166. Washington, DC: Brookings Institution Press, 2003.

Meier, Claudia, and C.S.R. Murthy. "India's Growing Involvement in Humanitarian Assistance." *Berlin, Global Public Policy Institute*, Research Paper, no. 13 (March 2011). www.gppi.net/2011/03/14/indias-growing-involvement-in-humanitarian-assistance. Accessed January 12, 2019.

Menon, R. "Birth of Social Security Commitments – What Happened in the West." In *Refugees and the State: Practices of Asylum and Care in India, 1947–2000*, edited by Ranabir Samaddar, 152–186. New Delhi: Sage, 2003.

Messina, Anthony M., and Gallya Lahav, eds. "Chapter 2.3." In *The Migration Reader: Exploring Politics and Policies*, 24–30. Boulder, CO and New Delhi: Lynne Rienner Pub., and Viva Books Ltd., 2006.

Mezzadra, Sandro. *Borders, Confines, Migrations, and Citizenship*. Translated by Maribel Casas Cortes and Sebastian Cobarrubias, 2006. www.observatario.faidaiat.net/tiki-index.php?page=borders,+migrations+citizenship. Accessed 12 June 2013

Mezzadra, Sandro. *The Gaze of Autonomy: Capitalism, Migration and Social Struggles*, September 19, 2010. Reprinted in *The Contested Politics of Mobility: Borderzones and Irregularity*, edited by V. Squire, 121–143. London: Routledge, 2011. www.uninomade.org/

the-gaze-of-autonomy-capitalism-migration-and-social-struggles/. Accessed December 2, 2016.

Mezzadra, Sandro. "What's at Stake in the Mobility of Labour? Borders, Migration, Contemporary Capitalism." *Migration, Mobility, and Displacement* 2, no. 1 (2016): 31–43.

Mezzadra, Sandro, and Brett Neilson. *Border as Method: Or, the Multiplication of Labour*. Durham, NC: Duke University Press, 2013.

"Migration, Risk and Resilience in the Context of Sudden and Slow-Onset Disaster." *International Organization for Migration*, Global Compact Thematic Paper (September 2016): 1–6. www.iom.int/sites/default/files/our_work/ODG/GCM/IOM-Thematic-Paper-Migration-Risk-and-Resilience-in-the-Context.pdf. Accessed August 17, 2018.

Mirowski, Phil. *Never Let a Serious Crisis Go to Waste: How Neoliberalism Survived the Financial Meltdown*. London: Verso, 2013.

Mishra, Omprakash, ed. *Forced Migration in the South Asian Region: Displacement, Human Rights, and Conflict Resolution*. New Delhi: Centre for Refugee Studies, Jadavpur University, Brookings Institution, and Manak Publications, 2004.

Mittal, Malini. "Work, Mobility, and Changing Family Relations: A Study of a Section of South Asian Pink-Collar Workers in Kuwait." Unpublished PhD diss., Delhi School of Economics, University of Delhi, 2017.

"Mixed Migration: Policy Challenges." *The Migration Observatory*, March 24, 2011. www.migrationobservatory.ox.ac.uk/resources/primers/mixed-migration-policy-challenges/. Accessed January 15, 2017.

Mohapatra, P.P. "Coolies and Colliers: A Study of the Agrarian Context of Labour Migration from Chotanagpur1880–1920." *Studies in History* 1, no. 20 (1985): 297–298.

Monsutti, Alessandro. "Migration as a Rite of Passage: Young Afghans Building Masculinity and Adulthood in Iran." *Iranian Studies* 40, no. 2 (April 2007): 167–185.

Monsutti, Alessandro. "Mobility as a Political Act." *Ethnic and Racial Studies* 41, no. 3 (2018): 448–455.

Moreno-Lax, Violeta, and Eithymios Papastavridis. *"Boat Refugees" and Migrants at Sea: A Comparative Approach*. Leiden: Brill Nijhoff, 2017.

Mukhopadhyay, Amites. "Cyclone Aila and the Sundarbans: An Inquiry into the Disaster and Politics of Aid and Relief." *Policies and Practices*, no. 26 (2009): 1–24. www.mcrg.ac.in/PP26.pdf. Accessed February 14, 2015.

Mukhopadhyay, Bhaskar. "Crossing the Howrah Bridge: Calcutta, Filth and Dwelling – Forms, Fragments, Phantasms." *Theory, Culture, & Society* 23, no. 7–8 (2006): 221–241.

Mukhopadhyay, Bhaskar. *The Rumor of Globalization: Desecrating the Global Forms from the Vernacular Margins*. London: C. Hurst & Co., 2012.

Nag, Sajal. "Disciplining Villages and Restoring Peace in the Countryside." In *Government of Peace: Social Governance, Security and the Problematic of Peace*, edited by Ranabir Samaddar. New Delhi: Routledge, 2015.

Nagel, Caroline R. "Review of *The Age of Migration*, by Stephen Castles, Hein de Haas and Mark J. Miller." *Political Geography* 19 (2000): 661–665.

Nail, Thomas. *The Figure of the Migrant*. Stanford, CA: Stanford University Press, 2015.

Nair, Arjun. *National Refugee Law for India: Benefits and Roadblocks*. ICPS Research Paper, no. 11 (December 2007): 1–10.

Narahari, N.S. *Security Threats to Northeast India – The Socio-Ethnic Tensions*. New Delhi: Manas Publications, 2002.

"New York Declaration for Refugees and Migrants." *UNHCR*, 2016. www.unhcr.org/newyorkdeclaration. Accessed August 1, 2018.

Nikhil, Kumar. "Reprisals, Rape, and Children Burned Alive: Burma's Rohingya Speak of Genocidal Terror." *Time*, December 12, 2016. https://time.com/4596937/burma-myanmar-rohingya-bangladesh-refugees-crimes-against-humanity/. Accessed March 2, 2017.

Noll, Gregor. "Why Human Rights Fail to Protect Undocumented Migrants." *European Journal of Migration and Law* 12, no. 2 (2010): 241–272.
"Non-Paper on the Asylum Capacity Support Group." *UNHCR*, Proposed Global Compact on Refugees, June 4, 2018. www.unhcr.org/publications/legal/5b1558104/non-paper-asylum-capacity-support-group-4-june-2018.html. Accessed August 15, 2018.
Norbu, D. "Refugees from Tibet – Structural Causes of Successful Settlements." In *Refugees and Human Rights*, edited by S.K. Roy. New Delhi: Rawat Publications, 2002.
Nordland, Rod. "A Mass Migration Crisis, and It May Yet Get Worse." *International New York Times*, November 2015.
Novak, Paolo. "Back to Borders." *Critical Sociology* 43, no. 6 (September 2017): 847–864.
Nunthara, C. *Impact of the Introduction of Grouping of Villages in Mizoram*. New Delhi: Omsons Publications, 1989.
Oberoi, Pia. *Exile and Belonging: Refugees and State Policy in South Asia*. New Delhi: Oxford University Press, 2006.
Omata, Naohiko. "Refugees' Engagement with Host Economies in Uganda." *Forced Migration Review*, Economies: Rights and Access to Work, no. 58 (June 2018): 19–21.
Ong, Aihwa. "Making the Biopolitical Subject: Cambodian Immigrants, Refugee Medicine, and Cultural Citizenship in California." *Social Science and Medicine* 40, no. 9 (1995): 1243–1257.
Ong, Aihwa. *Flexible Citizenship: The Cultural Logics of Transnationality*. Durham, NC: Duke University Press, 1999.
Ong, Aihwa. *Buddha Is Hiding: Refugees, Citizenship, the New America*. California Series in Public Anthropology. Berkeley, CA: University of California Press, 2003.
Ong, Aihwa. "A Milieu of Mutations: The Pluripotency and Fungibility of Life in Asia." *East Asian Science, Technology, and Society: An International Journal* 7, no. 3 (2013): 69–85.
Papadopoulos, Dimitris, Niamh Stephenson, and Vassilis Tsianos. *Escape Routes: Control and Subversion in the Twenty-first Century*. London: Pluto Press, 2006.
Papadopoulos, Dimitris, Niamh Stephenson, and Vassilis Tsianos. *Escape Routes: Control and Subversion in the 21st Century*. London: Pluto Press, 2008.
Parker, Roy. *Uprooted: The Shipment of Poor Children to Canada, 1867–1917*. Chicago: Chicago University Press and University of Bristol Press, 2008.
Parveen, Gulshan. "Watery Zones of Refuge: State Practices, Popular Politics and Land in the *Chars* of Assam." In *Political Ecology of Survival – Life and Labour in the River Lands of East and North-East India*, edited by Basu Madhurilata, Rajat Ray, and Ranabir Samaddar, 121–141. Hyderabad: Orient Blackswan, 2018.
Pathiraja, Dinusha. "Compare and Contrast the Situation of Conflict Related IDPs and Tsunami Related IDPs in Sri Lanka." *Calcutta Research Group*, October Issue (2005): 1–9. www.mcrg.ac.in/DP.pdf. Accessed 20 June 20, 2015.
"Pathways to Employment: Expanding Legal and Legitimate Labour Market Opportunities for Refugees." *Regional Support Office – The Bali Process*, Background Papers, 2016. www.baliprocess.net/UserFiles/baliprocess/File/FINAL_Pathways%20Background%20Papers_050417.pdf. Accessed August 26, 2017.
Patrick, Barnard. "Notes on Syria and the Great Refugee Crisis." *Montreal Serai* 21, no. 9 (March 2016). http://montrealserai.com/2016/03/28/notes-on-syria-and-the-great-refugee-crisis/. Accessed April 5, 2016.
Paul, Nelson. "Turning Migration Challenges into Opportunities to Build Resilience." *100 Resilient Cities*, October 5, 2017. www.100resilientcities.org/turning-migration-challenges-into-opportunities-to-build-resilience/. Accessed August 15, 2018.
Perouse de Montclos, Marc-Antoine, and Peter Mwangi Kagwanja. "Refugee Camps or Cities? Socio-economic Dynamics of the Dadaab and Kakuma Camps in Northern Kenya." *Journal of Refugee Studies* 13, no. 2 (2000): 205–222.

Petti, Alessandro. "Campus in Camps: A University in Exile." In *Permanent Temporariness*, edited by Sandi Hilal and Alessandro Petti, 209–214. Stockholm: Royal Institute of Art and Art and Theory Publishing, 2018.

Piore, Michael J. *Birds of Passage: Migrant Labor and Industrial Societies*. Cambridge: Cambridge University Press, 1979.

Postel, Hannah, Matt Juden, and Owen Barder. "What the EC's 17 Point Refugee Action Plan Ignores." *Centre for Global Development*, October 30, 2015. www.cgdev.org/blog/what-ec%E2%80%99s-17-point-refugee-action-plan-ignores. Accessed October 24, 2015.

Prakash, Amit. "The Capital City: Discursive Dissonance of Law and Policy." In *Migrant and the Neoliberal City*, edited by Ranabir Samaddar, 225–257. Hyderabad: Orient Blackswan, 2018.

Prins, Annemiek. "The Plight of Dwelling: East-Bengali Refugees and the Struggle for Land in Kolkata." *Refugee Watch*, no. 43–44 (June – December 2014): 32–52.

Pugliese, Joseph. "Race as Category Crisis: Whiteness and the Topical Assignation of Race." *Social Semiotics* 12, no. 2 (August 2002): 149–168.

Rahman, Md. Mahbubar, and Willem Van Schendel. "'I am Not a Refugee' – Rethinking Partition Migration." *Modern Asian Studies* 37, no. 3 (2003): 551–584.

Rahola, Federico. "The Space of Camps: Towards a Genealogy of Places of Internment in the Present." In *Conflict, Security and the Reshaping of Society: The Civilisation of War*, edited by A. Dal Lago and S. Palidda, 185–199. Milton Park: Routledge, 2010.

Rai, Om Astha, and Sonia Awale. "Killed in the Line of Duty: Nepali Migrant Workers Who Return in Coffins Are Too Young and Healthy to Die." *Nepal Times*, January 8–14, 2016. https://nepalitimes.atavist.com/nepalis-killed-in-the-line-of-duty. Accessed March 5, 2019.

Ramachandran, Sujata. "Indifference, Impotence, and Intolerance: Transnational Bangladeshis in India." *Global Migration Perspectives*, no. 42 (2005): 1–18.

Ray, Nihar Ranjan. *An Introduction to the Study of Theravada Buddhism in Burma: A Study in the Indo-Burmese Historical and Cultural Relations from the Earliest Times to the British Conquest*, 1946. Cited in Parimal Ghosh. *Brave Men in the Hills, Resistance and Rebellion in Burma, 1825–1932*. London: C. Hurst & Co., 2000.

"'Refugees' and 'Migrants': Frequently Asked Questions." *UNHCR*, March 16, 2016. www.unhcr.org/news/latest/2016/3/56e95c676/refugees-migrants-frequently-asked-questions-faqs.html. Accessed January 14, 2017.

Refugee Rights Europe. *The State of Refugees and Displaced People in Europe: A Summary of Research Findings Across Europe*. Refugee Rights Europe, 2017–18. http://refugeerights.org.uk/wp-content/uploads/2018/12/RRE_SummaryReport_2017-18.pdf. Accessed January 16, 2019.

Reinhold, Martin. *The Organizational Complex: Architecture, Media and Corporate Space*. Cambridge, MA: MIT Press, 2003.

Robert, Farley. "Four Myths About the European Refugee Crisis (And Why You Need to Know the Reality)." *Lawyers, Guns & Money*, October 13, 2015. www.lawyersgunsmoneyblog.com/2015/10/four-myths-about-the-european-refugee-crisis-and-why-you-need-to-know-the-reality#comments. Accessed October 15, 2015.

Robinson, W. Courtland. "Risks and Rights: The Causes, Consequences, and Challenges of Development Induced Displacement." *Brookings Institution*, Occasional Paper (May 2003): 1–96. www.brookings.edu/wp-content/uploads/2016/06/didreport.pdf. Accessed June 8, 2015.

Ronge, Volker. "Review of *The Age of Migration: International Population Movements in the Modern World*, by Stephen Castles and Mark Miller." *Journal of European Social Policy* 4, no. 2 (1994): 152–153.

Rosenberg, Clifford. *Policing Paris – The Origins of Modern Immigration Control Between the Wars.* Ithaca: Cornell University Press, 2006.

Rossiter, Ned. "Translating the Indifference of Communication: Electronic Waste, Migrant Labour and the Informational Sovereignty of Logistics in China." *International Review of Information Ethics*, no. 11 (2009): 35–44.

Rossiter, Ned. "The Logistical City: Software, Infrastructure, Labour." Paper presented at *Cities and Materialities Workshop*, Institute for Culture and Society, University of Western Sydney, April 11, 2012. http://nedrossiter.org/?p=324. Accessed June 15, 2015.

Rother, Bjorn, Gaelle Pierre, Davide Lombardo, Risto Herrala, Priscilla Toffano, Eric Roos, Greg Auclair, and Karina Manasseh. "The Economic Impact of Conflicts and the Refugee Crisis in the Middle East and North Africa." *IMF* Staff Discussion Note, SDN/16/08 (September 2016): 9–18.

Ruben, Andersson. "The Illegality Industry: Notes on Europe's Dangerous Border Experiment." In *LSE International Development: Social, Political and Economic Transformation in the Developing World*, October 26, 2015. www.law.ox.ac.uk/research-subject-groups/centre-criminology/centreborder-criminologies/blog/2015/10/illegality. Accessed November 7, 2017.

Rudolph Jr., Joseph. "The Doubtful Effects of Military Intervention on Forced Migration in Yugoslavia." In *The Politics of Forced Migration: A Conceptual, Operational, and Legal Analysis*, edited by Nina Nachmias and Rami Goldstein, 191–224. Baltimore: Publish America, 2004.

Ruiz, Hiram A. *Northeast India's Hidden Displacement.* Washington, DC: U.S. Committee for Refugees, 2000.

Said, Edward. *Reflections on Exile and Other Essays.* Cambridge, MA: Harvard University Press, 2002.

Samaddar, Ranabir, ed. *Reflections on Partition in the East.* New Delhi: Vikas, 1997.

Samaddar, Ranabir. *Memory, Identity, Power: Junglemahals: 1880–1950.* Hyderabad: Orient Longman, 1998.

Samaddar, Ranabir. *The Marginal Nation: Transborder Migration from Bangladesh to West Bengal.* New Delhi: Sage, 1999.

Samaddar, Ranabir, ed. *Refugees and the State: Practices of Asylum and Care in India, 1947–2000.* New Delhi: Sage, 2003.

Samaddar, Ranabir. "Governing Through Peace Accords." In *The Politics of Dialogue: Living Under the Geopolitical Histories of War and Peace*, 159–196. Aldershot: Ashgate, 2004.

Samaddar, Ranabir. "The Non-dialogic World of the Humanitarian." In *The Politics of Dialogue: Living Under the Geopolitical Histories of War and Peace*, 271–310. Aldershot: Ashgate, 2004.

Samaddar, Ranabir. "Primitive Accumulation and Some Aspects of Work and Life in India." *Economic and Political Weekly* 44, no. 18 (May 2009): 33–42.

Samaddar, Ranabir. "Empire, Globalisation, and the Subject." In *Emergence of the Political Subject*, 267–291. New Delhi: Sage, 2010.

Samaddar, Ranabir. "The Insecure World of the Nation." In *Migration and Circles of Insecurity*, edited by Paula Banerjee and Ranabir Samaddar, 1–69. New Delhi: Rupa, 2010.

Samaddar, Ranabir. "Refugees and the Dynamics of Hospitality: The Indian Story." In *Immigration Worldwide: Policies, Practices, and Trends*, edited by Uma A. Segal, Doreen Elliott, and Nazneen S. Mayadas, 112–123. New York: Oxford University Press, 2010.

Samaddar, Ranabir. "Rajarhat, the Urban Dystopia." In *Transit Labour: Circuits, Regions, Borders*, July 29, 2011. http://transitlabour.asia/blogs/dystopia. Accessed June 12, 2014.

Samaddar, Ranabir. "Introduction: Power and Care – Building the New Indian State." In *Refugees and the State*, edited by Ranabir Samaddar, 21–68. New Delhi: Sage, 2013.

Samaddar, Ranabir. *Memory, Identity, Power: Junglemahals: 1880–1950*. Reprint, Hyderabad: Orient Longman, 2013.

Samaddar, Ranabir. "Government of Peace." In *Government of Peace: Social Governance, Security, and the Problematic of Peace*, edited by Ranabir Samaddar, 19–56. Farnham, Surrey: Ashgate, 2015.

Samaddar, Ranabir. "Returning to the Histories of the Late 19th and Early 20th Century Immigration." *Economic and Political Weekly* L, no. 2 (January 2015): 49–55.

Samaddar, Ranabir. "Human Migration Appearing as Crisis of Europe." In *A Postcolonial Enquiry into Europe's Debt and Migration Crisis*, edited by Ranabir Samaddar, 87–116. Singapore: Springer, 2016.

Samaddar, Ranabir, ed. *Migrant and the Neoliberal City*. Hyderabad: Orient Blackswan, 2018.

Samaddar, Ranabir. "Pangs of Ambiguity: *Race, Nation, Class* Deciphered for India." In *Balibar/ Wallertstein's "Race, Nation, Class: Rereading a Dialogue for Our Times*, edited by Manuel Bojadzijev and Katrin Klingan, 171–198. Hamburg, Berlin: Argument Verlagand Haus der Kulturen der Welt, 2018.

Samaddar, Ranabir, and Paula Banerjee. *Migration and Circles of Insecurity*. New Delhi: Rupa & Co., 2010.

Sanyal, Kalyan. *Rethinking Capitalist Development: Primitive Accumulation, Governmentality, and Postcolonial Capitalism*. New Delhi: Routledge, 2007.

Sassen, Saskia. "Europe's Migrations: The Numbers and the Passions are Not New." *Third Text* 20, no. 6 (November 2006): 635–645.

Sassen, Saskia. *Expulsions: Brutality and Complexity in the Global Economy*. Cambridge, MA: Harvard University Press, 2014.

Scheel, Stephan. "Autonomy of Migration Despite Its Securitisation? Facing the Terms and Conditions of Biometric Rebordering." *Millennium: Journal of International Studies* 41 (2013): 575–600.

Scheel, Stephan. "Studying Embodied Encounters: Autonomy of Migration Beyond Its Romanticisation." *Postcolonial Studies* 16, no. 3 (November 2013): 279–288.

Scheel, Stephan. "Rethinking the Autonomy of Migration: On the Appropriation of Mobility Within Biometric Border Regimes." PhD diss., Department of Political and International Studies, The Open University, Milton Keynes, 2016.

Scheel, Stephan. "Appropriating Mobility and Bordering Europe Through Romantic Love: Unearthing the Intricate Intertwinement of Border Regimes and Migratory Practices." *Migration Studies* 5, no. 3 (2017): 389–408.

Scheel, Stephan. "Real Fake? Appropriating Mobility via Schengen Visa in the Context of Biometric Border Controls." *Journal of Ethnic and Migration Studies* 44, no. 16 (2018): 2747–2763.

Schmeidl, Susanne. "From Root Cause Assessment to Preventive Diplomacy: Possibilities and Limitations of the Early Warning of Forced Migration." PhD diss., Ohio State University, 1995.

Sebastian, Kohn. "Russia and the Baltics: The Great Statelessness Game." In *European Network on Statelessness*, October 25, 2012. www.statelessness.eu/blog/russia-and-baltics-great-statelessness-game. Accessed October 1, 2017.

Seifu, Yordanos Almaz. *Wayferers: Travel Journal*. Translated by Hiwot Tadesse. Addis Ababa: Friedrich Ebert Stiftung, 2018.

Sen, Anandaroop. "A Lost Population? East India Company and Arakanese 'Refugees' in Chittagong." *Refugee Watch*, no. 46 (December 2015): 1–20. www.mcrg.ac.in/rw%20files/RW46/RW46.pdf. Accessed October 1, 2017.

Sen, Uditi. "Memories of Partition's 'Forgotten Episode': Refugee Resettlement in the Andaman Islands." *South Asia Chronicle*, no. 7 (2017): 147–178. https://edoc.hu-berlin.de/bitstream/handle/18452/19503/07%20-%20Focus%20-%20Sen%20-%20Memories%20 of%20Partition%E2%80%99s%20%27Forgotten%20Episode%27.%20Refugee%20 Resettlement%20in%20the%20Andaman%20Islands.pdf?sequence=4&isAllowed=y. Accessed October 20, 2018.

Sengupta, Kaustubh Mani. "Taking Refuge in the City: Migrant Population and Urban Management in Post-Partition Calcutta." *Policies and Practices*, no. 72 (October 2015): 1–15. www.academia.edu/26461483/Cities_Rural_Migrants_and_the_Urban_Poor. Accessed February 8, 2017.

Sengupta, Sucharita, and Samir Purakayastha. "Politics of Immigration and Look East Policy: Reflections from Assam and the Northeast." In *Global Governance and India's Northeast: Logistics, Infrastructure, and Society*, edited by Ranabir Samaddar and Anita Sengupta, 260–287. London and New York: Routledge, 2019.

Shah, Alpa, and Barbara Harriss-White. "Resurrecting Scholarship on Agrarian Transformations." *Economic and Political Weekly* 46, no. 39 (September 2011): 13–18.

"Shared Responsibility, Shared Humanity." In *Communiqué from the International Refugee Congress*, 2018. http://jhrmk.org/index.php/2018/05/18/international-refugee-congress-2018-shared-responsibility-shared-humanity/?lang=en. Accessed August 13, 2018.

Siddiqi, A.R. *Partition and the Making of the Mohajir Mindset: A Narrative*. Oxford: Oxford University Press, 2008.

Sikdar, Sujit, and Devadas Bhorali. "Resource Mobilisation, Distribution Effect and Economic Development of the North-eastern Region." In *Liberalisation and India's North East*, edited by Gurudas Das and R.K. Purkayastha, 167–172. New Delhi: Commonwealth Publishers, 1998.

Singh, Anita Inder. *The Partition of India*. New Delhi: National Book Trust, 2006.

Singh, Simpreet. "The Emergence of the Migrant as a Problem Figure in Contemporary Mumbai: Chronicles of Violence and Issues of Justice." In *Migrant and the Neoliberal City*, edited by Ranabir Samaddar, 147–169. Hyderabad: Orient Blackswan, 2018.

Skeldon, Ronald. "What's in a Title? The Fifth Edition of the Age of Migration." *Ethnic and Racial Studies* 38, no. 13 (2015): 2356–2361.

Smith, Martin. *Burma: Insurgency and the Politics of Ethnicity*. London: Zed Books, 1991.

Stedman, Stephen John, and Fed Tanner, eds. *Refugee manipulation – War, Politics, and the Abuse of Human Sufferings*. Washington, DC: Brookings Institution, 2003.

Steinbeck, John. *The Grapes of Wrath*. London: Penguin Modern Classics, 1939.

Sword, Keith. "Review of *The Age of Migration: International Population Movements in the Modern World*, by Stephen Castles and Mark Miller." *The Slavonic and East European Review* 74, no. 1 (1996): 186–188.

"Syrian Refugees in Turkish Garment Supply Chains." *Business and Human Rights Resource Centre*, Briefing Note (February 2016): 1–7. https://business-humanrights.org/sites/default/files/160131%20Syrian%20Refugee%20Briefing%20FINAL.pdf. Accessed January 19, 2017.

"Syrian Refugees Working in Turkey's Garment Sector." *Ethical Trading Initiative*, n.d. www.ethicaltrade.org/programmes/syrian-refugees-working-turkeys-garment-sector. Accessed January 19, 2017.

Tacita, Vero. "The Grey Zone." *Slate*, March 13, 2017.

TAMPEP (European Network for HIV/STI Prevention and Health Promotion Among Migrant Sex Workers). *Sex Work in Europe: A Mapping of the Prostitution Scene in 25 European Countries*. Amsterdam: TAMPEP International Foundation, 2009. www.nswp.org/sites/nswp.org/files/TAMPEP%202009%20European%20Mapping%20Report.pdf. Accessed January 2, 2017.

Tarapot, Phanjoubam. *Bleeding Manipur*. New Delhi: Har-Anand Publications, 2003.

Tavares, Paulo. "Lines of Siege: The Contested Government of Nature." In *The Biopolitics of Development: Reading Michel Foucault in the Post-Colonial Present*, edited by Sandro

Mezzadra, Julien Reid, and Ranabir Samaddar, 123–164. New Delhi and Dordrecht: Springer, 2013.

Taylor, J. Edward, Mateusz J. Filipski, Mohamed Alloush, Anubhab Gupta, Ruben Irvin Rojas Valdes, and Ernesto Gonzalez-Estrada. "Economic Impact of Refugees." *PNAS (Proceedings of the National Academy of Sciences of the United States of America)* 113, no. 27 (July 2016): 7449–7453.

Teresa, Rehman. "Too Deep for the State." *Tehelka Magazine*, n.d. http://archive.tehelka.com/story_main41.asp?filename=Ws271208too_deep.asp. Accessed October 11, 2015.

"The Bali Process on People Smuggling, Trafficking in Persons and Related Transnational Crime." *The Bali Process*, n.d. www.baliprocess.net. Accessed October 10, 2015.

"The Global Compacts on Refugees and Migration." *Andrew & Renata Kaldor Centre for International Refugee Law*, January 2019. www.kaldorcentre.unsw.edu.au/publication/2018-global-compacts-refugees-and-migration. Accessed April 16, 2019.

"The Issue: The Growing Salience of Mixed Migration." *The Migration Observatory*, March 24, 2011. www.migrationobservatory.ox.ac.uk/resources/primers/mixed-migration-policy-challenges/. Accessed January 15, 2017.

"The Policy Study Report on the Waste Electrical and Electronic Equipment." Directive. *Friends of the Earth Report*, 2011. www.foe.co.uk/.../report-influence-eu-policies-environment-9392. Accessed March 13, 2016.

"The Responsibility to Protect." *International Commission on Intervention and State Sovereignty*, December 2001. http://responsibilitytoprotect.org/ICISS%20Report.pdf. Accessed August 12, 2018.

"The Responsibility to Protect." *e-International Relations*, November 2011. www.files.ethz.ch/isn/181082/R2P.pdf. Accessed August 12, 2018.

"The Rohingya Situation." *Presentation by Thailand Bali SOM*, February 24–25, 2009. www.baliprocess.net/UserFiles/baliprocess/File/Bali%20Process%20SOM%202009%20-%20Thailand%20Presentation%20-%20The%20Rohingya%20Situation.pdf. Accessed August 29, 2017.

"The Time for Action Children Uprooted Is Now." *UNICEF*, June 8, 2018. www.unhcr.org/5a4374d47.pdf. Accessed August 15, 2018.

"The Transcontinental Railroad." *American Experience*, January 27, 2003. www.pbs.org/wgbh/americanexperience/films/tcrr/. Accessed December 21, 2017.

Thucydides. *The History of the Peloponnesian War in Complete Works of Thucydides*. Translated by Benjamin Jowett. 2nd ed. Oxford: Clarendon Press, 1900.

Tilly, Charles. "Migration in Modern European History." In *Human Migration*, edited by W.H. McNeil and R.S. Adams, 48–72. Bloomington: Indiana University Press, 1978.

Tilly, Charles. "The Old New Social History and the New Old Social History." *Institute for Social Research University of Michigan, Ann Arbor*, Working Paper, no. 218 (October 1980): 1–49.

Tilly, Charles. "Transplanted Networks." *New School for Social Research, Centre for Studies of Social Change*, Working Paper Series, no. 35 (October 1986); and in *Immigration Reconsidered: History, Sociology, and Politics*, edited by Virginia Yans-McLaughlin, 79–95. New York: Oxford University Press, 1990.

Tilly, Charles. *Big Structures, Large Processes, Huge Comparisons*. New York: Russell Sage Foundation, 1994.

Tilly, Charles. "Trust Networks in Transnational Migration." *Sociological Forum* 22, no. 1 (March 2007): 3–24.

Tinker, Hugh. *A New System of Slavery: The Export of Indian Labour Overseas, 1830–1920*. London and Oxford: Institute of Race Relations and Oxford University Press, 1974.

Tometten, Christophe. "Judicial Response to Mixed and Massive Population Flows." *Refugee Watch*, no. 39–40 (June–December 2012): 125–140. www.mcrg.ac.in/rw%20files/RW39_40/11.pdf. Accessed December 1, 2017.

Tometten, Christophe. "Germany's 'Legal Entry' Framework for Syrian Refugees – A Tool for Containment?" *Oxford Monitor of Forced Migration* 7, no. 1 (August 2017): 47–59.

Torpey, John. *The Invention of Passport: Surveillance, Citizenship, and the State*. Cambridge: Cambridge University Press, 1999.

"Towards a Global Compact on Refugees: A Roadmap." *UNHCR*, May 17, 2017. www.unhcr.org/events/conferences/58e625aa7/towards-global-compact-refugees-roadmap.html. Accessed August 11, 2018.

"Towards a Global Compact on Refugees: Key Elements of the Roadmap." *UNHCR*, May 17, 2017. www.unhcr.org/58d135517.pdf. Accessed August 15, 2018.

"Towards a Global Compact on Refugees: Roadmap on the Formal Consultations." *UNHCR*, April 16, 2018. www.unhcr.org/5a60b9409.pdf. Accessed August 15, 2018.

"Transcontinental Railroad: Reports from the End of the Track." *American Experience*, n.d. www.pbs.org/wgbh/americanexperience/features/tcrr-reports/. Accessed February 1, 2019.

"Transit Labour." *About*. http://transitlabour.asia/about/. Accessed December 1, 2016.

Trilling, Daniel. "What to Do with the People Who Do Make It Across?" *London Review of Books* 37, no. 19 (2015): 9–12. www.lrb.co.uk/v37/n19/daniel-trilling/what-to-do-with-the-people-whodo-make-it-across. Accessed January 3, 2016.

Tseng-Puttermanwrites, Mark. "A Century of U.S. Intervention Created the Immigration Crisis." *Medium World*, June 20, 2018. https://medium.com/s/story/timeline-us-intervention-central-america-a9bea9ebc148. Accessed December 21, 2018.

"Tsunami: Learning from the Humanitarian Response." *Forced Migration Review*, Special Issue (July 2005): 4–51. www.fmreview.org/sites/fmr/files/FMRdownloads/en/tsunami.pdf. Accessed June 21, 2015.

Tumbe, Chinmoy. "Migration Persistence Across Twentieth Century India." *Migration and Development* 1, no. 1 (June 2012): 87–112.

Turk, Volker. "Prospects for Responsibility Sharing in the Refugee Context." *Journal on Migration and Human Security* 4, no. 3 (2016): 45–59.

UNHCR. "Coordination in Complex Emergencies." *UNHCR*, September 1, 2001. www.unhcr.org/partners/partners/3ba88e7c6/coordination-complex-emergencies.html. Accessed February 28, 2019.

UNHCR. "Bali Process on People Smuggling, Trafficking in Persons and Related Transnational Crime." *Senior Officials' Meeting, Brisbane, Australia*, February 23–24, 2009. www.baliprocess.net/UserFiles/baliprocess/File/UNHCRBalipresentation.pdf. Accessed August 29, 2017.

United Nations. "Migration Compact Support MPTF: Financial Reporting on Sources and Uses of Funds for the Period Ending 31 December 2017." *UNDP*, 2018. https://refugeesmigrants.un.org/sites/default/files/work_plan_gcm.pdf. Accessed August 1, 2018.

Upadhyay, Priyankar, and Anjoo Sharan Upadhyay. "Peacebuilding in India: Meghalaya's Experience." In *Cultures of Governance: A Comparison of EU and Indian Theoretical and Policy Approaches*, edited by J. Peter Burgess, Oliver P. Richmond, and Ranabir Samaddar, 172–189. Manchester: Manchester University Press, 2016.

"Urban Refugees." *UNHCR*, December 4, 2017. www.unhcr.org/5a33d4447.pdf. Accessed December 11, 2018.

Van Schendel, Willem. "Working Through Partition – Making a Living in the Bengal Borderlands." *International Review of Social History*, no. 46 (2000): 393–421.

Van Schendel, Willem. "Stateless in South Asia – The Making of India-Bangladesh Enclaves." *The Journal of Asian Studies* 61, no. 1 (2002): 115–147.

Van Schendel, Willem. *Bengal Borderlands: Beyond State and Nation in South Asia*. London: Anthem Press, 2004.

Vernon, James. *Hunger: A Modern History*. Cambridge, MA: Harvard University Press, 2007.

Visaria, Leela, and Pravin Visaria. "Population (1757–1947)." In *Cambridge Economic History of India*, edited by Dharma Kumar, Vol. 2, 463–532. Hyderabad: Orient Longman, 1984.

Vuolajarvi, Niina. "Precarious Intimacies: The European Border Regime and Migrant Sex Work." *Viewpoint Magazine*, October 31, 2015. https://viewpointmag.com/2015/10/31/precarious-intimacies-the-european-border-regime-and-migrant-sex-work/. Accessed January 20, 2017.

Vyas, Mouleshri. "The Cutting Edge: Death and Life of Safai Karmacharis and Elderly Security Guards in Mumbai." In *Migrants and the Neoliberal City*, edited by Ranabir Samaddar, 170–195. New Delhi: Orient Blackswan, 2018.

Walter, Chris. "Weaving a Future for Tibetan Refugees: Tibetan Rug Weaving Project." *Cultural Survival Quarterly Magazine*, June 2003. www.culturalsurvival.org/publications/cultural-survival-quarterly/weaving-future-tibetan-refugees-tibetan-rug-weaving. Accessed January 20, 2017.

Walters, William. "The Frontiers of European Union: A Geostrategic Perspective." *Geopolitics* 9, no. 3 (Autumn 2004): 674–698.

Walters, William. "Foucault and Frontiers: Notes on the Birth of the Humanitarian Border." In *Governmentality: Current Issues and Future Challenges*, edited by U. Bröckling, S. Krasmann, and T. Lemke, 138–164. London: Routledge, 2010.

Walters, William. "Migration, Vehicles and Politics: Three Theses on Viapolitics." *European Journal of Social Theory* 18, no. 4 (2014): 469–488.

Walters, William. "Reflections on Migration and Governmentality." *Movements: Journal for Critical Migration and Border Regime Studies* 1, no. 1 (2015). https://movements-journal.org/issues/01.grenzregime/04.walters – migration.governmentality.html. Accessed March 22, 2018.

Wareing, John. *Indentured Migration and the Servant Trade from London to America, 1618–1718*. Oxford: Oxford University Press, 2017.

Warner, Daniel. "We are all Refugees." *International Journal of Refugee Law* 4, no. 3 (1992): 365–372. www.mcrg.ac.in/RLS_Migration/Reading_List/Module_A/72.%20Warner,%20Daniel%20%E2%80%9CWe%20are%20all%20Refugees.pdf. Accessed October 28, 2015.

Westmoreland, Mark W. "Interruptions: Derrida and Hospitality." *Kritike* 2, no. 1 (June 2008): 1–10.

"Who Is Affected by Statelessness?" *Canadian Centre on Statelessness*, n.d. www.statelessness.ca/who-is-stateless.html#. Accessed January 1, 2019.

Wodak, Ruth, Majid Khosrav Nik, and Brigitte Mral, eds. *Right-Wing Populism in Europe: Politics and Discourse*. London: Bloomsbury, 2013.

Wolff, Larry. *Inventing Eastern Europe: The Map of Civilisation on the Mind of Enlightenment*. Stanford, CA: Stanford University Press, 1994.

Worster, Donald. *Rivers of Empire: Water, Aridity, and the Growth of the American West*. New York: Oxford University Press, 1985.

Yegar, Moshe. "The Muslims of Burma." In *The Crescent in the East: Islam in Asia Major*, edited by Raphael Israeli. London: Curzon Press, 1982.

Zetter, Roger. "Are Refugees an Economic Burden or Benefit?" *Forced Migration Review*, no. 41 (December 2012): 50–52. www.fmreview.org/preventing/zetter.html. Accessed January 19, 2017.

Zolberg, Aristide R., Astri Suhrke, and Sergio Aguayo. *Escape from Violence: Conflict and the Refugee Crisis in the Developing World*. Oxford: Oxford University Press, 1989, 1992.

C. Newspaper Articles

Alex, Needham. "The List: The 34,361 Men, Women and Children who Perished Trying to Reach Europe." *The Guardian*, June 20, 2018. www.theguardian.com/world/2018/jun/20/the-list-34361-men-women-and-children-who-perished-trying-to-reach-europe-world-refugee-day. Accessed November 1, 2018.

Aung, Zaw. "The Man Behind the Burma Independence Army." *The Irrawaddy*, August 25, 2017. www.irrawaddy.com/opinion/commentary/man-behind-burma-independence-army.html. Accessed March 3, 2019.

"Bali Process to Take up Rohingya Issue." *Mizzima News*, February 22, 2009. http://archive-2.mizzima.com/archive/1752-bali-process-to-take-up-rohingya-issue.html. Accessed October 10, 2015.

Bikash, Singh. "Disturbed Area Tag in Assam Extended for Another Six Month." *Economic Times*, September 7, 2019. https://economictimes.indiatimes.com/news/politics-and-nation/disturbed-area-tag-in-assam-extended-for-another-six-month/articleshow/71025014.cms. Accessed September 8, 2019.

Blitzer, Jonathan. "Letter from El Salvador: The Deportees Taking Our Calls, How American Immigration Policy Has Fuelled an Unlikely Industry in El Salvador." *The New Yorker*, January 23, 2017. www.newyorker.com/magazine/2017/01/23/the-deportees-taking-our-calls. Accessed March 11, 2017.

Brankamp, Hanno. "The Question of Internal Colonialism." *Pambazuka News*, January 13, 2015. www.pambazuka.org/global-south/question-%E2%80%98internal-colonialism%E2%80%99. Accessed January 5, 2019.

"Briefing Prostitution and the Internet: More Bang for Your Buck." *The Economist*, August 9, 2014.

Chowdhury, Sandip. "Civic Bosses Lay Out Vision 2020 for City." *Hindustan Times*, November 2, 2012. www.hindustantimes.com/kolkata/civic-bosses-lay-out-vision-2020-for-city/story-eoIhGUvZAG2fmuL6OEg7iK.html. Accessed September 23, 2017.

"Countries Under the Most Strain in the European Migration Crisis." *New York Times*, September 3, 2015. www.nytimes.com/interactive/2015/08/28/world/europe/countries-under-strain-from-european-migration-crisis.html?_r=0. Accessed October 1, 2016.

"Danish MEP Quits Ruling Party Over Plan to Seize Refugees' Valuables." *The Guardian*, December 20, 2015. www.theguardian.com/world/2015/dec/20/danish-mep-quits-ruling-party-plan-refugees-valuables. Accessed November 1, 2018.

Diarmaid, Ferriter. "This Brexit Plan Will Divide Britain and Ireland Once More." *The Guardian*, October 10, 2016. www.theguardian.com/commentisfree/2016/oct/10/brexit-plan-divide-britain-ireland-uk-border. Accessed December 8, 2018.

Douzinas, Costas. "Cities of Refuge." *openDemocracy*. www.opendemocracy.net/can-europe-make-it/costas-douzinas/cities-of-refuge. Accessed April 12, 2016.

Erika, Solomon. "Mixed Fortunes in Lebanese Refugee Economy." *Financial Times*, April 11, 2014. www.ft.com/content/c403e0a0-c098-11e3-8578-00144feabdc0. Accessed January 13, 2017.

Fulya, Ozerkan. "17 Migrants die off Turkey, 500 Rescued." *Asian Age*, September 27, 2015. www.asianage.com/international/17-migrants-die-turkey-500-rescued-285. Accessed November 1, 2015.

Ian, Urbina. "Tricked and Indebted on Land, Abused or Abandoned at Sea." *The New York Times*, November 8, 2015. www.nytimes.com/2015/11/09/world/asia/philippines-fishing-ships-illegal-manning-agencies.html. Accessed March 15, 2018.

Jerry, Markon. "Can a 3-year Old Represent Herself in Immigration Court? This Judge Thinks So." *Washington Post*, March 5, 2016. www.washingtonpost.com/world/national-security/can-a-3-year-old-represent-herself-in-immigration-court-this-judge-thinks-so/2016/03/03/5be59a32-db25-11e5-925f-1d10062cc82d_story.html?hpid=hp_hp-more-top-stories_immigrationkids-930am%3Ahomepage%2Fstory. Accessed October 5, 2018.

John, Cassidy. "The Economics of Syrian Refugees." *The New Yorker*, November 18, 2015. www.newyorker.com/news/john-cassidy/the-economics-of-syrian-refugees. Accessed January 4, 2017.

Juliet, Shwe Gaung. "Massive Loan from China to Fund Gas Investment." *Myanmar Times*, December 13, 2010. www.mmtimes.com/business/4457-massive-loan-from-china-to-fund-gas-investment.html. Accessed January 1, 2019.

Mayank, Aggarwal. "New Rules to Curb Illegal Sand Mining." *Livemint*, July 1, 2015. www.livemint.com/Politics/lFs1vaw0PHEMHizHgMk83N/New-rules-to-curb-illegal-sand-mining.html. Accessed October 13, 2015.

Mehul, Srivastava. "Syrian Refugee Entrepreneurs Boost Turkey's Economy." *Financial Times*, May 16, 2016. www.ft.com/content/93e3d794-1826-11e6-b197-a4af20d5575e. Accessed January 6, 2017.

"Merkel Calls on Europe for Joint Responsibility on Refugee Crisis." *The Toronto Globe and Mail*, September 20, 2015. www.theglobeandmail.com/news/world/merkel-calls-on-europe-for-joint-responsibility-on-refugee-crisis/article26449744/. Accessed October 1, 2015.

"Migrant Crisis: Many Stranded in Balkans." *The Statesman*, October 20, 2015.

Miller, John W., and Juliet Samuel. "Mining Companies Bury Dividends." *The Wall Street Journal*, December 10, 2016.

"More Neighbours Make More Fences." *The Economist*, January 7, 2016. www.economist.com/blogs/graphicdetail/2015/09/daily-chart-10?fsrc=rss. Accessed November 2, 2015.

"Myanmar Army Denies Ethnic Cleansing of Rohingya in Rakhine State." *ABC News*, March 1, 2017. www.abc.net.au/news/2017-03-01/myanmar-army-defends-operation-against-rohingya/8316654. Accessed March 9, 2017.

Oliver, Laughland. "Inside Trump's Secretive Immigration Court: Far from Scrutiny and Legal Aid." *The Guardian*, June 7, 2017. www.theguardian.com/us-news/2017/jun/07/donald-trump-immigration-court-deportation-lasalle?CMP=share_btn_fb. Accessed November 28, 2018.

Pankaj, Mishra. "The Malign Incompetence of the British Ruling Class." *The New York Times*, January 17, 2019. www.nytimes.com/2019/01/17/opinion/sunday/brexit-ireland-empire.html. Accessed January 20, 2019.

Paul, Taylor. "EU Offers Turkey Cash, Closer Ties." *The Canberra Times*, October 17, 2015.

Phillips, Kristine. "Thousands of ICE Detainees Claim They Were Forced into Labor, a Violation of Anti-slavery Laws." *Washington Post*, March 6, 2017. www.washingtonpost.com/news/post-nation/wp/2017/03/05/thousands-of-ice-detainees-claim-they-were-forced-into-labor-a-violation-of-anti-slavery-laws/?utm_term=.5c796b97f65a. Accessed March 8, 2017.

Prabin, Kalita. "Biggest Detention Centre on Way in Assam." *Times of India*, Kolkata. September 8, 2019.

PTI Report. "Germany and Austria Call for EU Summit on Refugee Crisis." *The Statesman*, September 17, 2015. www.thestatesman.com/news/world/germany-and-austria-call-for-eu-summit-on-refugee-crisis/90526.html#sauiiHlJ2ByvSe1l.99. Accessed September 30, 2015.

Rajeev, Dhavan. "India's Refugee Law and Policy." *The Hindu*, June 25, 2004. www.thehindu.com/2004/06/25/stories/2004062501791000.htm. Accessed February 22, 2015.

"Refugee Crisis: EU Deportations to Turkey from Lesbos Continue Despite Protests." *The Independent*, April 8, 2016. www.independent.co.uk/news/world/europe/refugee-crisis-eu-deportations-to-turkey-from-lesbos-continue-despite-protests-a6974266.html. Accessed February 5, 2019.

Sebastian, Kohn. "Fear and Statelessness in Mauritania." *openDemocracy*, October 3, 2011. www.opensocietyfoundations.org/voices/fear-and-statelessness-mauritania. Accessed October 1, 2017.

Sharma, Christopher. "Gulf Crisis Frightens 400,000 Nepalese Workers in Qatar." *Asia News*, June 14, 2017. www.asianews.it/news-en/Gulf-crisis-frightens-400,000-Nepalese-workers-in-Qatar-41011.html. Accessed February 5, 2019.

Smith, Helena. "Migration Crisis: Idomeni, the Train Stop That Became an 'Insult to EU Values'." *The Guardian*, March 17, 2016. www.theguardian.com/world/2016/mar/17/migration-crisis-idomeni-camp-greece-macedonia-is-an-insult-to-eu-values. Accessed November 26, 2018.

Stapinski, Helene. "When America Barred Italians." *The New York Times*, June 2, 2017. www.nytimes.com/2017/06/02/opinion/illegal-immigration-italian-americans.html. Accessed June 1, 2018.

Sue, Reid. "Germany in a State of SIEGE Germany in a State of SIEGE: Merkel Was Cheered When She Opened the Floodgates to Migrants. Now, with Gangs of Men Roaming the Streets and Young German Women Being Told to Cover Up, the Mood's Changing." *Mailonline*, September 26, 2015. www.dailymail.co.uk/news/article-3249667/Germany-state-SIEGE-Merkel-cheered-opened-floodgates-migrants-gangs-men-roaming-streets-young-German-women-told-cover-mood-s-changing.html. Accessed February 3, 2017.

Sylvia, Federici. "The Reproduction Crisis and the Birth of a New 'Out of Law' Proletariat." *Left East*, July 10, 2017. www.criticatac.ro/lefteast/the-reproduction-crisis-and-the-birth-of-a-new-out-of-law-proletariat-an-interview-with-silvia-federici/. Accessed September 19, 2018.

"The Andaman Sea Refugee Crisis a Year On: Is the Region Now Better Prepared?" *The Conversation*, May 27, 2016. https://theconversation.com/the-andaman-sea-refugee-crisis-a-year-on-is-the-region-now-better-prepared-59687. Accessed August 28, 2017.

"The Economic Impact of Europe's Refugee Crisis." *Euronews*, November 1, 2016. www.euronews.com/2016/11/01/refugees-in-germany-from-desperation-to-economic-fortune. Accessed January 1, 2017.

"The Economic Impact of Refugees, For Good or Ill: Europe's New Arrivals Will Probably Dent Public Finances, but Not Wages." *The Economist*, January 23, 2016. www.economist.com/finance-and-economics/2016/01/23/for-good-or-ill. Accessed January 20, 2017.

"Tony Abbott Rules Out Resettling Rohingyas in Australia, Indonesia Says It Is Obliged to." *ABC News*, May 21, 2015. www.abc.net.au/news/2015-05-21/rohingyas-migrants-indonesia-says-australia-obliged-resettle/6486590. Accessed March 10, 2019.

Vaidyanathan, A. "7 Rohingya Will Be Deported, Supreme Court Says Myanmar Has Accepted Them." *NDTV*, October 5, 2018. www.ndtv.com/india-news/supreme-court-refuses-to-stop-deportation-of-7-rohingya-to-myanmar-today-1926544. Accessed January 5, 2019.

"West Indians Arrive in Britain on Board the Empire Windrush – Archive, 1948." *The Guardian*, June 30, 2016. www.theguardian.com/uk-news/2016/jun/23/immigration-windrush-west-indians-jamaica-britain. Accessed April 20, 2018.

INDEX

Note: Page numbers followed by 'n' refer to notes.

Abbott, Tony 175
accumulation: primitive 51, 89, 102–103, 153
actors, economic 61, 62, 70
Adas, Michael 57n10
Adorno, Theodor 52
Afghanistan 25, 29, 75, 143, 191–192, 198, 203
Afghanistan-Iran migration system 79n25
Afghan refugees 81n36, 200
Afghans 76, 148, 178, 198, 200
African Charter on Human and Peoples' Rights 185
Agamben, Giorgio 23
agencies 2, 10, 11, 14, 69, 73, 121, 226, 231
age of globalisation 6, 7, 10, 43–60
The Age of Migration 1–22, 62, 73, 145, 213; dualities and paradoxes in 12–15
age of penalised labour 2–7
Agier, Michel 62
alien-hood 196
All Assam Tribal Students Union 137
Andaman Sea refugee crisis 176
Andersson, Ruben 159n5
Angles 144
Anglo-Burmese War 168
Annals of Rural Bengal 89
annus mirabilis 144
anti-citizenship 184
anti-immigrant movement 132
Arakanese refugees 167

Arendt, Hannah 5, 23, 36, 173
Armed Forces Special Powers Act 179
Arnold, David 87
Arunachal Pradesh 128–130, 134–135, 137, 138; state of 99, 198
ASEAN 177
Assam 91, 100, 127–129, 131, 132, 134, 135, 137, 138, 179, 180, 182–183, 204; anti-foreigner movement 131; chars of 181; plains of 100, 129
Assam Accord 137
Assam Citizens' Association 180
Assamese Muslims 132, 133
asylum 27, 31, 33, 65, 70, 193, 195, 196, 198, 199, 220, 225, 226, 229, 232
Asylum Capacity Support Group (ACSG) 222
asylum seekers 8, 14, 62, 64–65, 70, 71, 77n14, 121, 175, 177, 193–194, 199, 200, 205, 232
Aung Sang Suu Kyi 172
autonomy of migrant 15
autonomy of migration 12, 42n50, 71, 83n51, 84n53
avant-garde centres 29

Balibar, Etienne 38n19
Bali Process 9, 171, 175–177
Balkan wars 230
Bangladesh-India Initiative 97

Bangladeshis 171, 177, 178, 205
barbarians 52, 53, 125
Bardelli, Nora 78n23
BBC 55, 56
Behind the Wall – The Women of the Destitute Asylum, Adelaide, 1852–1918 45
Bellary mining 118
Berlin Congress 144
Betts, Alex 61, 63, 66, 69–73
bilateral agreements 184
Birds of Passage 65
Bolshevik Revolution 49
borderland existences 28, 182, 184, 206
border-making exercises 47
borders 2, 3, 5, 11, 12, 24–28, 35, 52, 103, 136–138, 143, 144, 148, 150, 151; age of globalisation 7–12; control 149, 155; management 5, 11, 12, 231; and migrant 52–57; regions 68, 170
boundaries, crossing: postcolonial context 24–26
boundaries, international 204
Bradley, Megan 41n37
Brahma, Upendra 137
Brecht, Bertolt 30
Buchanan, Francis 168
burden 10, 32, 69, 72, 152, 176, 184, 191, 196, 199–200, 202, 219–221, 227, 231
Burma 170
Burmese 172, 197–200; migrant workers in Thailand 54; nationals 197, 199

Calcutta Research Group 97
camps 5, 14, 25, 26, 30, 35, 36, 45, 62, 63, 71, 72, 155, 156, 182; detention 13, 180, 182, 183
capital 3, 45, 51, 56, 69, 87, 102, 103, 111, 113, 115, 117, 138, 144, 171
capitalism 2, 5, 8, 61, 65, 74–75, 102, 103; contemporary 15, 73
care, principle of 34–35
Cartagena Declaration on Refugees 185
Castles, Stephen 1–3, 6, 7, 11–12, 21n47, 43, 61–63, 65, 66, 70, 73, 145
Census of British Burma 169
Cesaire, Aime 155
Chakma population 136
Chakma refugees 13, 182, 197
Chakmas 134, 138, 198
Chakrabarty, Subhasranjan 89, 90
charlands 98
Chatterjee, Jaya 195
child labour 120
Child Protection by Indian Railways 114

Chimni, B.S. 40n36
China International Trust Investment Corporation (CITIC) 171
Chins 134, 136, 137, 169
Chittagong Hill Tracts 133, 134, 194
Chowk, Chandni 113
cities of refuge 223, 224
citizenship 4–6, 8, 13, 26, 100–101, 131, 146, 167–190, 203, 206; liberal theory of 4; policies 155, 167; rights 13, 132, 172, 182–184
Citizenship Act 203
citizens scrutiny cards (CRCs) 170
climate change 46, 47, 105–106, 146, 231
climate refugees 105, 106, 146
colonialism 8, 24, 26, 27, 30, 52–53, 88, 203
commodities 66, 72, 76, 111–113, 128; production 76
communal riots 202
communities: international 34, 177, 183, 225, 227
complex emergencies 47, 58n19
comprehensive refugee response framework (CRRF) 218, 219, 222, 223, 231
Constituent Assembly Secretariat (CAS) 180
construction 44–45, 47, 55–56, 66, 72–73, 79, 98–101, 103–104, 114–117, 120, 134, 137–138; workers 114, 138
contemporary capitalism 15
convention for refugee protection, 1951 33
convention on statelessness 171
countries: colonised 46, 87, 201; developing 55, 62, 111, 227; foreign 135; neighbouring 9, 72, 174; postcolonial 23, 64, 87, 125, 157, 167
courts 26, 54, 199–201, 205
Crépeau, François 232
criminalisation, migration 9
crisis: nutritional 90; refugee rights 232; resource 47, 89, 97
critical juridical discourse 29
crop production 132

Dadaab refugee camp 81n35
Davis, Mike 87, 88, 91, 146
de facto statelessness 13, 171, 174, 182
De Hann, Arjan 116
democracy 23, 36, 92–93, 172, 175, 181, 192, 195
Derrida, Jacques 27, 196, 224
destitute asylums 51
Dillingham report 154
disasters, natural 34, 47, 103–105

discourses 48, 51, 91, 94, 131, 136–139, 196, 197, 201, 229, 230, 233; political 131, 138, 139
discrimination 172–178; anti-immigrant 4
displacement 12, 31, 35, 87, 88, 94, 100, 101, 105, 133–135, 182, 192, 202; environmental 87, 99
diversity, immigrant labour market 62
durable solution 70, 214, 217, 219–221, 223, 225
Dutta, Akhilranjan 183

ecological disasters 110
ecological migrants 87–101; colonial background 87–91; hunger, disasters, and governing mechanisms 91–95; postcolonial footprints 87–109; primitive accumulation 102–106
ecology 95–102
economic activities 61, 62, 64, 65
economic spillover 63
The Economist 71, 142, 143
economy: fringe 89, 97, 102, 104, 177; immigrant 61, 66, 97; immigrant labour 167; local 63; plantation 43, 44, 47, 129; urban 111, 112
education 9, 55, 56, 64, 65, 72, 96, 100, 117, 129, 173, 223, 230, 231
emigrants 89, 90
empire 52–57; and migrant 52–57
enclave economy 129–131
epistemological category 26–31
Escape from Violence 193
Escape Routes 83n51
ethnic groups 6, 169; national 170
ethnicity 2, 3, 6, 27, 74, 126, 129, 137, 172
euphemism 120
EUROJUST 152
Europe 5, 6, 10, 11, 46, 64, 65, 75, 142, 143–149, 151, 154–157; borders of 14, 151, 154; countries of 65, 146, 158; crisis of 145; labour markets of 70, 220
European Asylum Support Office (EASO) 152, 224
European migration 12, 232
European Monetary Union 144
Europe's border-centric response 148–155
Europe's migration crisis 12, 220, 232; border-centric response 148–155; neo-liberal mechanisms of governance 155–158; postcolonial nature 142–166
EUROPOL 152
exercise 4–5, 27, 46–47, 57, 88, 137, 149, 158, 168, 174, 192, 194, 200, 203–204, 213
extraction 75, 103, 110–111, 113, 117, 119, 121, 129

Faist, Thomas 14
Falls, Sioux 86n65
famine 28, 44, 46–47, 50, 73, 87–91, 93, 103, 105, 133, 146, 155, 201
Famine Act 88
famine code 87, 91
famine foods 146
federalisation, care 34
Federici, Sylvia 2, 143, 160n7
figures of visibility 110–111
flood 46–47, 88–90, 95, 97–103, 121, 128, 146, 223
food insecurity 91, 94
food security 90, 92
Food Security Act 92
forced migrants 15, 25, 29, 61, 65
forced migration 2, 7, 9, 10, 13, 23–27, 29–31, 35–36, 61, 62, 64, 76, 181, 215–216, 226; and justice 201–206; nature of 30, 32; protection 228; studies 14, 23–32, 35, 36; victims of 31, 51, 61, 63–65, 201, 203, 226
forced migration and justice 201
Foreigners Act 203
"Forensic Oceanography: Mare Clausum" 149
Foucault, Michel 185, 205
Franks 144
French Communist Party (PCF) 49
FRONTEX 147, 152, 154
frontier 7, 12, 24–25, 28, 47, 51, 53, 67, 88, 126–127, 131, 143–144, 150, 153–155, 157–158, 200, 205

GCR 230
Geneva Convention 156
Geyer, Mary 45
global commodity 8
global compact 111, 214–215, 217–219, 221–222, 224–226, 228, 230, 232–233
Global Compact on Refugees (GCR) 225, 234
global conversations 217
global economy 69–71, 76, 111, 217, 227
global gaze 213–217
global governance 15, 68, 94, 146, 157, 174, 182, 191, 213–215, 217, 219, 221, 226, 233–234
globalisation 2, 4, 6–8, 10–11, 28, 31, 43, 45, 47, 53, 54, 56, 103, 150
global labour market 10, 112
global markets 4
global migration 3, 8, 10, 11, 14, 15, 105, 157, 217; flows 12; history 151; issue of 15, 215
global North 29
global power 213–242

Index **275**

global protection agenda 232–235
global protection regime 193
global realm of protection 213
global refugee forum 226–227, 230
global refugee regime 191–193
global security discourse 125
global South 28–29, 150, 193
Goldstein, Brooke 180
gorkha 135
Goths 144
governmentality 10, 33, 44, 50, 102, 104, 132, 204
governmental politics 100
government policies 93
Gramsci, Antonio 154
Great Calcutta Riot 201
The Guardian 147
Gujarat High Court 199
Guwahati Tea Auction Centre 128

Hajela, Prateek 179
Harvey, David 75
Heller, Charles 149, 161n24
Hindus 183
historical intelligibility 23, 25, 28–29, 35, 37, 43, 106; role of 23
history: colonial 87, 89, 91, 125, 151, 158; contemporary 105, 230; contentious 57, 137; heavy migration 145; nation-centric 43, 44, 47; received 8, 66
homeland 5, 104, 129, 131, 134, 144, 150
homogeneity 126
homo sacer 36
hospitality 14, 27, 34, 193–194, 196, 199, 213, 223; Indian story of 193–197
Hossain, Monirul 100
host communities 69, 71, 223, 224
humanitarian border 150
humanitarianism 8, 15, 26, 32, 34–35, 47, 51, 217, 220, 226, 228, 230–231, 234; figure of migrant and 47–52
humanitarian machine 221–228
human rights 8, 32, 35, 36, 144, 149, 176, 177, 183, 221, 224, 228, 229, 232, 233; of migrants 232
hunger 29, 44, 46, 88, 89, 91–94
Huns 144
Hunter, W.W. 89

immigrant economy 61, 66, 97
immigrant labour absorption policies 61
Immigrant Workers and Class Structure in Western Europe 1, 43
immobilization, institutional form 74
imperial sovereignty 52
Indian Famine Code 91

Indo-Burma border 137
industrial capitalism 66
informal labour 115
infrastructure 69, 71, 91, 111, 114–116, 121, 129
insecure migrant 125–141
insecure nation 125–141
internal displacement 3, 9, 13, 24, 32, 104, 157, 184, 217
internally displaced population groups (IDPs) 24, 25, 31
International Conference on Assistance to Refugees in Africa 69
International Organization for Migration (IOM) 9, 176, 233, 242n66
Iraq 29, 55, 56, 71, 143, 151, 191, 192

Jakarta Declaration 177
judicial reasoning 197–201

Kälin, Walter 105
Kant 191, 207n5
Kapadia, S.H. 118
Karbi Autonomous Council Demand Committee 137
Khosravi, Shahram 42n50, 184
Ki-moon, Ban 177
Kosack, Godula 1, 43
Kumar, Mithilesh 100

labour *see individual entries*
labour-centric history 43–60
labour form 8, 44, 52
labour market 2; age of penalised labour 2–7; integration, paradoxes of 64–70
labour migration 4, 7, 28, 29, 43, 52, 90, 91, 112, 178
labour mobility schemes 241n58
Late Victorian Holocausts: El Nino Famines and the Making of the Third World 87
legal pluralism 33, 228
liberal empire 143, 144
Libyan Coast Guard (LYCG) 149
living labour 72–75, 105, 181
logistics 76, 110, 111, 114, 115, 227
Lytton, Lord 91

Mablin, Lucy 193
MacLean, Ken 180
macro/micro insecurity 138, 203
Mahato, Nirmal Kumar 90, 91
Manto, Sadat Hasan 31
Mare clausum operation 149, 161n23
The Marginal Nation 25, 43, 97
marriage migration 157
Marshall Plan 142

Marx, K. 47, 102, 143
M B Shah Commission Report 119
mechanism 31, 34, 36, 54, 71, 76, 91, 95, 97, 103, 149, 152, 155, 174, 177, 202, 204, 205, 215, 218, 219, 226, 227
Mediterranean 49, 147–150, 177; boat tragedies 145
Mezzadra, Sandro 52, 73, 157
migrant labour 7, 18, 46, 50, 54, 56, 57, 66, 70, 73–76, 95, 97, 104, 105, 110, 111, 114–121, 138; and black hole of ecology 117–121; mediator of economic transformation 111–117
migrants: age of globalisation 43–60; conflict and civil war 137–139; spectral presence 110–124
Migration Museum 45
Miller, Mark 62, 63, 65, 70, 73
Mines Act of 1952 119
mining 45, 47, 76, 103, 117, 118; *see also individual entries*
mixed and massive population flows 14, 87
Mizos 136
modern humanitarianism 50
Mohajirs 211n36
Mohapatra, P.P. 91
Mongoloid 127
Monpa community 99
Monsutti, Alessandro 22n52
Moroccan enclaves 142
Mosaic Law 237n34
Mother Courage 30
Mukhopadhyay, Bhaskar 20n42
Muslims 169, 183
Muttahida Qaumi Movement (MQM) 211n36

National Hydro-electric Power Corporation 99
National Register of Citizens (NRC) 129, 135, 179, 183
National Rural Employment Guarantee Act 93
National Space Research Organisation (NSRO) 97, 101
nation-centric history 43–60
nation form 7, 8, 43, 44, 52, 143
natural calamities 30
negative dialectics 52
Nehru-U Nu agreement 137
Neilson, Brett 104
neo-liberal capitalism 73, 74
neo-liberal developmentalism 25
neo-liberalism 138, 221
neo-liberal mechanisms, governance: postcolonial gradient 155–158

neo-liberal urbanisation 111
Nepal Citizenship Act 189n49
Nepalis 184
New Poor Law of 1834 93
New York Declaration 214
non-refoulement 194, 200; principle 156
non-state persons 170
North Bihar labour 97
Northeast 25, 95–103, 125, 126–130, 133, 135, 136, 138, 171, 178, 179, 182, 183, 202, 204
nouvelles frontieres 200
Novak, Paolo 16n9, 166n71

Obama, Barack 177
Operation Relex 178

Papadopoulos, Dimitris 83n51
Paris Conference on Climate Change 146
partition 24–27, 29–31, 46, 94, 110, 125, 132–133, 154, 192, 194–196, 201–202, 204–206, 210, 213
Partition of 1947 24
Partition of India 210n31
partition refugees 195, 201
Parveen, Gulshan 100
passport 47, 197
persecution-centric approach 193
Pezzani, Lorenzo 149, 161n24
Piore, Michael J. 65
plantation 43, 44, 47, 129
political economy, resources 127–137
politics 95–102; of control 72
population politics 7
postcolonial age of migration 37, 76
postcolonial citizenship 167
postcolonial labour 112
power 191–193; *see also specific entries*
precarious labour: immigration and production 70–76
prima notteâ 153
primitive accumulation 51, 89, 102–106, 102–106, 103, 153
protection 9, 24, 26–28, 31–36, 49, 50, 56, 62, 64, 69, 74, 75, 94, 105, 110, 114, 117, 121, 125, 150, 152, 157, 158, 171, 173, 174, 176, 180, 184, 185, 191–197, 199–203, 205, 213–217, 219, 220–222, 225–234
public-private partnership (PPP) 102
public sector companies 128

race 2, 10, 13, 57, 74, 104, 121, 126, 137, 138, 154, 182, 228–231
racial mixing 138
Rahola, Federico 5, 155, 156
Rakhines 169

Reangs 136
reconciliation mechanisms 204
refugee activism 20n44
refugee burden 152
refugee care 24
Refugee Convention 33, 192
refugee economies 177; labouring subject of 61–86; site of several interfaces 61–64
Refugee Economies 61
refugee flows 65
refugee labour 36, 112, 113, 168
refugee like condition 13, 36, 75, 182
refugee protection 24, 28, 33, 34, 56, 152, 176, 191, 192, 195, 196, 203, 214, 225, 228–232; regime 230
refugee status determination (RSD) system 31, 222
reproduction crisis 2
responsibility 213–242; forced migration and justice 201–206; judicial reasoning 197–201; postcolonial marks 191–212; power and protection 191–193
Responsibility to Protect (R2P) 226
responsible agency 192
retrospective responsibility 192
riot 24, 27, 93, 131–133, 169, 201–203
Rivera, Miguel Primo de 49
river erosion 100
river lands 102
Rohingyas 168, 171, 172, 175–178, 180, 182, 219
Rosenberg, Clifford 48–50
Rossiter, Ned 104
Rothermund, Dietmar 129
rumor of globalization 20n42
Rwandan genocide 230

safe and orderly migration 216, 233
Said, Edward 5
sand mining 120, 121
Sanyal, Kalyan 113
Sassen, Saskia 28, 59n26, 68, 155
Second Anglo-Afghan War 91
security 127–137, 229
Sepoys in the British Overseas Expeditions 56
sex work 73
sex workers 74
Sierra Nevada 44
Singh, Tarlok 136
Skeldon, Ronald 3
slavery, abolition 46
social citizenship 43
social conflicts 4
Social Darwinism 91
social functioning 36
social governance 7

social transformation 3
sociological culture 2
South Bhutanese refugees 13
sovereignty 52, 53, 155
special economic zones (SEZs) 104, 114, 115
Srimavo-Shahstri Pact 184
Stanford, Leland 44
Stapinski, Helene 153
stateless migrant 181
statelessness 26, 167–190; history of situation 167–172; legal limbo 178–185
strategic hamlet 136
sudden unexpected death syndrome (SUDS) 141n29
survival migration 95–102
Sword, Keith 6
Sykes-Picot agreement 154
Syria 29, 32, 65, 67, 76, 143, 151, 191, 192
Syrian child labour 71
Syrian/Iraqi migrant labour 71
Syrian refugees 66, 67

TAMPEP Network 84n54
technocratic mode, protection 228–231
temporary registration cards (TRCs) 170, 171
10-point action plan 151–153
terrorist 138, 181, 223
Tibetan refugees 66, 196
Tilly, Charles 36, 54, 93, 157
Toba Tek Singh 31
trafficking 9, 14, 44, 73, 74, 76, 98, 113, 150, 157, 171, 174, 175, 177, 184, 187, 229, 231, 233
trans-border migratory movements 52
transitional justice 139, 205
transit labour 47, 66, 78n21, 116
trans-national corporations (TNCs) 50
transplanted networks 54
Treaty of Yandabo 168
Trilling, Daniel 148
Tripura Upajati Juba Samity (TUJS) 133, 134
Tseng-Putterman, Mark 165n53
Tusk, Donald 149

undocumented migrant 184
UNDP 217
UN Guiding Principles on Internal Displacement 16n4
United Nations High Commissioner for Refugees (UNHCR) 19n34, 31, 58n19, 64, 70, 71, 81n34, 148, 172, 173, 176, 186n17, 187n17, 197–200, 202, 206n3, 214, 215, 218, 219, 221, 223, 225, 227, 229, 232–234, 241n65
United Nations Refugee Convention. 176

United States 46, 143
Upheaval: The Refugee Trek through Europe 12
Uprooted: The Shipment of Poor Children to Canada, 1867 to 1917 44
urbanisation 128
urban resilience 223
US Immigration and Customs Enforcement (ICE) 86n65

Vernon, James 88, 94
viapolitics 10
Vijayanagara Empire 117
violence 143
visible/invisible 8, 25, 31, 50, 68, 116, 117, 154, 200

Walters, William 10, 11, 17n9, 150, 157
Warner, Daniel 146
waste 47, 48, 72, 73, 76, 103, 111–113, 116, 121; reprocessing 112
West Bengal Land Reform Act 98
"whole-of-society" approach 219
work permits 73
work place 72
World Bank 67
World Food Programme (WFP) 67, 68

year of 2015 *see* Europe's migration crisis

Za'atari 80n30

Made in United States
Troutdale, OR
07/07/2023